THE SCIENCE OF MIND

THE GPS GUIDES TO LIFE

Think and Grow Rich

As a Man Thinketh

The Power of Your Subconscious Mind

The Science of Getting Rich

The Richest Man in Babylon

THE SCIENCE OF MIND

The Complete Original 1926 Edition
The Classic Handbook for Creating a Life of Possibilities:
Plus Bonus Material

ERNEST HOLMES

ST. MARTIN'S
ESSENTIALS
NEW YORK

The information in this book is not intended to replace the advice of the reader's own physician or other medical professional. You should consult a medical professional in matters relating to health, especially if you have existing medical conditions, and before starting, stopping, or changing the dose of any medication you are taking. Individual readers are solely responsible for their own healthcare decisions. The author and the publisher do not accept responsibility for any adverse effects individuals may claim to experience, whether directly or indirectly, from the information contained in this book.

Published in the United States by St. Martin's Essentials, an imprint of St. Martin's Publishing Group

FOREWORD. Copyright © 2022 by Joel Fotinos. All rights reserved. Printed in the United States of America. For information, address St. Martin's Publishing Group, 120 Broadway, New York, NY 10271.

www.stmartins.com

The Library of Congress Cataloging-in-Publication Data is available upon request.

ISBN 978-1-250-85224-3 (trade paperback)
ISBN 978-1-250-85225-0 (ebook)

Our books may be purchased in bulk for promotional, educational, or business use. Please contact your local bookseller or the Macmillan Corporate and Premium Sales Department at 1-800-221-7945, extension 5442, or by email at MacmillanSpecialMarkets@macmillan.com.

The Science of Mind was first published in 1926.
What Religious Science Teaches was first published in 1944.
First St. Martin's Essentials Edition: 2022

10 9 8 7 6 5 4 3 2 1

This edition seeks to faithfully reproduce the original publications of the author's works and so has maintained the original spelling and grammar throughout, with only minor alterations for clarity or content.

CONTENTS

FOREWORD

You are holding a book that has influenced millions of people since its original publication in 1926. The ideas within the book are as current now as they were when it was written and will remain current for generations to come. I first encountered it in a bookstore in Denver, Colorado, in the 1980s—I saw a tall stack of thick hardcover books called *The Science of Mind*. Picking one of the copies up, I flipped through it and saw it was filled with concepts, ideas, meditations, even charts, all explaining a school of thought that would later change my life. I soon discovered that *The Science of Mind* is a foundational text in a larger school of philosophy commonly called "New Thought."

Ernest Holmes is known as the founder of the Religious Science philosophy, which is largely represented now by the Centers for Spiritual Living (CSL). There are hundreds of CSL locations around the United States, Canada, Mexico, and more around the world.

ERNEST HOLMES

Ernest Shurtleff Holmes was born in 1887 in Lincoln, Maine, and was born into a free-thinking family. At age fifteen, he moved to Boston, where he read *Science and Health* by Mary Baker Eddy, founder of the Christian Science movement. By all accounts, he had an extremely curious mind and read as many books as he could find, devouring the works of, among many others, Ralph Waldo Emerson and Henry David Thoreau, as well as early New Thought pioneers, such as Warren Felt Evans, Phineas P. Quimby, William Walker Atkinson, Christian D. Larson, and Emma Curtis Hopkins.

Another early influence seemed to be John Bascom, a late-nineteenth- and early-twentieth-century educator and philosopher, who briefly was the president of the University of Wisconsin. He wrote several dozen books with titles such as *Natural Theology; Science, Philosophy and Religion*; and *An Historical Interpretation of Philosophy*.

In 1881, Bascom published a book titled *The Science of Mind*, which reflected his on going adaptation of the ideas of the time with the concepts of religion, philosophy, psychology, and science. He called this philosophy New Theology. You can easily find copies of Bascom's *The Science of Mind* online, and reading through it, you can see how much it influenced Holmes's thought, though Holmes later both simplified and expanded the ideas in Bascom's book.

Holmes eventually moved to California and began work in the city government. He ended up giving a lecture at Los Angeles's Metaphysical Library, which ended up being a success. He continued to give lectures, and his audiences grew quickly. He was known for his brilliant mind, his humor, and his enthusiastic oratory skills. He soon traveled around the country giving lectures on the New Thought principles that had become his passion.

TWO VERSIONS OF *THE SCIENCE OF MIND* (1926 & 1938)

His audience increased, and eventually Holmes founded the Institute of Religious Science in 1926. This was the same year that Robert M. McBride & Company published Holmes's third book, *The Science of Mind*, a book that later became commonly referred to as "the textbook." It was Holmes's magnum opus, the overview of Religious Science. It expanded on his earlier books, and it met with early success, being reprinted several times in the first couple of years after it was published.

Twelve years after he published the first edition of the book you are holding now, he published a revised and expanded edition of *The Science of Mind* with the assistance of Maude Allison Lathem, a longtime editor of the Institute's magazine, *Science of Mind* magazine, which is still being published to this day. This new edition, which is still used as the main textbook in many CSL locations, added sections about spiritual thought and Jesus. It was more organized and clearly meant to be used in the classes of the Institute.

While much of the material from the 1926 edition was retained, much of it was also edited out. For example, Holmes removed nearly all of "Lesson Six: Psychic Phenomena." This lesson, which is faithfully included in this edition, contains Holmes's thoughts and teachings about subjects such as telepathy, apparitions, trances, psychic capacities, ghosts, clairvoyance, psychometry, black magic, crystal gazing, and more. Holmes continued to believe in these subjects but edited them out of the later 1938 edition as he felt they were being developed into their own science of study.

He also removed some of the "Special Articles" in his later edition, including those on sexuality, male and female psyches, psychoanalysis, and emotions. Many people have noticed that in this original 1926 edition, many of Holmes's ideas, which would have been forward-thinking at the time of publication, are remarkably in line with current human thought. One need only read his section on "Male and Female" and see how advanced and ahead of his time Holmes was.

Another change from this original edition to the later 1938 edition is that much of Holmes's teaching voice had changed. This makes the later 1938 edition less personal and urgent than the 1926 edition. Reading through this original edition, you can almost feel Holmes's excitement at the ideas he is sharing. While the 1926 and 1938 editions share a title and some material, they are two distinct books, and both deserve to be read.

THE ORIGINAL 1926 EDITION

The original 1926 edition itself is arranged in several parts. Part One is Holmes's introduction to the Religious Science philosophy. In this section, he makes the case of the evolution of thought and how metaphysics is expressing the highest ideal yet for humankind. He uses science, art, psychology, religion, philosophy, and more to substantiate his claims.

Holmes never claimed to receive direct revelations or any special divine knowledge. He believed that all traditions and disciplines could contain revelatory truths that could make life more complete. He blended the best of all of those disciplines listed in the previous paragraph into his philosophy and frequently would say that even the Religious Science philosophy was evolving. He called it being "open at the top," meaning to take the best ideas available at the time, but always remain open to more ideas and new concepts.

Part Two contains the six metaphysical lessons. In them, one can see the structure of how he would teach these lessons to his students. To make sure each idea was made clear to readers, each concept was explained thoroughly through glossaries, charts, introductions, and recapitulations.

Part Three is made up of "Special Articles," short essays about different topics that go beyond the six main lessons. These are meant to be responses to many of the questions that students had while going through the lessons.

Part Four has the inspirational meditations that many readers use in their daily spiritual reading. These meditations are short prayerlike, poemlike writings that are meant to focus the reader and help them raise their thoughts higher.

READING *THE SCIENCE OF MIND* NOW

As you read through this copy of the 1926 edition of *The Science of Mind*, I would suggest you keep in mind a few things that might be helpful.

Holmes includes mini-glossaries throughout the original 1926 edition. The philosophy he taught contained its own language to represent the thoughts and ideas he was trying to make clear. These glossaries are helpful to refer to as you read through the book, since he often ascribed different meanings to words that were common in religion and philosophy. And speaking of language, it's also good to remember that Holmes wrote this nearly a century ago. While he was well-read and advanced in his thinking, he was also a man of his time as well. For instance, his use of the male gender pronoun throughout was common at the time (and even still is today). He also occasionally has a few thoughts that feel very much of the time in which the edition was published.

Since this book was written as a series of lessons, I suggest that you might want to approach reading this book in that way. After carefully reading the Introduction to get a sense of his point of view, spend a week or so reading Lesson One. Read, study, highlight, underline, and even journal your thoughts about it before moving on to Lesson Two, and so on. In this way, you will not only understand the ideas, but you will be shown step-by-step how to use the ideas in a practical way in your own life. Holmes would often say that ideas that don't make your life better aren't worth practicing. Keep at it, soak up the wisdom, and see how it works in your life. We've added this volume to the GPS series (Good, Practical, Simple), a collection of classic books designed to bring life-changing teachings from the last couple of centuries to today's modern readers. The book's impact on countless men and women since its publication continues to this day, with many of today's most popular teachers and authors citing *The Science of Mind* as one of their main influences. As an added bonus for this edition, we are also including Holmes's short primer, *What Religious Science Teaches*, which succinctly summarizes the philosophy in *The Science of Mind* and shows how it synthesizes the world's wisdom traditions.

Now it is your turn. Whether you are reading it for the first time, or you have read it many times already, this edition holds something special for you if you only look for it. This is your time to let the timeless ideas of *The Science of Mind* become alive in you.

—Joel Fotinos

THE SCIENCE OF MIND

A COMPLETE COURSE OF LESSONS IN THE SCIENCE OF MIND AND SPIRIT

These lessons are dedicated to that truth which frees man from himself and sets him on the pathway of a new experience, which enables him to see through the mist to the Eternal and Changeless Reality.

CONTENTS

Our Thoughts Go • Suggestion Becomes Memory • Mental Medium Through All • Reading Thought • Mental Law • The Word of God as Law • Threefold Nature of God • Trinity of Being • Conscious Mind in God and Man • Unity • Worship of God • Many Gods • Belief in Duality—Its Results • Duality in Theology • Duality in Philosophy • Duality and Science • An Awakening • Philosophy Leads Man's Thought • A Deep Inquiry • The Great Difficulty • The Voice of God in Creation • The Word of God • Spirit Knows Itself • Law, Servant of the Word • Forms of Spirit or Creation • Meaning of Creation • The Word Alone Is Conscious • The Thought of God • Eternal Creation • The Universe Is Alive • Conclusion

Spirit • Soul • Two Ways of Reasoning • Body • The Changeless • Cause and Effect • Unity and Multiplicity • Immortality • Forms • Allness of Truth • Volition • Only One Mind • Individuality

The World Has Learned All It Can Through Suffering • What Individuality Really Means • The Meaning of Freedom • Sin and Punishment. Righteousness and Reward • The Incarnation of Spirit • Different Viewpoints • The Lesson of Nature's Laws • The Relation of Man to the Universe of Spirit • Man's Experience • Nature Waits on Man • Mental and Spiritual Laws • God and Man • Man Reenacts the Nature of God • The Two Ways to

Reason • Nothing Happens by Chance • Many Are Waking Up to the Facts • The Time Has Come to Know the Truth • A Wonderful Experiment • What Psychology Teaches About Man's Nature • The Self-Knowing Mind • Man's Unity with the Whole • Man a Center of God-Consciousness • Unity with Law • The Subjective Obeys the Objective • The Body • Last Stages of Matter • The Unity of All Body • The Formless and the Formed • Individuality Means Self-Choice • The Greatest Discovery Ever Made • A Complete Unity

Upper Section • Middle Section • Lowest Section

Spirit • Soul • Body • Limitless Medium • Christ and Antichrist • Man Is Identified in Mind • Treatment • The Aim of Evolution • Methods of Treatment • Subjective Law • Thought and the Creative Medium • Each Is the Logical Result of His Own Thinking • A Law of Belief • We Are Dealing with Law • The Cycle of Necessity and Karmic Law • The Law of Action and Reaction • We Argue in Mind • Wrong Use of Mind • Subjective but Not Unconscious • How Habits Are Formed • Law Is Mind in Action • We Are Bound by Our Own Freedom • Oneness with All Law • Demonstration • Karmic Law • Thought Force • Choosing Thought • Inducing Thought • Place No Limit on Principle

Healing • What We Understand About Healing • Thoughts Are Things

The Meaning of Immortality • Where Did Man Come from and Why? • Man Awakes with a Body • What Is the Body? • Matter • The Ether of Science • The Resurrection Body • Conclusive Facts • In What Mental State Do We Go Out? • What Causes Psychic Manifestations? • Telepathy Does Not Explain Everything • Spirit Communication • Communication Must Be Mental • We Do Not Control Spirits • The Psychic Power Should Not Be Forced

Me • The Personality of God • The Radiation of Life • Unity •
Within Thee Is Fulness of Life

PEACE BE UNTO THEE, STRANGER

Peace be unto thee, stranger, enter and be not afraid.

I have left the gate open and thou art welcome to my home.

There is room in my house for all.

I have swept the hearth and lighted the fire.

The room is warm and cheerful and you will find comfort and rest within.

The table is laid and the fruits of Life are spread before thee.

The wine is here also, it sparkles in the light.

I have set a chair for you where the sunbeams dance through the shade.

Sit and rest and refresh your soul.

Eat of the fruit and drink the wine.

All, all is yours, and you are welcome.

FOREWORD

In presenting these lessons on Mental Science, I do not claim to have discovered any new Truth. The Truth has been known in every age by a few; but the great mass of people has never even dreamed that we live in a mental and spiritual world. Today, however, there is a great inquiry into the deeper meaning of life because the race has reached a state of unfoldment where a broader scope is possible.

These lessons are an attempt to put into the spoken word and into print some of those great truths known to the enlightened of all ages.

To suppose that the Creative Intelligence of the world would create man in bondage and leave him bound would be to dishonor that Creative Power which we call God. On the other hand, to suppose that God could make man as an individual, without leaving him to discover himself, would be to suppose an impossibility. Individuality must be spontaneous and can never be automatic. The seed of freedom must be hid within the shell of the human.

But, like the Prodigal of old, man must make the great discovery for himself. Although the journey may at times seem hard and the burden too great to bear, man still feels within a subtle sense, a mystical presence, a divine Reality. Thus, the inherent nature of himself is forever seeking to express itself in terms of freedom. We will do well to listen to this inner voice, for it tells us of a life wonderful in its scope, of a love beyond our fondest dreams, of a freedom which the soul craves.

But the great love of the universe must be one with the great law of Its own Being, and we must approach love through the law.

This, then, is the teaching—Love and Law. As the love of God is perfect, so the law of God is also perfect. We must understand both. "Who hath ears to hear, let him hear."

I wish to express my appreciation to the authors whose names are mentioned following the different lessons in this course of instruction, as well as to many others whose names are not mentioned. The Truth comes to us from all sources, and our understanding of it is the result of the time, thought and effort of thousands of people who have given their lives to its study.

I wish to express special appreciation to Miss Anne Shipman, of Boston, Mass., without whose untiring efforts it is not probable that these manuscripts would have ever been gotten in shape for publication; and to my mother whose great faith in these teachings has inspired me with the hope and the belief that they may be of benefit to those who study them.

—E.S.H.

THE SCIENCE OF MIND
YOURSELF

Oh, weary heart, laden with earth's weight and care,
Oh, feet, stumbling on the way, bleeding and bare,
Oh, arms outstretched, and hands upheld in prayer,
Oh, back, which so oft has felt the lash and rod,
Oh, soul, which cries aloud for the living God,
Oh, life, struggling to free itself from the clod;
Know this: there is no power from without,
Yourself must answer every fear and meet all doubt
With some divine, indwelling power
Which you yourself, upon yourself, shall shower;
And giving, take, and taking, give
Unto that life which you, yourself, shall live.

PART I

THE EVOLUTION OF
MAN'S THOUGHT

INSTINCTIVE MAN

If we traced man's history back into the dim past we should come to a place where he did not consciously know himself. We should come to a place where Instinctive Man alone existed; for the self-conscious man had not yet evolved.

Nothing can be more apparent than that man, as he now appears, is the result of growth and unfoldment. But in order to unfold, he had to have something from which to unfold, and since he is intelligent, he must have unfolded from an intelligent cause.

Instinctive Man, then, means that Inner Something, or Life, which we do not see but which is, of course, there. We might say that Instinctive Life is God in man, or the idea of God, working through man. But if Instinctive Man is an idea of God, why is he not perfect? The answer is that he is perfect, but that as soon as individuality is evolved he must be left alone to discover himself. Even God could not make a mechanical Individuality. If man is created with the attributes of self-choice and free will, he must be let alone to make the great discovery for himself.

NATURE WAITS ON MAN'S SELF-RECOGNITION

We note, that from the day when Instinctive Life brought man to the point of self-choice, it let him alone, and from that day Instinctive Life has waited on man's unfoldment. It is true that during all this time it has carried on the automatic functions of the body and has even silently told man what to do; but it has let him alone in all other ways. It may, and must, hold man as a perfect being, but it also must let him discover this fact for himself. During all of this time, however, Instinctive Life, or God, must be silently waiting for the great discovery to be made and must always be ready to respond to man's advancement. We note this to be true along the line of man's progress. For instance, consider the discovery of any of nature's forces; we know that they must have always existed; but, so far as man is concerned, they exist to him only after he has discovered, and learned how to make use of them. Electricity was a reality in the universe when Moses led the Children of Israel from the land of Egypt, but neither Moses nor any of his followers knew anything about it, and so they did not receive any benefits from its use. This is true of any and all of the natural laws; they always existed, and as soon as understood may be used. In this way, Instinctive Life waits upon man's discovery of the natural laws and his discovery of himself and his relationship to the great Whole.

If this is so evidently true of all the forces in the natural world we must expect to find the same thing to be true of those inner and finer forces within man. The unfoldment of these inner and finer forces through man is what we call his evolution.

THE FIRST GREAT DISCOVERY

The first great discovery that man made was that he could think. This was the day when he rose from the ground and said, "I AM." This marked the first great day of personal attainment; and from that day man became an individual and had to make all further progress himself; any compulsory evolution stopped when man became an individual, and from that day he had to work in conscious union with Nature and Her forces; but he did not have to work alone, for Instinctive Life has always been with him and will never depart from him. Instinctive Life desires that man shall express more, and yet more, of its own limitless possibilities.

Man is evolving from an Infinite basis; behind him is the great Unknown but not the great unknowable; for the unknown becomes known through man, and whatever more Instinctive Life is to do for him must be done through him. Nature must work through man in order to work for him. This is true all along the line of life and endeavor.

The first great discovery of man was that he could think, plan and execute. As the result of this discovery he has built up a great civilization and all that goes with it. He has harnessed electricity to his inventions, tied steam and compelled it to do his bidding. He has laid waste forests, built cities, made the desert to bloom, and has thrown the lines of his commerce around the globe; indeed, he has seemed to possess the earth.

THE INNER SENSE AWAKENS

But with all of man's powers he has still felt a vague sense of something more, something greater, something further along; a sort of mystical inner sense of things, an instinctive urge, a blind groping after a greater light. Disregarding all of his apparent power, man has still been unhappy, sick, lonely and afraid. The cities which he built have crumbled into dust, the nations which he fostered have, one by one, fallen into ruin, and history alone remains to tell the tale of most of his endeavors.

In spite of man's apparent power he has suffered greatly, and death has crowned his life and work with a pall of darkness and uncertainty.

THE GREAT QUESTION "WHY"

The great question "Why" has forever been upon his lips. Few indeed have been able to answer this question; and these few have been passed by, unheeded, in the struggle for existence.

Man has struggled along the weary road with a heavy heart and bleeding feet, only to be met by the grave. The lack of a sense of completion has beset his every pathway; and in his blind groping he has held up his hands in speechless anguish, and his broken cries have rent the air with supplications to an apparently unheeding Deity.

Why the suffering, the sorrow, the sin, the sickness and a lifetime of trouble, only to be met at last by the grim and sinister tomb?

Why, why, why? Man has sought the wise only to discover their foolishness; he has sought the learned only to find a lack of wisdom. Why, why, why? His cry has appeared to go forth into an empty nothingness. But hark! from somewhere a vague answer has come, some subtle inner sense of things; some unknown presence has given answer and a still small voice has said to him, "Man, know thyself." The Instinctive Man has again spoken and told him to search more deeply into his own nature; to look deep within himself for the answer to life. The hour has struck in the evolution of man when he can understand this voice and do its bidding.

THE GREATEST DISCOVERY OF ALL TIME—MIND

Man's response to this inner Instinctive Voice has caused him to start on the greatest adventure of his career, the discovery of Mind.

Man's first discovery of his ability to think was set aside as being too evident to take any notice of; he could think, but what of it! Of course, it was a proof that he was, but that was all; he had always been able to think; this simply gave him the ability to know his needs and try to supply them. This he had always done.

The ability to think seemed to be an automatic thing; it

came with him and would doubtless die when he died; the brain seemed to be the organ of thought; and, of course, when death stilled the brain it would no longer operate—this was self-evident.

THE BRAIN DOES NOT THINK

But the day came when some wise man said that it is not the brain that thinks at all; for if the brain, of itself, could think, then one could cut it out and it would keep right on thinking.

No, the brain of itself could not think; and yet, without a brain man could not think; which simply means that man needs a brain while here, but that the brain, of itself, does not think. The brain does not think and yet man thinks; so behind the brain there must be a thinker. But where is this thinker? We do not see him. Have we a right to say that there is a thinker when no one has ever seen him? Yes; for can we name a single force of nature that we can see? Have we ever seen electricity or any of the other forces of nature? No; and the only evidence we have of their existence is that we see what they do. We have light and motive power, so we have a right to suppose that there is a force which we call electricity. This is true all along the line, for we see effects and not causes.

WE DO NOT SEE THE THINKER

But to return to the thinker; we do not see him, but the proof of his reality is in the evidence of his works. We know that the legs do not walk; for, if severed from the body, they could not carry anyone very far. Cut off the hand and see if it could still hold anything in its grasp! Pluck out the eye and it cannot see; and so it is with all the organs of the body. There is a thinker and doer back of the organism who is using it for a conscious purpose.

THE BODY UNCONSCIOUS WITHOUT THE THINKER

This is a great discovery; for it means that the body without the thinker could neither be sick nor suffer; for without the thinker there could be no movement of the body. Why then are we sick? This inquiry will not be answered until every form of disease is swept from the face of the earth and numbered with the things that were once thought necessary. For man has discovered that the body, of itself, has no life nor power to act.

Let us follow the course of man's thought since he first made this discovery about the body and began to apply his knowledge. He first realized that Instinctive Man built up the body through evolution; and, after having created and evolved a perfect body, left it in man's keeping to do with as he willed. At first, man was ignorant of this, thinking that the body was self-operating; but as soon as he discovered that such was not the case he began to formulate certain new theories about himself. He discovered that while he could consciously think and decide, something happened to his thoughts after he had thought them. They went somewhere; for soon they would come back as remembrance. Man had now discovered that he could consciously think and that his thought would come back to him again. This led to the conclusion that memory is an active thing, an inner mental action. He said, "Memory is the storehouse of all my conscious thoughts and it is active. My body is not conscious of life, but my thought is conscious of my body; my body is operated upon by my thought; and it must also be operated upon by my memory, since memory is active. But, since memory is only the result of conscious thought, memory, of itself, is an unconscious operation of what was once a conscious thought."

THE CONSCIOUS AND THE UNCONSCIOUS THOUGHT

Since man always has had the habit of naming things, he named his memory his "unconscious thought," and his conscious thought he called his "objective mind." He now came to the conclusion that he had two minds, one conscious and one unconscious, or sub-conscious. The conscious mind being the one that he used all of the time in his self-conscious state and the sub-conscious mind being the storehouse of all his conscious thoughts, as well as the seat of his memory. It follows, that as conscious thought acts, unconscious thought must also operate. This conclusion led to the discovery that the sub-conscious mind is the builder of the body; not that it really made the body in the first place, for Instinctive Man did that; but that the sub-conscious mind keeps the body going and is always acting on the thoughts of the conscious mind. After carefully watching this process, man discovered that he could consciously think and, by so doing, make such an impression on his unconscious thought that it would do what he directed. From these observations he deduced the law of suggestion to be one of action and reaction. Thus he found how habits are formed; that they are conscious ideas fallen into the inner thought and carried out to logical conclusions.

A NEW BASIS OF THOUGHT

Therefore, he began to reason: "Instinctive Man within me is perfect and yet I appear to be imperfect. My apparent imperfection must be the result of an imperfect thinking; in reality I am, and always have been, perfect. I will now begin to think differently about myself and see what happens." And as he began to think from the new basis he found that the body responded and was healed. So he came to this conclusion: "God made me perfect but He also made me an individual, which means that I can do with myself as I will. I cannot really destroy my body but I can make it most uncomfortable. Since God made me and made me perfect, each one of the organs of my body represents a perfect idea."

Realizing this to be true, he began to think from this basis, and the organs of the body responded. He found that thoughts of peace produced a peaceful condition while thoughts of fear produced a disturbed condition; that confidence made him strong while fear made him weak. In fact, he was able to trace each mental attitude to its physical correspondent. He discovered that, asleep or awake, the inner mind works all the time. He also found that by analyzing his thought he could discover what ailed him. This he called psycho-analysis.

THE LAW OF MIND

Then another idea came to him: the whole thing was in accordance with law. He had discovered a law of mind just as he, at another time, discovered a law of electricity. If it were law, then he could always use it and it would always respond. From this he gradually built up a definite technique for the practice of right thinking.

He found that if he always thought of himself as being perfect he would always feel better. But what should he do with his body when it appeared sick? How was he to think of himself when he was sick? Could he deny that he was sick when he was suffering? Yes; for his sickness was the result of thought, and by changing the thought he could change the effect. He learned to turn away from the body when it was sick and go back into mind and think of the body as being perfect; for his thought worked independently of the body. He turned from the image of sickness to the idea of health and said, "I am perfect, no matter what the appearance may be."

UNCONSCIOUS MIND AT WORK

But some kinds of sickness had never entered his mind at all; that is, he had never consciously thought of them. How was he to reconcile this fact with his new theory? For a while this was a hard problem to solve; but by a still more careful study of his inner self, he discovered that what he called his subjective mind took all of his thoughts and did something with them. He found that there were certain combinations of thought which, brought to their logical conclusions, would produce certain kinds of diseases. He did not have to consciously think of a certain disease to have it; but if he thought certain kinds of thoughts they would produce their logical results. For instance, if he were excited all the time it would produce nervousness; if he became angry it would secrete poison in his system, and so on through the whole category of the human ailments; somewhere in mind they had their reason for being. Perhaps he could not always tell exactly where, but, by knowing that his body was perfect, he could still heal himself. He knew that as time went on and his knowledge grew he would find out more and more about himself and so be better able to heal himself. He was glad that he had started on the right track; he believed that he would know all in time and never be sick again.

ANOTHER GREAT DISCOVERY—THOUGHT REACHED OTHERS

Then a new discovery came, which was that he could think of others and heal them. It seemed to make no difference where they were; he could think of them and heal them. This was a most astounding fact, for it meant that there was a common mind somewhere through which his thought operated; for he could not reach another unless there were a medium between himself and the other person. This seemed strange; for what he had learned to think of as his individual subjective mind, was, after all, only the personal use that he was making of something which was around every one. He began to think for others, and found that mind responded to his thinking for them and caused some action to take place in their bodies. He called this medium "Universal Mind," or "the Law of God." It seemed to be as omnipresent as the law of electricity or any of the other forces of nature.

THE DISCOVERY OF RACE-THOUGHT

In this way he discovered how it was possible that the whole race might have held certain kinds of thoughts and how they might have operated through anyone who was receptive to them. That is, if anyone should feel discouraged, other thoughts of discouragement might gain entrance also and make him feel worse. This he called race-suggestion. But how was he to protect himself from it? By knowing that it could not operate through him; that he was a perfect idea and could not be affected by suggestion; for, after all, it was nothing but thought. He learned to build a mental wall around himself which could not be entered unless he chose. This he called "Divine Protection."

A UNIVERSAL MEDIUM WHICH ALL MUST COME TO BELIEVE IN

Man had now discovered that he could help and heal himself and others by thinking into some kind of a Universal Law of Mind. He found that, like all other forces of nature, it was a great Impersonal Law and could be consciously used whenever he wished to use It and that the use of It was through right thinking. He realized that the time must come when the race would be healed by knowing the Truth about itself. But because the Law was mental it could only work for those who believed in It, and since many did not believe, the thing to do was to heal himself and others who wished to be healed, waiting for the rest of the world to realize the fact.

ANOTHER QUESTION COMES UP—WHY ARE PEOPLE POOR?

But another thought came to him. If he could think into some kind of a Universal Medium of Mind and heal himself and others; if this Mind could produce such a physical effect on the body, why could it not also produce the same kind of an effect on conditions and the affairs of life? Why was it that some were rich and some poor? Was this fate, or was it because there was not enough for all? If the One Mind made bodies, why did It not also create conditions? And if It did, why did it not give to all alike?

Why were some people happy and prosperous and others unhappy, weak and poor? Could the answer to this also be in

Mind? Could it be that just as man had thought of himself as sick, and so made sickness, he had thought of poverty and made this condition possible in his experience?

Questions like these and many others came into the mind of man and caused him to search even more deeply into the nature of things. Looking about, he saw some succeed and some fail, though all was taking place in the same world and under common conditions. So he knew that it must be something *in* man, and not *outside* of him, that made all these things possible. He realized that conditions did not make themselves. Everything in man's life was run by man himself.

MAN BEGINS TO REALIZE THAT HIS CONDITIONS ARE CONTROLLED BY THOUGHT

In this way man realized that even his affairs were controlled by thought working through the avenue of the One Mind. He discovered that by changing his thought he could remold his affairs, and that by right thinking he could bring into his life new conditions. But would there be enough to go around should every one become prosperous? Yes, for Instinctive Life is Limitless.

REALIZES THAT HE MUST THINK CORRECTLY

So man discovered that he could control his affairs by right thinking; he could bring into his experience the things he wished to enjoy if he thought correctly; and since this was all in accordance with law he could do so consciously. He realized that the time would come when every one would think correctly; and poverty, unhappiness, and all that goes with them, would be swept from the face of the earth. They were never intended to be, but man had misused his power; now that he understood, he would change his whole manner of thinking and consequently he would become happy and have plenty. But every one did not believe this. Many said that it was a foolish idea, while others said that it was too good to be true. However, it was soon proven that whoever would believe and comply with the Law could prove it to be true. If some did not wish to believe, that was all right; there were plenty who would, and the direct proofs of their lives would in time convince others. In this way, eventually, all would be saved from unbearable conditions. The thing to do was to teach the Law to those who did believe.

And so the lessons which follow are for this purpose, to teach those who believe in the Law how to use It.

The race is made up of individuals, and the place to begin is with the person who believes in the greater possibility. Each one, for himself, must work out the law of his own being. It is within the power of every man to completely change his environment and completely heal his body. Whether or not he will do this depends entirely upon his own conviction and his own determination. Nature attends him on the way and is always ready to serve; but he is an individual and nothing will ever be forced upon him. Let anyone follow the Law, comply with Its nature, and consistently apply himself to right thinking and living, and he will prove to himself that life holds all and more than he has ever imagined.

PART II

THE LESSONS

LESSON ONE

In presenting these lessons in Mental Science to the public, it is my desire to make it possible for anyone, who cares to take the time to study them, to demonstrate the truths that will be discussed. It is, perhaps, hard to set down in writing a complete teaching in Mental Science that will not appear difficult to understand; but this could be said as well of any science, and the Science of Mind is no exception to the general rule.

SCIENCE

Science is knowledge of facts built around some proven principle. All that we know about any science is that certain things happen under certain conditions. Take electricity as an example; we know that there is such a thing as electricity; we have never seen it, but we know that it exists because we can use it; we know that it operates in a certain way and we have discovered the way it works. From this knowledge we go ahead and deduce certain facts about electricity; and, applying them to the general principle, we receive definite results. No one has ever seen the power or the energy that we call electricity; and the only proof we have that it really exists is that from it we receive light, heat and motive power.

No one has ever seen any of the great causes that lie back of the manifestations of life, and perhaps no one ever will; but we know that such principles exist because we can use them.

HOW LAWS ARE DISCOVERED

The discovery of a law is generally made more or less by accident, or by some one who, after careful thought and observation, has come to the conclusion that such a principle must exist. As soon as a law is discovered experiments are made with it, certain facts are proved to be true, and in this way a science is gradually formulated; for any science consists of the number of known facts about any given principle. As more and more facts are gathered and proven, the science expands and gradually becomes accepted by all and used by those who understand it. In this way all of our sciences have been evolved until today we have the use of powers and unseen forces of which our ancestors never even dreamed.

PROOF OF MIND

This is true of the Science of Mind. No one has ever seen Mind or Spirit, but who could possibly doubt their existence? Nothing is more self-evident than that we live; and since we live, we must have life; yet who has ever seen this life? The only proof of life we have is that we live; and the only proof we have of Mind is that we can think; so we are perfectly justified in believing that we have a mind and that we live.

WHERE OUR THOUGHTS GO

As we watch the processes of thought we find that we think consciously, and we also find that something happens to our thoughts after we have thought them; for instance, they become memory. This proves that we have a deeper aspect of mind, which is called subjective, lying just below the threshold of the conscious. This subjective mind is the place where our thoughts go and from whence they eventually return to us again as memory. Observation proves this to be true; for it always happens this way.

Observation has proven that the subjective mind is the seat of memory and that it contains mental pictures, or impressions, of all that has ever happened to the individual. As these mental impressions come to the surface of the conscious mind they are called memories.

Moreover observation has shown that the subjective mind is the builder of the body. It has proven that it is not only the seat of memory; it is also the avenue through which Instinctive Man works. We mean by Instinctive Man that part of the individual which came with him when he was born—that inner something which makes him what he is. For instance, we do not have to consciously think to make the body function; so we say that the inner, or the Instinctive, Man, does this for us. This is true of most of the functions of the body; they appear to be automatic; they came with us and are nature's way of working through us. So we say that in the unconscious or the sub-conscious or the subjective, there is a silent process forever working away and always doing its duty, carrying on all of the unconscious activities of the body without effort on our part.

SUGGESTION BECOMES MEMORY

It has been observed that suggestions, planted in the subconscious, become memories, and eventually tend to externalize in the body. From this it has been deduced that the sub-conscious mind is the builder of the body and is the creative factor in man. It has also been proven that certain types of thought produce certain kinds of results. This shows that the subjective mind takes our suggestions and tends to act upon them, no matter what the suggestion may be.

While the Instinctive Man, or the Natural Man, must be perfect, it is known that the thoughts of the conscious man may hinder instinctive action, through adverse suggestion. That is, conscious thought, acting as memory, may build a false condition in the body, which condition we call disease. Conscious thought may also erase this memory and thereby heal the disease.

Through observations such as these, a science of the subjective mind has gradually been formulated, many facts have been put together; and, today, these facts constitute what we call the science of the subjective life in its relationship to mental healing.

MENTAL MEDIUM THROUGH ALL

It has also been proven that thought operates in such a manner as to make it possible to convey mental impressions from one person to another, showing that there is a mental medium between all people. When we think of it, how could we talk with each other unless there were some kind of a medium through which we talked? We could not; and so we know that there really is such a medium. While there is a place where our bodies begin and leave off, as form, there does not appear to be a place where our thought leaves off. Indeed, the observations made and the facts gathered show that the medium between men's minds is omnipresent; that is, it seems to be everywhere present. Radio also shows this, for messages are sent out through some kind of a universal medium, and all that we can say of it is that we know the medium is there. So it is with Mind; all that we can say is that everything happens just as though it were there. We have a perfect right, then, to say that such a medium exists.

This opens up a far-reaching theory, for it leads to the conclusion that we are surrounded by a Universal Mind which is the Medium of the communication of our thoughts. Perhaps this is the Mind of God! Who knows? That It is there, we cannot doubt.

READING THOUGHT

Other observations have shown even more wonderful possibilities. It is known that certain people can read our thoughts, even when we are not aware of the fact, showing that thought operates through a medium which is universal, or always present. This also shows that the medium is subjective; for it retains our thoughts and transmits them to others. This leads to the conclusion that what we call our subjective mind is really the use that we, as individuals, make of something which is universal. Perhaps, just as radio messages are operative through a universal medium, our thoughts are operative through the medium of a Universal Mind. Indeed, this has been believed for thousands of years by some of the deepest thinkers.

MENTAL LAW

As we think of the medium of radio transmission in terms of law, so we should think of the Mental Medium in terms of law; for it must be the law of mental action. While we might think of it as the Mind of God, we surely could not think of it as the Spirit of God; for the Mental Medium is automatic, while the Spirit must be Self-Knowing. We could not call the Universal Medium of Mind God, any more than we could call electricity God. It is but one of the many attributes of God or the Universe of Life. It is the avenue through which God operates as Law.

THE WORD OF GOD AS LAW

Since man has a self-conscious mind, a subconscious mind and a body, we know that he is threefold in his nature. First, he is conscious mind or spirit; next, he is subconscious mind or mental law; and then, he is body. The conscious mind controls the subconscious; and in its turn, the subconscious controls the body.

It is evident that man comes from God, Life or Nature, whichever we choose to call It. It is also evident that we can get from Life only that which is in It. Man must partake of the Divine Nature if he comes from It or is made out of It; for what is true of the Whole must also be true of any of Its parts. Something cannot come from nothing; something must come from something; for nothing comes from nothing and nothing is the result; but man is something, else he could not declare himself; and since he is something, he must be made from, or come out of, something; and that something must be what we call God.

THREEFOLD NATURE OF GOD

If we study the true nature of man, then, we shall have delved into the real nature of God, or First Cause, from which man springs; and as we have found that man is threefold in his nature, so we must also deduce that God is threefold in His Nature; that is, God is Spirit, or Self-Knowingness; God is Law and action; and God is Result or Body. This is the inner meaning of the teaching of "the Trinity." But let us elaborate: God, as Self-Knowing Spirit, means the Divine Being Whom we have always thought of and believed in; the Being to Whom we have prayed and Whom we have adored. God, as Law, means the way in which the Spirit works; and Law in this sense, would be the servant of the Spirit. God, as Body, means the manifestation of the Spirit. We might put it in another form and say, there is the Thing, the way that It works and the result of Its work. Still another form would be to say, Cause, Medium and Effect.

TRINITY OF BEING

A trinity of being appears to run through all Nature and all Life; for instance, there is electricity, the way it works and its result, which is light or motive power. There is the seed, the creative medium of the soil and the plant. Turn it as we may, we are confronted with the necessity of a trinity of being. There must always be the thing, what it does and the way that it operates. Always a trinity runs through life and through everything in it. But through the Trinity of God and man there runs a Self-Conscious Spirit, and this is what distinguishes man from the brute, or from a purely mechanical creation; and is the only thing that could make God a Self-Knowing Power.

CONSCIOUS MIND IN GOD AND MAN

In God and in man there is a power that, while it may not transcend law, yet consciously uses it for definite purposes. In God this knowledge must be complete, but in man it is, of course, but dimly perceived. Jesus, the wisest Man who ever lived, said that God and man are One in real nature, and no doubt this understanding was what gave Him His marvelous power.

UNITY

It is well to remember that the enlightened in every age have taught that back of all things there is One Unseen Cause: In studying the teachings of the great thinkers we find that a common thread runs through all—the thread of Unity. There is no record of any deep thinker, of any age, who taught duality. One of the great teachings of Moses was, "Hear, O Israel, the Lord our God is One Lord"; and the saying, "I AM that I AM," was old when Moses was yet unborn; for it had been inscribed over the temple entrances for generations. We may go back much farther than Moses and find the same teaching, for it crops out from the literatures and sayings of the wise of all ages. Jesus taught this when He said, "I and the Father are One," and in the saying, "The Father that dwelleth in me."

This teaching of Unity is the chief cornerstone of the Sacred Scriptures of the East as well as of our own Sacred Writings. It is today the mainspring of the teachings of the modern philosophies, such as Christian Science, Divine Science, The Unity Teachings, The New Thought Movement, The Occult Teachings, The Esoteric or Inner Teachings, and even of much that is taught under the name of Psychology. Without this basic teaching of Unity these movements would have but little to offer. Science has found nothing to contradict this teaching, and it never will, for the teaching is self-evident.

WORSHIP OF GOD

That there is a God or First Cause no one can doubt. That the Being Whom we call God really exists from eternity to eternity is self-evident. In every age people have worshipped some kind of Deity. It is true that as the evolution of man has progressed the idea of God has expanded, and the more that people have realized of life, and of nature and her laws, the clearer has been the concept of Deity, for this is the logical result of an unfolding mentality.

MANY GODS

The first stages of human thought brought out the idea that there were many gods, the natural outcome of a life which experienced many kinds of misfortune and difficulties. As there were many gods so there were many devils or evil powers; but as the understanding of man grew he began to realize that there could not be so many powers, since the Cause back of everything must be a Unity, else It could not exist. More than one power would indicate a universe divided against itself, and this kind of a universe could not hold together. However, it has taken a long time to come to this conclusion, and in the stages between many weird ideas have been formulated and believed in. At first there were many gods and many devils; but as thought progressed, this was narrowed down to One God and one devil or evil power. Duality has been believed in since time immemorial, and, indeed, is still believed in by many. By duality we mean a belief in more than One Power back of all things.

BELIEF IN DUALITY—ITS RESULTS

The belief in duality has robbed theology of power and has polluted philosophy with untruths; it has divided science against itself and has made countless thousands go through life with saddened hearts.

DUALITY IN THEOLOGY

The belief in duality has given rise in theology to the idea of a God and a devil, each with equal power to impose upon man a blessing or a curse, and men have worshiped a devil just as truly as they ever worshiped God. Even today this monstrous thought is robbing men of their birthright to happiness and a sense of security. Even today, and openly, men still teach that there is an evil power in the universe, that there is damnation to the souls of those who do not fall down and worship—they know not what. But the time is rapidly coming when such teachings will be thrown on the scrap heap and numbered among the delusions of a frantic mentality. It has been the habit of many religious teachers of all times to hold the crowd in awe before a mighty throne of condemnation and utter destruction, till the poor, ignorant population have rent the air with their lamentations of complete despair. This, indeed, was a good method to compel the attention with the hope of salvation through some sacred rites to be performed by those whom God had appointed. In justice to such an awful performance, we would better give to these religious teachers the benefit of the doubt and say that they themselves have believed in the atrocious teachings which they have so unhesitatingly given out.

Be this as it may, the time has now come for a clearer understanding of the true nature of the Deity, in Whom we all believe, and Whom we all seek to know and to understand. That there is a God no sane person would deny; that there could be a God of vengeance and hate, having all the characteristics of a huge man in a terrible rage, no person can well believe and keep his sanity.

We will say, then, and without mincing matters in the least, that the most we had better believe about such a God is that there is no such being.

DUALITY IN PHILOSOPHY

As the belief in duality has robbed theology of its greater message, so it has robbed much of the philosophy of the ages of a greater truth; for in philosophy the belief in duality has created a confusion that is almost as great as that in theology. It has made a philosophy of good and evil in which men have come to believe. True philosophy in every age, however, has perceived that the Power back of all things must be One Power; and the clearer the thought of Unity, the greater has been the philosophy. It has shone forth as a beacon light toward which weary souls have traveled, hoping to find reality. To the great philosophers of all times we owe the advancement of the world; for they have been the great way-showers and helpers of mankind. In reverence, we humbly bow before them as Messengers of the Most High; for God has spoken through their lips and has told us that we are not creatures of the dust but that we are Divine Beings, made in the image of Perfection and with an endless destiny.

DUALITY AND SCIENCE

The belief in duality has robbed science, in that it has created Spirit and matter; i.e., a dual universe. However, modern science is rapidly giving out a different idea of the universe; for with the passing of matter into a hypothetical and theoretical ether there is but little left on which to hang any belief in materialism. We now are told that all matter is in a constant state of flow; that it all comes from one source; and that it will eventually return to that source.

AN AWAKENING

The world is waking up to the fact that things are not at all what they appear to be; that matter and form are but the one substance appearing and disappearing; and that form is simply used to express something which is formless, but self-conscious life. What this life is, science does not attempt to explain. This has been left to theology, and whether or not it has been delegated to those competent to handle the problem time alone will tell.

PHILOSOPHY LEADS MAN'S THOUGHT

Philosophy has always transcended science and always will; for philosophy deals with causes while science deals with effects. A scientist observes the result of nature's work while a philosopher speculates as to its cause. Many things which philosophy has taught for thousands of years are today being demonstrated by science. The two should really go hand in hand; for one deals with causes and the other with effects. True philosophy and true science will some day meet on a common basis; and, working together, will give to the world a theology of reality. Then, indeed, will "God go forth anew into Creation."

A DEEP INQUIRY

The deep thinkers of antiquity as well as the philosophers of all ages have meditated long and earnestly on the nature of the Divine Being. Knowing that there could be but One Ultimate Reality back of all things, they have pondered deeply upon the nature of that Reality; and it is a significant fact that all of the greatest thinkers have come to about the same conclusion.

THE GREAT DIFFICULTY

The difficulty that has beset the path of true philosophy has been the necessity of explaining a multiplied Creation with a Unitary Cause. Nothing is more evident than that we live in a world of constant change. Things and forms come and go continuously; forms appear only to disappear; things happen only to stop happening; and it is no wonder that the average person, unused to trying to discover causes, is led to feel and to believe that there is a multiple cause back of the world of things.

The philosophers of all times have had to meet the difficulty of explaining how One Cause could manifest Itself in a multiplicity of forms without dividing or breaking up the One. This has not been easy, yet, when understood, the explanation becomes very apparent.

THE VOICE OF GOD IN CREATION

The argument has been something after this manner: The Ultimate Cause back of all things must be One, since Life cannot be divided against Itself; the Infinite must be One, for there could not be two Infinites. Whatever change takes place must take place within the One; but the One must be Changeless; for, being One and Only, It cannot change into anything but Itself. All seeming change, then, is really only the play of Life upon Itself; and all that happens must happen by and through It. How do these things happen through It? By some inner action upon Itself. What would be the nature of this inner action? It could not be physical, as we understand physics, but would have to be by the power of the inner Word of Life; that is, the Voice of God, God standing for the First great and Only Cause of all that Is.

THE WORD OF GOD

It is impossible to conceive of anything other than the Word of God being that which sets power in motion. This is why the Scriptures announce that, "In the beginning was the Word, and the Word was with God and the Word was God. All things were made by Him, and without Him was not anything made that was made." God speaks and it is done.

It is evident that First Cause must be Self-Existent; that is, It must be Causeless. Nothing came before That Which was First; and, while it may be a little hard to understand this, yet we can all grasp the fact that whatever the Being is Whom we call God, It must be Self-Existent.

SPIRIT KNOWS ITSELF

God speaks and it is done; but if God speaks, His Word must be Law. The Word of God is also the Law of God. God is Word, God is Law and God is Spirit; this is self-evident. We arrive at the conclusion that God, as Spirit, is Self-Conscious Life. That Spirit is conscious is proven by the fact that we have evidence of this consciousness strewn through all time and space. God must know that God Is. This is the inner meaning of the teaching of the "I AM," handed down from antiquity. "The Spirit is the Power that knows Itself," is one of the oldest sayings of time.

LAW, SERVANT OF THE WORD

Spirit knows Itself, but the Law is the servant of the Spirit and is set in motion through Its Word. It is known that all law is some form of universal force or energy. Law does not know itself; law only knows to do; it is, therefore, the servant of the Spirit. It is the way that the Spirit works; and is the medium through which It operates to fulfill Its purpose.

Did God make law? As it is not possible to conceive a time when law did not operate, it is impossible to conceive that it was ever created; therefore, law must be coexistent and coeternal with Spirit. We might say that law is one of the attributes of Spirit.

The Spirit [operates]* through law which is some part of Its own Nature; therefore, all action must be some action of Spirit as Law. The Word of Spirit sets Its purposes in motion through the law; and since the law must be as Infinite as the Spirit, we could not think of a time when it was not, or a time when it would cease to be; neither can we imagine the law ever failing to operate when set in motion.

We have, then, an Infinite Spirit and an Infinite Law; Intelligence and the way that It works; God, working through Law, which is unfailing and certain.

FORMS OF SPIRIT OR CREATION

Next, we come to the forms of Spirit, which forms we call matter. But what is matter? Science tells us that matter is eternal and indestructible; that, at first, it is an invisible cosmic stuff; and that it gradually takes form through some law working within it. The worlds were formed by the power of His Word. We know that right now worlds are being formed in the vast reaches of space, and worlds are also ceasing to be; that is, they are gradually losing their form. In this way Creation is eternally going on. This proves a definite purposefulness, a definite law set in motion to work out this purposefulness, and a definite form as the result of the operation of this purposefulness. In other words, it shows that there is an Intelligence inherent in the universe which knows what It is doing, and how to do it, and which knows why It does it; and that there is a law obeying Its will. It also shows that there is something upon which It operates. This "something" we will call matter in its unformed state. Perhaps this is "the ether" of science; it is impossible to say; but surely there is something upon which the Spirit works.

The teaching of the great thinkers of all times is that we live in a threefold universe of Spirit, Soul and Body—of Intelligence, Substance and Form.

MEANING OF CREATION

With this in mind, we shall be better able to realize that Creation does not mean making something out of nothing, but means the passing of Substance into form through a law which is set in motion by the Word of Spirit. Creation is eternally going on; for we could not imagine a time when the activity of Spirit would cease. It is "the same yesterday, today and forever."

The whole action of Spirit must be within Itself, upon the Law, which is also within Itself, and upon the Universal Stuff, or matter, which is also within Itself. The three must in reality be One; hence, "The Trinity."

THE WORD ALONE IS CONSCIOUS

One of the main facts to bear in mind is that, of the three attributes of Spirit, the Word alone is conscious of Itself. The Law is force, and matter is simply stuff ready to take form. Since law or energy is proven to be timeless, that is, not added to or taken from; and since matter is known to be of the same nature, we have a right to suppose that both matter and law are coexistent and coeternal with Spirit. But Spirit alone is Conscious. Law, of itself, is only a force, and matter has no mind of its own. Law is not a thinker but is a doer, while matter cannot think but is thought upon.

THE THOUGHT OF GOD

Just what is meant by the Word of God? This must mean the Inner Consciousness, or Self-Knowingness, of Spirit; the Thought of God. The word "thought" seems to mean more to us than any other word; it seems to cover the meaning better, for we know that thought is an inner process or consciousness.

The Thought of God must be back of all that really exists, and, as there are many things that really exist, there must be many thoughts in the Mind of the Infinite. This is logical to suppose; for an Infinite Mind can think of an infinite number of ideas. Hence the world of multiplicity or many things. But the world of multiplicity does not contradict the world of Unity; for the many live in the One.

ETERNAL CREATION

There may be confusion in the minds of men but not in the Thought of God; and so we have a universe expressing the limitless Ideas of a Limitless Mind, and without confusion. We have, then, a Cosmic World, and an infinite and endless Creation. This is the inner meaning of those mystic words, "World without end." Creation always was and always will be. Things may come and things may go, but Creation goes on forever; for It is the Thought of God coming into expression. This is, indeed, a wonderful concept, for it means that there will always be a manifestation of the Divine Ideas. We need not worry about whether it will ever cease; it cannot cease so long as God exists; and since God will be forever, there will forever be some kind of manifestation.

THE UNIVERSE IS ALIVE

The universe is alive with action and power, with energy and life. We touch it only in parts, but from these parts we do catch a glimpse of the nature of the Whole. "He hath not left Himself without a witness." Modern science is revealing many things that the great thinkers of the ages have announced. One of them is that matter is in a constant state of flow; it is like a river flowing in, out and on; it is operated upon by an unseen force or law and takes its form through some agency which science supposes to be the Will and Purpose of Spirit. This we call the Word. All things were made by the Word.

CONCLUSION

To sum up: There is a power in the universe which acts as though It were Intelligent and we may assume that It is. There is an activity in the universe which acts as law. We know this to be true. And there is a formless stuff in the universe, forever taking form, and forever changing its form; this also is self-evident. We have every right, then, to assume that there is a threefold nature of Being which we will call Spirit, Soul and Body. We will think of the Spirit as the great Actor, the Soul as the medium of Its action, and the Body as the result of this action. We will think of Spirit as the only Conscious Actor, the only Power that knows Itself. We will think of Soul as a blind force, obeying the Will of Spirit; and we will think of Body as the effect of the Spirit, working through law, thus producing form. We will say that neither the Law nor the stuff from which form comes has any conscious intelligence, but must, because of its nature, take the form of the Word. This simplifies the whole matter and enables us to see that in the entire universe One Power Alone really acts, the Power of the Word of God.

LESSON ONE

METAPHYSICAL MEANING OF WORDS
USED IN UNIVERSAL CHART

The chart in lesson one of this series is an attempt to portray the Threefold Nature of the Universe; to show how the Spirit, acting through Law, becomes Form; for this is the inner meaning of Creation.

UPPER SECTION

SPIRIT—The Intelligent Power back of and through everything; the First Person of The Trinity.

ABSOLUTE—The Unconditioned, that which nothing can limit.

FIRST CAUSE—That from Which everything comes. The Cause of all that is made manifest on any plane. That Which comes first. The first in any creative series. The Life back of Things.

GOD—The same as Spirit. The Self-Knowing Mind back of everything. The Heavenly Father and the Eternal Mother of all. The Being Whom we worship and adore. The One and Only Conscious Mind in the Universe, personal to all who believe in

Him. It is impossible to conceive of such a vast idea as God, and the only way that we can conceive of the Divine Being is through our own nature, for His Spirit is Our Spirit.

THE GREAT "I AM"—Revealed to Moses as the One and Only Real Mind or Power in the Universe. That beside Which there is no other. I Am is another way of saying God. The "I AM" in man is the Life of man; without this "I AM," man could not be.

CONSCIOUS MIND—That Power of Consciousness which knows Itself. That which is conscious of Its Own Being. "The Spirit is the power Which knows Itself." The Self-Knowing God. The Intelligence in the Universe which reveals Itself in all of Its Creation. If God were not Self-Conscious, then man could not be self-conscious. It is impossible for us to conceive of such a Universal Consciousness. We touch It only in spots, but the evidence of this Conscious Mind is strewn throughout all time and space; and the eternal activity of the Cosmos is proof enough that such a Conscious Mind really exists.

SPIRIT
ABSOLUTE
FIRST CAUSE – GOD
THE GREAT I AM
CONSCIOUS MIND

ONLY – ALL   PURPOSEFULNESS   PERSONALNESS
KNOWING NO OTHER   SELF-PROPELLING   CONSCIOUS IDEA
FATHER–MOTHER GOD   SELF-EXISTENCE   CHANGELESS
UNCONDITIONED ONE   VOLITION – LIFE – TRUTH   ONMISCIENCE
UNITY – MACROCOSM   POWER – CHOICE – WILL   OMNIPOTENCE
THE GREAT HOUSE   FREE SPIRIT PEACE – POISE   OMNIPRESENCE
MASCULINE   THE WORD   REASON DEDUCTIVE ONLY
ACTIVE   PERFECT LOGOS

SOUL
CREATIVE MEDIUM
BLIND FORCE – LAW   SUBJECTIVE – UNCHOOSING   KARMIC LAW
NOT KNOWING – ONLY DOING   SUBCONSCIOUS MIND   KNOWN AS
MEDIUM OF ALL THOUGHT,   IMMATERIAL   THE SERVANT OF THE
POWER AND ACTION   ILLUSION OF MIND   ETERNAL SPIRIT
CINEMA PICTURES   IMPERSONAL   THROUGHOUT
REASON DEDUCTIVE ONLY   FEMININE   THE AGES
PASSIVE AND RECEPTIVE   NEUTRAL
                             PLASTIC
                             MAYA

REFLECTION   BODY   RELATIVE MIRROR
ILLUSION OF MATTER   EFFECT   EMANATION
MULTIPLICITY – MANY   FORM
                             OBJECTIVE
                             CONDITIONS
                             RESULTS
                             TIME
                             SPACE
                             THINGS

Lesson One: Metaphysical Chart No. I.

This chart, which is called the Universal Chart, shows the Universe as a Trinity of Being. The upper section designates those attributes of Spirit which are Self-Conscious. The middle section shows the subconscious aspect of Law; and the lowest section shows the effect of Spirit working through the medium of Universal Mind. Read and carefully study the full explanation and meaning of the words used in this chart.

PURPOSEFULNESS—When we speak of the purposefulness of Spirit we mean that Conscious Mind has the ability to know what It wishes to express and the power to express it. Dean Inge says that there can be no such thing as an infinite purpose because this would be a contradiction of the meaning of Infinite. This is probably true; but it does not follow that there could be no such thing as an element of purposefulness running through the Eternal Mind. Indeed, the evidence of this quality of being is so complete in the Universe that we cannot deny it. The evolution of creation on this planet alone would presuppose some kind of a purposefulness.

SELF-PROPELLING—The Spirit must be Its own propelling power, Its own motive power. To suppose that Spirit had to go somewhere to get energy with which to energize Itself would be to suppose Spirit is not First Cause. Whatever the nature of that which comes first is, It must have within Itself all that It needs with which to express Itself. We must realize that, in dealing with Causation, we are dealing with That which is the First of everything and is absolutely Unconditioned. It does not need to be energized, but is the energy back of all form and all manifestation of Life.

SELF-EXISTENT—It is difficult to grasp the idea of self-existence; but we can do so to a degree at least. For instance, we might ask the question, "Why is water wet?" There is no reason why; it is wet simply because it is its nature to be wet. If we were to ask the question, "Who made Life?", it could not be answered; because if we were to assume that some power made Life we would not be supposing that Life is First Cause. We must grasp the fact that, in dealing with Real Being, we are dealing with that which was never created. When did two times two begin to make four? Never, of course. It is a self-existent truth. God did not make God; God is. This is the meaning of the saying, "I AM THAT I AM." All inquiry into Truth must begin with the self-evident fact that Life Is. The Truth is that which Is and so is Self-Existent.

"Never The Spirit was born;
The Spirit shall cease to be never; Never was time It
was not;
End and beginning are dreams."

VOLITION—Volition means the power of conscious choice. Choice—Choice means the ability to choose consciously. Will—Will means decision coming into execution.

Volition, choice and will must be attributes of Spirit. They mean practically the same thing. We must be careful, however, not to think of these qualities of Spirit in terms of human or limited thought. When we choose, we choose between different things; but when Spirit chooses, It simply announces that It is a certain thing. The Spirit does not have to will to make things happen; things happen because it is the will of Spirit that they should be. This will, then, is simply the execution of a purpose; and since Spirit is Absolute, there can be nothing to deny Its Will. Choice, volition and will are necessary and real attributes of Self-Existent Power; for without them there would be no channel through which the Ideas of God could be expressed. In man these qualities of mentality are limited but in God they are limitless.

POWER—The energy by which everything lives.

LIFE—Life means that Inner Something that makes everything live. Life and Power are necessary attributes of a Limitless Being, and go hand in hand to complete a Perfect Being. Life is That Which Lives, and Power is the Energy with which It operates. Considering Life and Power as a combined quality of Causation, we see that they combine to make the underlying basis of all manifestation visible and invisible. In the objective world, Life is the Power that binds everything together; It is the Intelligent Basis of all that exists.

For instance, in the material world, It is the Power that holds the atoms together that they may produce form. In the mental world, It is the Power that enables us to think; and in the Spiritual World, It is the Power that enables us to live at all.

It appears that Life manifests on different levels. In the mineral world, and in the world of all material form, It seems to be unconscious; that is, It is not manifesting in a self-conscious state. We know, however, that a certain degree of intelligence runs through all Creation. Chemical Affinity is a manifestation of Life as the attraction of Itself to Itself. In plant life It seems to have a more developed degree of consciousness. That is, It manifests in the vegetable world as a power to express in one spot, but without volition to move about. This, however, does not limit The Spirit but is simply one of the ways that It works. In the animal world, we see different degrees of Life's manifestation, from the first cell life up to Man. For instance, a dog is more intelligent than a fish, yet each has the power to move about. The fish seems to move by instinct alone; the dog appears to have some degree of conscious being, although there is a difference of opinion on this score. At least, in most animal life, we find the ability to move about and, either from instinct or self-choice, the ability to express a certain degree of freedom. In man, Life expresses in terms of Volition and Self-Will; It is manifesting at the level of Self-Consciousness. While The Spirit, of Itself, must always know Itself, yet we are perfectly justified in saying that It manifests on different levels. This does not limit The Spirit, but on the other hand proves that It is really Limitless. For if It had to manifest on one level only, It would then be limited, but because It can manifest on as many levels as It wishes It is Limitless.

When Spirit manifests in the purely mechanical and material world we say that It is Unconscious Life; when It manifests in the animal world we say that It is manifesting in a state of simple consciousness; and when It manifests in and through man we say that It is in a Self-Conscious State. As this Self-Conscious state of man's mentality reaches a larger world of realization and comprehends something of Its Unity with the Whole, we say that It is in a Cosmic State. We now know of four different levels upon which Spirit manifests:

- Unconscious State

- Simple-Consciousness

- Self-Consciousness

- Cosmic-Consciousness

All of these are but different ways through which the One Power operates. Life, then, is that quality of Being, running through all, which enables anything to be what It is.

TRUTH—The Truth is That which Is. It is the Reason, Cause and Power in and through everything. It is Birthless, Deathless, Changeless, Complete, Perfect, Whole, Self-Existent, Causeless, Almighty, God, Spirit, Law, Mind, Intelligence, and anything and everything that implies Reality.

FREE SPIRIT—Means that which cannot be bound; It is free to do as It chooses, but cannot, of course, do anything that denies Its own Nature.

PEACE—An inner calm so complete that nothing can disturb it. The Peace which comes only from the knowledge that It is All. Fathomless Peace is meant by the Peace of the Spirit. This is the peace to which Jesus referred when He said, "Peace I leave with you, My peace I give unto you." The Infinite is always at peace because there is nothing to disturb It.

POISE—That perfect balance which maintains everything in its proper place without effort. It is the law of equilibrium without which nothing could be maintained. It is the law of balance that must exist in the Infinite Mind, since there is nothing to disturb It. Poise or balance is the law back of what we call "the Law of Compensation." It is Life perfectly balancing Itself. Self-Existent Life alone could produce complete poise. We cannot fathom the full meaning of poise as it exists in Spirit; but we can understand that it means an Eternal Power, unruffled by conflicting emotions, always sure of Itself, unhurried and certain.

THE WORD—The Word means, of course, the ability of Spirit to declare Itself into manifestation, into form. The Word of God means the Self-Contemplation of Spirit. The Manifest Universe, as we see It, as well as the Invisible Universe that must also exist, is the result of the Self-Contemplation of the Lord. "He spake and it was done." "The Word was with God and the Word was God. All things were made by Him and without Him was not anything made that was made." The starting point of all Creation is in the Word of Spirit. The Word is the Concept, Idea, Image or Thought of God. It is the Self-Knowing Mind Speaking Itself into manifestation. Everything has a Word back of it as its Initial Cause.

THE PERFECT LOGOS—"The Divine Creative Word." The Perfect Word of God.

ONLY—ALL—Beside Which there is none other. That Which has within Itself all that really is. The Life of everything and the Love through everything. The One Presence and the One Infinite Person Whom we call God or Spirit. Within This One all Live.

KNOWING NO OTHER—The Spirit could know nothing outside Itself. It is The Center and Circumference of everything that exists. It has no enemies, no differences, no otherness, no apartness, no separation from Itself; is Undivided. Complete and Perfect within Itself. It has no opposites and no oppositions. It knows only of Its own ability to do; and, since It is All, It cannot be hindered in any way, shape or manner. It is not possible to conceive of such a complete Life and Power; but we do catch glimpses in moments of real inspiration when we realize, to a degree, at least, that God is All.

FATHER-MOTHER GOD—The Spirit contains within Itself the Life Principle of both the masculine and feminine. It is both combined in One.

UNITY—The Axioms of Reason declare that that Which is Infinite cannot be divided against Itself. The Infinite is, therefore, Indivisible and consequently a Perfect Unit. "Hear, O Israel, the Lord our God is One Lord." It is also, "That Whose Center is everywhere and Whose Circumference is nowhere." All of It is present at any and every point within It. It is not approaching a point nor receding from it, but is always at it. The Whole of God is present at any and every point within God. It was to this Indwelling Spirit that Jesus prayed; for God is within man as well as throughout all Creation. It is, "That thread of the All-Sustaining Beauty Which runs through all and doth all unite." "His lines have gone out into all places." "There is no place where God is not." This concept enabled Job to say, "In my flesh shall I see God." All Life is bound together by One common law of Love, and Love is the Self-Givingness of Spirit, manifested in and through all that is visible and invisible. It was the realization of this One Presence that illumined the saints and sages of the past. "I and the Father are One." "The Father dwelleth in Me,

He doeth the works." We must come to sense this Marvelous Presence; for It is the secret of metaphysical work; God in all and through all.

MACROCOSM—Means the Universal World. It is another word for the Whole.

THE GREAT HOUSE—Another way of saying The Universal.

MASCULINE—The Assertive Principle of Being. The Self-Conscious, Self-Propelling Power of Spirit. The Projective Principle of Life, impregnating the Universal Soul with its ideas and concepts.

ACTIVE—The Self-Realizations of Spirit constitute Its Active Being. It acts upon Itself. Since we could not conceive of an unconscious consciousness, we could not imagine an inactive consciousness. The Spirit, by reason of Its Infinite Capacity to know Itself, must always be acting upon Itself. This action is what we call Creation. Creation is eternally going on. It may stop in one place and begin in another, but It is always going on; and, as we know that God will always be God, we know that Creation will never cease. This is the meaning of those mystical words, "World without end." This point must not be overlooked, for there are people who believe that some day Creation will cease. No more unphilosophical position could be taken than to suppose that the activity of Spirit would ever cease. There is another philosophical delusion that many believe in, namely, that there are periods when Spirit does not create. This is impossible, since we cannot conceive of a time when Spirit will cease to be conscious of Itself. ITS SELF-CONSCIOUSNESS IS ITS ACTION. We might imagine that It would not create more worlds like the one in which we live; but to suppose that It could stop creating would be to suppose that It could stop Being.

PERSONALNESS—We do not think of God as a tremendous Person, but we do think of the Spirit as the Infinite Personalness in and through all Life. We must remember that Infinite as Spirit is, It is still Self-Conscious; and Infinite Self-Knowingness is the Infinite Essence of Personalness, or the Abstract Essence of all personality. To think of God simply as an Infinite Principle would be to resolve the Divine Being into an Infinite It, a cold Impersonal Law containing no warmth or color, and certainly no responsiveness. Such a concept of God would rob man of his Divine Birthright and throw him, empty-handed, into an abyss of Law and Action without motive or direction. No worse state of mentality could be imagined than one in which man thought of God simply as a Principle. The very fact that man comes from the Universe in a self-conscious state proves that behind all manifestation there is a Power that knows Itself; and a Power that knows Itself must be Personal. It is not, of course, limited but must be Infinite. As wonderful as the concept may be, God is Personal to all who believe in Him. God is responsive to all who approach Him, and God is the Element of Personalness back of all personality.

CONSCIOUS IDEA—No two ideas are alike. The Creative Mind of the Universe, being Infinite, thinks of a limitless number of things, and each thing is, therefore, separate and distinct in the great Whole. Just as the atoms of science are cemented together by the ether, so each idea of Divine Mind is united in One Spirit. No two things are alike; no two roses are alike; no two people are alike. All come from One Life; all are in One Life and all live by It; but each forever maintains its identity in the Perfect Whole.

CHANGELESS—The One cannot change by reason of the fact that, being All, there is nothing for It to change into but Itself. It, therefore, remains Changeless. The One Cause back of all never changes, but It does constantly remain active; and so we perceive a changing form within that which is Changeless. Nothing changes, however, but the form. We know that matter and energy are indestructible and eternal, but we also know that within them a change is forever taking place. If we realize that nothing changes but form we will not become confused over the idea of the Changeless. Water may turn into ice and ice may be melted and again become water. Where was the water when it was ice? Where was the ice when it was water? Nothing really happened, except that a form took shape and again became formless. The Principle back of it did not change.

OMNISCIENCE—The All-Knowing, All-Perceiving Mind of God.

OMNIPOTENCE—The All-Powerful One.

OMNIPRESENCE—The Constant Presence of the Undivided Whole. Read again the explanation of Unity.

REASON DEDUCTIVE ONLY—The Spirit does not reason as man reasons; that is, It makes no inquiry into Truth, but Itself is the Truth. It knows intuitively; therefore, It simply announces Itself to be That which It is. If we were to ascribe to It any reasoning power, we should be compelled to say that It reasons deductively only, or from the Whole to a part.

MIDDLE SECTION

SOUL—Used in the sense of the World-Soul, or Medium through which Spirit operates. It is the Holy Ghost or Third Person of the Trinity.

CREATIVE MEDIUM—Like the creative soil in which seeds are planted and from which plant life grows, the Soul of the

Universe is the Creative Medium into which the Word of Spirit falls and from which Creation arises. We must be careful not to think of Soul and Spirit as separate; for they are really two parts, or aspects of the same thing, each being Self-Existent and Coeternal with the other. The simplest way to think of the World-Soul is to think of It as we would the soil in which we plant seeds.

SUBJECTIVE—The dictionary defines subjective as "the impression which an object makes on the mind." The external object is a percept while the impression is a concept. The concept, or idea, would be subjective; for it would be the impression which the mind receives.

In the above chart we are interpreting the word subjective as meaning the receptacle of the thought forms of Spirit. The Soul is Subjective to the Spirit; that is, It receives impressions from It. Subjective always means something that receives.

SUBCONSCIOUS MIND—The same as Subjective. The Spirit is Conscious Mind; the Soul is Subconscious Mind; It is like the soil or ground; It receives and acts. It is not a Knower as Spirit is, but is a Doer, or Executor, of the Will of the Spirit.

UNCHOOSING—Unlike Spirit, the Soul has no choice of Its own. Being subjective, It is bound to receive but cannot choose. We must always bear in mind that Soul simply reflects the images that the Spirit casts into It.

IMMATERIAL—The Soul is immaterial, as we think of matter; but It is the substance of Spirit and might be considered to be the Matter of Spirit. As all matter in the physical world is supposed to finally resolve into the ether from which it came, so we may think of the Substance of Soul as we think about the ether and realize that everything in form finally becomes Soul-Stuff again. Perhaps the simplest way to think of It, however, would be to think of It as the last and final analysis of matter. We know that matter comes from somewhere, and the teaching is that Soul-Stuff is the thing from which it comes. We must, however, distinguish Soul-Stuff from Soul. Soul is Subjective Intelligence; for, while It may not have the ability to choose, It certainly has the ability to intelligently work out the commands of Spirit. We must never think of the subconscious as though it were unconscious. The Soul of the Universe is next in Principle to Spirit and but little lower than Spirit. Subconscious means subjective consciousness but not unconsciousness. While the Soul may not choose, having no self-knowing consciousness of Its own, yet It has an intelligence of Its own, which is Infinite compared to the power of intelligence which we exhibit. For instance, the whole intelligence of the race could not create a buttercup or a pansy; yet the Intelligence in the creative soil in the earth will produce as many for us as we ask it to; that is, of course, if we plant the seeds. This same idea holds good in that greater Creative Medium of the Spirit which we call the Soul of the Universe. It has the intelligence and the power to produce things but no choice as to what It is to produce.

Soul and Soul-Stuff are two different things; but they belong together and must be placed in the category of the Creative Medium. Soul is Subconscious Mind working on Immaterial Stuff and creating from It the many forms which we see. Think of It as a seed working in the soil and the soil working on the seed.

ILLUSION OF MIND—This does not mean that Subjective Mind is an illusion, but it does mean that forms could be projected into It which were not really true. For a more complete explanation of this, see chart in the lesson on Psychic Phenomena.

IMPERSONAL—The Creative Medium is Impersonal, having no personality of Its own as the Spirit has. It neither knows nor cares who uses It, but is always ready to work for any or all alike. Remember this.

FEMININE—The Universal Medium or Soul has been called the "Womb of Nature" and "The Holy Mother," because It is receptive to the Spirit and is impregnated with the Divine Ideas. It gives birth to the Ideas of the Spirit and is, therefore, the Feminine Principle of Nature.

NEUTRAL—Soul is neutral. Like the soil it will produce any or all kinds of plants. Having no conscious mind of Its own, It receives all ideas and works them out into form. We must always remember that the Creative Medium is neutral. If It could choose, It could reject, and this is just what It cannot do. It is bound to accept and act, just as the soil does when we plant cabbages in the ground. It does not argue, but at once goes to work to produce cabbages. When we plant potatoes it does the same thing. We may plant cabbages and potatoes with roses and pansies; and we shall receive all four plants from the one neutral creative medium which knows neither good nor bad, but is conscious only of its ability to do.

PLASTIC—This refers to Soul-Stuff, either formed or unformed. It is entirely an indeterminate stuff; that is, it has no mind of its own. Matter has no intelligence at all, but is the material which is formed by the power of the Word.

MAYA—Refers to the illusion of mind.

BLIND FORCE—Some of the early philosophers referred to the Soul or Creative Medium as a "Blind force not knowing, only doing." This we know to be true of all law. Law knows only to do but has no conscious volition of its own.

LAW—It will be apparent by now that the Creative Medium of Spirit is the great Mental Law of the Universe. It is the Law obeying the Will of the Spirit. It is the Universal Law of Mind. All law is Mind in action.

MEDIUM OF ALL THOUGHT, POWER AND ACTION—It is the one Medium through which all Law and all Power operate. It is the One Law within which all the lesser laws work.

CINEMA PICTURES—Means that It is the Medium of all thought forms. See explanation of chart covering the lesson on Psychic Phenomena.

PASSIVE AND RECEPTIVE—Means neutral and feminine.

REASON DEDUCTIVE ONLY—Being subjective, the Creative Medium cannot analyze, dissect nor deny. Because of Its nature, It must always accept.

Consequently, It is always deductive in Its reasoning powers.

KARMIC LAW—Karmic Law means the law of cause and effect. The Karmic Law works through the Medium of the World-Soul.

THE SERVANT OF THE SPIRIT THROUGHOUT THE AGES—The Universal Soul, being the Creative Principle of Nature and the Law of Spirit, has been called "The Holy Ghost" or "The Servant of the Eternal Spirit throughout the Ages."

Let us realize that neither the Soul of the Universe nor the Spirit were ever created. Each is Eternal.

LOWEST SECTION

BODY—The entire manifestation of Spirit, both visible and invisible, is the Body of God. Within this One Body of God is included all lesser bodies. This One Body, coupled with the Intelligence running through it, is called the Son, or the Second Person of the Trinity. This, of course, includes man, both visible and invisible. It also includes every gradation of consciousness from the simple to the complex, from a cell to an archangel.

> *All are but parts of One stupendous Whole,*
> *Whose body Nature is, and God the Soul.*

In short, it is the entire manifestation of Spirit on any and all planes. "In my Father's House are many Mansions." We do not, of course, see all these mansions, but science has revealed to us that many exist which we do not see, and revelation has shown that the Universe is Infinite. "For we know in part."

EFFECT—That which follows cause. Effect is that which did not make itself, but which must have a power back of it causing it to be. All manifestation is effect and all effect is subject to its cause. The Creator is greater than His Creation. Everything that we see, touch, taste, feel, hear or sense with the physical senses is an effect. "Things which are seen are not made of things which do appear." This means that what we see comes from what we do not see.

FORM—Form is definite, the result of a definite idea. Form is real as form, but is not self-conscious; it is subjective to the power that created it. Forms come and go, but the power back of them remains forever and is changeless. Form is temporary, but Mind is Eternal. It is necessary that Spirit should manifest in SOME KIND OF FORM in order that It may come into Self-Expression through Self-Realization. This is the meaning of that Creation which is eternally going on.

OBJECTIVE—Means the object, the external, the effect.

CONDITIONS—The result of causes, another word for effect.

RESULTS—What happens as a necessary result of the law of cause and effect. Results follow causes mathematically.

TIME—Dean Inge says that "Time is a sequence of events in a Unitary Whole." This is an excellent definition; for, of course, time is not a thing of itself; it is simply a measure of experience in eternity. Time does not contradict Eternity, but allows It to become expressed in terms of definite experience. Time is necessary since it allows experience to take place within the One, but time is never a thing of itself. It is really impossible to measure time; for yesterday is gone and tomorrow has not come, and today is rapidly slipping into the past. If we were to attempt to put a finger on any period of time it would be gone before we could point to it. But, illusive as time is, it is still necessary to experience.

SPACE—Space, like time, is not a thing of itself, but is only the outline of form. It is a relative distance within the Absolute. Space, also, is necessary to the expression of Spirit; for without it no definite form could be produced. We must not be confused over the ideas of time and space, as they are not things of themselves. They are entirely relative, but none the less necessary.

THINGS—Means form in time and space. Things are always results and never make themselves; they are the objectifications of Spirit. Things are necessary to the manifestation of Spirit. They are the result of the Self-Knowingness of the Word of God. Things vary in size and shape, in time and duration, from the planet to the peanut, from a moment to an eternity.

REFLECTION—The world of matter reflects the Thoughts of God.

ILLUSION OF MATTER—Refers to false forms.

MULTIPLICITY, MANY—From One come many. From Unity comes multiplicity, but multiplicity does not contradict Unity. It is like the soil from which come many plants. We grow many plants from one soil, but the Unity of the soil is never disturbed in the least. So the One Mind, working through the Creative Medium of the Universe, produces many things.

RELATIVE MIRROR—Both the Absolute and the relative are reflected in the mirror of matter.

EMANATION—Projection of Spirit into form.

LESSON ONE

THE NATURE OF BEING

The circle in Chart No. I signifies Universal Life, because it is without beginning and without end. We have divided it into three parts, calling one Spirit, one Soul and the other Body; not because the nature of Being is three distinct things, but because It is a Unity with three distinct attributes, i.e., Spirit, Soul and Body.

SPIRIT

We treat of Spirit as the Active and the only Self-Conscious Principle. We define Spirit as the First Cause or God; the Absolute Essence of all that is. It is also called the great, or the Universal, I AM. When Moses asked God who he should tell the Children of Israel had sent him, the answer was, "Thus shalt thou say, I AM hath sent me unto you." The reason why "I AM" was given is because this is an absolute statement. Spirit is Conscious Mind, and is the Power Which knows Itself; It is conscious of Its own Being. The Spirit is Self-Propelling; it is Absolute and All. It is Self-Existent, and has all life within Itself. It is the Word, and the Word is volition. It has choice because It is Volition; It is will because It chooses; It is Free Spirit because It knows nothing outside Itself, and nothing different from Itself.

Spirit is the Father-Mother God because It is the principle of Unity back of all things. The masculine and feminine principles both come from the One. Spirit is all Life, Truth, Love, Being, Cause and Effect; and is the only Power in the Universe that knows Itself.

SOUL

The Soul of the Universe, not as opposed to the Spirit, but as the principle just beneath It, has always been taught as the receptive medium into which the Spirit lets fall the forms of Its thought. It is subjective to the Spirit; that which is subjective is always impersonal, neutral, plastic, passive and receptive. Wherever you find subjective law you will find something that is compelled to receive and to act upon; consequently the Soul of the Universe has been called a "blind force, not knowing, only doing," and "The servant of the Eternal Spirit throughout the ages." It is the medium of the thought, power and action of the Spirit.

TWO WAYS OF REASONING

There are but two processes of reasoning known to the human mind; one is inductive and the other is deductive. Inductive reasoning is an inquiry into the truth; it is a process of analysis. Deductive reasoning is that process of reasoning which follows an already established premise. It is from the whole to a part. Here is an example of inductive reasoning: I look about and say, "John Smith is good; Mary Jones is good; my neighbors are good; consequently, God must be good." This is a process of analysis which leads to the conclusion that the Cause back of all things must be Good. Deductive reasoning would operate this way: "God is Good; consequently, Mary Jones, John Smith and my neighbors must be good"; because God is Good they cannot be otherwise.

Since inductive reasoning is an analysis, which is always an inquiry into truth, it follows that God can reason only deductively. That which is Infinite does not have to inquire into the Truth; consequently, there can be no inductive process of reasoning, either in the Spirit or the soul of the Universe. There cannot be any inductive reasoning in the Spirit, because It already knows all things. There cannot be any inductive reasoning in the Soul of the Universe, because It is the Creative Medium, and, if It could reason inductively, It could reject certain thoughts, because It could analyze; and soul or subjectivity can never reject; but is bound by its own nature to accept. It is impersonal, and neither knows nor cares who uses it. It is plastic, because It is immaterial. It is formless, having no mind of Its own. It has been called the Universal Feminine or Holy Womb of Nature, because It is receptive and creative. It is Karmic Law, because It is subjective to the self-knowing mind. It is the medium of all Karmic Law and of all race suggestion.

BODY

The Universe has been called the Great Trinity, or Triune Unity of Spirit, Soul and Body. The body is the result, the effect, the objectification of Spirit. Soul is the Immaterial, plastic and receptive medium; It is primordial or Cosmic Stuff; It is unmanifest form. Body is the result of Spirit working through Soul or Law. There is but one Body of the Universe; It is both visible and invisible; and within this one body are all of the lesser bodies, all of the manifest Universe, including the body of man. "But now are they many members yet but One Body."

Spirit is the Absolute Being; and is the only power in the universe which has self-knowingness, volition, choice or will. The soul has no will; It has no purpose to execute other than the purpose that is given It. Soul is the servant of the Spirit, while body is the result of the union of Spirit with Soul. There is the Power, the way that It works and the result of Its operation; the Word, the law, and the effect; Intelligence, substance, and form; the Active Principle, the passive receptivity, and the relative condition. The

Spirit of the Universe cannot change; the Soul of the Universe cannot change; the Body of the Universe cannot help changing.

THE CHANGELESS

The Spirit cannot change because there is nothing for It to change into, Spirit being All; this is axiomatic. The Soul of the Universe cannot change; for it is simply Universal Substance and Law; and we know that energy and substance are indestructible and eternal. The Soul of the Universe cannot change; but, as stated above, the body of the universe is forever changing; and this is what constitutes the eternal activity of Spirit within Itself.

Creation does not mean making something out of nothing. If by Creation we mean making something out of nothing, there is no such thing; but if we mean the passing of Spirit into form, then Creation is eternally going on.

It is necessary to understand that the only Active Principle is Spirit—Self-Conscious, Self-Knowing Life, and that all else is subject to Its will. The Spirit is conscious of Its own Thought, Its own Desire and manifestation; and It is conscious that Its desire is satisfied; consequently, It is conscious of that which It manifests; but It is not conscious of any effort or process in Its manifestation.

It is necessary that Soul and Body should exist, because Spirit, without manifestation, would construct only a dream world, never coming into Self-Realization. Since Spirit must be manifested, in order to be Spirit, there must be a way in which It manifests, and there must be a manifestation; hence, Soul and Body.

CAUSE AND EFFECT

If all Cause is existent in Spirit, and if the Law which executes the volition of Spirit is entirely subconscious, or subjective to the Will of the Spirit, and if the body is only an effect, it follows that both cause and effect are spiritual.

Involved within the seed, which the Spirit drops into the Creative Medium, is everything necessary to unfold the seed into form. This is why the Spirit never thinks of methods or processes; for that which the Spirit involves must evolve.

UNITY AND MULTIPLICITY

From Unity—which is the One back of all things, through the One Law, which is the medium of the One—multiplicity is manifested, but it never contradicts Unity. When we realize that we are dealing with an Infinite Intelligence, and with an Infinite Law within this Intelligence, we see that there can be no limit placed upon Creation. We think of the world as we see it, but we see it from the viewpoint of only one plane. We see it as matter, which we have divided into eighty or ninety odd elements; but we discover that all of these elements come from one substance. Suppose we should view it from ten different planes, what would happen? We should see ten times as much as we now see. The present hypothesis of science is that the ether is more solid than matter; and this means that there could be a form within the very form that one's body now occupies in space; there might even be a million bodies, each within the other; and each would be just as real as the one that we now think we occupy. The Universe, as we see it, is not even a fractional part of the Universe that actually is. "Eye hath not seen," because it sees only on one plane, i.e., in part.

IMMORTALITY

From the standpoint of immortality, we may have a body within a body to infinity; and when this body is rendered useless, and is no longer a fit instrument through which to function, another one may be already there.

The physical disappearance of Jesus after His resurrection was the result of the spiritualization of His consciousness. This so quickened His mentality that His body disintegrated; and His followers could not see Him because He was on another plane. Planes are not places; they are states of consciousness.

Is it apparent that the Spirit can know nothing outside It-self; that whatever the Spirit knows must be a definite mental image, concept, or idea, in the Consciousness of the Spirit? Is it clear that as the Self-Consciousness of Spirit knows within Itself, It knows upon Itself as Law? Is it clear that the Law can never say, "I will not," but can only act? And is it clear that as the Spirit lets fall the forms of Its thought into the Soul, or Subjectivity of the Universe, these thoughts must manifest as things?

FORMS

Let us take a look at these forms. As we look at the many millions of forms, and see that they are all of different shape and color, and yet we know that they all came from One Stuff, are we not compelled to accept the fact that there is a specific cause, or concrete mental image, back of every idea or thing, a Divine Mental Picture? In the subjective world there must be a correspondent of everything in the objective world; and since the subjective world is a receptive or plastic substance, this correspondence can find its initial starting point only in real Intelligence. Therefore, Intelligence is ultimately all there is in the universe.

ALLNESS OF TRUTH

By a process of axiomatic reasoning, we arrive at the conclusion that Spirit knows nothing outside Itself. The Truth is that which Is; and being that which Is, It must be Infinite and All. Being Infinite or All, the Truth can have nothing outside Itself, other than Itself, or unlike Itself, by which to divide Itself; consequently, the Spirit is Indivisible, Changeless and Complete within Itself. Itself is all that is—both Cause and Effect, the Alpha and the Omega.

VOLITION

There is but one volitional factor in the Universe, and this is Spirit or the Self-Knowing Mind. God did not make God; this is self-evident; hence God is Self-Existent. God did not make Law; Law is coeternal with God. God did not make Substance; this, also is coexistent and coeternal with God. But God did make, and does make, and is making, and will continue to make, from eternity to eternity—forms. We live in a universe of Infinite Substance and numberless forms wherein nothing is moved unless Intelligence moves it.

Mind is dual in its aspect; it is conscious, as the active principle of conscious intelligence, and subconscious, as the passive principle of impersonal receptivity. Body is the result of the knowing of Spirit through Soul. Matter, of itself, has no intelligence, no volition, no power. Since the Law is but a Universal Potential Possibility through which anything might happen, and since it is set in motion by the Word, it follows that every word specializes its own law and carries its own mathematics along with it.

It follows that everything that the Spirit thinks must take form. The Spirit, being Self-Conscious Life, knows and cannot stop knowing. To suppose that it could stop knowing would be to suppose that It could stop being. Since It cannot stop knowing, It must be forever setting in motion the Law of Its own Being, which Law must be forever projecting the forms of Its thoughts, thereby producing things. Creation is always beginning, but never ending. The slightest thought of Intelligence sets in motion a power in the Law to produce a corresponding thing.

When we speak of every thought dropped into the Creative Medium, do we think of God's thought and man's as the same? We think of each as thought; but, whereas man thinks both inductively and deductively, God thinks only deductively. "As he thinketh in his heart, so is he," i.e., as he lets fall the forms of his thought.

God is not conscious of matter, as we are. God is conscious of Himself as form, but not as size. God is conscious of Himself as definite purposefulness, but not as space. God is conscious of Himself as definite outline, but not as limitation. God is conscious of Himself as many, but not as division.

Would there be any difference between a conscious thought, for the purpose of a direct manifestation, and one that might be thought with no idea of the form that would be manifested? There would be a great difference. Trained thought is far more powerful than untrained. If this were not true, the thoughts of the metaphysical practitioner could not neutralize those that caused his patient to be sick. We know a little right thought puts to rout that which is wrong. The day that you say to yourself, "My thought is powerful," you would better be careful. *Every thought must manifest according to its intensity.*

Ponder over the meaning of the words in Chart No. I. Think what Self-Existent Life is—Life within Itself; get an understanding of the Law which is the Servant of it, and what matter is, until you begin to feel your own self as part of this great scheme of Existence.

ONLY ONE MIND

There is no such thing as your mind, my mind, his mind, her mind and God's Mind; there is just Mind in which we all live, move and have our being. There is Mind and nothing but Mind. We think of Conscious Mind and Spirit as One and the Same.

Things are ideas. What else could they be? There is nothing out of which to make things, except ideas. In the beginning we behold nothing visible; there is only an infinite possibility, a Limitless Imagination, a Consciousness; the only action of this Consciousness being idea.

That which we call our subjective mind is, in reality, our identity in Infinite Mind; in other words, it is the result of our mental attitudes. It is our mental atmosphere or center in universal Subjective Mind, in which are retained all the images, impressions, inherited tendencies and race suggestions as far as we accept them.

We see, then, that this is the Medium through which everything comes to us.

There is One First Cause, having three aspects: Spirit, Soul and Body, i.e., Cause, Medium and Effect; the Father, Son and Holy Ghost; Masculine Activity, Feminine Activity and Result.

We should not think of three Gods, but of the Triune Nature of the One God, the One Cause. We think of Spirit as Absolute, Self-Conscious Intelligence. We think of Soul as Receptive to Intelligence; and of the Intelligence as always acting upon It. Spirit and Soul intersphere each other; i.e., both have Omnipresence. The Spirit of the Universe permeates the Soul of the Universe, eternally impregnating It with ideas. The Soul of the Universe is the "Holy Womb of Nature," producing the forms which appear in the physical Universe.

The Body of the Universe is the result of the thought of Spirit, operating through the medium of Soul. This Trinity is called the Father, the Son and the Holy Ghost. The Father is Absolute, Positive Intelligence; the Son is the Offspring of the Father; the holy Ghost is "the Servant of The Eternal Spirit throughout the Ages." Spirit is Absolute Intelligence, operating through the Soul of Receptive Intelligence, impregnating It with "The Divine Ideas."

Neither the Spirit nor the Soul of the Universe can change. That which changes is the Body of the Universe. Planets may appear and disappear as do people and things; but the Substance from which things are formed is Changeless.

INDIVIDUALITY

Individuality emerges from the Universal. Psychology teaches the personification of this individuality, which is true as far as it goes; but Metaphysics universalizes individuality by unifying it with the Whole.

There is a Universal Nature of Man, inherent within him, which causes the manifestation of his personality, i.e., The Spirit of God.

The next chart will be about man, and when that is explained you will begin to see the way out of your difficulties if you have any.

LESSON ONE

RECAPITULATION

Note: Study carefully "The Edinburgh Lectures on Mental Science," by T. Troward; "Creative Mind," by Ernest S. Holmes; "The Axioms of Truth," by Burnell; "Philosophy of Plotinus," by Dean Inge.

The evolution of man brings him automatically to a time when real individuality is produced. From that day any further evolution must be through his conscious cooperation with Life. All nature waits on man's self-recognition and is always ready to obey his will; but he must use nature's forces in accordance with her laws.

Science is the knowledge of certain facts built around some known principle of being. Man never creates; he discovers and uses. In this way all sciences are evolved. We live in a Universe of Law through which runs an element of Self-Knowing Intelligence. "All's Love, yet all's Law."

The Law has done all that it can do for man automatically. It has brought him to the point of individuality, and must now let him alone to make this discovery for himself. Man is potentially perfect, but free will and self-choice cause him to appear imperfect. In reality, all that he can destroy is the embodiment of himself, for the Divine Spark is always intact in Instinctive Man.

Man awakes to self-consciousness, finding himself already equipped with a mentality, a body and an environment. Gradually he discovers one law of nature after another until he conquers his environment through his acquisition of natural forces. Everywhere he finds that nature does his bidding, in so far as he understands her laws and uses them along the lines of their inherent being; for he must first obey nature, then she will obey him.

Man discovers his ability to think, and begins to realize that from within comes a reaction to his thought. He comes to realize that he is threefold in his nature; that he can consciously think; that he has within a mentality which acts upon his thoughts; and that he has a body which is affected by his thinking.

He next discovers that he can think for others, causing a corresponding action in and through their bodies. In this way he discovers that there is a mental medium through which thought operates. He now realizes himself to be a thinking center in a Universal Mind.

Man next discovers that his affairs are also controlled by thought, and that he can likewise think for others and aid in the control of their affairs.

He now realizes that everything in the visible world is an effect; that back of all effects there are ideas which are the real causes of these effects. The Divine Ideas are perfect, but man has the ability to cause them to appear imperfect. Through right thinking he is able to uncover the appearance of imperfection and reveal the Perfect Idea.

Man's idea of the Deity evolves with his other ideas. After a belief in many gods, he comes to realize that there is One Mind and One Spirit back of all manifestation.

There is One Spirit or Self-Conscious Life acting through the Medium of One Mind or Subjective Law, producing many manifestations. Multiplicity comes from Unity without breaking up the Unity of the Whole.

Spirit is Self-Knowing, but Law is automatic and obeys the will of Spirit, having no alternative other than to obey.

Like all law, the Law of Mind is an Impersonal Force, and because of Its nature is compelled to act.

Soul and Universal Subjective Mind have the same meaning and are the Creative Medium of all thought and action. Soul is also the Substance of Spirit; i.e., It is the unformed Stuff from which all forms are evolved.

Spirit, acting upon Soul, produces Creation; Spirit, Soul and Substance intersphere each other; each has omnipresence. Creation takes place *within* Spirit and is the result of the *Contemplation of Spirit.*

Creation is eternally going on; change is always taking place within that which is changeless; forms appear and disappear in that which is formless.

God thinks or knows within Himself; and as the result of this inner action Creation manifests. Creation is the play of Life upon Itself through Divine Self-Imagination. Spirit must create in order to be expressed. Spirit, Life, Soul, Substance, Law and Unity are all coexistent and coeternal with each other. The only thing that changes is form.

Life makes things out of Itself by becoming the thing that It makes; there is no effort in the process.

Conscious Mind and Spirit mean the same; they denote that part of the Trinity which is Self-Knowing or God.

Subconscious and Subjective Mind, Soul and Mental Medium, Universal Subjectivity or Law, all have the same meaning; they denote that part of the Trinity which acts as Law.

Body, Creation or the manifest Universe, is simply the result of the Trinity which acts as Law.

Body—Creation or the manifest Universe—is simply the result of the Knowingness of Spirit through Law.

One element alone is really self-conscious and that is Spirit.

Both Law and Manifestation are automatic and must react to Spirit.

Soul or Subjective Mind, Substance or unformed matter, and Conscious Spirit permeate all things and all people. There is an Intelligence acting through everything, and everything responds to intelligence.

It cannot be too plainly stated that Spirit, or Conscious Intelligence, is the only Self-Assertive Principle in the universe. "Spirit is the power that knows Itself," and is the only power that is Self-Knowing. Everything else is subject to Spirit. The sole and only operation of Spirit is through Its Word. The Word, acting as Law through Substance, produces Creation.

LESSON TWO

Mental Science, which is the Science of Mind and Spirit, makes a tremendous claim when it states that it can free the individual from the bondage of sickness, poverty and unhappiness; but it makes this statement without hesitation and without qualification; it does not retract from that claim and it never will. It does, however, carefully set forth the conditions under which it operates and the laws governing Life, warning man that, unless he understands these conditions and obeys these laws, he will not receive full benefit from the Science of Mind.

THE WORLD HAS LEARNED ALL IT CAN THROUGH SUFFERING

The world is beginning to realize that it has learned all it can through suffering and pain. Perhaps they were good in their place, but surely there can be no power in the Universe which wishes man to be sick, to suffer pain, to be unhappy and end up in the grave. Surely God could not ordain that man should ultimately be other than a perfect expression of Life.

We should have no intellectual difficulty in realizing that even God Himself could not make an automatic individuality, and this explains why man must suffer on the road to self-discovery. He must suffer, not because pain is a necessity, but because he must have experience in order to become individualized.

WHAT INDIVIDUALITY REALLY MEANS

Perhaps it would be a good idea to elaborate on this and explain just what individuality really means. Individuality means self-choice, volition, conscious mind, personified Spirit, complete freedom and a POWER TO BACK UP THAT FREEDOM.

We cannot imagine a mechanical or unspontaneous individuality. To be real and free, individuality must be created IN THE IMAGE OF PERFECTION AND LET ALONE TO MAKE THE GREAT DISCOVERY FOR ITSELF.

The answer to the question, "Why did not God make us free and compel that freedom?" is apparent when we realize that even God could not do this. A freedom under compulsion would produce a freedom that would ultimately amount to the very worst kind of bondage. There is no such thing as compulsory freedom; even God Himself could not ordain this; for He could do nothing that would violate His own nature. No; man must be created with the possibility of limitless freedom and then be let alone to discover the fact for himself. On the road to that discovery he must be subject to the Law of all Life, and if in ignorance he violates that Law, he must thereby suffer. This is not, however, because God imposes the suffering or desires it, but simply because it is the necessity of the case.

THE MEANING OF FREEDOM

Freedom of will means the ability to do, say and think as one wishes; to express life as one personally desires. To be able only to think and dream of freedom would not be liberty. To imagine, without the power to manifest that imagination, would be to remain in a sort of dream world which would never come to complete self-realization. This is not the world in which man lives at all, for man's world is one of self-expression, even though that expression appears at times to destroy him.

SIN AND PUNISHMENT. RIGHTEOUSNESS AND REWARD

We do not wish to enter into theological discussions in this course of instruction, but we do wish to make the thought clear to those who care to study it. There is no sin but a mistake and no punishment but an inevitable consequence. Wrong doing must be punished, for the Law of cause and effect must be eternally operative. Right doing must be rewarded for the same reason.

We do not say that man cannot sin; what we say is, that he does sin or make mistakes and that he is thereby automatically punished, AS LONG AS HE CONTINUES TO MAKE MISTAKES. This does not mean that there is an evil power in the Universe; but it does mean that there is an immutable Law of cause and effect running through everything. Sin is its own punishment and righteousness ITS OWN REWARD.

The age-long discussion of the problem of evil will never be answered until we realize that it is not a thing of itself but is simply A MISUSE OF THE LAW OF FREEDOM. The problem of evil will be met only to the degree that we *cease doing evil and do good*, for evil will disappear when we no longer indulge in it. When the whole world sees the right and does it; then, and not until then, will the problem of evil be solved for the entire race.

THE INCARNATION OF SPIRIT

To return to individuality; it is that which distinguishes man from the mere brute creation; it is the greater Incarnation of God in the human; the Indwelling Spirit of the Most High.

Man is created and left to discover himself, and on the road to this self-discovery he experiences the creations of his own imaginations which ultimately show him the Truth and lead to real freedom.

There is an interesting myth in regard to the creating of man which may serve to point out this fact. It is said that when the gods decided to make man, and make him a Divine Being, they held a long discussion as to where would be the best place to hide his Divinity. Some of the gods suggested that it be hidden in the earth, but others argued that some day man would penetrate the earth and so discover himself; it was then suggested that it be hidden in the depths of the sea, but this idea was rejected, for man would go under the sea and there discover his true nature; it was next suggested that his real nature should be deposited somewhere in the air, but this also was rejected, for he would surely fly through the air and find himself. After a long discussion it was finally agreed that the best place to hide man's Divinity would be IN THE INNERMOST NATURE OF MAN HIMSELF—this being the last place he would look to find it!

This discovery would not be made until he had had all the experience necessary to complete a well-rounded life. "The Word is very nigh unto thee, in thy mouth, and in thy heart, that thou mayest do it."

Of course, this is a fable, but how clearly it sets forth the reality of the case! The word is really in our own mouths, and every time we say "I AM" we are repeating it; for "I AM" is the secret of nature and the emblem of Eternity.

The story of "The Prodigal Son" is the story of man's return to "His Father's House." How truly the poet puts it when he says that "Trailing clouds of Glory do we come from Heaven which is our home." This is the mystical meaning of that marvelous poem of Robert Browning's, called "Saul." Saul had lost his sense of real life and lay in a stupor in his tent when David came to sing to him, to awaken him to the realization of his true nature. At first David sings of the wonders of Creation and of the delights of life; he tells Saul of his power and glory as a human being; and, as the song expands, he touches the secret spring of Saul's being—"He is Saul ye remember in glory, ere error had bent the broad brow from the daily communion." Then, he plainly tells Saul of the Christ. This revelation finally awakens Saul to "His old motions and attitudes kingly." The healing has taken place and the realization of the Truth has freed Saul from the thraldom of false belief.

DIFFERENT VIEWPOINTS

Some take the viewpoint that man was cast forth to discover himself; and others contend that man decided to do this for himself. It makes no difference what the case may be; man is certainly on the pathway to self-discovery, and everything in his experience points to the truth of this fact. We know that the forces of nature wait on man's discovery of them and obey his will as soon as he understands how to make use of her laws. We certainly have freedom enough when we understand how to use that freedom. The Pilgrim Fathers might have had steam cars if they had understood the nature of steam. It was not pushed into man's experience by any autocratic power, but served him only after he had discovered how to use it. We might say the same of any and all of the laws that we now understand and utilize.

THE LESSON OF NATURE'S LAWS

If we find this to be true of the laws of the mechanical world, why should we not also find it true of those Mental and Spiritual Laws which transcend the mechanical world? No doubt, we shall find latent powers and capacities of which we have never dreamed; powers and abilities waiting to be understood and used. "Behold I stand at the door and knock." It certainly will pay man to spend much time and thought in the study of his own nature; for he will discover things about himself that will cause him to "Arise and shine." Man is today, more than ever before, awakening to the real facts of the case, and from now on his evolution will become very rapid. Nothing is impossible;

all things are possible to the Great Whole, and man is a part of
that Whole.

THE RELATION OF MAN TO THE UNIVERSE
OF SPIRIT

As the evidence of design in the Universe proves a Designer,
so the evidence of self-choice shows a Power that Knows Itself. The Spirit is Self-Knowing; God knows that God Is. But
a Universal Self-Knowingness really means a Universal Personalness; and so we see how God can be Personal to every
living soul who believes in Spirit. We could truthfully say—so
it seems to me at least—that there is One Infinite Person, in
whom we all "live, and move and have our Being"; for we all
live in the One.

MAN'S EXPERIENCE

Let us assume that man is on the road to self-discovery. What
is he to discover?—That he is really free, but that, in order to be
free, he must first go through experiences which will teach him
how to use his freedom properly; and, after the lesson is learned,
he will be free indeed. Everything seems as if this were true.
We have traced man's progress carefully through his journey on
this planet from the time when the first face "Was turned from
the clod," to now, and what have we discovered? That all nature
waits upon man's self-discovery and is ever ready to serve him
and do his bidding. Laws and forces undreamed of by our ancestors are now being employed; powers and forces which to
prehistoric man would have seemed as gods, are today called
nature's forces, and we consciously make use of them. Man has
gradually merged with nature and her laws, and today stands
forth as a new being so far as the mechanical world is concerned.
It seems as if he had conquered nature and compelled her to
serve him.

NATURE WAITS ON MAN

Nowhere on this path has he found nature opposed to him. She has silently waited for his recognition and as silently done his bidding. She will never contradict herself nor operate contrary to her inherent laws; but she will serve whoever comes to understand and use them along the lines of her way of working. Man never created any of these laws but simply uses them, and he can do this only as he first obeys them. "Nature obeys us as we first obey it" is an old saying and a true one. We learn the fundamental principle of a law, obey its mode of operation and then have conscious use of it. It would be absurd to say that nature punished us because we did not make proper use of her laws. She simply will not work harmoniously for us until we harmonize with her; she will obey us only after we have obeyed her. This is, of course, true of any and all law. If we obey, it serves; if we disobey, it seems to punish us.

MENTAL AND SPIRITUAL LAWS

It is the same with those great Mental and Spiritual Laws of our Being. We must come to discover and utilize the inner forces of Mind and Spirit, for they are the highest powers.

Man will be delivered from sin, sickness and trouble in exact proportion to his discovery of himself and his relationship to the Whole.

Law is law wherever we find it, and we shall discover that the Laws of Mind and Spirit must be understood if they are to be consciously used for definite purposes. THE SPIRIT KNOWS AND THE LAW OBEYS.

Hidden away in the inner nature of the real man is the Law of his life, and some day he will discover it and consciously make use of it. He will heal himself, make himself happy and prosperous, and will live in an entirely different world; for he will have discovered that LIFE IS FROM WITHIN AND NOT FROM WITHOUT.

GOD AND MAN

Man is made out of and from Life; and, as effect must partake of the nature of its cause, so man must partake of the Divine Nature from which he springs.

MAN REENACTS THE NATURE OF GOD

If we realize that God is "Triune" and that man is made in the Image and Likeness of God, we shall see that the whole scheme of Life and the whole nature of the Divine Being is reenacted through man. This, of course, does not mean that man is God; it means that, in his small world of individual expression, his nature is identical with God's. This is what Jesus meant when he said, "As the Father hath Life within Himself so hath He given to the Son to have Life within himself."

A single drop of water is not the whole ocean, but it does resemble the ocean and does contain within itself the same qualities and attributes. We might say that man is in God and that God works through man. "I and The Father are One," "The Kingdom of God is within you"; and we might add, "God's in His Heaven, all's right with the world."

THE TWO WAYS TO REASON

There are but two processes of reasoning known to the human mind: inductive and deductive; and from these two ways of reasoning all our knowledge of life has come. Inductive reasoning is the systematic process of reasoning from a part to the whole. Deductive reasoning is the process of accepting certain conclusions as truths and drawing other conclusions from them; it is reasoning from the whole to a part. For instance, in inductive reasoning we would say that everything happens just as if there were what we call electricity and that it is everywhere present. Deductive reasoning says that since electricity is everywhere present, it is always where we are and can always be generated from any center.

Using these two methods of reasoning to deduce the nature of God, we may start with the assumption that God IS, drawing all our conclusions from this premise; or we may carefully study the nature of man and the Universe and so draw the conclusion that a God must exist. Whichever method we use will lead to the same conclusion; namely, that there is a Divine Being and that man is made in His Image and must reenact and portray the same attributes as the Life from which he came.

NOTHING HAPPENS BY CHANCE

Nothing in the Universe happens by chance. All is in accordance with Law, and the Law of God is as Omnipresent as is the Spirit of God. This Law is a Law of Mind, but back of the Law is the Word. "All things were made by Him and without Him was not anything made that was made."

Back of our lives is the Law of our Being; and through that Law runs the word which we speak; for "What things soever He (the Son) seeth the Father do, these also doeth the Son likewise."

MANY ARE WAKING UP TO THE FACTS

Thousands of people today are beginning to realize this and put it into operation, and the results attained would fill more books than one man could read in a lifetime. Thousands today are using the silent power of Mind to heal their bodies and bring prosperity into their affairs; and the Law is always working in accordance with the belief of those seeking to use It. As the Universe is run by an Infinite Mind, so man's life is controlled by his thinking; ignorance of this keeps him in bondage; knowledge will free him.

One by one, people will investigate the Truth and put It into operation, and the time will come when disease and poverty will be swept from the face of the earth, for they were never intended to be. They are simply the by-products of ignorance, and enlightenment alone will erase them.

THE TIME HAS COME TO KNOW THE TRUTH

The hour of freedom has struck, the bell of Liberty is ringing, and "Let him that is athirst come." Let us, then, plunge more deeply into our own natures and into the nature of the Universe and see if we shall not find treasures undreamed of, possibilities never imagined and opportunities which the fond thought—yearning for freedom—has often, in our vision of the greater Life, given us.

"Prove me now, herewith, saith the Lord of hosts, if I will not open you the windows of heaven, and pour you out a blessing that there shall not be room enough to receive it."

A WONDERFUL EXPERIMENT

It would be a wonderful experiment for anyone to make to begin to live as if this promise were true; to talk, think and act as though there were a Limitless Power attending him on his journey through life; as though his every act were directed and guided into expressions of peace, health, happiness and harmony. It is surely worth while, and understanding will make the way so clear before us that we shall some day come to see the logic of it; and then, indeed, shall we really begin to live. Our lives, fortunes and happiness are in our own hands to mold as we will—provided we first obey the Law and learn how to make conscious use of It. "With all thy getting get understanding"—an old adage—but today as true as ever.

It has been the teaching of all times that man reproduces the Divine Nature; and if he does, we shall expect to find in his nature the same qualities that we suppose must be in the Nature of Life Itself.

WHAT PSYCHOLOGY TEACHES ABOUT MAN'S NATURE

A study of the psychological nature of man verifies the belief in "The Trinity" running through all Life. Man is self-conscious; of this we are sure, for he can say "I AM." This fact alone proves his claim to immortality and greatness. In psychology we learn that man is threefold in his nature; that is, he has a self-conscious mind, a subconscious mind and a body. In metaphysics we learn that the three are but different attributes of the same life. Man's self-conscious mind is the power with which he knows; it is, therefore, one with the Spirit of God; it is, indeed, His only guarantee of conscious being.

THE SELF-KNOWING MIND

It is from this self-knowing mind that man is able to realize his relationship with the Whole; for without it he would be unhuman and most certainly not Divine; but since he has it, he must be Divine.

It is the self-knowing mind alone that constitutes reality, personality and individuality. It is the "Image of God," the essence of Sonship, and the "Personification of the Infinite."

MAN'S UNITY WITH THE WHOLE

We recognize, then, in man's self-knowing mind his Unity with the Whole. For while a drop of water is not the ocean, yet it does contain within itself all the attributes of the limitless deep.

Man's self-knowing mind is the instrument which perceives reality, and cognizes or realizes Truth. All illumination, inspiration, and realization must come through the self-knowing mind in order to manifest in man. Vision, intuition and revelation proclaim themselves through man's self-knowing mind; and the Saints and Sages, the Saviours and Christs, the Prophets and Seers, the Wise and Learned, have all consciously perceived and proclaimed this fact. Every evidence of human experience, all acts of kindness and mercy, have interpreted themselves through man's self-knowing mind. All that we know, say or think, feel or believe, hope or long for, fear or doubt, is some action of the self-knowing mind. Subjective memories we have, and inner, unexpressed emotions we feel; but to the self-knowing mind alone does realization come. Without this capacity to consciously know, man would not exist as an expressed being; and, so far as we are concerned, would not exist at all. The self-knowing mind of man proclaims itself in every thought, deed or act, and is truly the only guarantee of his individuality.

MAN A CENTER OF GOD-CONSCIOUSNESS

With this vast array of facts at our disposal it would be foolish to suppose that man's self-knowing mind is any other than his perception of Reality. *It is his Unity with the Whole, or God, on the conscious side of life, and is an absolute guarantee that he is a Center of God-Consciousness in the Vast Whole.*

UNITY WITH LAW

We will say, then, that in Spirit man is One with God. But what of the great Law of the Universe? If we are really One with the Whole we must be One with the Law of the Whole, as well as One with the Spirit. Again psychology has determined the fact to be more than a fancy. The characteristics of the subconscious mind of man determine his Subjective Unity with the Universe of Life, Law and Action.

THE SUBJECTIVE OBEYS THE OBJECTIVE

In the Subjective Mind of man we find a law obeying his word, the servant of his Spirit. Suggestion has proved that the subconscious mind acts upon our thought without question or doubt. It is the mental law of our Being and the creative factor within us. It is unnecessary, at this point, to go into all the details of the Subjective Mind and its mode of action; it is enough to say that within us is a mental law, working out the will and purposes of our conscious thoughts. This can be no other than OUR INDIVIDUAL USE OF THAT GREATER SUBJECTIVE MIND WHICH IS THE SEAT OF ALL LAW AND ACTION, AND IS

"THE SERVANT OF THE ETERNAL SPIRIT THROUGH ALL
THE AGES."

Marvelous as the concept may be, it is none the less true
that man has at his disposal, in what he calls his subjective mind,
a power which seems to be Limitless. This is because he is One
with the Whole, on the subjective side of life.

Man's thought, falling into his subjective mind, merges
with the Universal Subjective Mind and becomes the law of his
life, through THE ONE GREAT LAW OF ALL LIFE.

There are not two subjective minds. *There is but one subjective mind; and what we call our subjective mind is really
only THE USE THAT WE ARE MAKING OF THE ONE LAW.*

Each individual maintains his identity in Law through
his personal use of It; and each is drawing *from* Life what HE
THINKS *INTO* IT.

TO LEARN HOW TO THINK IS TO LEARN HOW TO
LIVE, for our thoughts go into a Medium that is Infinite in Its
ability to do and to be.

MAN, BY THINKING, CAN BRING INTO HIS EXPE-
RIENCE WHATSOEVER HE DESIRES, IF HE THINKS COR-
RECTLY AND BECOMES A LIVING EMBODIMENT OF HIS
THOUGHTS. *This is not done by holding thoughts but by
KNOWING THE TRUTH.*

THE BODY

But what about man's body? Is that, too, one with the Body of
the Universe? Let us briefly analyze matter and see what it really is. We are told that matter is not a solid, stationary thing;
but is a constantly flowing, formless substance which is forever
coming and going. Matter is as indestructible as God, as eternal
as Timeless Being; nothing can be either added to or taken from
it. The very bodies we now have were not with us a short time
ago. As Sir Oliver Lodge says, we discard many of them on the

path through this life, for the material from which our bodies are composed is in a constant state of flow. Vistas of thought open up along the line of mental healing when we realize this fact; later we will thoroughly discuss and work out a definite technique for the purpose of healing.

Matter is not what we thought it to be; it is simply a flowing stuff taking the form that Mind gives it. How about the matter from which other things than the body are made? It is all the same—ONE SUBSTANCE IN THE UNIVERSE TAKES DIFFERENT FORMS AND SHAPES AND BECOMES DIFFERENT THINGS.

LAST STAGES OF MATTER

The last analysis of matter resolves it into a universal ether and leaves nothing more than a stuff which may be operated upon.

Matter, in the last analysis, is composed of particles so fine that they are simply supposed to be. In other words, it disappears entirely, and the place where it once was is again "without form and void." Matter, as we know it, is only an aggregation of these particles arranged in such order as to produce definite forms, which are determined by something *WHICH IS NOT MATERIAL*.

There is no difference between the particles which any one form takes and the particles which all forms take; the difference is not in the minute particles but in their arrangement.

THE UNITY OF ALL BODY

Our bodies are One with the Whole Body of the Universe. Seeds, plants, cabbages and kings are made of the same substance; minerals, solids and liquids are made from *THE PRIMORDIAL SUBSTANCE WHICH IS FOREVER FLOWING INTO FORM AND FOREVER FLOWING OUT AGAIN INTO THE VOID.*

THE FORMLESS AND THE FORMED

Nothing could form a formless stuff, which has no mind of its own, except Intelligence operating upon it. Again we come back to the Word as the starting point of all Creation—God's Word in the Great World, man's word in the small world.

ONE SPIRIT, ONE MIND, AND ONE SUBSTANCE; ONE LAW BUT MANY THOUGHTS; ONE POWER, BUT MANY WAYS OF USING IT; ONE GOD IN WHOM WE ALL LIVE, AND ONE LAW WHICH ALL OPERATE; ONE, ONE, ONE. NO GREATER UNITY COULD BE GIVEN THAN THAT WHICH IS ALREADY VOUCHSAFED TO MANKIND.

But why is man so limited? Why is he still poor, sick, afraid and unhappy? Because he does not know the Truth—that is the only "Why." But why was he not so made that he would *have* to know the Truth? The answer is that even God could not make a real man, that is, a real Personified Expression of Himself, without **creating him in freedom and leaving him TO DISCOVER HIMSELF.** This is the meaning of the story of the Prodigal Son and the whole meaning of it.

INDIVIDUALITY MEANS SELF-CHOICE

Individuality means real individualized being and real personified self-choice. We could not imagine an individuality without self-choice; but what would be the use of self-choice unless the ability to choose were backed with the power to externalize that choice? It would remain simply an idle dream, never coming into real self-expression. A little thought will make it clear that, if man is created to express freedom, he must be left to discover himself. Of course, during the process he will have much experience, but in the end he will come out a real being.

The day of man's discovery of himself marked the first day of the record of human history on this planet; and from the day when he first made this discovery he has constantly risen and continuously progressed. All the forces of nature attend him on his way, but he must first discover them in order to make use of them.

THE GREATEST DISCOVERY EVER MADE

The greatest discovery that man ever made was that his thought has creative power; that is, that it uses creative power. His thought, of itself, would have no power unless it were operative through a creative medium. We do not have to compel Law to operate; all that we have to do is to use It. The Law of Mind is just like any and all other laws of Being. It simply Is.

A COMPLETE UNITY

We have now discovered a Unity with the Whole on all three sides of life or from all three modes of expression. We are One with all matter in the physical world, One with the Creative Law of the Universe in the Mental World, and One with the Spirit of God in the Conscious World.

What more could we ask or hope for? How would it be possible for more to be given? We could ask for no more, and no greater freedom could be given. From now on we will expand, grow and express, only to the degree that we consciously cooperate with the Whole.

LESSON TWO

UPPER SECTION

Spirit—That part of man which enables him to be self-conscious. That which he really is. We do not see the spirit of man any more than we see the Spirit of God. We see what man does; but we do not see the doer.

Christ, Logos—The Word of God manifest in and through man. In a liberal sense the Christ means the Entire Manifestation of God and is, therefore, the Second Person of the Trinity. Christ is a Universal Idea, and each one "Puts on The Christ" to the degree that he surrenders a limited sense of Life to the Divine Realization.

Sonship—We are all Sons of God and all partake of the Divine Nature.

Microcosm—The individual world as distinguished from the Universal.

Emmanuel-God-with-us—Means that Christ is in every one.

Personality—The external evidence of individualized being.

Individuality—Each one is a separate identity in Mind and no two are alike. Each is an Individualized Center of God-Consciousness. Our personality is the use that we make of our Divine Individuality.

Conscious-State—The conscious-state is the self-knowing mind of man. It is the only thing that distinguishes him from brute creation. Without a conscious-state of mind man would not be at all; or, at least, he would not know that he is. The conscious mind should be carefully guarded, as it is the real man.

Mental—Means that man is mentally conscious.

Spiritual—Means that man is a Spiritual Being.

Reason: Inductive and Deductive—The conscious mind of man can reason both inductively and deductively. It can reason from the Whole to a part or from a part to the Whole.

Will—Means conscious ability to determine.

Choice—Ability to differentiate and choose.

Volition—Power to act independently.

Intellect—Mental quality of analysis.

Purpose—Determination with incentive.

Decision—Ability to choose.

MIDDLE SECTION

Soul—*The Subjective Side of Life.* Man's place in the One Subjective Mind of the Universe; his identity in Mind. Man's soul life reenacts the Soul Life of the Universe with which it is at One.

Subjective—The Soul is subjective. Read again the meaning of subjectivity as given in the Universal Chart.

Subconscious—The Soul is subjective to the conscious thought.

Unconscious—Word used in psycho-analysis to denote soul. It is a poor way of expressing soul-life, for it really is not unconscious. It is subconscious but certainly not unconscious.

Consciousness—Another way of saying soul. The Bible says, soul; the psychoanalyst says, unconscious; the psychologist says, subjective or subconscious; and the metaphysician says, consciousness. All have the same meaning.

Karma—The subjective law of tendency set in motion by the individual. The mental law acting through him. Karmic Law means the use that man makes of his mentality. Karma is not Kismet; for Kismet means "fate," and Karma simply means "the mental tendency." Karma is both individual and Universal.

Aura—Mental atmosphere or vibration. It extends from a few inches to a few feet around the individual and can be seen by many people.

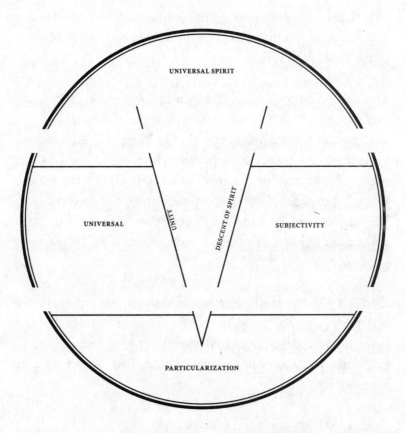

Lesson Two: Metaphysical Chart No. II-A.

This chart shows first the Universal Spirit; then the Universal Soul or Subjectivity, which is the medium of all thought, power and action; then the particularization or manifestation of Spirit.

The point drawn down through the center symbolizes the descent of Spirit into matter, or form. It is necessary that Spirit be manifested in order to express Itself. The word Unity on the descending line shows that all come from the One. Man reenacts the whole Universal Life, and his nature is identical with Spirit. What is true of the Whole is true of any one of Its undivided parts. Man comes to a point of individualization in the Whole and is subject to the Law of the Whole.

Memory—The soul, or subjective mind, is the seat of memory, and retains within itself everything that the individual has ever said, thought, seen, heard, felt, read or been told; and, indeed, everything that has ever happened to him. It also contains race memory, and may, or may not, contain much of what we call Cosmic Purposes. Cosmic Purposes mean the Ideas of God. The soul of man, being in constant contact with the Soul of the Universe, might contact tremendous powers if it would turn to the One.

Conflict—In the study of psycho-analysis, which means the analysis of the soul, we learn that the subjective side of thought, being the seat of memory, often retains thoughts and suppressed emotions which more or less tear or bind. This is what is meant by inner conflict.

Psyche—Means soul.

Inherited Tendencies—The subjective, being the seat of memory, contains the race characteristics and tendencies. We do not inherit diseases, but we do inherit tendencies. This is the way that family and race traits are handed down.

Race-Suggestion—The tendency to reproduce what the race has thought and experienced.

Prenatal Conditions—The tendency to inherit family traits.

Images of Thought—The soul, or subjective mind, contains all of our thoughts as mental images or pictures.

Auto-Suggestion—The soul receives the suggestions of the individual.

Reason Deductive Only—That which is subjective can reason deductively only.

LOWEST SECTION

Body—The definite outline of flesh, containing all of the ideas which go to make the complete physical instrument.

Effect—That which follows cause. The body is always an effect.

Affairs—That which happens to the external man.

Conditions—External things, the result of thought.

Results—Conditions.

Health—Result of correct thinking.

Disease—Result of wrong thinking.

Destiny—Result of what man thinks.

Riches—Result of a consciousness of supply.

Poverty—Result of limited thought.

Business—Also result of thought.

Vocation—The thing that our thought causes us to do.

Profession—Same as vocation.

Occupation—Same as vocation.

Reason, None—Everything in the body of man, as well as in his affairs, is the result of what he thinks. Nothing in the external is a cause, and nothing that happens causes itself to happen. Things have no power to reason, but are always the result of some inner cause.

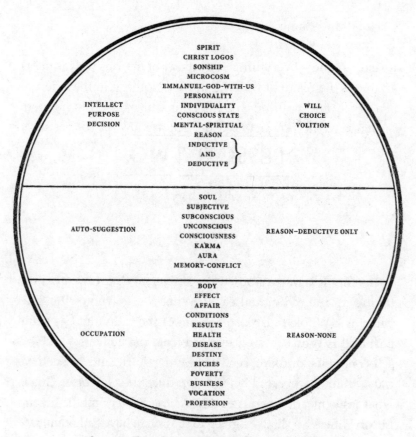

Lesson Two: Metaphysical Chart No. II-B.

This chart shows how man reenacts the Whole and is subject to the law of his own being. If the meaning of this chart is carefully studied it will be made plain that man thinks consciously and that his conscious thought becomes the law of his life. The upper section stands for the Self-Conscious man; the middle section stands for the subconscious man; and the lowest section stands for the man as he appears in the flesh and in the conditions of his life.

LESSON TWO

THE NATURE OF MAN

In the first lesson we studied the Universal Chart; we are now taking up the individual chart. Whatever is true of the Universe as a Whole must also be true of the individual as some part of this Whole. Man is evolved from the Universe, and is a self-conscious, thinking center of Living Spirit, and, as such, he must, in his nature and being, reproduce the Universe. This is what Jesus meant when He said, "As the Father hath (Inherent) Life in Himself, so hath he given to the Son to have (Inherent) Life in Himself." Inherent Life means real Life. The whole Cosmic Scheme must be reproduced on the plane of the individual, if there is an individual.

We must expect to find in man, therefore, the same inherent attributes that we find in the universe from which he springs.

Chart No. II-A symbolizes, first, the Universal Spirit; next, the Universal Subjectivity, which is called the Soul of the Universe; and third, the particularization or manifestation of Universal Spirit. We have marked Unity on the descending line, because the Spirit emanates, or particularizes Itself, at the point of our personality becoming what we call man. It is essential that we realize the Unity of life, i.e., the Unity of God and man on all three planes.

Let us start with the objective plane: matter or body, devoid of mind or intelligence, has no volition; it may be permeated with intelligence, but it is not intelligent. It is one with the Body of the Universe.

Now, what do we know about the soul? Remember the things that were discussed in connection with the qualities of the Soul of the Universe; and you will find all of them depicted in what is called the psychological, subjective nature of man; for our subjective or subconscious mind reproduces all the attributes belonging to the Universal Mind. When we turn to the spirit of man, we find that it is one with the Spirit of God—that is, man is a self-conscious, thinking, choosing center of individualized intelligence, or God-Consciousness in the great Whole.

So we find man is one with all matter in the material world, one with the Soul of the Universe in the subjective world, and one with the Spirit of God in the conscious world. What we call our objective or conscious mind is as much as we know of God and Life. The objective mind is the spiritual mind for which we have been looking, but it is not fully developed; if this were not so there would be no mind with which to look. The objective mind must be the spiritual mind of man, since it is the only thing about him which knows that it has life and is conscious of itself.

The whole of Spirit is potentially focused in our individual, objective consciousness; but we have not yet evolved to a realization of this, except in a small degree. Back of the objective mind is the subjective mind or soul, which is the medium through which intelligence operates.

There is but One Universal Subjective Mind or Soul; and what we call our subjective mind is simply our use of Universal Subjectivity; for our subjective mind is not a thing apart, but is our place in Universal Subjective Mind; and our place in It is the use that we make of It.

SPIRIT

Turning to the chart of man, Chart No. II-B, we find that the spirit of man is his conscious state of mental and spiritual being; that this mental state is equipped with decision, will, choice, volition, intellect and purpose. We find that it is individuality, personality, and is called Emmanuel or God with us. It is the microcosm within the Macrocosm, which means the little world within the big world; it is also called the Image of God; it is Sonship, the Sonship of the Father; it is the Christ or Logos, which means the Word. It can reason both inductively and deductively, and is the only thing known to us that can reason both ways.

SOUL

We find that on the subjective or soul side man is subconscious; but subconscious does not mean unconscious. Subconscious means subjective to the conscious thought, compelled by reason of its subjectivity to receive what is put into it. The term "unconscious" is used by psycho-analysis. Consciousness is the word that some use in speaking of the soul side of life. It is Karmic Law, because it is the use that we are making of Universal Subjectivity; Karma means the law of cause and effect. Soul contains the memory, because it is the receptacle for the seeds of our thought. It is psyche, soul, psychic; this is where we get the word "psycho-analysis," analysis of the soul. It contains the inherited tendencies, because it is the seat of memory. It also contains race-suggestion; for we are not dealing with a separated and isolated subjective mind, but with the one Subjective Mind. There is a vast difference between thinking of having three or four minds and thinking of having but One which all use. Its reasoning capacity is deductive only, yet it contains an intelligence which is infinite compared with the human concept of intelligence.

BODY

Next we come to the body of man, which is simply the effect of what his thought has been in Mind. Body, effect, affairs, conditions, health, disease, destiny, riches, poverty, business, vocation, profession, results, occupation, any word that stands for the externalization of man's thought and endeavor, we class as a part of the body.

"What a man has, as well as what he is, is the result of the subjective state of his thought." The thinker is conscious mind, but when he thinks, he lets fall the forms of his thought into Subjective Mind, which is the Universal Medium of all thought and action, and as the result of this, the Creative Medium at once sets to work to produce the thing thought of. This is the way that Nature works and it is the way that man works, although he is just waking to this realization.

Plotinus, who was one of the Neo-Platonic philosophers, personifying Nature, said, "I do not argue; I contemplate; and as I contemplate, I let fall the forms of my thought." This is the way Nature creates; It contemplates through Its Conscious Mind. As the result of Its contemplation, It lets fall the seeds of Its thought into the Universal Subjective, which, being Law, produces the thing thought of. Now we must expect to find, and we do find, the same thing reenacted in man. This means that whatever man thinks (whether it is what he calls good or bad) falls into this Universal Creative Medium, is accepted by It, is at once acted upon, begins to take form, and, unless neutralized, tends to become a thing in the objective world.

LIMITLESS MEDIUM

When we realize that as we deal with our own individuality we are dealing with Self-Conscious Mind, and when we realize that as we deal with subjective mind we are dealing with the Universal Subjectivity, we see at once that we have at our disposal a Power compared to which the united intelligence of the human race is as nothing; because the Universal Subjective Mind, being entirely receptive to our thought, is compelled by reason of Its very being to accept that thought and act upon it, no matter what the thought is. Since we are dealing with an Infinite Power, which knows only Its own ability to do, and since It can objectify any idea impressed upon It, there can be no limit to what It could or would do for us, other than the limit of our mental concept. Limitation could not be in Principle or in Law but only in the individual use that we make of It. Our individual use of It can only equal our individual capacity to understand It, to embody It. *We cannot demonstrate beyond our ability to mentally conceive, or to mentally provide, an equivalent.* We must have a mental equivalent of the thing we want, in order to demonstrate.

Subjectivity is entirely receptive and neutral, as we have learned, and It can take our thoughts only the way we think them. There is no alternative. If I say, "I am poor," and keep on saying, "I am poor," subconscious mind at once says, "Yes, you are poor," and keeps me poor, as long as I say it.

This is all there is to poverty. It comes from impoverished thinking. We deal only with thoughts, for thoughts are things, and if the thought is right the condition will be right. An active thought will produce an active condition. Suppose I have thought poverty year after year, I have created a law, which keeps on perpetuating this condition. If the thought be unerased, the condition will remain. A law has been set in motion which says, "I am poor," and sees to it that it is so. This is, at first, auto-suggestion; then it becomes an unconscious memory, working day and night. This is what decides the law of attraction, because the laws of attraction and repulsion are entirely subjective. They may be *conscious to start with, but they are subconscious as soon as they are set in motion.* Now suppose I did not say I was poor, but came into the world with an unconscious thought of poverty; so long as that thought operated, I would be poor. I might not have understood the Law, but it would have been working all the time.

There is also a race-suggestion which says that some people are rich and some are poor; so we are all born or come into this world with a subjective tendency toward negative conditions. But we are also dealing with a subjective tendency toward ultimate good; because, in spite of all conditions, the race believes more in the good than in the evil; otherwise, it would not exist. It believes that everything will come out all right, rather than all wrong. This is the eternal hope and sense of all life.

No matter what may be in the soul, or subjective state of our thought, the conscious state can change it. This is what treatment does. How can this be done? Through the most direct method imaginable—by consciously knowing that there is no subjective state of poverty, no inherited tendency toward limitation, no race-suggestion operating through subjectivity; nothing in, around or through it that believes in or accepts limitation in any way, shape, form or manner. The conscious state must now provide a higher form of thought. What does it do? It supplies a spiritual realization, a self-conscious realization, and says, "I partake of the nature and bounty of the All Good and I am now surrounded by everything which makes life worth while." What happens then? This Soul side of life, this Universal Medium, at once changes Its thought (because Its thought is deductive only) and says, "Yes, you are all of these things." *Whatever is held in consciousness until it becomes a part of the subjective side of thought must take place in the world of affairs. Nothing can stop it.* The reason we do not demonstrate more easily is that the objective state of our thought is too often neutralized by the subjective state. There is more fear of poverty than there is belief in riches. As long as that fear remains it is sure to produce a limited condition. *Whatever is subjective must objectify.* Matter is immaterial, unknowing, unthinking, and plastic in the hands of Law or Mind; and Law or Subjective Mind, which is entirely unvolitional, but not unintelligent, is compelled by its own subjectivity to receive the thought of the conscious mind, which alone can choose and decide. It follows then that whatever the conscious mind holds long enough is bound to be produced in external affairs; nothing can stop it, because we are dealing with Universal Law. This is called Divine Principle. It is the Medium in which we all live, move and have our being on the subjective side of life; our atmosphere in Universal Subjectivity; the medium through which all intercommunication takes place on every plane.

It follows from what we have said that any suggestion held in Creative Mind would produce its logical result, no matter what that suggestion might be. If it were a suggestion of destruction, it would destroy; for this is a neutral field. If it were a suggestion of good, it would construct.

CHRIST AND ANTICHRIST

The Spirit of Christ means that mentality which recognizes the Law and uses It for constructive purposes only. The spirit of Antichrist is the spirit of the individual, or class of individuals who, understanding the Law, use It destructively. The meaning of the Flood or Deluge (which is recorded in every sacred scripture we have read or heard of) is that a race of people were upon the earth who came to understand psychic, or subjective, law as being the servant of the Spirit. They understood themselves to be Spirit, but they did not understand the harmonious Unity of Spirit. They had arrived at an intellectual concept of the Law—a very clearly defined mental concept; but that knowledge and wisdom were not used for constructive purposes. They used it destructively, and what happened? The confusion which took place in the psychic world (or the psychic atmosphere of this planet) caused its physical correspondence in the form of the Deluge or Flood.

Psyche also means "sea," and it was into this psychic sea that Jonah fell. This is the meaning of the story of Jonah and the whale and is also why, in Revelation, it says: "There was no more sea." It does not mean that Law shall be eliminated, but that the time will come when It will be used for constructive purposes only. The misuse of this Law today is called "Malpractice." We have no fear of malpractice, because it can be practiced only upon the person who believes in it. If we say to Mind: "There is no such thing as malpractice," there being only One Ultimate Reality, as far as we are concerned, we are free from it. "Against such there is no law." We recognize Subconscious Mind as the Great Servant of our thought. It is the Medium through which all treatment operates. How do we contact this Universal Subjective Mind, which is the Medium through which healing and demonstration take place? *We contact It within ourselves and nowhere else.* It is in us, being Omnipresent. Our use of It, we call our subjective mind; but It is Universal Subjectivity.

MAN IS IDENTIFIED IN MIND

Mental treatment recognizes that each individual has his identity in mind and is known in Mind by the name he bears. This Subjective Law knows there is a John Smith and a Mary Jones. Why? Because John Smith and Mary Jones know that there is a John Smith and a Mary Jones. *But It only knows about them what they know about themselves.* Being subjective to their thought, It could not know anything else; consequently, whatever John Smith and Mary Jones say, It says, accepts and does. This is a marvelous concept. Unless we have thought it out, it may seem rather startling. But it means this: that *the Law absolutely accepts us at our own valuation.* Now this does not mean that it accepts us at an *assumption* of *valuation*, but at the *actual valuation*. It can reflect to us only the actual embodiment of ourselves. *It is the deep inner conviction that we carry which decides what is going to happen.* So we are each known by the name we bear, and each is daily making some statement about that name. When we say "I am this or that," we are involving in Mind statements which Mind in turn produces as conditions.

TREATMENT

In treatment we turn entirely from the condition, because so long as we look at a condition we cannot overcome it. That is why the mystic said: "Behold my face forevermore." "Look unto me and be ye saved, all the ends of the earth." That is, look up and not down. It is useless to treat one's business, because business is an immaterial thing. It is an unthinking, unknowing thing—a lot of stuff in form, a lot of forms in stuff. That which decides what the business shall be is in Consciousness or Mind. Consequently, we must involve in Mind a correct concept of the business, seeing it as we want it to be; and when we have seen it that way long enough, it will be so. How long will it take? *Until the subjective side of thought accepts the new concept as true, or until we have neutralized the old concept.*

Jesus had a great understanding and He gave a clue to that understanding when He said: "The Prince of this world cometh and findeth nothing in me." He meant that race-suggestion found no mental correspondence or equivalent in Him. His consciousness was so clear that it operated directly from the Spirit.

THE AIM OF EVOLUTION

The aim of evolution is to produce a man who, at the point of his objective thought, may completely manifest the whole idea of life—i.e., bring the concept of Unity to the point of particularization, finding nothing in the Law to oppose it. The reason Jesus was able to become the Christ was, that at the objective point of His thought there was a complete realization of the Unity of the Spirit and the Absoluteness of his word. His spiritual and psychical faculties, his objective and subjective mind, were completely poised and perfectly balanced.

It is evident that if this took place in any individual his word would be manifested likewise. It would have to be, because behind the word is Universal Soul, Omnipotent Law. Divine Principle is Limitless, but *It can only be to us what we believe It is.* Why must we believe It is? Because until we believe It is, we are believing It is not. The reason some people cannot demonstrate the Truth is, they do not realize It. The whole thing is a matter of belief; *but belief is scientifically induced into a subjective state through conscious endeavor and effort.* Treatment is the science of inducing within Mind concepts, acceptances, and realizations of peace, poise, power, plenty, health, happiness and success, or whatever the particular need may be.

What does a practitioner do? He sets the Law in motion in Universal Mind. Let us suppose that Mary is sick, and that John is a practitioner. She comes to him, saying, "I am sick." He, being a metaphysician, understands that Mind is all; she does not understand this. She feels that she is sick. But he knows that all sickness is mental. He does not try to hold a thought over her, nor does he try to suggest anything to her; for that is not mental treatment. He simply declares the Truth about her; he speaks her name and says: "This word is for her; she is perfect; she is well." In other words, he contradicts what appears to be and declares the Truth about her. What happens? A law is being enacted on the subjective side of life. His word, operative through the Universal Sea of Mind (in which both live) sets in motion a law which objectifies through her body as healing.

Mary thinks a miracle has been performed. She exclaims: "I am healed. I did not have a bit of faith, but John healed me." No miracle has been performed. He used a law which all may use if they will. Suppose Mary were perfectly well, but wanted a position—what would the treatment be? It would be the same. John would state in Mind what should be done for Mary. There is only One Law, and Mary could demonstrate just as well for herself if she understood It, but she must first see It demonstrated to realize It. This is the state of mind of most people who come for healing. They do not know what ails them; they think their condition is due to some external cause. Nevertheless, they are healed and exclaim: "This is a marvelous thing, though I do not understand what it is all about." Often they become superstitious about it, as people do about the things they do not understand; once they understand the law, however, healing is no longer a mystery.

The only reason a man has difficulty in throwing off some weakness of character, while believing in Spirit implicitly and having faith that he is going to overcome his limitation, is because he has not induced the necessary mental images in Mind. If he had, he would have overcome his trouble; thinking of his weakness keeps the image of it before him.

In treating, turn entirely away from the condition. Disease and limitation are neither person, place nor thing; they are simply images of thought. Turn entirely from the condition, or the limited situation, to its opposite, that is, to the realization of health, happiness or harmony.

METHODS OF TREATMENT

Although several methods of treatment are used, there are but two distinct methods; one is called argumentative, and the other realization. The argumentative method is a process of mental argument in which the practitioner argues to himself about his patient. He is, consequently, presenting a logical argument to Universal Mind, or Divine Principle; and if that argument carries with it a complete evidence in favor of his patient, it is supposed that the patient will be healed.

The method of realization is one whereby the practitioner realizes within himself the perfect state of his patient; it is purely a spiritual and meditative process of contemplating the Perfect Man; and if the embodiment of the idea is really made, it will at once produce a healing. Treatment is for the purpose of inducing an inner realization of perfection in the mentality of the practitioner, which inner realization, acting through Mind, operates in the patient.

Between John and Mary there is One Universal Medium which is also in John and Mary; It is not only between them, but in them. As John knows right where John is (since there is only *One*), he is at the same time knowing right where Mary is, because his work is operative though a field which is not divided but which is a complete Unit or Whole, i.e., Universal Subjectivity. As he knows within or upon himself, he is setting in motion the Law, which operates through the person whom he mentions in his treatment, no matter where the patient may be. There is no such thing as an absent treatment, as opposed to a present treatment.

Mary must have a consciousness of health before the healing can be permanent. It will have to become a part of her subjective thought. If the consciousness did not change she would perpetuate the old thought images and would get sick again; and that is why, in treating, people get well for a while and then become sick again. They are not permanently healed unless the consciousness is healed.

A treatment begins and ends within the thought of the one giving it. The practitioner must do the whole work within himself. He must know the Truth, and as he does that, he sets in motion the Law. A thing which is known by any part of the Universal Mind is known by every part of It, for It is an Undivided Whole. When you know in one place you know everywhere. When you give a treatment you do not send out a thought, or hold a thought, or give suggestion. A treatment is a positive thing.

If you are treating a certain John Smith, you say (if he is not present), "I am treating John Smith of such and such a place." Then you forget all about him as a personality and give your treatment. It is not necessary to specify the trouble. Once in a great while, you might find yourself mentioning a thing in order to make some statement against it, but probably that is not the best way. Of course there are certain thoughts back of certain things, and a knowledge of the disease might enable you to know better what thought to destroy.

It is like this: Mary Jones comes to John Smith and says, "I have tuberculosis." In answer to this he declares, "This word is for Mary Jones. She is a perfect and complete manifestation of Pure Spirit, and Pure Spirit cannot be diseased; consequently she is not diseased." This is an argument, trying to bring out the evidence in favor of perfection. It is an argument which produces a certain conclusion in the mentality of John Smith, and, consequently, it sets in motion a certain law for Mary Jones. As John does this, day after day, he gradually becomes convinced of her perfection and she is healed. If he could do it in one minute, she would be healed in one minute. *There is no process in healing. It is a revelation, an awakening, a realization of Life.* Man exists in Divine Mind as a Perfect Image; but he covers himself with the distorted images of his own thought along the pathway of his mental experience.

If using the method of realization, say, "This word or this thought is for Mary Jones." Then begin to realize the Perfect Presence, the *Only* Perfect Presence. "God is all there is; there is no other Life"; very little argument, but more and more a complete realization. This is very powerful, although it makes no difference which method you use, as they produce the same result. It is a good idea to combine both.

In the case of a child, the treatment should be the same. *It would have an effect commensurate with the absolute conviction that the practitioner has.* But in the case of an infant, who is subjective to the conscious thought of the people around it, you must teach those people how to think about the child, and see that they do think that way; else you might heal the child and their thought might make it sick again.

In case of failure, it is probable that the trouble is more with John than with Mary, as far as the immediate healing is concerned. However, diseases are the direct results of certain habitual mental attitudes which people entertain, and unless those mental attitudes are changed, there will be no permanent healing. It is the business of the practitioner to discover what those attitudes are and to change them. It is also the business of the practitioner to show people why they are as they are, and to teach them how to overcome undesirable attitudes.

In giving a treatment, you talk to yourself about somebody else.

We must grasp the idea of Universal Subjectivity, the Potentiality of all things, the Divine Creative Medium. This is the Principle through which we are to demonstrate the healing of the body or of the condition; and It acts accurately and mathematically, because It is the Law of cause and effect.

SUBJECTIVE LAW

When we think, we think from conscious intelligence, or Spirit. We will say that the thought becomes subjectified; i.e., it goes into the subconscious mind. But what is man's subconscious mind? It is his atmosphere or mental vibration in Universal Subjectivity. There is no such thing as your subjective mind and my subjective mind, meaning two, for this would be duality. But there is such a thing as the subjective state of your thought and of my thought in Mind. This should be made very clear, for here is where psychology and metaphysics separate; i.e., their understandings are different. When we think, we think into a Universal Creative Medium, a receptive and plastic substance which surrounds us on all sides, which permeates us and flows through us. We do not have to think that we are thinking in It or upon It; for when we think we do think into and upon It; there is no other place that we could think, since It is Omnipresent.

As each subjectifies himself in consciousness he is building around himself a mental atmosphere; and nothing can enter this unless he allows it to, through the avenues of his own thought; but this thought might be conscious or unconscious; in most cases it is unconscious, but the student of Truth is learning to consciously control the stream of thought that he allows to enter his inner and creative mentality.

THOUGHT AND THE CREATIVE MEDIUM

Thought is an inner movement which is the result of one's perception of life and his reaction to it. Every time this movement takes place it takes place within Mind, upon Cause, according to law. We are, without question, dealing with the same Power that molds the planets and all that is upon them; and the limit of our ability to prove this is not in Principle, but is in our understanding of It; in our ability to incorporate within ourselves an embodiment of our ideals.

EACH IS THE LOGICAL RESULT
OF HIS OWN THINKING

We are dealing with a neutral, creative power, just as we would be in the case of electricity or any other natural force. It is on a higher plane; for it is the power of intelligence. As we think into this Universal Mind, our thought, in its externalization, will reach its own level, just as water will reach its own level by its own weight and without effort. This is in line with necessity; for the Universe, in order to be at all, must be Self-Existent.

What is meant by the Self-Existence of the Universe? This means a Universe which is Its own reason for being; a Universe which exists by virtue of Itself, being All.

Each one of us is today the result of what has gone before, either consciously or unconsciously, no matter what kind of a condition he may be in. As soon as we realize this we shall be better off, because we shall see that since what we now are, or what we now have and experience, is the result of what we have thought; the answer to what we shall be is contained in what we now are; for we *can change* our thinking.

Man thinks and supposes that he lets go of the thoughts

he thinks. But such is not the case; for thought becomes sub-jectified in Mind, like a seed planted in the soil; it stays there, unless neutralized, and decides the attraction and repulsion in the experience of the one thinking. There is a constant action on the subjective side of life; and it is this unconscious process which decides what is going to happen in the outer expression. Whatever we think, act, believe in, feel, visualize, vision, image, read, talk about, in fact, all processes which affect or impress us at all, are going into the subjective state of our thought, which is our individualized use of Universal Mind. Whatever goes into the subjective state of thought tends to return again as some condition.

A LAW OF BELIEF

Jesus said, "As thou hast believed so be it done unto thee." Knowing the nature of the law, He did not say, "It is done unto you as you wish." He announced the universality of law when He said, "As thou hast believed so be it done unto thee."

WE ARE DEALING WITH LAW

Someone may say, "I can't imagine God not caring." I cannot ei-ther; but we are dealing with law. Does the law of electricity care whether it cooks the dinner or burns the house down? Whether it electrocutes a criminal or warms the feet of a saint? Of course it does not care at all! Does the urge, which impels people to express, care whether a man kneels in ecstasy or lies drunk in the gutter? We are dealing with law. And it follows that, since we are dealing with law, it will ultimately bring back to us the results of the forces which we set in motion through it. Conse-quently, no person who is enlightened would seek to use this law destructively; for he would know that, sooner or later, the very power set in motion by himself would ultimately destroy him. "All they that take the sword shall perish with the sword." The Spirit of Christ is the spirit which constructively uses the

law. The spirit of Antichrist is the destructive use of law. The
Spirit of Christ, being in line with the Cosmic Life, will always
transcend, neutralize, destroy, and utterly obliterate the spirit of
Antichrist; and ultimately only the Spirit of Christ can succeed.
"He that hath an ear, let him hear."

THE CYCLE OF NECESSITY
AND KARMIC LAW

The cycle of necessity means that those things which the individual sets in motion through the law must ultimately swing
back to him again. This is the Karmic Law; "The law that binds
the ignorant but frees the wise." This law has been announced
by every great teacher who has ever lived. Jesus referred to this
law when He said, "As thou hast believed so be it done unto
thee"; and when He said, "Heaven and earth shall pass away:
but my words shall not pass away." It is the law to which Isaiah
referred when he said, "So shall my word be that goeth forth
out of my mouth; it shall not return unto me void, but it shall
accomplish that which I please." This is the law which today is
called "Divine Principle," or the law of cause and effect; it means
that once a tendency is set in motion through law, it is bound to
objectify at the level of the subjective concept which entertains
it. There is nothing fatalistic about this, for we may consciously
change the currents of subjectivity with the conscious thought.
Indeed, this is what treatment does.

THE LAW OF ACTION AND REACTION

This is simply the law of cause and effect, and instead of getting
too occult or mystical a concept of it we would better think of it
simply as something into which we think, and which returns to
the thinker what he thinks into it. This law can be applied for
concrete purposes, and once it is set in motion the rest works
automatically. This is why we may absolutely trust Principle
when we understand how it operates. It knows everything and

can do anything; but in order to work for us, we must let it work through us. This is the power that Jesus used when He withered the fig tree and when He raised Lazarus from the dead.

WE ARGUE IN MIND

So we argue in Mind; and if we argue toward a belief in health, we will be healed. It isn't a question of suggestion or of the power of thought making us well, for this is but a limited sense of will power. It isn't something over which we must clinch our teeth and will to be; it is something which we have to know. Water doesn't have to will to be wet, it is wet; and if we go into it we will get wet. Life doesn't have to claim to be Life; It simply announces Itself to be what It knows that It Is. So we argue in Mind, not to convince Mind that It is or can accomplish, but to convince ourselves that we are *now* perfect.

WRONG USE OF MIND

There have been many controversies about the use and the mis-use of this power. Some claim that we cannot misuse this power, since there is but One Mind, and It cannot act against Itself. Mind cannot act against Itself; and any person who knows this, and who knows that there is no human mind to destroy, or to be destroyed, is immune from malpractice. But let anyone believe in malpractice, and he will open mental avenues of receptivity to it; for we can receive only that to which we vibrate.

Malpractice is the ignorant use of something which of itself is good. It is the wrong use of mental power and will never be indulged in by anyone who understands the Truth; neither can one who understands the Truth be affected by it. There could be innocent, ignorant and malicious malpractice. Innocent mal-practice, in the form of sympathy with disease and trouble, thereby accentuating these conditions, is often prolific of dire results. Ignorant malpractice would be about the same thing; for instance, when one sees a criminal, thinking of him as such helps to perpetuate the state in which he is manifesting. Malicious malpractice would be an act of centering thought for destructive purposes. When Jesus said, "The prince of this world cometh and hath nothing in me," He meant that he had neutralized all race thought about destruction and so was immune to all false suggestion. This we should all try to do.

SUBJECTIVE BUT NOT UNCONSCIOUS

The subjective mind can deduce only; it cannot, of itself, initiate anything; but this does not mean that it is unintelligent. We must be very careful not to labor under the delusion that because the subjective mind cannot reason it is unintelligent, for it is infinitely more intelligent than our present state of conscious mind, but is, nevertheless, controlled by it.

If our subjective consciousness were always clear, that is, if it never received any false impressions, the Spirit would always flow to the point of objectivity and we would never make mistakes; we would never be sick, poor, or unhappy.

HOW HABITS ARE FORMED

Back in the subjective are the images of thought surrounding us, all acting as living intelligences. It is here that habits are formed; for when one has a habit that he cannot seem to break he is hypnotized by the thought and desire back of that habit; the thought force has grown too strong to be controlled. Habits are healed by neutralizing the thought forces behind them.

LAW IS MIND IN ACTION

There is One Infinite Life acting through Law, and this Law is mental; Law is Mind in action. We are surrounded by an Infinite, Subconscious, Impersonal, Neutral, Plastic, Creative, Ever-Present, Thinking Stuff from which all things come, which, in Its Original State, permeates and penetrates all things. By impressing our thought upon this Substance we can cause It to produce for us that which we think, to the limit of our ability to mentally embody the idea. Impressing our thought upon It is not an external act, for when we impress our thought upon ourselves, we are thinking into It; this is because of the Unity of all Mind. This is one of the great lessons to learn; we do not know anything outside ourselves. This is what Jesus meant when He said, "Ye shall know the Truth and the Truth shall make you free." When we know within ourselves we are knowing at the point of that Individualized Spirit which we are; upon the very Heart of the Infinite, the Ever-Present Substance, which is ever responsive to Itself.

WE ARE BOUND BY OUR OWN FREEDOM

We are all bound, tied hand and foot, by our very freedom; our free will binds us; but, as free will creates the conditions which externally limit us, so it can uncreate or dissolve them. The Universe, being deductive only, cannot refuse man anything.

The very force that makes us sick can heal us; the force that makes us poor can make us rich; and the power that makes us miserable can make us happy. If this were not true there would be duality in the Universe, and this is impossible.

ONENESS WITH ALL LAW

When we know of our Oneness with God and Law, what a great burden will be removed which otherwise would cause us to struggle in making a demonstration! The sense of opposition must forever be removed from the consciousness which perceives Unity.

Instead of saying, "Here is a sick man to heal and I shall have to work hard on this case," we should realize that there is nothing but concept in the Universe and, therefore, say, "I am going to conceive of this man as being absolutely perfect," then the same power which made him sick will heal him. This is the reversal of thought.

That which we call our subjective mind is but a point in Universal Mind where our personality maintains its individualized expression of Spirit. If we think of ourselves as being separated from the Universe we will be limited by this thought; for it is a belief in separation from Good which binds and limits; we are bound by nothing except belief. "They could not enter in because of unbelief," and because they "limited the Holy One of Israel."

There is but One Mind. Here is the point: everything we experience, touch, taste, handle and smell; environment, bodies, conditions, money, happiness, friends; all are effects. Is it clear that the infinite and limitless possibilities of that One of which man is a part, depend, in man's expression, upon his own concepts? If he is a point of personality in limitless Mind, which he is, and if all of his life must be drawn from this One Mind, which it must, there cannot be anything else, can there? And if there is nothing else, if there is nothing to move but Mind, and if man is a thinking center in Mind, nothing is going to happen to him that does not happen through him, whether this is the result of his own erroneous conclusions, those of his grandfathers, or the race to which he belongs. It is impossible to conceive of anything ever happening to anyone unless the force back of it was set in motion by himself, sometime or somewhere. But this is not fatalistic, for we may change the chain of causation which we have set in motion.

Everything comes from Intelligence; there is nothing but Unity; there is nothing but freedom; there is nothing but completeness; there is nothing but Totality. Begin at the beginning and reason this out time after time till doubt disappears; for you will be neutralizing that subjectivity which rises to slay you. It is necessary that each do this for himself.

DEMONSTRATION

As far as making a demonstration is concerned, when we get the correct consciousness this is the easiest thing in the world; but we cannot demonstrate beyond our ability to mentally embody an idea. The argument is between our experience, what the world believes, and what we are convinced is the Truth.

It should be understood that we can demonstrate in spite of our own selves, in spite of all weakness, in spite of every fear, in spite of all that is in us, because such is the power of the Truth. If we waited to be good before demonstrating, the wheel might turn a million times; but law is neither good nor bad; law is and responds.

The possibility of demonstrating does not depend upon environment, conditions, location, personality or opportunity. It depends upon ourselves and upon nothing else. The Universe will never deny man anything, unless we conceive that it is possible for man to think of something that it is impossible for the universe to produce. Every one who asks receives, according to his belief.

KARMIC LAW

Annie Besant said of Karma, "It is the law that binds the ignorant but frees the wise." That which is called Karma in the Orient, we call cause and effect. The subjective state of consciousness is our Karma; this is the result of the thinking that has gone before, and of the race-suggestion operating through us. Karma is not fate; it is mental law; and it can be changed by right thinking and right action. Karma is not Kismet.

THOUGHT FORCE

Thought force is the movement of consciousness which sets law in operation. The movement of consciousness upon itself creates a motion or vibration in Intelligence and upon Substance, the force of which is equal to the reality of the thought set in motion. For everything that happens in the objective world, there must be something in the subjective world to perfectly balance it. Just suppose for a moment that the Universe is nothing but water, permeated by an Infinite Intelligence. Imagine that every time this Intelligence moves or thinks an icicle is formed in the water, exactly corresponding to the thought. We might have countless numbers of icicles of different forms, colors and sizes; but these icicles would still be water. If we could heat the whole mass, it would melt, and all the forms would again become fluent; nothing would have changed but form. This is all there is to matter; it is Spirit in Form; and as such is perfectly good; to deny matter is poor logic.

First is Intelligence; then the Word, the vision, the image, the concept; then the movement to the thing. Remember, thought is an actual working power; otherwise there would be nothing with which the Universe could be run.

CHOOSING THOUGHT

We have a right to choose what we shall induce in Mind. The way that our thoughts are to become manifested we cannot always see; but we should not be disturbed if we do not see the way, because effect is potential in cause; "I am Alpha and Omega" and all that comes between cause and effect. Cause and effect are really One, and if we have a given cause set in motion the effect will have to equal this cause. One is the inside and the other the outside of a concept or idea.

A practitioner's work begins and ends within himself. If, in doing mental work, the thought should come that the thing cannot be done, you must treat this thought as having no power, but only as an impersonal suggestion trying to gain entrance to your mentality. Realize that there is nothing in you that can hinder you from demonstrating the Truth.

If one says to himself, "I am filled with life, health, strength and vigor," and then goes down the street saying, "I see a poor blind beggar, a criminal and a sick person," he is still treating himself just as much as when he affirmed that he was perfect. We are only as perfect as we perceive others to be. This does not mean that we shut our eyes to those who are in trouble; for we may have sympathy with the one having trouble without having sympathy with his trouble. We must have sympathy with all, for, as one of the great prophets of the new age said, "The Divinity of Christ was made manifest through the Humanity of Jesus."

A certain, specific, intelligent form, or idea in Mind, will produce a certain, specific, concrete manifestation in matter, equal to itself. There is one Infinite Principle, One Infinite Thought-Stuff, One Infinite Creative Power and countless numbers of forms, which appear and disappear as the definite, specific, concrete thought behind them changes.

A practitioner is one who changes the false thought and builds on the Principle of Truth, which executes and manifests the truth that the practitioner embodies. He can demonstrate to the limit of his mental ability and his spiritual capacity to conceive of the Truth.

If one wishes to demonstrate prosperity he must first have a consciousness of prosperity; if he wishes health he must embody the idea of health. A consciousness of health, happiness and prosperity can be induced within through right mental and spiritual practice. By consciousness is meant the inner embodiment of an idea; the subjective image of the idea; the mental and spiritual equivalent of the idea.

INDUCING THOUGHT

While a certain consciousness may be mechanically induced, of course, the more spontaneity put into the mechanical word, the more power the word must have. Since we all must begin right where we are, most of us will be compelled to begin with a mechanical process. This is more than faith, for it is a sure knowledge that we are dealing with Law.

Principle is Changeless Reality. That which we call personality is the instrument through which Principle operates, but It can operate for the individual only by operating through him. It is never bound by the form that It takes, but is forever free. Principle fills all form, and not only fills all forms but surges around them, and is in and through them. Ice is water and water is ice; so God and man exist in an Eternal state of Unity.

When one realizes that he is depending upon Principle, he should educate himself to the point of realization of his ability to use It.

We should always be impersonal in mental work. We do not have to be impersonal in life, for we are brought to the point of personality in order that we might enjoy each other. But in mental work we are dealing with an impersonal Principle. It will operate for one just as quickly as for another, because It is Law. Dare to speak and to know that what you speak is the law unto the thing spoken. One, alone in consciousness with the Infinite, constitutes a complete majority.

Knowing this in your own thought, work in perfect peace and calm; always expect; have enthusiasm; and have a consciousness of love; that is, a radiant feeling flowing through the personality at all times. If one hasn't this he should treat himself until he does have it; for without it, he is diseased in mind. Treat until you feel an inner sense of Unity with the all Good. There is One Mind, and the moving impulse of this Mind is Love.

In choosing words in treatment, say anything that will induce the right mental attitude. Giving formulas is a mistake, for how can anyone put a spontaneous thought into the mind of another? Anyone can stand in front of a dead man and say, "Arise," but who is going to have the consciousness to make this happen?

PLACE NO LIMIT ON PRINCIPLE

Know your own mind; train yourself to think what you wish to think; be what you wish to be; feel what you wish to feel; and place no limit on Principle. The word which you speak would be just as powerful as the words which Jesus spoke, if you knew it; but know this within and not only without.

After all, all there is, is mental action and reaction. If you have reached the point where the inner consciousness produces all things, then your word is simply an announcement of reality. There will come a time when demonstration will no longer be necessary.

Know that when you give a treatment, the act takes place in Infinite Mind. Infinite Mind is the Actor and you are the announcer. If you have a vague, subtle, unconscious fear, get still and think, "Who am I? What am I? Who is speaking? What is my life?" Think right back to Principle until your thought becomes perfectly clear again.

Such is the Power of right thinking that It cancels and erases everything unlike Itself. It answers every question, solves all problems, is the solution to every difficulty. It is like the sunlight of Eternal Truth, bursting through the clouds of obscurity and bathing all life in glory. It is the Absolute with which you are dealing and nothing less.

Note: Read carefully "Being and Becoming," F.L. Holmes; "Doré Lectures," T. Troward; "From Existence to Life," James Porter Mills; "Mind's Silent Partner," James Porter Mills; "History and Power of Mind," Richard Ingalese.

LESSON TWO

Man reenacts the Divine Nature on all three planes; he is self-knowing in his conscious mind, creative through his subconscious mind, and has a body. He reenacts the Trinity of Being.

Man is in perfect unity with the Whole. His conscious mind is his understanding of God; his subjective mind is the use that he makes of the Universal Creative Medium; and his body is one with the Body of God.

There is but One Mind in the Universe, and man uses It. Man is an identity in the Universe; he is a center of God-Consciousness. At first he is ignorant of this and misuses his power, consequently bringing upon himself misfortune and sickness.

Man's thought operates through the medium of Universal Creative Mind. As he thinks within himself, he thinks upon Creative Mind and sets Law in motion. Since there is but One Mind a person may think for himself, or for some one else, and cause the Law to operate as he directs.

The use of Creative Mind is like the use of the creative soil. Man never creates; he simply uses a Creative Law.

Objective, conscious and self-knowing mind, all have the same meaning; they mean that part of man which knows that it exists.

THE SCIENCE OF MIND

Subjective, subconscious, unconscious, soul and consciousness have the same meaning; they mean the inner creative medium.

Body, effect and outward conditions all respond to the inner thought.

The Spirit of man, which is his self-knowingness, is the only part of him which has volition or self-choice; all else is automatic law.

Man's conscious thought, acting through law, may change any condition in his experience, provided he can clearly conceive of that condition as being changed. There is no limit to the Law. The limit is not in the Law but in man's ability to embody the Truth and constructively use the Law.

Remember, there is but One Mind and One Law which all people use, consciously or unconsciously, constructively or destructively; One Spirit, One Mind, One Law, One Substance, but many forms. There is only One Ultimate Reality, but within this One there are many experiences. Man is within the One and draws from It any and all experiences in which he believes.

As man thinks he subjectifies thought and sets Law in motion through the Medium of the Universal Mind. *This Law works automatically until It is consciously changed.*

Man uses a Power which is Infinite as compared with the power of his conscious thought.

Divine Principle means Universal Subjective Law; It is the Medium of all thought and action.

Freedom and bondage, sickness and health, poverty and riches, heaven and hell, good and bad, big and little, happiness and misery, peace and confusion, faith and fear and all conditions that appear as opposites, are not really opposing powers, but are the way that the One Power is used.

Man has within himself the key to every situation, but he must come to realize his relation to the Whole. That relationship is one of Perfect Unity.

LESSON THREE

HEALING

Mental healing means mind healing. The possibility of healing physical diseases through the power of right thinking rests entirely on the theory that we are surrounded by an Infinite Mind which reacts to our thought.

That people have been healed through prayer and by faith in all ages, there is no question. But we live in a Universe of Law and Order, and at no time can that Law or Order be broken; therefore, if people have been healed through prayer and faith, it is because they have somewhere contacted a Law which really exists. To suppose that God would heal one man any more readily than another, would be to suppose that God is human and subject to the changing emotions that we ascribe to the human mind. To believe that the Divine Power would operate for one man simply because he asked It to, but would not operate for all, would be to believe in a God more human than man himself. It is very evident, however, that many times people have been healed through prayer; and either God has especially answered them, while He left others to suffer, or else by the act of prayer they have complied with some law. Again, many people have prayed and their prayers have not been answered; yet they have prayed to the best of their ability. Why have some been heard and others not heard? The only possible answer is that some reached a place in their mentality where they believed, while others fell short of this mental attitude. After all, prayer is a certain mental attitude, a certain way of thinking, a certain way of believing. All prayer is mental; some prayers reach a state of belief, while others fall short of that state. This leads us to suppose that *the answer to prayer is in the prayer when it is prayed*. True prayer stimulates a belief in Good which nothing else can, and often causes the one who prays to rise to a point in mentality where the healing work may be done according to the Law of the Universe, which is a Law of Mind.

We have no objection to any form of healing. Anything that will help to overcome suffering must be good, whether it takes the form of a pill or of a prayer. We do not oppose doctors nor medical practitioners, but gratefully acknowledge the wonderful work that they have done and are doing. We hold no controversy with anyone on the subject of healing. We are glad when anyone is healed, or helped, by any method. We believe in any and all methods, and know that each has its place in the whole. We know that man's life is a drama which takes place on three planes—the physical, the mental and the spiritual. We know that each needs to be taken into account. We believe in proper food, proper exercise, proper clothing, proper sanitation and in everything that is real and sensible. We include all and exclude none.

But, while we do not hold arguments with anyone, neither will we allow anyone to hold controversies with us. We know that man's life, in reality, is spiritual and mental; and that until the thought is healed, no form of cure will be permanent. We will gladly cooperate with any and all; but we will not accept the judgment of any and all. We know that there is a Law higher than the physical, and we seek to use It. We, perhaps, shall not always succeed, but we shall not become discouraged or confused over the issue, but will continue until we arrive.

We hold no arguments over any form of theology. We believe in any and every church and in all forms of worship. Above all, we certainly believe in God. But we will not allow anyone to tell us how to worship God, nor compel us to worship in any way other than the way we choose.

We reject the theory that the Truth has been once and for all time given and that It cannot be added to nor taken from. We know this to be true about the Truth; but we also know that no one, so far, has arrived at a complete understanding of the Truth. We expect more light all along the line, and we repudiate any belief that says that all truth has been given.

We know that the authority of man is, in most cases, an assumption and not a reality, and we refuse to be hypnotized into believing in any man-made mandate.

WHAT WE UNDERSTAND ABOUT HEALING

We understand that health is a mental and not a physical state. We seek to heal men's mentalities, knowing that to the degree in which we are successful we shall also be healing their bodies. We know that to the degree in which we are able to see a perfect man he will appear. We feel that man is really perfect, no matter how he appears; and we seek to uncover that perfection which is within every man's life, for this is healing.

We realize that mental healing must also be spiritual healing, for the two cannot be divorced. We know that *a belief in duality has made man sick and that the understanding of Unity alone will heal him.* We seek to realize that Unity with God in all our healing work. Every treatment must carry with it a realization of God if it is to be a good treatment.

We are not superstitious about this, but understand that it is necessary since all Life is One. God stands to us for the One Life in which we all live.

THOUGHTS ARE THINGS

We know that thoughts are things. We know that thought is intelligent and has power within itself to objectify itself. We know that belief makes thought very powerful. We know that our thought lays hold of Causation and manipulates real Substance. We know that the word of man is the law of his life, under the One Great Law of all Life. We know that thoughts of sickness make man sick, and that thoughts of health and perfection will heal him. We know that a realization of the Presence of God is the most powerful healing agency known to the mind of man. We do not argue over the issue, nor seek to convince anyone of its merits. We have passed the stage of doubt and uncertainty; for we KNOW. We also know that we can heal only to the degree that we can think from the higher motive; and we know that we should be constantly on the alert, seeking to embody higher thoughts.

Meanwhile, we will use the best thought that we have and will expect to heal and help all who ask our aid.

Thought is the conscious activity of the one thinking, and works as he directs; it works through Law, but that Law is *consciously* set in motion. We know that Law will operate for us to the fullest extent of our belief in, and understanding of, it.

We realize that since our understanding is not yet complete, it is legitimate to use any and all methods that will help humanity; but we do look forward to the day when Truth alone will answer every need. That day will come to the degree that we know it is already here. The mental healer will do all of his work in Mind and will give his whole time and attention to correct knowing; but he will leave his patient free to use any method that will help him. In this way he will get the best results, for everything is good so far as it goes; but a consciousness of Truth alone can really and permanently heal.

LESSON THREE

METAPHYSICAL MEANING OF WORDS
USED IN CHART NO. III

Universal Spirit—Means the universe of conscious mind and self-determination. The Universal Subjectivity means the Creative Medium of the Spirit, or the Subjective law of the Universe. Particularization means the world of matter and forms. Read again the explanation to Chart Number One. The descent of Spirit means the passing of Spirit into form—the particularization of Spirit into many things. The point, drawn from the top of the chart to the bottom section, symbolizes the Unity of all Life. Spirit passes through Law into Form. Multiplicity comes from Unity, but never contradicts Oneness. The many are within the One.

Man's life partakes of the Divine Nature, and this chart may be used in the Individual or the Universal sense. Our conscious mind is some part of the One Conscious Mind of the Whole. The Complete Nature of God is reflected in man, and he uses the same law that God uses; for there is but One Law, as there is but One Spirit. Both God and man use the same Creative Medium or the Universal Subjectivity. It is the law of all thought and all action. Things come from One Source through One Common Law and One Common Creative Medium. We think of our lives as One with the Whole on all three planes of expression. We are one with the Conscious Mind, one with the Creative Law, and in our bodies we are one with all matter.

No matter what we are treating or for what purpose, the Medium of all thought is the Universal Law. It particularizes Itself through the power of the word that is spoken into It. The word alone is conscious. The Law is Automatic and the form is without self-determination.

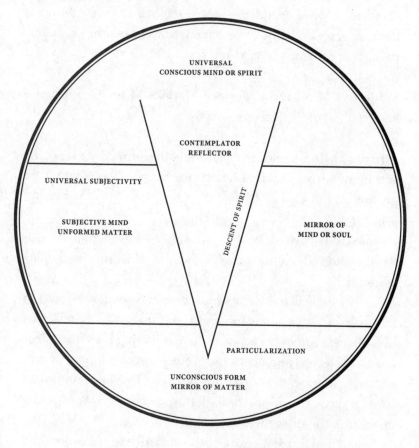

Lesson Three: Metaphysical Chart No. III.

The upper section of this chart shows how the conscious mind, or spirit of man, reflects or contemplates itself, through the medium of soul or subjectivity, into form or matter. The middle section represents the World-Soul or Subjectivity; the Mirror of Mind and unformed matter; the Servant of Spirit; the lowest section shows the result of self-contemplation as it takes form in the world of matter. Read and carefully study the metaphysical meanings of the words used in the Individual Chart.

Conscious Mind or Spirit—Means the Self-Knowing Mind of the Universe. Contemplator, or Reflector, means the conscious thought of the Conscious Mind.

Subjective Mind and Unformed Matter—Mean the Substance and the Soul of the Universe.

Mirror of Mind, or Soul—Means that the Subjective side of life acts like a mirror; that is, It reflects the forms of thought that are given It.

Unconscious Form or Mirror of Matter—Means that the material world reflects the forms of thought which the Soul holds before it.

This depicts the Creative process and sequence—first in the chain of Causation is the Word, and this Word is conscious of Itself; next comes the action of Law, reflecting the Word. (This Law is subjective and obeys the Word, reflecting It into form or matter; matter, being at first unformed, or a Universal unformed stuff.) It then takes form, through the power of the Word acting upon It, on the subjective side of life.

Soul and Substance are both subjective to the Spirit; and form, or matter in form, has no volition.

In the Trinity of Unity, one attribute alone is really self-conscious, namely, the Spirit, or the Word.

This chart may be used in either the individual or the

universal sense, for the individual reenacts the Universal on all three planes.

The manifest Universe is the result of the self-contemplation of Spirit or God. This self-contemplation, through law, reflects its images into the world of form or manifestation.

Man's world of affairs and his body are the result of his inner self-knowingness. He is the result of his self-contemplation.

LESSON THREE

MENTAL HEALING

Whatever exists at all must be the result of a definite image of thought held in the Mind of God or the Absolute, Who is the cause of all. Whether we think of man as a projection of God, an emanation of God, a manifestation or a reflection of God, we must realize that God, or the First Cause, holds man in His Consciousness as a Perfect Being, since the Perfect Mind could not conceive of an imperfect idea. If, on the other hand, we think of man as a part of God, which some schools of thought teach, we should then have to realize that man, as a part of the Divine Being, must inherently be perfect. This is a conclusion which is unavoidable. But man does not appear to be perfect; he certainly appears to have many experiences which are far from ideal. There can be no question but the human man suffers, is sick and has pain and eventually dies. To doubt this would be to doubt the evidence of the only quality we possess whereby we may consider ourselves conscious beings at all. We must, then, reconcile our conclusion of perfection with an experience which is apparently not perfect.

INDIVIDUALITY

While man must be, and is, a Divine Image or a Perfect Idea, yet he suffers and is sick. The answer to this is the same answer which can be given, philosophically, to the whole problem of evil—that man is an individual and does with himself what he wills. The Scriptures say, "God hath made man upright; but they have sought out many inventions." Individuality cannot be automatically produced but must be spontaneous. It could not be real individuality unless it had the ability to think as it chose; and it could not be individuality unless its ability to think as it chose were backed by a power to produce this choice; because, if nothing ever happened as the result of man's choice, he would live in a dream world, and his dreams would never come to objectification. This would be a world of illusion. But man has the ability to choose and is unified with a Law which automatically produces his choice; whereas he does not have the ability to destroy the idea of himself, he does have the ability to deface it, to make it appear discordant; but he cannot destroy the Divine Image.

We live in a Universe of Love as well as in a Universe of Law. One is the complement of the other—the Universe of Love pulsating with feeling, with emotion; and the Universe of Law, the Executor of all feeling and all emotion.

In taking up this lesson on healing, then, let us remember that back of the man which we see is the Divine Image. There is a Perfect Concept, held in the Mind of the Universe as an already accomplished fact, but man is subject to the law of his own individuality.

Let us turn to the Law, and find what It says, in Chart No. III, viz., that man is conscious mind or spirit; this stands for his objective faculty. The objective mind of man is his recognition of life in a conscious state; it is the only attribute of man that is volitional, or self-choosing; consequently, it is the spiritual man. The conscious mind of man is the contemplator, the reflector. The Universe is the result of the Contemplation of the Divine Mind, or the Holy Spirit, which is God. God creates by contemplating His own I-AM-NESS; and this contemplation, through law, becomes the objectification of the Self-Realization of the Infinite Mind.

MAN REENACTS GOD

The Divine nature is reeenacted in man; he is conscious mind and spirit; and, as he contemplates, he reflects his thought into the Universal Subjectivity; it is received and acted upon.

As Mind, or Soul, accepts these images of thought, It operates upon unformed substance and causes it to take definite form as body, which is unconscious form. It becomes definite form, but the form itself is unconscious, because it is made of immaterial substance. Body of itself, without Mind, has no consciousness nor volition. Devoid of mentality, the body neither thinks, sees, hears, feels, touches nor tastes. Take the mentality away from the body and it becomes a corpse. Having no conscious intelligence, it at once begins to disintegrate and to resolve again into the Universal Substance, or unformed matter, from which it came.

Conscious thought or contemplation is a reflector, reflecting through mentality into matter, the forms which consciousness entertains. Although man is inherently a perfect idea, his individuality covers this idea with the forms of thought which he images. Of course, these forms of thought may, or may not, be conscious. Man comes into this life subjective to the race consciousness and with a belief in his own environment; and as he unfolds his own personality he begins to create new subjective thought. He thinks and observes, draws certain conclusions and deductions, and incorporates them within his mentality, until, at last, they also become a part of the relative cause of his objective existence.

Healing is accomplished by uncovering, neutralizing and erasing false images of thought, and letting the perfect idea, or ideal, reflect itself through subjective mind into the body.

When one realizes that *everything is Mind and that nothing moves but Mind*, and that the only instrument of Mind is thought (which is contemplation in some form or other), he will see that nothing can permanently heal but right thinking. It is the only permanent form of healing that is known, i.e., mental and spiritual healing.

NOT LIMITED BY PRINCIPLE

Realizing that conscious thought operates through a Power which is Infinite, we see that there can be no limit to the power to heal, other than the limit of our ability to conceive that Power as healing. We are limited, not by Principle, but by our ability to conceive perfection. Our thought can bring out a condition as perfect as we can conceive; therefore, the man whose thought is the most God-like will be the best healer. That is why we cannot divorce true mental healing from true spiritual work. The man whose thought is the most God-like, i.e., the truest, the highest, the most noble, the most complete, the most peaceful, will be the best healer because his thought reflects a greater perfection. When thought reaches a higher degree of perfection, it will bring out a still greater development, i.e., as the race consciousness unfolds and evolves.

MENTAL TREATMENT IS REAL

Never forget that the Conscious Mind is the only Actor in the Universe and in man; that the unconscious or subjective mind is compelled, by reason of its nature, to accept; and that it can never reject; that the body is an effect, with no intelligence of its own. We can now see that a mental treatment is a real, tangible, specific operation, working in perfect accord with scientific Law.

When a practitioner treats anyone, he does not just hope that his patient will get well; he does not ask that he may be healed; he does not simply desire that he may be healed; he is busy doing a definite piece of mental work, bringing out in his own consciousness (in his own self-contemplative, conscious mind) an understanding that the patient is healed and is perfect.

Treatment is the act, the art and the science of inducing thought within the mentality of the one treating, which thought shall perceive that the body of the patient is a Divine, Spiritual and Perfect Idea. Treatment does not necessarily treat every organ of the body specifically, but it does declare the body to be harmonious and that every specific idea within it is harmonious. It then pays especial attention to what appears to be the physical disorder.

As the result of this treatment which the practitioner gives, Subjective Mind (which is Universal and Omnipresent) accepts the images of his thinking and reflects them in the direction that he specifies.

He is not trying to send out a thought, hold a thought, or suggest a thought. Be sure that you differentiate between suggestion (which is all right, so far as it goes, but is limited) and real metaphysical healing. In metaphysical healing we are conscious that we are dealing with a Universal Principle, or Law, which takes the impress of our thought and acts upon it. Nothing can stop It. Some day we shall know that not even the thought of the patient can stop It, and then that argument will be ended! We are dealing with Something that cannot and does not answer back nor argue. We are directing It for definite purposes, telling It to do certain things which It does. This is what happens when we give a treatment.

Since the Law is Infinite, there is no incurable disease, as opposed to a curable one. The Law knows nothing about disease. It only acts. The practitioner says: "My word is the presence, power and activity of the Truth which is within me, which is Almighty, which is God. There is none other." This word then is the law of the thing whereunto it is spoken and has within itself the ability, the power, and the intelligence to execute itself through the great Law of all Life. This word, being the spontaneous recognition of Living Spirit—Infinite, Ever-Present, and Active—is now completely manifested in and through this person, or thing, about which the practitioner is thinking.

MAN COMES THROUGH SUBJECTIVITY

When man is born, he is born from pure subjectivity into objectivity. He is born from a subjective state of consciousness into an objective state, and he gradually grows into intelligent, self-conscious, objective understanding.

When a baby is born into this world, it is purely subjective; it does not know enough to feed itself; it has no objective
faculties, no judgment, no thought processes. But the minute it
is born it begins to develop an objectivity through observation;
however, it takes a baby longer than it does any other animal,
as it is more helpless. A child does not always gain its objective
faculties quickly—sometimes it never does during this lifetime.
Irresponsible people never become completely objectified on
this plane; they are still instinctively subjective.

BORN PERFECT

Since babies are born from subjectivity, they are born, generally
speaking, from a perfect condition. You will find that practically
everything, when it comes into the world, is perfect; it then takes
on objectivity; but it brings with it, subjectively, certain tendencies.
Very seldom does it bring disease. Very few diseases are inherited,
in spite of all the claims that people make that they inherit heart
trouble, tuberculosis, etc. They do not! What they do, however, is to
inherit a subjective receptivity toward, and a belief in, those things.

At first, children are happy, free, spontaneous. That is why
we like them; they live instinctively. As they grow older and
their emotions become more complex and they hear people talk
about death, trouble, divorce, love and marriage, and everything
else that is good, bad or indifferent, they begin to react to these
emotions subjectively.

Everything that opposes harmony and Spontaneous Unity
will prove disastrous to the child's health, sooner or later. The
inherited part is simply an inherited subjective tendency.

RACE-SUGGESTION

Another prolific source of disease is race-suggestion. RACE-
SUGGESTION MEANS THE ACCUMULATED SUBJECTIVE
TENDENCIES OF THE HUMAN RACE; these tendencies are
operative through any person who is receptive to them.

These, then, are the sources from which most diseases come—conscious observations, suppressed emotions, subjective inherited tendencies, and, perhaps three-fourths of them, from race-suggestion.

DISEASE IS IMPERSONAL

Disease is an impersonal thought force operating through people, which does not belong to them at all. Recognize that it is neither person, place, nor thing; that there is no law to support it; that it is a coward, fleeing before the Truth; that there is nothing but the Truth. There is no limitation imposed upon man anywhere. You must know that the Power you are using is definite, scientific, dynamic, Spiritual, Absolute and complete, and that It will work. Let no fear come into your thought.

Remember that nothing can come through consciousness into objectivity but such thoughts as you claim. The person who has clearly and subjectively realized the Unity of Mind, the Unity of Good, the Presence of God, the Absoluteness of his own Being, the totality of things existing at the point of his own personality, is immune from mental suggestion. He can surround himself with an armor of protection so that false suggestion cannot enter.

As a matter of fact, practically all the world is hypnotized through race concept, and what we need to do is to dehypnotize it.

HOW TO HEAL

Disease is mentally contagious through suggestion; so we must surround our patients with an aura, or atmosphere, of protection. This is nothing less than the realization of the presence and the power of God, or Spirit, as their Life, as the only Life there Is, as Complete and Perfect in them.

First recognize your own perfection; then build up the same recognition for your patient; then directly attack the thought that binds him, recognizing that your word destroys it, stating that it does, taking into account and specifically mentioning everything that needs to be changed, every so-called broken law or false thought. Then finish your treatment with a great realization of peace, sitting there a few moments in silent recognition that it is done, complete and perfect.

The work must not be thought of as hard; and when we know that there is but One Mind, we shall realize that it could not be hard. *Mental treatment is a direct statement in Mind of what we wish to have done and a complete realization that it is done.*

MIND IS THE ACTOR

We recognize that everything is in Mind and that nothing moves but Mind; that Intelligence is back of everything, acting through a thought force which is concrete, definite and real. The reason people do not realize that mental healing is possible is that they do not understand the meaning of Causation; they do not realize that Intelligence is back of all things; that there is but One Fundamental Intelligence in the Universe, One Common Mind or One Mind, Common to all people. *That which we appear to be is simply the point where this Mind manifests through us.* (Man is an Individualized Center of God-Consciousness. Remember, all Law is Mind in Action.)

Every disease that we have must come through Mind in order to operate through us. There is but One Subjective Mind in the Universe. Upon this understanding alone is mental treatment possible (whether it be present or absent); if there were more than One, it would be impossible, for then there would be no Common Medium through which to work, think or act.

There is but One, and we are always thinking into It; so whether a patient is present or absent makes no difference. The only advantage in having him present is that you may talk to him and teach him, and, by analyzing his thought, remove any mental complex or conflict.

The question is often asked: "Is this Subjective Mind, or Law, all that there is to the Divine Nature?" No, of course not. There is the Spirit and the Soul of the Universe, a dual aspect of that which is One; but when you are practicing mental healing, you are dealing with Law, just as definitely as a physicist deals with law.

DISEASE IS NOT ALWAYS DUE TO CONSCIOUS THOUGHT

Any disease, in order to operate through the body, must first be a mental picture in the inner mentality; it must first be subjective, if it is to become objectified. "Disease is an image of thought held in Mind until it appears in the body." This is all there is to it. While every disease is an effect and must first have a subjective cause, the subjective cause, nine times out of ten, is not conscious in the thought of the person who has it; but is, perhaps, largely the result of certain combinations of thinking, which, gathering together around and through the individual who thought and received them, becomes operative through him. Certain combinations of thought, coalescing, produce a definite manifestation.

So, while it is true that every disease has a direct prototype in subjective mind, it is also true that the individual who suffers from the disease, nine times out of ten, never thought he was going to have that particular kind of trouble.

WE DEAL WITH IDEAS

You are dealing with ideas only. Let the physicians deal with bodies, if necessary. There is nothing wrong with medicine or manipulation, provided it relieves suffering, but lest the suffering come again, the mental cause must be removed. Never say to patients: "Don't take medicine, because if you do, the treatments will do you no good"; for this is untrue. Say, instead, "If you feel like taking medicine or going to the doctor, do so." If you follow this method, the time will generally come when your patient will realize that he no longer needs the medicine; *he will have unfolded out of the disease, rather than have broken away from it.*

Actually speaking, no one needs to be healed; that is, health is an omnipresent reality, and when the obstructions that hinder healing are removed, it will be found that health was there all the time. So, in your work, do not feel that you must heal anyone. In fact, assume no responsibility for anyone's recovery.

HAVE NO DOUBTS

Suppose, when you treat a patient, you begin to feel a terrible sense of responsibility—what should you do? You should begin at once to treat yourself against that thought, for as long as you have it there is a barrier to healing. Why? Because when you sift that sense of responsibility down to its last analysis, it is a belief that you cannot heal. Do not give in to that belief, because it is nothing but a thought which says that you cannot heal. Nothing but a thought is saying, or could be saying, it. A chair could not say it, and since it is only a thought that says it, it is only a thought that can unsay it.

Declare: "My word has the power to heal," and you will find that doubt has gone.

THINKING IN TREATMENT

When you are giving a treatment, you are thinking; you are meeting, opposing, neutralizing, erasing and obliterating all suppression, fear, doubt, failure, morbid emotion and sense of loss—whatever the trouble may be. Every time your thought hits fairly and squarely, it erases just as definitely as one would erase a chalk line. Such is the mystery of appearance and disappearance.

Why doesn't God heal us? Because we are independent. We have made ourselves sick and we must heal ourselves. In the Great World War ten or fifteen million people suffered agony, pain, sorrow and grief—it staggers the imagination to conceive of it. But water was just as wet and the birds sang just as sweetly through it all. Nothing happened, except in man's thought and act; he fought until he tired of fighting; then he stopped. We will be sick until we tire of it; then we will inquire into the cause, eliminate it and be healed.

DO NOT TRY TO GO BEYOND YOUR UNDERSTANDING

Our understanding is not sufficient to enable us to set bones, and, since we cannot walk on the water, we take a boat. We can go only as far as we know. Principle is Infinite, but we can demonstrate only at the level of our own concept.

If a man struggles against a habit, he is building up a mental resistance, but if he does not resist it while you treat him, he will soon find himself liberated.

People say: "I can't take off my glasses." Then wear them; but begin to make the declaration that there is One Perfect Vision seeing through you. This is the Truth. *When this statement shall have become a subjective realization, you will be healed and will no longer need glasses.*

If a plaster will relieve, use it. If a pill does any good, take it; but gradually lead thought from where it is into the higher realms of consciousness where neither plasters nor pills are needed.

WHAT A PRACTITIONER MUST KNOW

A practitioner knows that disease is mental. He not only knows this; he knows that disease is simply an impersonal thought force, operating through whatever channel it may find. He knows that it is a direct thought force; that there is nothing but Mind in the Universe; nothing to move but Intelligence. He is not dealing with a physical body, nor trying to heal a physical condition.

Right here, let me mention that many people think they

must put their hands on their patients to heal them—that there is a certain magnetism, potent in healing. This has nothing to do with the power of which we are talking. Magnetic healing is the transmission of vital energy from one body to another and soon exhausts itself.

We treat man, not as a patient, not as a physical body, not as a diseased condition; neither do we treat the disease as belonging to him, the reason being that if we do, we will fasten the disease to him. We must not think of the disease as being connected with him or as a part of him. The practitioner realizes that man is born of Spirit and not of matter. Spirit is Changeless, Perfect, Complete, and in every respect Pure, Undefiled and Uncontaminated. He realizes this until he sees his patient as a living embodiment of Perfection.

A practitioner, then, is one who, recognizing that there is nothing but Mind to move, definitely, specifically, concretely and consciously speaks from his objective mind into subjectivity and gives direction to Law, which is the Actor.

HEALING IS CLEAR THINKING

Healing is the result of clear thinking and logical reasoning, which presents itself to consciousness and is acted upon by it. It is a systematic process of reasoning which unearths the mental cause or idea underlying disease, and presents the Truth about man's Being, thereby healing him.

For instance, say to yourself: "God is All there is. There is only One Life." When you are treating, if there is any little point that is not clear, stop at once and go back to the last analysis of Ultimate Reality and Absoluteness and build your whole argument upon It, in order to get a clear consciousness.

Repeat: "God is All. There is only One Power, Intelligence and Consciousness in the Universe, only One Presence. Now, that One Presence cannot change. There is nothing for It to change into but Itself. It is Changeless and It is My Life now. It is in me now." Claim that no form of race-suggestion, belief in limitation, subjective idea of limitation, thought of Karma, fatalism, theology or hell, horoscope, or any such beliefs have power. Accept none of them. If you have ever believed in them; if you have ever believed that the stars govern you, or that your environment governs you, or that your opportunities govern you, if you have ever been led to believe by anyone that any of these things govern you, recognize that it is a hypnotic condition into which you have fallen, and deny every one of them, until there is no longer anything in you that believes in them.

This is the way to get your consciousness clear. You see what it does; it induces a clear concept of Reality which must reproduce Itself. This process of clear thinking, if carried out every day, would heal any disease, because it would bring a complete recognition of Life.

ONLY ONE LAW

The thing that makes you sick can heal you. You do not need to look for a law of health as opposed to a law of disease; for there is only One Law. This will give a great sense of relief, since it means that there is no power to oppose a correct mental treatment.

People often say to a practitioner: "I want you to hold a strong thought for me." This is a misconception; for there are no strong and weak thoughts in this sense. The most powerful thought is the one that carries the greatest conviction with it. We do not hold thoughts; we simply think them and let Mind operate upon them.

People often say: "It must be a drain to treat so many people; I should think that your will power would become exhausted." This also is a misconception; for will power has nothing whatever to do with real mental healing; its use would imply that the practitioner exercises a personal thought force over his patient. This is false suggestion, which is always some form of hypnotism.

NO SENSATION IN TREATMENTS

It is sometimes thought that in giving or receiving a treatment one must experience some physical sensation. A patient sometimes says, after having received a treatment: "I felt nothing during the treatment." It is not necessary that the patient should feel anything during the treatment, neither is it necessary that the practitioner should feel anything, other than the truth about the words that he speaks.

When we plant a seed in the ground, we do not have a great sensation, and it is not probable that the soil has any sensation. But the seed, planted in the creative soil, will, nevertheless, produce a plant. "What is true on one plane is true on all." Know that you are doing things just as definitely as the gardener. It is the person who knows what he is doing who gets results.

HOW TO REMOVE DOUBT

All thoughts of doubt concerning one's ability to heal come from the belief that it is the personality which does the healing, and not the Law. Never say: "I am not good enough to heal," or "I do not know enough to heal," or "I haven't understanding enough to heal." Know that you are dealing with Law and that It is the Actor. Recognize all such arguments as some form of suggestion and refuse to let them operate through you. You can heal; but you must know that you can.

The day will come when the entire world will believe the Truth, because of the great neutralizing power which It is exercising upon the race consciousness.

THE TRUTH DEMONSTRATES ITSELF

The reason people do not get better results is that they do not understand that principle works independently; the Truth demonstrates Itself. At the root of every one's personality there is One Common Mind. There is but One Subjectivity in the Universe, and all use It. Think of yourself as being in Mind as a sponge is in the water; you are in It and It is in you.

DISEASE IS MENTAL

Every disease that comes up through subjectivity, or appears in the body, must come up through Mind. Bodies, of themselves, do not get sick. For instance, when the Life Principle deserts the body, it is what we call a corpse—a lifeless and inanimate thing; it no longer becomes sick; we understand that it could not get sick unless there were intelligence there to cognize the trouble.

Since the body, of itself, cannot become ill, or hurt, or contract disease, unless there is intelligence there to recognize and feel it, disease is primarily a mental thing. Without mentality it is not; and yet with mentality it appears to be.

For instance, a contagious disease is physically contagious between two living people; but it is not contagious between two dead people. There must be intelligence, even in a contagious disease, for the body to contract it. The dead body cannot catch it from the living because the intelligence has departed.

THE MEDIUM OF HEALING

The thing to *remember always* is, that *there is just One Subjective Mind in the Universe.* This is a point that people often do not realize, and because they do not, they cannot see how a person may be treated without touching him; or that a person can be healed at a distance through absent treatment.

If there is but One Subjective Mind in the Universe (and we all remember the meaning of Subjective Mind; It is Deductive, Receptive, Plastic, Neutral, Impersonal and Creative; It is the Stuff from which all things are formed)—you can impress upon It a certain image of thought, or a certain process of realization, and you will get a result; for it is the Actor.

DEPEND ON PRINCIPLE

Through the proper use of this great Subjective Law you can impress upon It a definite idea; and if you, yourself, do not withdraw that idea, or neutralize it by an opposite one, the law will bring it into manifestation.

What we need, then, is to learn the law governing this Principle. When you give a treatment, you are definitely setting in motion a Universal law which must not only accept what you say, but the way in which you say it. If your treatment is given with a sense of struggle, it will manifest that way; if it is given with a sense of peace, then it will manifest in that manner.

Remember that you need assume no personal responsibility for the recovery of your patient. All that you have to do is to make certain statements which Mind is going to carry into effect through him.

One who understands the use of Divine Principle never tries to suggest, hypnotize nor personally influence anyone; he is always impersonal in his work; he is stating in Mind directly what he wishes to have done.

When you have occasion to treat yourself, call your own name and then proceed with the treatment, as though you were treating some one else.

Disease will be healed, provided you get at its cause and remove it, and provided the one for whom you are working is willing to surrender that cause. *You cannot heal anyone of his trouble if it is the result of some mental attitude which he will not surrender.* In this case, find out what the mental attitude is and remove it. It is a practitioner's duty to uncover false ideas of Life and replace them with the Truth. If this can be done before the disease destroys the body, a healing will always follow.

DEFINITE WORK IN HEALING

Principle is the Power that made everything; it is Absolute; It will not and cannot be denied. The only thing that can deny God is yourself.

Do not think of disease as an entity, but as an impersonal thought-force. In healing, you are separating the false from the true; the work is definite and dynamic, and is consciously done with a clear purpose always in mind.

If your own thought is clear, and you are able to completely realize the presence of Spirit in your patient, all the power on earth cannot hinder you from healing.

REPEATING TREATMENTS

Always come to a complete conclusion while giving a treatment; always feel that it is done, complete and perfect. In the intervals between treatments, do not carry the thought of the patient around with you; to do so is to doubt, and this mental attitude must be completely overcome. Each treatment is a complete statement of the Reality of Being. The treatment should be repeated daily until a healing takes place. If it takes five minutes, five hours, five days or five years, the treatment must be kept up until a healing is accomplished. This is the only method that we know. It is not enough to say that everything is all right; this is true in principle, but in fact, it is only as true as we make it. Treat until you get results. A healing takes place when the patient is no longer sick, and until that time mental work must be done.

REMOVE THE COMPLEX

Suppose one is constantly saying: "Everything is all wrong in the world; people are wrong; things are wrong; conditions are wrong; every one is sick; every one is unhappy; nothing is worth while." You, as a practitioner, must remove this complex; for these inner emotions create outer conditions in and through the body and are what cause a great deal of the sickness in the world.

Treatment straightens out consciousness by clear thinking. When the inner consciousness agrees with the Truth, when there is no longer anything within which denies the outer word of Truth, then, and not until then, a demonstration takes place. Specifically go over the thoughts that are wrong and use the power of your word to heal them.

THE SCIENCE OF MIND

HEALING PAIN

Use the thought of peace and the realization of a Perfect Presence; know that in this Presence there is no tension, there is no struggle, there is no fear, there is no sense of conflict. Know this until there comes to your own consciousness a deep, calm sense of peace and ease, and until every thought of pain is eliminated.

Do the same in the case of fever; treat until it is gone; usually it will go like heat off a stove.

HEADACHE

Suppose that every little while you have a headache. A physician may say that it is caused by some nerve strain; a chiropractor may say that it is something out of joint; the osteopath may say that it is something else; and some other practitioner may say that it is something else; for each has found some twist in the body to fit his theory. All of these twists may be there; but the body could not twist unless you were there to twist it. The metaphysician goes to the twister and untwists his thought, thus freeing the twists in the body. We recognize all the good that doctors are doing, but we insist that the mentality must also be taken into account.

Back of nearly every disorder there is some complex, or mental knot, that needs to be untied; generally, some suppressed emotion which, perhaps, is centered around the affections—the likes and dislikes, the loves and passions, and everything that goes with them. All these knots must be untied and it is the business of the practitioner to untie them.

WHAT RIGHT THOUGHT DOES

Right thought, constantly poured into consciousness, will eventually purify it. Disease is like a bottle of impure water; healing might be likened to the process of dropping pure water into the bottle, a drop at a time, until the whole is clean and pure. Some one might ask why the bottle could not be turned upside down and at once drain out all the impurities. Sometimes this happens, but not often; meanwhile, a drop at a time will finally eliminate the impurities and produce a healing.

In treating, go beyond the disease and supply a spiritual consciousness; never leave a person without the Great Realization of Life and Love, of God and Perfection, of Truth and Wisdom, of Power and Reality. Sense the Divine Presence in and through the patient at all times.

HOW HABITS ARE HEALED

What is a habit? A habit is the form that desire takes; it is a desire for something that will give satisfaction. At the root of all habit is one basic thing, the desire to express life. There is an urge to express in all people, and this urge, operating through the channels of Creative Mind, looses energy into action and compels the individual to do something.

Back of all desire is the impulse of Spirit to express. In man, this impulse must express at the level of his consciousness:

"For each, for the joy of the working and each in his separate star, Shall paint the thing as he sees It for the God of things as they are."

Some express constructively and some destructively.

Suppose a man who has the liquor habit comes to you to be healed. You would not pray that he be healed, for you would know that you are dealing with a man who has the desire to express life and who thinks that he must express it in terms of intoxication. He once thought this expressed reality to him; he now knows that it does not, but he has not the will power to stop; for the habit has appeared to take complete possession of him. (It is well to remember that unless we control thought, it will control us.)

In giving the treatment, first recognize who and what he is, saying something like this: "He is the full and complete expression of the Truth, and, as such, he is free from any sense of limitation. He is free from any delusion or fear of delusion. He knows that the Spirit of Truth within him is complete and always satisfied. That thing which calls itself the liquor habit has no power over him and cannot operate through him. By the power of this word, it is now completely destroyed and forever obliterated." Then see him free and satisfied. Wait until you, yourself, are sure of the statements made, realizing that the work is done. This is the treatment.

THE SEED OF THOUGHT

Whether we say our thought goes out, or whether we say it is operated upon by Principle, makes no difference; it is very evident that until a thought is created there is no operation. For instance, a person is sick and he remains sick until some one knows that he is well. It is very evident, then, that as the result of some one's thinking he is healed. We know that the thinking sets in motion some law. Whether the word used heals, or whether it simply sets the Law in motion, really makes no difference. The practitioner is in the same Mind in which his patient lives; consequently, since each is in One Mind, the patient is sick in the same Medium and, in a certain sense, in the same Mind in which the practitioner lives; and because this Mind is Indivisible, the practitioner can, in his own mentality, reach the thought which causes the patient to be sick. Whether we say he sends out a thought, or whether he simply thinks a thought, makes no difference. *The simplest way is to say that the practitioner realizes within himself upon the One Mind, through the One Medium, in the One Law.*

The practitioner realizes a certain truth for his patient—within himself. Therefore he sets the Law in motion for his patient. (The operation of this Law may be thought of as the same as that of the law whereby water reaches its own level by its own weight.) The practitioner knows within himself; and that self-knowingness rises into the consciousness of his patient. So we do not have to worry about sending out thoughts. It is just like planting a seed in the ground; the practitioner sows the seed and the Creative Mind produces the plant. Does the ground operate on the seed, or does the seed operate upon the soil? We do not know, but we do know that when a seed is put into the ground, something operates upon it and a plant is produced; and that unless a seed is put into the ground, no plant will be produced.

WHAT CAN BE HEALED

What should we try to heal mentally? If we were dealing only with the power of our own thought, our limited concept, we could not heal anything mentally; but if we realize that we are dealing with Universal Principle, how can we set any limit to Its Power?

People are sick because they cover a perfect idea with imperfect thoughts; for sickness is the result of subjectified thinking. Everything which the objective mind has consciously thought has fallen into the subjective. All suggestions received have also fallen into the subjective thought; these suggestions may or may not have been consciously received. This will explain why people may be taken sick with diseases of which they never heard; somewhere, on the subjective side of thought, certain forces have been set in motion which, when objectified, produced certain conditions.

WHY PEOPLE GET TIRED

Let a person say to himself; "I have overworked," and at once there will come up through his consciousness a belief in weariness. People who are constantly complaining of being tired are simply hypnotized into this belief through the law of race-suggestion.

Suppose one had dropped complexes into his subjective thought; suppose desires had torn him, and conflicts had entered into his life; what would have happened? He would have been continually dropping opposing thoughts and concepts into his mentality; and as the mental action took place, they might produce a twisted body; and if over-chaotic, they might produce what is called nervous prostration. It would not, however, be the body that was sick but would be a condition brought about through wrong thought.

Now, if subjective thought were a thing apart from us, if we did not have conscious access to it, we could not change it; but being the result of the way thought has worked, we *can* consciously change it. If this were not true mental healing would be impossible.

THE IDEA MUST TAKE FORM

Healing, then, takes place to the degree that we send down the right kind of thoughts into subjectivity. This does not mean that we must sit around holding thoughts. We do not hold a seed in our hand when we wish to plant it, and it is the same in healing; we do not hold the thought but seek to realize it and let it work. By thinking consciously and with deep feeling, we implant the right idea in Mind, and Mind reproduces this idea as effect in the body. We must realize that we are using a power compared to which the united intelligence of the human race is as nothing. This should not seem strange; for we know that the united intelligence of the entire race cannot produce a single rosebud, yet any gardener may produce as many roses as he wishes, if he goes about it in the right way. We must remember that what is true on one plane is true on all. Involution and evolution are the law, cause and effect. The practitioner involves an idea in Mind; it is Law and must operate.

If one wishes to treat a patient, he must first treat himself; as he treats himself, that is, as he treats his own mentality, which is simply a point in Mind, he reaches the mentality of his patient. The practitioner cannot erase the thought in the patient's mentality until he has first neutralized the idea in his own thought.

RESOLVE THINGS INTO THOUGHTS

A treatment is a specific thing. If you are treating some one against the belief in scarlet fever, you are making your word operate in such a way as to neutralize a belief in this disease. Each treatment must have, in itself, everything necessary to cover the case. When you treat, resolve things into thoughts; bodies, people, objects and all things. Having resolved everything into thoughts, know that disease is neither person, place nor thing; it has no location, does not belong to anyone, cannot operate through anyone, is not believed in by anyone. Know that it is a false belief, a false image, with no power. Know that the whole thing is mental; then mentally dissolve it.

HEALING INSANITY

In treating someone whose mind appears to be deranged, realize that there is but One Mind, which Mind is God, and is Perfect. This is the only Mind that is; It is the Mind of your patient; It is your own Mind. This Mind, being a Complete, Perfect and Indivisible Whole, cannot labor under a delusion, cannot, for one moment, lose Its Self-Consciousness. After you have realized this Truth about Life, realize that it is also true about the one you are treating; his thought is perfect. If you have this realization in your own mentality, knowing there is just the One Mind, there will be no doubts or confusions; and the mentality of the patient will cease to be deranged.

WHAT A PRACTITIONER DOES

What a practitioner really does is to take his patient, the disease and everything that appears to be wrong right into his own mentality, and here he dissolves all false appearances and all erroneous conclusions. He takes the condition, not as a reality, but as a belief; and right at the center of his own being he neutralizes the whole false thought, thus healing the condition.

The more completely the practitioner is convinced of the power of his own word, the more power his word will have. There must be a complete realization that the power of the word, operating as the Truth and the Reality of Being, can do all things. Therefore, the person whose consciousness is the clearest, who has the most complete idea of Life, will be the best healer.

BACK OF THE APPEARANCE IS THE REALITY
HEALING IS NOT CREATING A PERFECT BODY OR A PERFECT IDEA; IT IS REVEALING AN IDEA WHICH IS ALREADY PERFECT. HEALING IS NOT A PROCESS. IT IS A REVELATION, through the thought of the practitioner to the thought of the patient. There may be a process *in* healing but not a process *of* healing. The process in healing is the mental work and the time it takes the practitioner to convince himself of the perfectness of his patient; and the length of time it takes the patient to realize this perfectness.

It is necessary that the practitioner realize a perfect body; he cannot realize this unless he has already become convinced that the perfect body is there. If he has come to this conclusion, he must not deny it. There is a perfect heart and a perfect idea of heart; there is a perfect head and a perfect idea of head; perfect lungs and a perfect idea of lungs. The practitioner must realize that back of the appearance is the Reality, and it is his business to uncover this Reality. He does this through a process of obliterating false thought; he must deny false conclusions, bring out the evidence of perfection, and produce the healing. Disease is a fact but not a truth; it is an experience but not a reality.

SEEING PERFECTION
When Jesus said to the man, "Stretch forth thine hand," He undoubtedly saw a perfect hand. Did he see the without or the within as being perfect? If everything is mental, and if he saw

an imperfect hand instead of a perfect one, no good result could have come through His seeing, according to the law of cause and effect. This is true of all demonstration in healing. A practitioner does not treat a sick man; if he does, he not only will not heal him, but he might become sick himself. The reason for this is simple; he will have entered into the vibration of the patient's thought, and will, himself, experience the results of that vibration. This is an experience that many have when they first begin to practice; they take on the conditions of their patients. So, from what we know, Jesus must have seen only the perfect hand. Even though He might have recognized the false condition, as far as His word of healing was concerned it must have been a recognition of perfection, else it could not have healed.

We must think of the subjective state of our thought as our atmosphere in the Universal Mind; for we cannot separate ourselves from the Universe. There is but One Mind and we are in It; we are in It as intelligence; It accepts our thought and acts upon it. Destructive emotions, desires or ideas, unless they are neutralized, will grow into some bodily condition, and may produce disease. Disease is thought manifested, no matter what the disease may be. We are surrounded by a Receptive Intelligence which receives the impress of our thought and acts upon it.

HEALING LUNG TROUBLE

Suppose a person comes to a practitioner and says: "I am dying of tuberculosis." What is tuberculosis? It is a belief in lung trouble; but lung itself is a universal idea, a perfect idea; and nothing has ever happened to it. It was, is, and will be; but man, through the creative medium of his thought, has caused an appearance of disorder and disease in the lung. Back of all such trouble is a consuming passion, an unexpressed emotion, a strong desire. Healing will take place to the degree that the practitioner neutralizes this belief and perceives the presence of a perfect lung. He realizes that there is a perfect body, perfect lung, perfect being, perfect God, perfect man, perfect expression; he must bring his own thought up to this perception. The word he speaks is law; it is power; it knows itself to be what it is. It is the law unto the case. He is now conscious that the word he speaks will neutralize and entirely destroy the false thought and condition. He says: "There is one body; this body is the Body of God; and it is Perfect; it is never depleted; its vitality is never lowered. There is no wasting away of substance or burning up of substance; for substance is eternal, changeless and perfect." He goes on until he covers what in his own thought appears to be the cause of the false condition. If he does this day after day, the patient begins to get better; though the practitioner never thinks of his patient, other than that his word is being spoken for him; and he never wonders whether his word is taking effect, because he speaks into Intelligence and lets It act. Perhaps, if it is a case that requires a great deal of attention, he treats morning, afternoon, and evening, each time for a few moments; otherwise ten or fifteen minutes each day should be sufficient.

Never think that a sick person is one who simply has a sick *body*. If you do you will find yourself treating the body. Why shouldn't we treat the body? Because the cause of the disease is not in the body. The body is an effect and not a cause. KNOW THAT BODIES AND CONDITIONS NEVER MOVE; THEY ARE ALWAYS MOVED UPON. A sick person is one who has a sick thought.

What about accidents? It is part of our belief that as soon as, and to the degree that, our minds become adjusted harmoniously to the Universe, we will be less likely to have accidents.

WE DO NOT SEND OUT THOUGHTS

In practice, we do not try to send thoughts to our patients; for there is but One Mind in the universe. We will say "A" represents a man who is sick; "B" represents a practitioner. "B" thinks into

Mind; and whether we say he is thinking within himself or somewhere else does not matter; he is always thinking into Mind,
because he is in Mind. "But," one might say, "the patient thinks
into his own subjective mind"; yes, but his subjective mind is
only his atmosphere in the One Mind. We must get this very
clearly, else some day there will be a wall between our thought
and its ability to heal some condition, or some person who is at
a physical distance.

Both the patient and the practitioner think into One Common Mind; therefore when a patient comes to a practitioner for
healing the practitioner does not try to hypnotize him or suggest
anything to him; he declares the Truth about him. And to the degree that he brings his own consciousness to a true recognition
of perfection—provided there is a receptivity in the thought of
the patient—that man will be healed; nothing can hinder it. The
practitioner does not try to hold a thought or send out a thought;
he simply tries to convince himself of the perfection of his patient. He does not try to make his word operate through his
patient but only attempts to know the Truth of what he states.
The patient must be receptive to the Truth, and then the Truth
will heal him. The practitioner is dealing with Universal Law,
backed by Omnipotent Power, which is Divine Principle. This is
what Jesus meant when He said: "Ye shall know the Truth and
the Truth shall make you free."

Every time we think, we are thinking into a receptive, plastic Substance, which receives the impress of our thought. When
we stop to realize how subtle thoughts are, how unconsciously
we think negation, how easy it is to get down and out, we will see
that each is perpetuating his own condition. This is why people
go from bad to worse, or from success to a greater success.

VISION

Eye trouble is a belief in limited vision; it is a belief in a separated vision. God sees, and His is the Only Mind there is. It is

our Mind; consequently, man sees, whether he knows it or not. Do not fear to claim this; because it is the truth. There is no obstruction to vision; there is no near vision nor far vision; there is no false vision; there is no weak vision nor blurred vision. There is One Perfect Seeing, which is Now seeing through and in me.

HEALING CONSTIPATION

Constipation is due to a belief in limitation or burden and is healed by knowing that there is no restriction, no inaction, no limited action, no bondage, no fear, no congestion. Make the thought realize that there is nothing but freedom; that all action is normal, harmonious and perfect.

Very often the word of healing is spoken and does not appear to operate because some obstruction hinders it. Some people are obstinate, resistant, stubborn; and they must be healed of these beliefs. There is no resistance to Truth, no thought anywhere which can hinder consciousness from perceiving the Truth. Whatever the false condition is, ARRAY MENTAL ARGUMENT AGAINST IT IN AN OPPOSITE MANNER. Turn the thought over and over, until, either by reason or by chance, you hit upon the thing that is wrong. Anyone can heal if he will do this, just as anyone, if he goes into the garden and drops seed into the ground, will cause plants to grow. Anyone can heal who can get away from the effect long enough to perceive a different cause.

In every treatment the thought of fear must always be handled. One should realize that there is no fear, nothing to be afraid of; and that fear cannot operate through man.

DISEASE NOT AN ENTITY

Man is fundamentally perfect; this is our whole premise; Perfect God, Perfect Man, Perfect Being; this is the whole basis of the argument. Always separate disease from the person suffering with it. Declare very frequently that disease is neither person,

place nor thing; that it has no location, no avenue through which
to express itself, no expression, no one through whom to express.
Never locate disease, because thoughts are things, and if located
they will operate. Always separate the belief from the believer,
for nothing ails the real man; nothing ever did or ever will.

THROAT TROUBLE

In treating throat trouble the thought to handle is sensitiveness.
No one would ever have throat trouble if his feelings were never
hurt. You heal a person of sensitiveness by teaching him that no
one desires to hurt him, and that no one could if he did so desire.
When one becomes really individualized his feelings cannot be
hurt; for he will feel complete within himself.

CONGESTION

In colds, congestion and like conditions, the thought to heal is
confusion. There should be a consciousness of poise, a recognition of peace; and when this comes into the individual's experience he will no longer have colds.

PARALYSIS

People could be healed of all forms of paralysis through the
elimination of the belief in bondage. Use the thought that Life
cannot become paralyzed or inactive. As in constipation, there
is a thought of restriction back of the thought of paralysis; and
often there is a very emotional nature to deal with; and often,
though not always, a lot of stubbornness and resistance to heal.

GROWTHS

If the thought of false growths can be erased the manifestation
can be healed. Declare, "Every plant which my Heavenly Father
hath not planted shall be rooted up." The Heavenly Father is
the Reality of Man and is Eternal Presence and Perfection. Dissolve the idea of false growths by knowing that there is nothing

for them to feed upon. Erase the belief in your own mentality and you will remove it from the mentality of your patient, and thereby heal his body.

TREATING CHILDREN

In the case of children, remember that the thoughts of the parents influence the child. We will suppose the child's mother is constantly saying: "The poor thing; the poor, little, sick thing!" From the human standpoint this is natural, but it makes the child sick just the same, no matter how loving it may be. This is called unconscious, or innocent, malpractice. It is malpractice, because it is the wrong use of thought; innocent, because it is not intended to harm; unconscious, because she doesn't know what she is doing; ignorant, because she doesn't know the results of such mental action. In such a case the practitioner must realize that there is no mental influence operating through the child, except a belief in perfection.

POWER OF THE WORD

Be specific in treating, be definite and direct in your mental work. You are dealing with Intelligence, so deal with It intelligently. The treatment must realize the patient as perfect; must recognize the word as power; must know that it breaks down every man-made law and casts it out; that it is the law of harmony and the recognition of the Presence of Good; that within itself it is unbounded, and equipped with the power to execute itself; and it must know that it does this. It must know that there is nothing that can change it; that there is no belief which can hinder it; that it cannot be reversed, mislaid, misplaced, neutralized or destroyed by any opposing force; but that it does the thing that it is supposed to do. And it must know that it is continuous and will operate until it does all that it is supposed to do.

Jesus said: "Heaven and earth shall pass away: but my

words shall not pass away." Isaiah understood something of this when he said: "So shall my word be that goeth forth out of my mouth: it shall not return unto me void."

NO AGE

There are certain thoughts that should always be handled, such as thoughts of race-suggestion, inherited tendencies, prenatal conditions, environment, and mental influences and suggestion. A treatment must be so formulated as to recognize that there is but One Mind; consequently, no thought can flow through It of depression, fear, or suggestion of imperfection. Man is Birthless, Deathless, Ageless Spirit; and this should be the consciousness of our work. This leaves nothing to be born, mature, decay and die. When this thought shall be made clear in the consciousness of the race, people will no longer grow old. Life cannot grow old; It is always the same.

MEMORY

Locke, in "Human Understanding," defines memory as: "The power to revive again in our minds those ideas which, after imprinting, have disappeared, or have been, as it were, laid aside out of sight." Memory is the ability to remember things that have happened; therefore, if something happened two years ago, of which we are not at present thinking, we can remember it, because it is in our subjective thought. We say that we are getting absent-minded, which means that we cannot recall thoughts. A person may be healed of this belief by knowing that the One Mind never forgets Itself. This Mind is our Mind now.

GUIDANCE IN TREATING

If, in treating, it seems impossible to know just what thought to handle, it is well to be still and know that Intelligence within will tell you what to say and how to say it. By doing this some idea will come and you will find that, by using it, you will reach the case.

HOW TO HEAL

Never say: "Here is a patient whom I must heal"; for, if you see him from this angle, how are you going to heal him?

If you see a sick man he will remain sick, so far as you are concerned; you cannot heal while you see sickness. Disease is neither person, place nor thing; nobody believes in it; it has no action or reaction; it is neither cause nor effect; it has no law to support it and no one to operate through; there is no one to talk about it or believe in it.

You have nothing to do with the patient's thought as a personality, for as your own thought clears it will heal him. When you give a treatment, first eliminate all doubt and fear from your own thought. Realize that you are a Divine Idea and that your word is the law unto the thing unto which it is spoken. This is what gave Jesus his power; "For he taught them as one having authority, and not as the scribes."

REMOVE DOUBT

Suppose a practitioner is not able to convince himself of the Truth of the statements which he makes; how is he going to bring himself to the point of belief? By repeating the affirmation, dwelling on its meaning, meditating upon the spiritual significance of it until the subjective state of his thinking becomes clarified. This is the only reason for repeating treatments; for one treatment would heal anything if there were no doubts. Repeated treatments induce within consciousness a definite concept of an already established fact, even though the fact may not already have become objectified; this is why mental healing is a science. There is no room for doubt in a treatment.

Realize that you treat with your understanding through the Law. Never say: "I am not good enough to treat." There are no good, better and best; this is a delusion; for one is as good as another in the Truth.

Do not allow yourself to become superstitious; for you are

dealing with a normal, natural law in the mental and spiritual world. This law is just as real as any other known law. Don't say: "I am not sure that I have enough power to treat"; you cannot heal with this mental attitude. Say, "As I let fall the forms of my thought they are operated upon by Principles I believe. This is the Law of God, the law of man and the Law of the Universe." Never say: "This disease is hard to heal while another is easy." If you find yourself saying this, at once heal yourself. This comes from a belief that we are dealing with a limited power.

NO FEAR

Suppose when you begin to treat, a great surge of fear comes over you and attempts to tell you that you cannot give a good treatment. The thing to do is to treat this fear as a suggestion which has no power and which cannot convince you that you lack the power to heal. Say: "There is nothing in me which can doubt my ability to heal." This will neutralize the fear and free the effort to accomplish.

How do we know when we have treated a patient long enough? When he is well he will need no more treatments; until this time comes treat every day for a realization of perfection.

Does it make any difference whether or not the patient is taking medicine? Not a bit. If this form of healing gives him any relief, let him have it. We all need all the relief we can get. The patient is healed when he no longer needs medicine. Forget the medicine and heal him mentally and he will no longer take pills.

Some think that they dishonor God when they take a pill. God knows nothing about pills; this is superstition, pure and simple; mostly simple. Discard all such thoughts and give your entire attention to realizing perfection for your patient.

Healing is not accomplished through will power but by knowing the Truth; this Truth is that man is already Perfect, no matter what the appearance may be. Holding thoughts has nothing to do with treatment. If you find, when you begin to give treatments, that the process gives you a headache, know that you are doing your work on the mental plane and not through spiritual realization. A treatment should leave the practitioner in a better condition than before he gave it; otherwise it is not a good one.

One might ask: "Is all disease a thought held in the conscious mind of the patient?" No, not necessarily; it may be a subconscious thought; or it may be the result of many thoughts which, gathered together, produce a definite result.

PSYCHO-ANALYSIS

It may be necessary for the practitioner to diagnose the thought of his patient; in fact this is one of the main points in healing. This is psycho-analysis (from psyche or soul). Psycho-analysis is the analysis of the soul or subjective mind. Its teaching is, that within the soul, or subjective mind, all the seeds of our thought fall; and that most of man's physical troubles are caused by some conflict of the emotions and the will. The conscious mind, desiring certain things which it cannot have, sends into the subjective thought opposing desires, which conflict with each other and mentally tear or bind; and as they manifest in the body, they produce disease. It is claimed that seventy percent of all diseases are the results of suppressed emotions; these emotions are not necessarily sex emotions, but may be any suppressed desires. These suppressed emotions cause what are called complexes.

It is probable that when Jesus forgave the man his sins, He realized that the man had a complex of condemnation within himself. The sense of condemnation which the race holds about itself weights it down, and it must be removed. This explains why Jesus said: "Thy sins be forgiven thee." It is feeling that hurts. The thinking man thinks things out, resolves everything into its normal parts and so avoids complexes. It has been said:

"Life is a comedy to him who thinks, a tragedy to him who feels."

The practitioner talks to his patient, shows him the Law of Mind, teaches him the way, diagnoses his thought, points out to him that certain mental attitudes produce certain physical results, teaches him how to be harmonious in his thinking, how to be at peace, how to trust and believe in the Good, lifts him up mentally and spiritually and supports his thought until he can stand alone.

A practitioner must be filled with a spirit of Divine Compassion; he must have a deep, underlying sense of unity and sympathy, else he will do but little good; but he must not have sympathy with the disease. The only guarantee of our Divinity is in its expression through our Humanity. Consequently an enlightened soul understands the meaning of sympathy and exercises it, but not morbidly.

DEAL ONLY WITH THOUGHTS

In mental treatment, the practitioner deals with thoughts and does not treat bodies or conditions. He never manipulates, nor need he lay his hands on his patients. He does not hypnotize them; he does not care where they are when he is treating them, or what they are doing; for this would be a limited concept. The practitioner's work begins and ends within his own consciousness.

NERVOUSNESS

The thoughts to cover in nervousness are ones of peace, poise and power. There is no twitching of the nerves; there is no strain or struggle in the universe. Things move harmoniously, quietly and normally; and this action, which is the action of Life, is the truth about the one you are treating. A treatment lasts until the one treating is convinced of the truth which he states; it might last one minute or one hour, or longer.

STAMMERING

The treatment for stammering is one that covers the idea of correct speech. Speech is the Word of God and cannot become impaired, but must be a flow from that One Life which knows Itself to be what it is. Speech is perfect.

ARGUMENT IN TREATMENT

Just a word about argument in treatment; we do not argue to make principle work but to convince our own thought that it already is operating.

To sum up the idea of treating, then—you are conscious mind: your patient is conscious mind; he has thought, or is thinking, or there has been thought through him, consciously or unconsciously, an idea of imperfection. You, as conscious mind, remove this something which says that he is imperfect. The treatment begins and ends within your own mentality; it must cover the case and leave nothing to be sick, sin or die; then it will be effective. Meditation in treatment; an uplifted receptivity to Spirit will always produce good results. A deep inner sense of the unity of all life enables one to feel that the Great Conscious Mind and Spirit of the Universe, flowing through his mentality, is the Presence and the Power of an Infinite Life, Truth and Love. We should sense that back of the word which we speak is the Power of the Universe surging to express Itself. Then speak the word consciously, knowing that it is Law.

Note: Read and carefully study "Teaching and Addresses," Edward S. Kimball; "The Law of Mind in Action," F. L. Holmes; "The Faith That Heals," F. L. Holmes; "Christian Healing," Fillmore; "Lessons in Truth," Cady; "Primary Lessons," Militz; "Outwitting Our Nerves," Jackson.

LESSON THREE

Sickness is an experience but not an Ultimate Reality; it is an effect and not a cause. The body, devoid of mentality, could neither know nor have sensation; it is entirely an effect. The body is made of the same unthinking stuff from which all Creation is formed.

Instinctive Man is Perfect, but his individual use of Life and Law enables him to cover a perfect idea with an apparently imperfect cloak.

Man comes into objectivity with the tendency of the race already subjectified within him, through race-suggestion. The race believes in sickness and limitation, and this suggestion is more or less operative through all people. This suggestion works through the field of the subjective state of the race thought, and will operate through any individual who is receptive to it.

As man becomes individualized, he consciously thinks and continuously pours suggestions into his subjective thought which is the silent builder of the physical body. Through the field of subjectivity thought always works out to a logical conclusion.

Man does not, necessarily, consciously think that he is to

have a certain type of physical trouble, but the physical correspondent is a logical outcome of what he thinks.

Disease, of itself, is neither person, place nor thing; it is an image of thought, consciously or unconsciously held somewhere in Mind and will externalize wherever it finds an avenue of operation.

Disease is entirely mental in its origin, since no person could be sick unless he had intelligence; it is the result of thinking about, and believing in duality, or a power apart from God.

Disease can be healed through reversing the thought and turning to the Spiritual Realization of Life. It is impossible to divorce real mental healing from true Spiritual Realization, since God is ALL.

The use of mental argument in healing rests upon the theory that we are surrounded by a Universal Mind which reacts to our thought.

Right mental practice is the constructive use of Mind, i.e., a mental argument given for the purpose of presenting the Spiritual Truth about man. Wrong mental practice is the destructive use of Mind, i.e., a mental argument given for the purpose of presenting a false claim about man.

Right mental practice is called the Spirit of Christ. Wrong mental practice is called the spirit of Antichrist; it is malpractice and may or may not be consciously used. To think of anyone in a negative way is some form of malpractice and is harmful. Malpractice may be ignorant, innocent or malicious. It is always some form of suggestion.

Man is known in Mind by the name he bears, and any statement made in Mind about his name will cause some action to take place through Law towards him. This is the basis of all mental healing.

A practitioner is one who recognizes Man as a spiritual reality. *Since there is but One Mind, the practitioner does this within himself.* Through the medium of the One Mind these statements rise to objective conditions in his patient, according to the practitioner's belief and according to the ability of his patient to receive the Truth. Healing is accomplished through the act of setting Subjective Law in motion. The more Spiritual or Godlike the mentality of the practitioner, the more powerful the treatment.

A mental treatment begins and ends within the thought of the practitioner because he is in the same Mind in which his patient lives. Treatment is inducing right concepts within the subjective side of life.

Absent and present treatments are the same; *for there is no absence in the One Presence.*

One disease would be as easily healed as another if the thought were as sure of itself in one case as another.

There is no personal responsibility in healing; the practitioner directs the Power and lets It work. One does not hold thoughts in mental healing; he looses thought. A practitioner does not try to suggest, hypnotize or mentally influence; he simply knows that man is now a spiritual being and holds to that belief, no matter what the appearance may be. Right mental treatment does not tire the one giving it.

Personal magnetism has nothing to do with mental healing. The whole basis of the possibility of mental healing rests upon the premise that we all live in One Creative Mind which reacts to our belief. It is as though there were a Universal Ear listening to, and hearing, everything that we say, feel or think, and reacting to it.

Healing is not a process, but a revelation; for the revealing of the perfect man always heals. The process is the time and thought that it takes to arrive at the correct understanding of man's perfect state in Spirit.

Anyone can heal who believes that he can, and who will take the time to put that belief in motion through the Law.

To daily see the perfect man and to daily declare for his objective appearance is correct mental practice and will heal.

A treatment recognizes that all is Mind and that everything is mental; it resolves all disease into thought; neutralizes the false thought and recognizes the true. Nothing can stop it from operating except a lack of faith in the reality of the Truth and man's ability to use It.

In giving mental treatment the practitioner first realizes his own being as spiritual; he then recognizes the perfect state of his patient's being; then he attacks the false claim and brings the evidence of Truth to bear against it, thinking in such a manner as to completely destroy the false claim and to realize the Truth.

LESSON FOUR

INTRODUCTION

Mental Science is not a "get-rich-quick scheme," neither does it promise something for nothing. It does, however, promise the one who will comply with its teaching that he shall be able to bring into his life and experience greater possibilities and happier conditions.

The Science of Mind is based entirely upon the supposition that we are surrounded by a Universal Mind into which we think; this Mind, in Its original state, fills all space with Its Presence. Since It fills all space, It fills the space that man uses in the Universe. It is *in* man as well as outside of him. As he thinks into this Universal Mind he sets in motion a Law which is creative, and which contains within Itself a limitless possibility.

THE LAW IS INFINITE

The Law through which man operates is Infinite, but man appears to be finite; that is, he has not yet evolved to a complete understanding of It. He is unfolding from a limitless potential but can bring into his experience only that which he can conceive. There is no limit to the Law, but there appears to be a limit to man's understanding of It. As his understanding unfolds, his possibilities of attainment will increase.

It is a great mistake to say: "Take what you wish; for you can have anything you like." We do not take what we wish, but we do attract to ourselves that which is like our thought. MAN MUST BECOME MORE IF HE WISHES TO DRAW A GREATER GOOD INTO HIS LIFE. We need not labor under the delusion that all we have to do is to say everything is ours. This is true in reality; but in fact, it is only as true as we make it. We provide the mold for the Creative Law, and unless the mold which we provide is increased, the substance cannot increase in our experience; for Mental Science cannot hold forth a promise that will do away with the necessity of complying with law.

The Law is a law of liberty, but not a law of license. It is exact and exacting, and unless we are willing to comply with Its nature and work with It, along the lines of Its inherent being, we will receive no great benefit. Every man must pay the price for that which he receives, and that price is paid in mental and spiritual coin. An avenue must be provided through which the Law may work as a law of liberty, if It is to free us. This does not mean that we must please the Law; for It is impersonal and neither knows nor cares who uses It, nor for what purpose; but, because It is impersonal, It is compelled, by Its very nature, to return to the thinker exactly what he thinks into It. The Law of mental equivalents must never be overlooked; for "Whatsoever a man soweth, that shall he also reap."

THE POSSIBILITIES OF THE LAW

The possibilities of the Law are infinite; and our possibilities of using It are limitless. We may, and should, receive full benefit, and we will to the degree that we understand and properly use It.

There is a law of unfoldment in man which says that he can advance only by going from where he is to the place where he would like to be. This is not because the Law is limited but because It is law. As man unfolds in his mentality, the law automatically reacts to him. The way to work is to begin right where we are, and, through constantly applying ourselves to the Truth, to gradually increase in wisdom and understanding; for in this way alone will good results be obtained. If, day by day, we have a greater understanding and a clearer concept; if daily, we are realizing more of Truth and applying it in our actions, then we are on the right path, and eventually we will be made free.

SPIRIT AND MENTAL LAW

It is impossible to divorce spiritual understanding from the proper use of mental law. The Spirit within man is God, and only to the degree that we listen to, and seek to obey that Spirit, shall we really succeed. The Law is a blind force, and lest we misuse It, we should be very careful to FOLLOW ONLY A CONSTRUCTIVE COURSE. But the Law is Absolute, and we should trust Its impersonal action implicitly. It can do anything for us that we can conceive of Its doing. It is the law of freedom to all who believe in and obey It.

The highest realization that we can have is a recognition of the Omnipresence of Spirit. This will set in motion greater possibilities and will, automatically, provide a larger concept of life. We should daily train our thought to recognize the Spirit in everything we do, say, or think. There is no other way, and to try any other way would be to make a complete failure. "Render to Cæsar the things that are Cæsar's; and to God the things that are God's."

A constant realization of the Presence of Spirit will provide a sense of Divine Companionship that no other attitude could produce. Why should we not take the highest and best? God Is—and we should realize this fact and make use of it; as soon as we recognize that God Is, we can turn to the Law and tell It what to do.

We have no record of Jesus ever asking God to do things for Him; He gave thanks, and then commanded the Law to work. This is the correct manner of approach to the Spirit and the Law. This is not superstition but the fact in the case, and we would better realize it.

The Law is subject to the Spirit and is Its servant. Man is Spirit, but until he knows this he will be only half using the Law; for he will not have a clear understanding to fall back upon.

DEMONSTRATION, OR BRINGING THINGS TO PASS

We hold no argument with anyone over the possibility of demonstrating the Law. There is such a thing as Universal Law and Mind, and we can use It if we comply with Its nature and work as It works. We do not argue, ask, deny, nor affirm; WE KNOW. Thousands are today proving this Law, and in time, all will come to realize the Truth.

We can demonstrate to the level of our ability to know; beyond this we cannot go. But we will constantly expand and increase in knowledge and understanding, thereby continuously growing in our ability to make use of the Law; in time we will be made free through It.

It is a wonderful experiment and a great adventure to make conscious use of the Law, to feel that we can plant an idea in Mind and see it gradually take form.

The student should take time every day to see his life as he wishes it to be, to make a mental picture of his ideal. He should pass this picture over to the Law and go about his business with the inner assurance that on the invisible side of life something is taking place. There should never be any sense of hurry nor worry about this; just a calm, peaceful sense of reality. Let the Law work through, and express Itself in, the experience. There should be no idea of compulsion; we do not have to make the Law work; it is Its nature to work, and all that we need to do is to make use of It. In gladness, then, we should make known our desires, and in confidence we should wait upon the Perfect Law to manifest through us.

OUR PART

Our part is to be ready and willing to be guided into truth and liberty. If, in the making of a demonstration, it becomes necessary to change our mode of living, then the Law will point the way and we will follow. Our correct choice will be part of the working out of the Law. All doubt and fear must go, and in their place must come faith and confidence; for we shall be led by the Spirit into all good.

TREATMENT

Treatment is not for the purpose of making things happen; it is to provide, within ourselves, an avenue through which they may happen. Treatment opens up the avenues of thought, expands the consciousness, and lets Reality through; it clarifies the mentality, removes the obstructions of thought and lets in the Light. We already live in a Perfect Universe, but It needs to be mentally seen before It can become a part of our experience. Treatment removes doubt and fear; lets in the realization of the Presence of Spirit; and is necessary while we are confronted by obstruction or obstacles. Every problem is primarily mental, and the answer to all problems will be found in Spiritual Realizations.

MEDIUM BETWEEN MAN AND HIS MANIFESTATION

The subjective state of man's thought decides what is to happen to him. The subjective state of his thought is the sum-total of his thinking and knowing; It is the medium between the relative and the Absolute, between the Limitless and the conditioned. Whatever is involved in it will evolve; therefore, treatment is the act, the art and the science of systematically and consciously inducing such thoughts as we wish to see expressed. When there is no longer anything within our mentality that denies our word, a demonstration will be made; nothing can stop it, for the Law is Absolute. The question might be asked: "If this is true, why not affirm that we have what we desire and let it go at that?" This is true in Principle, but in practice and in fact, it is only as true as we make it; that is, we cannot demonstrate beyond our ability to know the Truth. We should begin, then, with the things that we do know, and from that basis evolve a greater knowledge.

We should approach the Law normally and naturally and with a sense of ease. There is nothing peculiar or weird about this; it is a natural Law, working in a normal way, and must be thought of in this light.

We should come to consider the Law and the Spirit as friends and think of them as such; in this way we will gradually go from good to more good and from peace to a greater peace. This is the natural unfoldment of Reality through man. We should expect the best and so live that the best may become a part of our experience.

LESSON FOUR

THE CONTROL OF CONDITIONS

In taking up this subject, let us very clearly understand that we do not differentiate between Conscious Mind and Spirit; there is no difference, for they are One.

The Spirit of Intelligence, which is God, in order to do something for us must do that thing through us, and what It is to do must first become a part of our mentality before it can become an individual experience. OUR MENTALITIES ARE BUT THE SPIRIT WORKING THROUGH US AS INDIVIDUALS.

In the new schools of thought there are those who claim to demonstrate only by the Spirit; also those who claim to demonstrate only by the Mind. This is a distinction which is suppositional rather than real and is impossible, because, if there were two powers, we would at once have duality and our philosophy of Unity would be contradicted. There is but One Active Intelligence, whether it be the Universal Intelligence or Universal Spirit individualized in us.

We do, however, distinguish between the phase of mind which we call conscious and the phase which we call unconscious or subjective, as has already been explained.

In demonstrating conditions, the only inquiries we need to make are: Do the things that we want lend themselves to a

constructive program? Do they express a more abundant life, rob
none, create no delusion, but instead, do they express a greater
degree of livingness? If they do, then all the power in the universe must be behind them. If it is money, automobiles, houses,
lands, stocks, bonds, dresses, shirts or shoestrings, cabbages or
kings—all of which come from the same source—there can be
nothing, either in the Law or in the Spirit back of the Law, to
deny us the right to the greatest possible expression of life.

So we need not hesitate to use the Law for personal mo-
tives, for we have a perfect right to do so. It is good for everyone
to express himself, provided that in so doing, he does not destroy the independence of others.

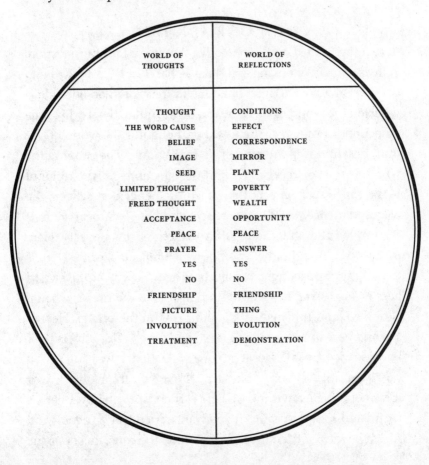

WORLD OF THOUGHTS	WORLD OF REFLECTIONS
THOUGHT	CONDITIONS
THE WORD CAUSE	EFFECT
BELIEF	CORRESPONDENCE
IMAGE	MIRROR
SEED	PLANT
LIMITED THOUGHT	POVERTY
FREED THOUGHT	WEALTH
ACCEPTANCE	OPPORTUNITY
PEACE	PEACE
PRAYER	ANSWER
YES	YES
NO	NO
FRIENDSHIP	FRIENDSHIP
PICTURE	THING
INVOLUTION	EVOLUTION
TREATMENT	DEMONSTRATION

Lesson Four: Metaphysical Chart No. IV.
HOW IDEAS MANIFEST AS THINGS.

The upper section of this chart shows how the conscious mind, or spirit of man, reflects or contemplates itself, through the medium of soul or subjectivity, into form or matter. The middle section represents the World-Soul or Subjectivity; the Mirror of Mind and unformed matter; the Servant of Spirit; the lowest section shows the result of self-contemplation as it takes form in the world of matter. Read and carefully study the metaphysical meanings of the words used in the Individual Chart.

LAW OF REFLECTION

In turning to the Law, then, realize that It is a Law of reflection. "Life is the mirror of king and slave." Chart No. IV is divided into two parts with a suppositional line in the center; on one side is depicted the world of thought and on the other, the world of the reflections of thought. The world of thought is the world of our individuality; it is the part of us that knows. The other is the world of soul or receptivity and of reflections. In the thought is the cause that reflects the effect; the belief that reflects the correspondence. Here is the image; and here is a form. Here is the limited thought, the result of which reflects poverty. Here is the freed thought, the result of which reflects wealth. Here is a thought of peace which reflects peace. Here is a prayer and here is its answer; the answer to prayer is in the prayer when it is prayed, and the answer is identical with the prayer. Here is Yes and here is Yes; and here is No and here is No. Why is this? Because the Law takes us at our own valuation; if we say "Yes," It says "Yes"; and if we say "No," It says "No"; for It can only reflect; It cannot initiate anything. So here is friendship and over here is friendship. Emerson said: "If you want a friend, be a friend"; and so, as the idea of friendship dawns upon the consciousness, the law of attraction produces friends; for one is the picture and the other is the thing. This is the great teaching of Involution and Evolution, the thought involved and the result evolved; one is the treatment and the other is the demonstration.

We mean by demonstration, bringing into our experience something which we had not experienced before; bringing it in as the result of conscious thought; and unless it is possible to do this the whole science is a mistake and a delusion.

Unless there is a Divine Principle, Universal Soul or Subjectivity, or Medium, which, of Itself, without any help or assistance, can produce things, and will, then there is nothing in this teaching. But there is Divine Principle; and what It does for us, It must do through us. Our part in the demonstration is to set the word in motion, thus compelling, through the law of subjectivity, the result or manifestation.

ATTRACTING FRIENDS

When we are dealing with Causation, we are dealing with that which has involved within Itself all effect, as it unfolds. We may leave it to the Law to compel right action. With this in mind, let us go on to treatment.

Suppose we wish to attract friends. We must begin to image ideal relationships, be they social or otherwise; to sense and feel the presence of friends; to enjoy them in our own mentalities, not as an illusion, but as a reality; not as a dream, but as an experience; to declare that their presence is now here; that they know it and that we know it. But we must never look to see if they are here, because this would imply doubt and would neutralize our word. We can attract the kind of friends we wish if we specifically designate the kind; but we must never think of certain people, or that a particular individual must be one of them, for this would be hypnotic; just thinking the idea will bring the right kind of friends.

In order to have this friendship enduring, true, really

worth while and a thing of beauty, we should cultivate an attitude of friendship toward everybody and everything.

THE PRINCIPLE OF PROSPERITY

We are surrounded by a Universal Subjectivity, a Subjective, Creative Consciousness, which is receptive, neutral, impersonal, always receiving the impress of our thought, and which has no alternative other than to operate directly upon it, thus creating the things which we think.

Each one should realize that there is nothing in him that denies that which he desires. Our unity with our good is not established while there is anything in us that denies it.

People often say: "How shall I know when I know?" If you knew you would not ask this question; the very fact that you can ask it proves you do not know; for when you know that you know you can prove it by doing.

Thought sets definite force in motion in Mind, relative to the individual who thinks. For instance, I am known in Consciousness as Ernest Holmes, for that is my name; and every claim made for me, which I accept, operates through avenues of mind-activity and returns to me as some condition.

In practice, always forget the limitations of individuality. Each treatment should embody a recognition of the Whole, because It is Omnipresent.

WE DEAL WITH ABSOLUTENESS

We deal with Absoluteness; this is the attitude that we should have. What we need is to know the Truth. This does not mean that we need not be active; of course we shall be active; but we need not compel things to happen. A good demonstration is made when the Truth, gathering Its own power, lifts one out of his environment; and until that time comes he should stay where he is, in order that he may know when he has made a demonstration.

It is not a good demonstration if, when we give our treatments, we have to struggle just as before. Principle is Absolute, and in so far as any individual can actually induce, within consciousness, upon Principle, a definite, concrete acceptance of his desire, it will manifest, even if every thought on earth had to change to compel it. If it were a bit of information that only one person on earth knew, and he was in the center of Africa, it would be produced.

PRAYER IS ITS OWN ANSWER

Cause and effect are but two sides of thought; and Spirit is both Cause and Effect. Prayer is its own answer. Now, if the one who prays only partly believes, then there is a tendency to set an idea in motion; if the next day he wholly doubts, this idea must be wiped out. In dealing with Mind, we are dealing with a Force which we cannot fool. We can fool ourselves; we can fool others; but we cannot cheat Principle out of the slightest shadow of our most subtle concept; for this is impossible. The hand writes and passes on, but the writing is left there, nevertheless; and the only thing that can erase it is a writing of a different character. We must either transcend all that has gone before, by walking above it, neutralize it by an opposite state of consciousness, or endure it.

Get a sense of self-mastery, of being equal to every occasion. There is nothing too great; there is no obstacle that you cannot surmount; no obstruction that you cannot dissipate by the power of Truth, if your concept of Truth is dynamic enough and clear enough, and if the embodiment is complete.

IF YOU KNOW

If you know that the Power with which you are dealing is Principle and not personality; if you know and believe that Mind is the only Actor, Cause, Effect, Substance, Intelligence, Truth and Power that there is; and if you have a real embodiment of your desires, then you can demonstrate.

If you lack, if you are poor, if you are without friends, if you are without opportunity, don't fight anything; but be sure to erase from your consciousness any sense of that lack.

You erase thought from consciousness by pouring in an opposite thought; this opposite thought meets the other and neutralizes it; that is, it rubs it out, just as we rub a chalk mark off a board. Take a consistent, positive, aggressive mental attitude in the Truth.

We walk by falling forward; water falls by its own weight; the planets are eternally falling through space; for everything sustains itself in nature. The only reason that man is limited is that he has not allowed the Instinctive Life to come out through him, and the reason why this is possible, is that his own Divine Individuality, as soon as it was evolved, compelled Infinity to appear in his experience as duality, because he believed in duality.

Take no personal responsibility for making anything happen. Throw your word into Mind, and know that Mind receives it; Mind believes it; Mind accepts it; Mind acts upon it; and Mind produces it.

NO PERSONAL RESPONSIBILITY

No matter how great a responsibility may rest in that which must be done, never let one minute's responsibility rest in your own thought about it, because that to which the mind gives birth is, and EVERY IDEA IS BOUND TO PRODUCE AN EFFECT EXACTLY LIKE ITS CAUSE.

When we make a demonstration we must take what goes with it. Therefore, all demonstrations should be made in peace, confidence and joy and in the realization of Divine Love and Perfection as permeating everything. The reason for this is evident, for we are dealing with the law of cause and effect. We are not depending upon chance, but upon Law.

We must know that we are dealing with the substance from which all things are made—people, brains, monkeys—everything that is. Nothing moves but Mind, and we are dealing with the Mind that is the Mover, the Creator, the Cause of all that is or is to be.

HELPING AN INVENTOR

Suppose an inventor came to you and said: "I am trying to perfect a piece of machinery and have not been able to work out the right plan." You sit with him for treatment; that is, you concentrate in Mind, in order to produce the desired idea through him. You know that all ideas come from Mind and that Mind is always unfolding Its Ideas through man. You say: "John Smith is an inventor; a certain idea is trying to operate through him and there is nothing in him that can obstruct this idea." Then state that this idea is known in Mind, and is now flowing through him. If you do this, thinking clearly, new ideas will begin to operate through him and he will discover the thing he needs.

LOOK ONLY AT WHAT YOU WANT

Never look at that which you do not wish to experience. No matter what the false condition may be, it must be refuted.

The proper kind of a denial is based upon the recognition that, in reality, there is no limitation; for mind can as easily make a planet as anything else. The Infinite knows no difference between a million dollars and a penny. It only knows that IT IS. It would be just as easy to demonstrate a million dollars as it would be to demonstrate ten cents, if the mental concept embodied the idea of a million dollars.

It is the consciousness back of the word that forms the word. Consciousness means the inner embodiment of an idea through the recognition of Truth and a direct relationship to the Divine. The greatest Teacher Who ever lived was the most spiritual man; for the more universal and comprehensive the thought, the more Godlike it must become.

A good treatment is always filled with the recognition of the Presence of God or Good. Even in Spiritual Things we are still dealing with the law of cause and effect, for God is Law. The more exalted the thought, the more heavenly, the more boundless, the more Godlike or Christlike the thought, the more power it will have. This is why the greatest Teacher should become the Saviour; He couldn't help it. A great teacher would have to be a Saviour.

DEFINITE PLAN

We will say that there are four men, "A," "B," "C," and "D." "A" receives $15 a week, "B" receives $50, "C," $75, and "D," $100. Now these four are all without positions and they come to a practitioner for mental treatment. The practitioner takes the thought that there is nothing but activity; he neutralizes, in his own thought, any belief in inactivity and declares that each of these four men is divinely active and occupied. Without question he has set in motion a law which will respond and will reproduce something for each of these four. We will suppose that his treatment is a good and an effective one; they receive it, and consequently each one of them receives a position. You will find that each does not receive the same compensation, for in all probability "A" will receive $15 per week; "B," $50; "C," $75, and "D," $100. "But," one might say, "he spoke the same word for each; why did they not all receive $100 per week?" Because, while his word was used for each in a like manner, each could receive only his fill, his mental capacity to comprehend. Each was full, and no doubt running over; but the molds which their perceptions of life provided were limited to the subjective remembrance already set in motion by themselves. Each attracted to himself, out of the Universal Good, that which he could comprehend. It is the old statement that water will reach its own level by its own weight, and without effort. So a treatment will only level itself in the objective world at the level of the subjective thought and realization.

This does not mean that each of the above-stated men will always have to receive the same compensation; for with an enlarged consciousness he would receive more.

ATTRACTION

Every one automatically attracts to himself just what he is, and you may set it down that wherever you are, however intolerable the situation may be, it is just where you belong. There is no power in the Universe but yourself that can get you out of it. Some one may help you on the road to realization, but substantiality and permanence can come only through the consciousness of your own life and thought. Man must bring himself to a point where there is no misfortune, no calamity, no accident, no trouble, no confusion; where there is nothing but plenty, peace, power, Life and Truth. He should definitely, daily, using his own name, declare the Truth about himself, realizing that he is reflecting his statements into Consciousness, and that they will be operated upon by It.

This is called, in mysticism, High Invocation; invoking the Divine Mind; implanting within It seeds of thought relative to one's self. And this is why some of the teachers of older times used to teach their pupils to cross their hands over their chests and say: "Wonderful, wonderful, wonderful me!" definitely teaching them that, as they held themselves, so they would be held. "Act as though I Am and I will Be."

One of the ancient sayings is that, "To the man who can perfectly practice inaction, all things are possible." This sounds like a contradiction until one gets down to the inner teachings; for it is only when one completely practices inaction that he arrives at the point of the true actor. For he then realizes that the act and the actor are one and the same, that cause and effect are the same; which is simply a different way of saying: "Know the Truth and the Truth shall make you free." To reduce the whole thing to its simplest form, whatever one reflects into Mind will be done.

HOW TO DEMONSTRATE A HOME

Suppose you wish to demonstrate a home; daily, looking into Mind, visualize it just as you wish it to be, making the picture as clear as possible; for it is a lack of clearness of thought that hinders demonstration. Then sit there about ten minutes, saying, "It is, it is, it is." Perhaps thoughts will come in which say "that it is not." Pay no attention to such thoughts but return to your meditation, and seeing the picture anew, say again, "It is, it is, it is." Use no effort, but simply see the picture very clearly and declare for its presence.

Never look for results from treatment; for if you do you will not find them. This is in accordance with law, for what you look for you know that you do not have and are only trying to fool yourself into thinking that you do have. Treatment is not a process of hypnotism; it is a process of self-knowing; and if you really know you will be sure to demonstrate.

Treatment is the art, the science and process of systematically inducing within consciousness concepts of definite desires as already accomplished facts and experiences in life.

RESIST NOT

When Jesus said "Resist not evil," He meant that non-recognition of evil is the only way to avoid it. This is true according to the law of cause and effect; for what we persist in recognizing, we persist in holding in place. That which we non-recognize, we neutralize, and it is no longer there, so far as we are concerned. In making a demonstration, don't try to demonstrate; for demonstrations are not made through effort, because this would contradict one of the fundamental principles of the universe, which is the Self-Existence of Causation. In other words, nothing can come before that which is, consequently everything must come out of that which is; and within that which is, is the inherent possibility of that which is to be. All things exist as a potentiality, as a possibility, now. "I Am Alpha and Omega." Try to get a recognition of your desire and pass the whole thing over to Mind, and let It operate. Just know that the desire is already a fact, and quietly say to yourself, as often as the thought comes into mind: "It is done." The lighter the thought is, the less care or worry over it, the better. The best work is done when the element of struggle is entirely left out.

HEALING A MISUNDERSTANDING

Suppose one says: "I have had a terrible misunderstanding with a friend of mine and it has come to a point where we do not even speak to each other." What is the fundamental error which has brought about this condition? A lack of the realization of the Unity of all life, a belief in duality. Destroy this belief in duality; recognize that there is but One Mind; see God in each, and the trouble will be healed. We all live in the One Mind of God.

FATE

If one believes in fate he must be healed of this thought, for there is no such thing as fate. If one believes that planetary forces have anything to do with life he must be healed of this thought. Break down everything except the recognition of the One Perfect Power, which is not contingent upon any place, person, condition, time of year, or anything but Itself. A demonstration is made when it comes through straight from the Truth.

The one who wishes to make a demonstration must first clear up his own subjective atmosphere; the reason being that he may be objectively making statements which his subjective thought may be denying. In this way we often neutralize our word as fast as it is spoken.

A treatment is scientific in that it is the act of inducing into Subjectivity ideas which neutralize false images of thought and which let the Truth come through into expression. The reason that we need such a science is that we do not have a perfect faith; for if we had a perfect faith we would have washed clean the subjective thought and no doubts would be there. Until the time comes when one can say to the sick, "Get up and walk," and have them do so; or say, "There is money," and have it appear, he must take the process of inducing thought for the purpose of accumulating a subjective belief in the things which he desires; this belief, as soon as it is complete, IS THE DEMONSTRATION. The demonstration takes place within and not without.

ATTRACTION OF PERSONALITY

One might say, "I have no personality with which to attract people." There is but One Person; this Person is manifested through every living soul. It is radiant, vibrant, dynamic; It is *The* Personality; It is Complete; It is, It is.

The ones to whom we are the most strongly attracted are not necessarily the ones who are the most beautiful physically; but are the ones from which we receive that subtle emanation, "that something." What is "that something"? It is not that which shows, but that which floats through from within. It is the inner recognition of Reality.

SEE LIFE EXPRESSED

One should analyze himself, saying, "Do I look at myself from a standpoint of restriction? Do I see life as limited to the eternal round of getting up in the morning, eating, going to work, coming home, going to bed, sleeping, getting up again?" and so on. Break the bonds of necessity and see life as one continuous expression of the Infinite Self; and as this conception gradually dawns upon the inner thought, something will happen in the outer conditions to let up on the greater demands of the law of necessity. If one were doing the work he should be doing, he would never become tired, because the energy which holds the universe in place is tireless. The reason why we become tired is that we have cross currents of thought over our work. This arises from a belief in duality.

A treatment is the scientific act of inducing concepts in Mind, which operates upon them and manifests them in external affairs, just as the picture is held subjectively. During the process we meet, contact, neutralize and erase any and all opposing mental forces or conditions which deny our greater good.

Never limit your view of life by what you or anyone else has ever accomplished. The possibility of life is inherent within the capacity to imagine what life is, backed by the power to produce this imagery or Divine Imagination. It is not a question of failing or of succeeding; it is simply a question of sticking to an idea until it becomes a tangible reality.

The illusion is in the way that we look at things. We have looked at some things and they have looked evil to us; we must look at them until they look good. We have looked at some one and he has looked sick to us; we must look at him until he looks well. We have seen discord; we must see harmony.

Look [at]* harmony and people will become harmonious. We have looked at poverty, degradation and misery until they have assumed a gigantic form. Now we must look at harmony, happiness, plenty, prosperity, peace and right action until it appears.

LOOK TO THE ULTIMATE

In treating, we conceive of the ultimate of the idea, but never of the process. Never treat a process; never look for one. We plant a seed, and there is in that seed, operating through the creative soil, everything that is going to happen until it comes up, unfolds, and produces a plant. The ultimate of effect is already potential in cause. This is the mystical meaning of those words, "I am Alpha and Omega." Our word should be the alpha and the omega, the beginning and the end of the thing thought of. All cause and effect are in Spirit. Cause and effect are bound together into one complete whole. One is the inside and the other is the outside of the same thing.

Once you have driven the peg into the ground, stick to it. Never let anything cause you to doubt your ability to demonstrate the Truth. Conceive of your word as being the thing. See the desire as an already accomplished fact and rest in perfect confidence, peace and certainty, never looking for results, never wondering, never becoming anxious, never being hurried nor worried. Those who do not understand this attitude will think that you are inactive, but remember, "To him who can perfectly practice inaction, all things are possible."

NO MISTAKES

In mental work, we must realize that there is One Infinite Mind, which is consciously directing our destiny. Declare every day that "no mistakes have been made, none are being made, and none can be made"; declare, "There is One Supreme Intelligence which governs, guides and guards, tells me what to do, when to act, and how to act"; then act with perfect assurance. Declare, "everything necessary to the full and complete expression of the most boundless experience, joy and life, everything is now"; know this, see it, feel it and be it. Do this every day for a few minutes; we should all do this until the time comes when it will no longer be necessary. When that time comes, we will know it, because our demonstrations will have been made.

Suppose one says: "I have made a lot of mistakes in my life. I had opportunities which I did not grasp." This is a direct belief that there is but one opportunity which comes to man, and if he does not take it he will have no more. This is a belief in limited opportunities, and it must be denied completely and specifically. We exist in Limitless Opportunities, which are forever seeking expression through us, and are expressed in and through us.

Know that there is no condemnation; for nothing can condemn unless we believe in condemnation. Destroy the thought that would lay limitation or bondage upon any situation or condition. "Loose him, and let him go."

Talk to yourself, not to the world. There is no one to talk to but yourself, for all experiences take place within. Conditions are the reflections of our own meditations, and nothing else. There is but One Mind to think, but one thing that It can think; that Mind is our Mind now. It never thinks confusion; It knows what it wishes, and how to accomplish what it desires. It is what It desires.

CAUSES AND CONDITIONS

Pay no attention to what happens in the objective world when you are making a demonstration. We interpret causes by conditions only as we realize that a condition must partake of the nature of its cause. If there appears to be confusion in the condition, then there must have been confusion in the thought back of it. Pay no attention to the objective expression so long as you know you are getting the right subjective recognition. The way to work out a problem scientifically is to take it up in thought daily and conceive of it as already being an accomplished fact in experience. Get the idea of the desire as already embodied in the Absolute. Unless one believes that there is an Absolute, how can he do this? We must believe that we are dealing with Reality and with nothing less than the Absolute.

If we are radiating thought into Divine Mind, what is there that can hinder It from operating on this thought? Nothing, for It knows no hindrances. Be sure that there is nothing destructive in the reaction; for there must be no element of destructiveness in our work. Daily hold your desire as an already accomplished fact and go about your business with joy and gladness, with peace and quiet confidence; the Law is then sure to act. During the process many things may happen that will appear to be destructive. You may pass through good fortune and bad; but if you can come to the point where you are not disturbed by what happens on the outside, you have found the secret. If, as Jesus said, we "Judge not according to the appearance, but judge righteous judgment," remembering that "things which are seen were not made of things which do appear"; out of any chaos we can produce harmony, provided we keep our thought steady. The answer to prayer is already in the prayer when it is prayed.

PERFECT ACTION

Assume a case of treatment for prosperity. Suppose one comes to you and says: "Business is bad; there is no activity." How are you going to treat him? Are you going to treat activity or business, customers, conditions or what? There is but one thing to treat, as far as the practitioner is concerned, and that is HIMSELF. The practitioner treats himself, the reason being that his patient's and his own mind are in the One Mind.

There is but one activity, which is perfect. Nothing has happened to it; nothing can cut it off; it is always operating. There is no belief in inactivity. What is this statement for? To neutralize the belief in inactivity. A word spoken in Mind will reach its own level, in the objective world, by its own weight; just as in physical science we know that water reaches its own level by its own weight. You must destroy the thoughts of inactivity. Man cannot become either discouraged or afraid if he realizes that there is but One Mind which he may consciously use. The real man knows no discouragement, cannot be afraid and has no unbelief.

"Who plants a seed beneath the sod and waits to see it turn away the clod, Has faith in God."

And he who knows of the power with which he is dealing, and who plants a seed of thought in Subjectivity, knows that it will come up and bear fruit.

Bring out the idea of Substance. Make consciousness perceive that Substance is Spirit, Spirit is God, and God is all that there is. Once you acquaint the consciousness with this idea, it is implanted in the Creative Power which is externalizing in your life.

MENTAL EQUIVALENTS

The Law is Infinite and Perfect; but in order to make a demonstration we must first have a mental equivalent of the thing we DESIRE. Consequently, the range of our possibilities at the present time does not extend far beyond the range of our present concepts. As we bring ourselves to a greater vision, we can then induce a still greater concept and thereby demonstrate more in our experience. In this way there is a continuous growth and unfoldment taking place. We do not expect to give a treatment today and have a million dollars tomorrow. But, little by little, we can unfold our consciousness through the acquisition of greater and still greater mental equivalents, until at last we shall be made free. The way to proceed is to begin right where we are. It is not scientific to attempt to begin somewhere else. This would be chaotic. One who understands the systematic use of the Law will realize that he is where he is because of what he is; but he will not say, "I must be where I am because of what I am." Instead, he will begin to disclaim what he appears to be. As his statements loosen wrong subjective tendencies and false mentality, providing in their place a correct concept of life and Reality, he will automatically be lifted out of his conditions; and impelling forces, which will sweep everything before them, will set him free, if he trusts in Spirit and in nothing else.

Stay with the One and never deviate from It; never leave It for a moment. Nothing else can equal this attitude. To desert the Truth in the hour of need is to prove that we do not know the Truth. When things look the worst is the supreme moment to demonstrate to yourself that there are no obstructions. When things look worst is the best time to work, the most satisfying time. The person who can throw himself, with a complete abandon, into that Limitless Sea of Receptivity, having cut loose from all apparent moorings, is the one who will always receive the greatest reward.

TREATING FOR ACTIVITY

Suppose you have a store and wish to attract customers, which means activity in this kind of business. Every day see the place filled with people. Make a mental picture of this. You are dealing with Intelligence, so work intelligently. Ask for what you wish and take it. If you were treating for activity in a store in Boston you would not be treating some one in Kalamazoo for the mumps. Remember that you are dealing with Intelligence; IT IS GOING TO EVOLVE YOUR CONCEPT EXACTLY AS YOU INVOLVE IT. If one could take a picture of his objective circumstances and his subjective mentality, he would find that they would be identical; for one is the cause of the other; one is the image and the other is the reflection of that image.

RECEIVING INFORMATION

Suppose that we wish a special piece of information; we should say, "I wish to know this thing and I do know it. Whatever instrument is necessary to present it to me is now in full operation." This is a direct declaration that we have the desired knowledge, that that which we wish to know we do know. Say, "The Spirit of Intelligence within me tells me what I should know," or, "Everything that I should know I do know." It does not matter how we get this knowledge; we would not care if we read it on a sign, or in the dictionary, or if it were told us, or if it were sent to us; but we should consider the demonstration complete provided we received it. Say, "Everything necessary for the complete fulfillment of this idea is now in full operation, and I accept it."

NO FAILURES

If one appears to have failed he should realize that there are no failures in the universe. We should completely erase the idea of failure by stating that there are no failures. If one believes that he failed last year he will be likely to fail again this year, unless the false thought should be erased.

Now here is a place where it looks as though one were lying to himself, but he is not; for he is declaring the truth about the Spirit that indwells him; this Spirit never fails. Affirm, "This word blots from the book of my remembrance any sense of lack, limitation, want or fear of failure. There is no failure, no person to fail; failure is neither person, place nor thing; it is a false thought and has no truth in it; it is a belief in lack and there is no lack; it is a belief in a limitation which does not exist."

Thought is very subtle, and sometimes you may find, when you are making such a statement, that arguments will rise against it. Stop right here and meet those arguments; refuse to accept them.

OPPORTUNITY

Suppose you are treating your business and something from within says, "There are too many people in this business"; handle the thought of competition at once; say, "There is no competition or monopoly." You must do something to free the endeavor to express itself. Treatment is a thing of itself; it is an entity of Infinite Intelligence, Life and Action, and nothing can hinder its operation except unbelief or a lack of adequate mental equivalents. "They could not enter in because of unbelief," and they "tempted God and limited the Holy One of Israel."

Never depend upon people, or say that things must come

from this or that source. It makes no difference where things come from. Say that they are and let them come from where they will; and then, if something appears to happen which points to a place for them to come from, it is correct to say, "If this is the place, then there is nothing which can hinder." This is not hypnotic, for you are simply guarding against the possibility of some false thought coming in and hindering your demonstration.

Nothing moves but Mind. God makes things through the direct act of becoming the things which He creates. This is what we do, for our thought becomes the thing thought of. The thought and the thing are one, in reality. "WHAT A MAN HAS AS WELL AS WHAT HE IS, IS THE RESULT OF THE SUBJECTIVE STATE OF HIS THOUGHT." Keep on subjectifying thought until the balance of your consciousness is on the affirmative side, and nothing can hinder it from demonstrating. This is inevitable, for this is the way that the Law operates.

NO MISTAKES

Regarding mistakes—declare that there are none, that there never were and never will be any. Say, "I represent the Truth, the whole Truth and nothing but the Truth; It is unerring, It never mistakes; there are no mistakes in the Divine Plan for me; there is no fear; there is no limitation, poverty, want nor lack; I stand in the midst of eternal opportunity, which is forever presenting me with the evidence of its full expression. I am joy, peace and happiness; I am the spirit of joy within me; I am the spirit of peace within me, of poise and power; I am the spirit of happiness within me; I radiate life; I am Life. There is One Life; that Life is my Life now." It is not enough to say, "There is One Life and that Life is God." We must complete this statement by saying, "That Life is my Life now," because we must couple this Life with ours in order to express It. We are not becoming This Life, but are now, in, and of, This Life. There is no other Life.

God is not becoming; God Is. God is not growing; God is Complete. God is not trying to find out something; God already knows. Evolution is not the expression of a becoming God, but is simply one of the ways that a God Who already Is expresses Himself; and as such, it is the logical result of involution and is eternally going on.

DEMONSTRATION BY PROOF

If one is in a position which is distasteful, subject to circumstances over which he apparently has no control at the time, how should he act? He should not leave the place where he is until his thought has drawn him to a better one. In making a demonstration, we should not shove anything before us, carry anything with us nor drag anything after us. We should stay where we are until our word takes us somewhere else; for this is the only proof that we have demonstrated.

HANDLING A SCHOOLROOM

A teacher, in dealing with the thought of pupils, should treat their thought as a unit. The individuality of the room, of which each pupil is a part, is a perfect idea. There is One Mind operating in, around and through all these pupils, controlling them, directing them and inspiring them; there are peace, calm, satisfaction and enlightenment here. Realize the Active Presence of the One Mind, working in, around and through all, and you will find that this will harmonize the most discordant state, provided the teacher, the one who is thinking, really knows the Truth.

THE LAW OF CORRESPONDENCE

The limit of our ability to demonstrate depends on our ability to provide a mental equivalent of our desire; for the law of correspondences works from the belief to the thing. But we can provide a greater mental equivalent through the unfolding of consciousness; and this growth from within will finally lead to freedom.

What we demonstrate today, tomorrow and the next day is not as important as THE TENDENCY WHICH OUR THOUGHT IS TAKING. If, every day, things are a little better, a little happier, a little more harmonious, a little more health-giving and joyous; if, each day, we are expressing more life, we are going in the right direction.

And so we meditate daily upon the Universe of the All Good, that Infinite Indwelling Spirit which we call God, the Father, Incarnate in man; trying to sense and to feel this Indwelling Good as the Active Principle of our lives. This is what the mystics call "The Man of the Heart," or "The Angel of God's Presence." This is why they taught that there are always Two; for there is what we seem to be and what we really are; and as we contact this Higher Principle of our own lives—Which is Perfect and Complete, needing nothing, wanting nothing, knowing everything, being happy and satisfied, and as we daily meditate upon this Indwelling God, we shall acquire a greater mental equivalent.

For those who have thought small thoughts all of their lives a very good practice is to dwell upon the bigness of the universe. Think how many stars there are; think of how many fish there are in the seas, and how many grains of sand on the beach. Think of how big the ocean is; of the immensity of space, the bigness of everything, the grandeur of everything, Mechanically, if necessary, compel the mentality to cognize Reality. Compel the consciousness to recognize the Truth through pure reason, if no other conviction comes.

Think, see and feel activity. Radiate Life. Feel that there is that within which is the center and circumference of the universe. The universe is the result of the Self-Contemplation of the Lord. Our lives are the results of our self-contemplations, and are peopled with the personifications of our thoughts and ideas. Accept this without question, for it is true.

Nothing is real to us unless we make it real. Nothing can touch us unless we let it touch us. Refuse to have the feelings hurt. Refuse to receive anyone's condemnation. In the independence of your own mentality, believe and feel that you are wonderful. This is not conceit; it is the truth. What can be more wonderful than the manifestation of the Infinite Mind?

"Awake thou that sleepest, and arise from the dead, and Christ shall give thee light." "Prove Me, now herewith, saith the Lord of Hosts, if I will not open you the windows of heaven, and pour you out a blessing, that there shall not be room enough to receive it." "Be firm and ye shall be made firm." "Act as though I am and I will be." "Onlook thou the Deity and the Deity will onlook thee." "As thou hast believed so be it done." "Ask and it shall be given unto you." "So shall my word be that goeth forth out of my mouth—it shall prosper."

Note: Read and study "That Something"; "The Edinburgh Lectures," T. Troward; "The Law and the Word," T. Troward; "Creative Mind and Success," E. S. Holmes; "How to Visualize," Behrend; "Financial Success Through Creative Thought," Wattles.

LESSON FOUR

RECAPITULATION

Limitation and poverty are not things but are the results of restricted ways of thinking. We are surrounded by a Subjective Intelligence which receives the impress of our thought and acts upon it. This Intelligence is a natural Law in the Mental World, and consequently It is neither good nor bad. It can only be said of It, that It Is, and that we may consciously use It.

The Law is a Law of Reflection; for life is a mirror, reflecting to us, as conditions, the images of our thinking. Whatever one thinks tends to take form and to become a part of his experience.

The Medium of all thought is the Universal Mind, acting as Law. Law is always impersonal, neutral, receptive and reactive.

A sense of separation from good causes us to feel restricted; and a sense of our Unity with Good changes the currents of Causation and brings a happier condition into the experience.

Everything in the so-called material universe is an effect and exists only by virtue of some mental image behind it.

Man's individuality enables him to make such use of the Law as he desires; he is bound, not by limitation, but by a limited thought. The same power which binds him will free him when he understands the Law to be one of Liberty and not one of bondage. The power within man can free him from all distasteful conditions, if the Law governing this power is properly understood and utilized.

The Law of Mind, which is the Medium of all action, is a Law of perfect balance; the Objective World perfectly balances the images within the Subjective World. Water will reach its own level by its own weight; and, according to the same law, consciousness will externalize at its own level by its own weight. Cause and effect are but two sides of the same thing, one being the image in Mind and the other the objective condition.

The manifest universe is the result of the Self-Contemplation of the Lord. Man's world of affairs is the result of his self-contemplation. He is, at first, ignorant of this, and so binds himself through wrong ideation and action; reversing this thought will reverse the condition.

There is neither effort nor strain in knowing the Truth. Right action will be compelled through right knowing; therefore, when we know the Truth, It will compel us to act in the correct manner.

Attraction and repulsion are mental qualities, and may be consciously utilized for definite purposes. Man, automatically and according to Law, attracts from without the correspondences of his inner mental attitudes. Inner mental attitudes may be induced through right thinking and correct knowing. The subjective state of thought is the power always at work; it is the result of the sum total of all beliefs, consciously or unconsciously held. The subjective state of thought may be consciously changed through right mental action. The conscious thought controls the subconscious, and in its turn, the subconscious controls conditions.

Visualizing, or mentally seeing right action, tends to produce the picture in external affairs.

Since the Law is mental, one must believe in It, in order to have It work affirmatively for him; but It is always working according to our belief, whether we are conscious of this fact or not.

Demonstration takes place through the field of the One

Universal Mind; we set the Power in motion; the Law produces the effect. We plant the seed and the Law produces the plant.

One should never allow himself to think of, or talk about, limitation or poverty. Life is a mirror and will reflect back to the thinker what he thinks into it.

God's plan for man is a perfect one, and when we harmonize with it we will become free from all bondage. The more spiritual the thought, the higher the manifestation. Spiritual thought means an absolute belief in, and reliance upon, Truth; this is both natural and normal.

All is Love yet all is Law; Love is the impelling force and Law executes the will of Love. Man is a center of God-Consciousness in the great Whole; he cannot deface his real being, but may hinder the Whole from coming into a complete expression through his life. Turning to the One with a complete abandonment and in absolute trust, he will find that he already is saved, helped and prospered.

There is One Infinite Mind from which all things come; this Mind is through, in and around man; It is the Only Mind that there is, and every time man thinks he uses It. There is One Infinite Spirit, and every time man says, "I am," he proclaims It. There is One Infinite Substance; and every time man moves, he moves in It. There is One Infinite Law, and every time man thinks he sets It in motion. There is One Infinite God, and every time man speaks to This God, he receives a direct answer. One! One! One! "I Am God and there is none else." There is One Limitless Life which returns to the thinker what he thinks into It. One! One! One! "In all, over all and through all."

Talk, live, act, believe and know that you are a center in the One. All the Power there is; all the Presence there is; all the Love there is; all the Peace there is; all the Good there is and the Only God that is, is Omnipresent; consequently, the Infinite is in and through man and is in and through everything. "Act as though I am and I will Be."

LESSON FIVE

A mystic is not a mysterious person; but is one who has a deep, inner sense of Life and Unity with the Whole; mysticism and mystery are entirely different things; one is real while the other may, or may not, be an illusion. There is nothing mysterious in the Truth, so far as It is understood; but all things, of course, are mysteries until we understand them.

A mystic is one who intuitively perceives Truth and who, without mental process, arrives at Spiritual Realizations. It is from the teachings of the great mystics that the best in the philosophy of the world has come.

The civilization of today is built around the teachings of a few people who have intuitively perceived Spiritual Truth. Our great code of law was given by Moses, a man who through the mystic sense perceived that we live in a Universe of Law. Our greatest code of ethics was given through the perception of the prophets, culminating in such teachings as those of Jesus and Buddha. Who was there who could have taught such men as these? By what process of mentality did they arrive at their profound conclusions? We are compelled to recognize that Spirit Alone was their Teacher; they were, indeed, taught of God.

The mystic intuitively senses Reality and instinctively

knows The Truth; and in this way all of the best in literature, music and art have come.

Our great religions have been given by a few who climbed the heights of spiritual vision and caught a fleeting glimpse of Ultimate Reality. No living soul could have taught them what they knew, and it is doubtful if even they themselves knew why they knew.

The great poets have been true mystics and have revealed, through their poems, the Presence of God. Men like Robert Browning, Tennyson, Wordsworth, Homer, Walt Whitman, Edward Rowland Sill, and others of like nature, have given us poetry which is immortal, because they had a mystic sense of life: the perception of a Living Presence. All true philosophers are mystics; the old prophets were mystics; David, Solomon, Jesus, Plato, Buddha, Plotinus, Emerson, and a score of others, all had the same experience: the sense of a Living Presence.

The greatest music ever composed was written by the hand of a mystic; and the highest and best in art has come from the same source.

Man has compelled nature to do his bidding; he has harnessed electric energy, caught the wind, trapped steam and made them all obey his will. He has invented machines to do the work of thousands; he has belted the globe with his traffic and built up a wonderful civilization; but in few cases has he conquered his own soul.

The highest and best that we have in civilization is the result of the mystic sense which has been perceived by a few in each age. All that modern appliances and inventions give us in the way of comfort and luxury, good and necessary as they are, may be counted as nothing compared to the teachings of Jesus. By this, we do not mean to decry modern civilization, education or anything that goes with it; for we are firm believers in anything and everything that makes life interesting and worth living. We believe in science, art, religion, education, commerce, government, industry, agriculture, and all that goes to make up a well-rounded experience in life; but we repeat, what would they amount to, if thought of in any other light than as passing things?

The mystic has revealed things that do not pass as ships in the night; he has revealed Eternal Verities and has plainly taught us that there is a Living Presence indwelling All.

TRUE MYSTICISM AND THE PSYCHIC SENSE

There is a vast difference between mysticism and psychism, between a mystic and an ordinary psychic. The psychic capacity will be thoroughly discussed in Lesson Six, and the reader will remember that it is the power to read subjectively; it may be dealing with a reality or with an illusion. The average psychic must become more or less subjective in order to do good work. At best, and even though in a normal state of mind, he can only read subjective pictures and tendencies; at best, he is generally dealing with human thought. Should he penetrate that thought, he would then become a mystic.

A mystic does not read human thought but senses the Thought of God. The question might be asked, "How do you know that he senses the Thought of God?" Because the mystics of every age have seen, sensed and taught THE SAME TRUTH. Psychic experiences more or less contradict each other, because each psychic sees a different kind of mental picture; but the mystic experiences of the ages have revealed ONE AND THE SAME TRUTH.

WHAT THE MYSTICS HAVE TAUGHT

Without exception, all of the mystics have taught that there is but One Ultimate Reality; and that this Ultimate Reality is HERE NOW, IF WE COULD BUT SEE IT.

Strange as it may seem, the great mystics have all believed in a Personal God; that is, a God who is Personal to all who believe in Him. They have not, of course, believed in an AN-THROPOMORPHIC GOD; but they have believed in a God who consciously works in and through man; and they have adored and worshiped this God.

The great mystics have been illumined, that is, they have, at times, seen through the veil of matter and perceived the Spiritual Universe. They have taught that the Kingdom of God is NOW PRESENT AND NEEDS BUT TO BE REALIZED; and they have, apparently, sensed that this Kingdom is within.

A psychic sees only through his own subjective mentality; consequently, everything that he looks at is more or less colored by the vibration of his own thought; he is subject to hallucinations and false impressions of every description. This is why, generally speaking, no two psychics ever see the same thing.

Mystics have all seen the same thing, and their testimony is in no way confusing; this is because the Spirit within them has borne witness to the Truth.

NO ULTIMATE EVIL

One of the most illuminating things that mysticism has revealed is that evil is not an ultimate reality. Evil is simply an experience of the soul on its journey toward Reality; it is not an entity but an experience necessary to self-unfoldment; it is not a thing of itself but simply a misuse of power. It will disappear when we stop looking at, or believing in, it. We cannot stop believing in it as long as we indulge in it; so the mystic has always taught the race to turn from evil and do good.

ULTIMATE SALVATION OF ALL

The mystics have taught the ultimate salvation of all people and the immortality of every soul. Indeed, they have taught that immortality IS HERE AND NOW, IF WE WOULD BUT WAKE TO THE FACT. "Beloved, now are we the Sons of God." Since each soul is some part of the Whole, it is impossible that any soul can be lost. "God is not the God of the dead, but of the living." Damnation has been as foreign to the thought of the mystic as any belief in evil must be to the Mind of God.

FREEDOM FROM BURDEN

The great mystics have taught that man should have no burdens, and would have none, if he turned to "The One." "Come unto Me all ye that labor and are heavy laden and I will give you rest." As Jesus must have known that it would be impossible for all men to come unto Him as a Personality, He must have meant that we should come into His understanding of Life and Reality; that is, to come unto the Great God. Some day we will learn to lay our burdens on the Altar of Love, that they may be consumed by the fire of faith in the Living Spirit. Man would have no burdens if he kept his "High watch" toward "The One"; that is, if he always turned to God.

UNITY OF ALL

Jesus prayed that all might come to see the Unity of Life. "That they may be One, even as we are One," was His prayer as He neared the completion of His great work on this planet. All mystics have sensed that we live in One Life. "For in Him we live, and move, and have our being." The Unity of Good is a revelation of the greatest importance; for it teaches us that we are One with the Whole, and One with each other. This realization alone will settle the question of human inequality. The real Fatherhood of God and the Actual Brotherhood of Man will be made apparent on earth to the degree that men realize True Unity.

REALIZATION OF INDIVIDUALITY

No great mystic ever lived who denied the reality of individuality. The higher the sense of Truth, the greater will be the realization of the uniqueness of individual character and personality. The Real Self is God-given and cannot be denied; it is the place where God comes to a point of Individualized and Personified Expression, and should be thought of in this light. "I am the Light of the world."

NORMALCY

All mystics have been normal people, that is, they have lived just as other people have lived. The only difference has been that they have sensed a greater Reality; namely, the Presence of the Living Spirit. The true mystic in every age has come into the world of affairs and lived among men, sometimes as a teacher, and sometimes in the ordinary walks of life, but always in a perfectly natural way. There is nothing peculiar or strange about a mystic. People who shroud themselves in a cloak of mystery are not true mystics but are laboring under mental delusions and subjective hallucinations. They may be sincere in their beliefs, but they are none the less wrong in their methods. It is a question if a real mystic would even realize that he is a mystic. He would be more liable to think of himself simply as one who understands that he is One with the Whole.

THE GREAT LIGHT

It is impossible, perhaps, to put into words or into print what a mystic sometimes sees, and it is as hard to believe it as it is to put it into words. But there is a certain inner sense which, at times, sees Reality in a flash which illuminates the whole being with a great flood of light. This, too, might seem an illusion unless the testimony were complete; for every mystic has had this experience; but some have had it to a greater degree than others. Jesus was the greatest of all the mystics; and once, at least, after a period of illumination, His face was so bright that His followers could not look upon it.

In moments of deepest realization the great mystics have sensed that One Life flows through ALL; and that all are some part of that Life. They have also seen Substance, a fine, white, brilliant stuff, forever falling into everything; a Substance, indestructible and eternal. At times, the realization has been so complete that they have been actually blinded by the light. There are instances where for several days after such an experience, the one having it could not see on the physical plane; for he had seen the Inner Light. Remember, all this takes place when in a perfectly normal state of mind and has nothing whatever to do with the psychic state. It is not an illusion but a reality; and it is during these periods that real revelation comes. Perhaps a good illustration would be to suppose a large group of people in a room together, but unaware of each other's presence; each is busy with his own personal affairs. We will suppose the place to be dark and that some one comes in and takes a flash-light picture of the room and its occupants. Should this picture be shown to anyone who was in the room before it was taken, it might be hard for him to believe that all of the objects in the picture were actually in the room. This is, of course, a poor analogy, but it does serve to elucidate a point. In flashes of illumination, the inspired have seen INTO THE VERY CENTER OF REALITY, and have brought back with them a picture of what they have seen and felt. Again, we know that this has not been an illusion or simply a subjective hallucination, for each age has had its mystics, and every age has produced the same results. ALL HAVE SEEN THE SAME THING. The testimony is complete and the evidence is certain.

WHAT THE MYSTICS HAVE TAUGHT ABOUT THE INDIVIDUAL

All of the great mystics have taught practically the same thing. They have all agreed that the soul is on the pathway of experience, that is, of self-discovery; that it is on its way back to its Father's House; and that every soul will ultimately reach its Heavenly Home. They have taught the Divinity to Man. "I have said, Ye are gods; and all of you are children of the most High." They have told us that man's destiny is Divine and sure; and that Creation is Complete and Perfect NOW. The great mystics have all agreed that man's life is his to do with as he chooses; but that when he turns to "The One," he will always receive inspiration from On High.

They have told us of the marvelous relationship which exists between God and man, of a close Union that cannot be broken; and the greatest of the mystics have consciously walked with God and talked with Him, just as we talk to each other. It is difficult to realize how this could be; it is hard to understand how a Being, so Universal as God must be, can talk with man; here, alone, the mystic sense reveals the greater truth and knows that, Infinite as is the Divine Being, It is still Personal to all who believe in Its Presence. It is entirely possible for a man to talk with the Spirit; for the Spirit is within men, and "He who made the ears" can hear.

INSTINCT AND INTUITION

That quality in an animal which directs its action and tells it where to go to find food and shelter, we call instinct. It is, really, Omniscience in the animal. The same quality, more highly developed, makes its appearance in man; and is what we call intuition. Intuition is God in man, revealing to him the Realities of Being; and just as instinct guides the animal, so would intuition guide man, if he would allow it to operate through him. Here again, we must be careful not to mistake a psychic impression for an intuitive one. *Psychic impressions seek to control man; intuition always remains in the background and waits* for his recognition. "Behold, I stand at the door."

All arbitrary control of man stopped as soon as he was brought to a point of self-knowingness. From this point he must discover himself; but intuition, which is nothing less than God in man, silently awaits his recognition and cooperation. The Spirit is always there if we could but sense Its Presence. Mystics have felt this wonderful power working from within, and have responded to it; and, as a sure evidence that they were not laboring under delusions, they have all sensed the same thing; had the impressions been psychic only, each would have seen and sensed a different thing; for each would have seen through the darkness of his own subjective mentality.

ILLUMINATION AND COSMIC
CONSCIOUSNESS

There is such an experience as Illumination and Cosmic Consciousness; It is not a mystery, however, but is the Self-Knowingness of God through man. The more complete the operation of that Power, the more complete has been man's conscious mentality; for the illumined do not become less, but more themselves. The greater the consciousness of God, the more complete must be the realization of the True Self—The Divine Reality.

Illumination will come as man more and more realizes his Unity with the Whole; and as he constantly endeavors to let the Truth operate through him. But since the Whole is at the point of the Inner Mentality, it will be here alone that he will contact It. "Speak to Him, thou, for He hears."

The only God man knows is the God of his own Inner Life; indeed, he can know no other. To assume that man can know a God outside himself is to assume that he can know something of which he is not conscious. This does not mean that man is God; it means that the only God man knows is within. The only place that man contacts God is within; and the only life man has is from within. God is not external, but is Indwelling, at the very center of man's life. This is why Jesus said that the Kingdom of Heaven is within, and why He prayed, "Our Father Which art in Heaven."

THE HIGHEST PRACTICE

The highest mental practice is to listen to this Inner Voice and to declare for Its Presence. The greater a man's consciousness of this Indwelling I AM is, the more power he will have. This will never lead to illusion but will always lead to Reality. All great souls have known this and have constantly striven to let the Mind of God come out through their mentalities. "The Father that dwelleth in Me, He doeth the works." This was the declaration of the great Master, and it should be ours also; not a limited sense of life but a limitless one.

THE POWER OF JESUS

The occult significance of the power of Jesus is easily understood when we study His method of procedure. Consider His raising of Lazarus from the dead. He stood at the tomb and gave thanks; this was recognition. He next said, "I Knew that Thou hearest me always"; this was unification; then He said, "Lazarus, come forth"; this was command. The method is perfect and we will do well to study and follow it. This method can be used in all treatment. First, realize that Divine Power Is; then unify with It, and then speak the word as "one having authority," for the Law is "the servant of the Eternal Spirit throughout all the ages."

TURNING WITHIN

We should turn within, then, as have all of those great souls who have blessed the world with their presence; we should turn within and FIND GOD. It should seem natural to turn to the Great Power back of everything; it should seem normal to believe in this Power; and we should have a sense of a Real Presence when we do turn toward the One and Only Power in the entire Universe. This method is by far the most effective. It gives a sense of power that nothing else can, and, in this way, proves that it is a Reality. It would be a wonderful experiment if the world would try to solve all of its problems through the power of Spirit. Indeed the time will come when every one will, "From the highest . . . to the lowest."

A sense of real completion can come only to that soul which realizes its Unity with the Great Whole. Man will never be satisfied until his whole being responds to this thought, and then, indeed, "Will God go forth anew into Creation."

"To as many as believed gave He the Power."

LESSON FIVE

THE PERFECT WHOLE

Chart No. V represents the Triune Unity. The other charts were divided into Spirit, Soul and Body, symbolizing the Conscious part of Existence; the Law through which It operates; and the result of the operation. But those lines were entirely arbitrary. No such lines could exist, for the threefold Universe, with all of Its attributes, interspheres Itself. We find the Spirit, or Conscious Mind, the Soul or Subconscious Mind, and the Body, which is the manifestation of the union of Spirit and Soul, simultaneously present at every point. This chart represents the Indivisible Whole, within which are all of Its parts; the Absolute, within which is the relative; the Uncreated, within which is all Creation.

Creation is the giving of form to the Substance of Spirit. Spirit, being All and Only, there is nothing for It to change into but Itself; therefore, It is the Changeless, within which must take place all change or manifestation of Itself. Change is simply motion within Life.

The Infinite, of Itself, is Formless, but within It are contained all of the forms which are the expressions or the outlines of Its experiences.

Spirit is the Limitless, within which is all space; Spirit is Timeless, within which is all time. "Time is the sequence of events in a Unitary Whole." Creation and experience are eternally going on, but a particular experience is measured by time and has a beginning and an end.

The big circle represents the Universal, within which is the individual; the One Person within Whom are all people. There is really but One Person in the Universe; but within this One Person all people live, "for in Him we live, and move, and have our being." It is the Source and center of all Life, Power, Action, Truth, Love, Mind, Spirit, the Ever and the All. It is, of course, God.

THE TRIUNE UNITY

THE INDIVISIBLE WHOLE

WITHIN WHICH IS ALL OF ITS PARTS

THE ABSOLUTE WITHIN WHICH IS THE CREATED

THE UNCREATED WITHIN WHICH IS THE CREATED

THE CHANGELESS WITHIN WHICH IS ALL CHANGE

THE FORMLESS WITHIN WHICH IS ALL FORM

THE LIMITLESS WITHIN WHICH IS ALL SPACE

THE TIMELESS WITHIN WHICH IS ALL TIME

THE UNIVERSAL WITHIN WHICH IS THE INDIVIDUAL

THE ONE PERSON WITHIN WHOM ARE ALL PEOPLE

SOURCE AND CENTER OF ALL LIFE, POWER AND ACTION

TRUTH, LOVE, MIND, SPIRIT, THE EVER, AND THE ALL

GOD

Our Father
which art
in
Heaven

THE SON

PERSONALITY . . . INDIVIDUALITY

MAN

Lesson Five: Metaphysical Chart No. V.

This is the Mystic's chart and shows how Universal becomes Particularization of Itself through man. Man comes to a point in the Universal, or God, and is the Idea of God as man. The Father is represented as the Whole just back of, or above, or within, man. This is the Indwelling God to Whom we pray and with Whom we talk. The mystic has the ability to consciously talk to God and to consciously receive a direct answer from the Spirit. In this chart it is shown that the Absolute contains the relative, within Itself, but is not limited by the relative. We must remember that the relative does not limit, but expresses, the Absolute. All change takes place within the Changeless. All form subsists within the Formless. All conditions obtain within that which is Limitless; and Creation is eternally going on within that which is Uncreated. All are activities of the One Mind and Spirit of God. All people come to a point of individuality within that which is Universal.

INDIVIDUALITY

The point within the big circle represents the personality and individuality of man, indicating that he is a center in the Divine Mind or God.

Man is the Personification of the Infinite Life; and so we place, just above this point and on the inside of it, "The Son"; and just above this (with no line to divide them) are written the words, "Our Father which art in Heaven," taken from the Lord's Prayer. There is no difference between God, the Absolute, which is Our Father in Heaven, and the Son, so far as actual Being is concerned. The Son is simply a point where God recognizes Himself as Personality or Individualized Being. It is within that we find the Unity of God and man; there is no separation.

Man, having his existence in the Unitary Whole, which is Indivisible, is compelled to accept the fact that his life is God or Spirit; but to say that man is God, which is equivalent to saying that any part equals the whole, is to contradict logic and reason, and limit the Limitless Idea. It is enough to say that we are at one with the Whole. It is both within and without. In perhaps a more liberal sense we could say man is in God; immersed in God; saturated with God. God permeates all life, and in man we find that this Infinite Mind or Intelligence comes to a point of Individualized Self-Consciousness.

Theoretically, we believe that the personality which we possess is on the pathway of self-discovery; for everything bears witness to this belief; as fast as we discover any truth, it is there to use. We never create Truth—we discover and use It. We believe, then, that as man continuously unfolds his personality, he will find latent capacities of which he has never dreamed.

FURTHER EVOLUTION

Since his whole life is the unfoldment of intelligence, according to law, man can only evolve as he recognizes greater possibilities—there could be no other way. The arbitrary process of evolution ceased when man became an individual; and any further evolution will be through self-recognition; but back of him is the whole of Life surging to express Itself. This is what is known as the Divine Urge. It is that Instinctive, Omniscient "I am" in man, always pushing him on and up; but It can only express for him as It flows through him. That person has the greatest power who the most completely recognizes himself to be one with this Infinite Mind. That is why Jesus said: "I speak not of myself" (it is not this individualized point); "but the Father that dwelleth in Me" (that is, God, our Father, Which is in Heaven); "He doeth the works."

The evolution of man, which is the unfoldment of Spirit through his personality, will be more complete when his objective and subjective faculties are more perfectly balanced; that is, when he has conscious control of the spiritual forces which surge for expression. The psychological nature has to change somewhat, and the subjective tendencies that hinder the Whole from coming to a point of conscious contact must be neutralized. This would produce illumination or the consciousness of his Unity with the Whole.

In treatment, we work until we penetrate the false thought within and break through to Reality. There is no limitation, either in Infinite Intelligence or in Infinite Law. The whole limitation which we experience is not, of itself, a reality or an entity, but is simply one of the forms within the formless which we are outlining.

THE TRUTH IS KNOWN

Our conscious intelligence is as much of Life as we understand. We have stopped looking for the Spirit, because we have found It; It is what you are and It is what I am; we could not be anything else if we tried. The thing that we look with is the thing that we have been looking for. That is why it is written: "I have said, Ye are gods; and all of you are children of the most High." We have stopped looking for the Law. We have found It. In the Universe we call It Universal Subjectivity or Soul; in our own experience we call It the subjective state of our thought, which is our individual use of Universal Law. We have found the Law and demonstrated It. We find that both the Law and the Spirit are Limitless. What is it that we need for a greater freedom? Nothing but a greater realization of what we already know.

We should never hesitate to say that we know the Truth, because we do; for the realization of the Unity of God and man *is* the Truth. We simply need a greater realization of this. How are we to get it? Only by penetrating deeper and yet deeper into our own Divine Nature; pushing farther and farther back into the Infinite. Where are we to do that? There is no place except within that we can do it. Who is to do it for us? No one. No one can. People can heal us; they can set the Law in motion for us and help us to become prosperous—that is good and helpful— but the evolution of the individual, the unfoldment of personality, the enlightenment of the Soul, the illumination of Spirit, can come only to the degree that the individual himself purposes to let Life operate through him. "Let this Mind be in you which was also in Christ Jesus." This is the Mind of God—the only Mind—the Supreme Intelligence of the Universe.

THE ANSWER IS IN MAN

The answer to every question is within man, because man is within Spirit and Spirit is an Indivisible Whole. The solution to every problem is within man; the healing of all disease is within man; the forgiveness of all sin is within man; the raising of the dead is within man; Heaven is within man. That is why Jesus prayed to this indwelling "I am" and said: "Our Father Which art in Heaven." He also said: "The Kingdom of God is within you."

Each of us, then, represents the Whole. How should we feel toward the Whole? In the old order, we thought of the Whole as a sort of mandatory power, an autocratic government, an arbitrary God, sending some to Heaven and some to hell; and "all for His glory." Now we are much more enlightened and we realize that there can be no such Divine Being. We have meditated upon the vastness of the Universe of Law, and we have said: "God is Law; there is a Divine Principle Which is God." In the new order, we are liable to fall into as great an error as the old thought fell into, unless we go much deeper than thinking of God simply as Principle. God is more than Law or Principle. God is the Infinite Spirit, the Limitless, Conscious Life of the Universe; the One Infinite Person within Whom all people live. The Law is simply a Force.

GOD—INFINITE PERSONALITY

God or Spirit is Supreme, Infinite, Limitless Personality. And we should think of the Divine Being as such—as completely responsive to everything we do. There should come to us a sense of communion, a spontaneous sense of Irresistible Union. If we had that, we would demonstrate instantaneously.

An evolved soul is always a worshiper of God. He worships God in everything; for God *is* in everything. God not only is *in everything, but He is more than everything He is in.* "Ye are the light of the world"—that is, God in us. All that we are is God; yet God is more than all we are.

The nearer consciousness gets to the Truth, the more Cosmic sweep it has, the more power it has. Angels wait upon individuals who perceive Cosmic Purposes and Powers, because the Whole is crowding forth into expression. Let a man recognize a Cosmic Purpose, which is the expression of Life, Truth and Love; let his thought vibrate to the higher and grander realization of life, and see how—automatically—he becomes more powerful.

The process of healing and demonstration is, at first, mechanical and scientific; then the fire of Spirit is added to make it real. One is technique—the other is the pulsating life and glow. We need the recognition of love, coupled with a scientific understanding of what we are doing. Thoughts are things, and diseases are the direct result of specific thoughts somewhere in consciousness. Poverty is the direct result of a subjective state of thought which binds.

UNITY

All Manifestation of Life is from and invisible to a visible plane; and it is a silent, effortless process of spiritual realization. We must unify, in our own mentalities, with Pure Spirit. To each of us, individually, God, or Spirit, is the Supreme Personality of the Universe; the Supreme Personality of that which we, ourselves, are. It is only as the relationship of the individual to this Deity becomes enlarged that he has a consciousness of power.

There should always be a recognition in treatment of the Absolute Unity of God and man; the Oneness, Inseparability,

Indivisibility, Changelessness; God as the Big Circle, and man as the little circle. Man is in God and God is in man; just as a drop of water is in the ocean, while the ocean is in the drop of water. This is the recognition Jesus had when He said: "I and my Father are One." There is a Perfect Union; and to the degree that we are conscious of this Union we incorporate this consciousness in our word, and our word has just as much power as we put in it, no more and no less.

Within this Infinite Mind each individual exists, not as a separated, but as a separate, entity. We are a point in Universal Consciousness, which is God, and God is our Life, Spirit, Mind and Intelligence. We are not separated from Life, neither is It separated from us; but we are separate entities in It, Individualized Centers of God's Consciousness.

We came from Life and are in Life, so we are One with Life; and we know that Instinctive Life within, which has brought us to the point of self-recognition, still knows in us the reason for all things, the purpose underlying all things; and we know that there is nothing in us of fear, doubt or confusion which can hinder the flow of Reality to the point of our recognition. We are guided, daily, by Divine Intelligence into paths of peace wherein the soul recognizes its Source and meets It in joyful Union, in complete At-One-ment.

HOLD TO THE GOOD

Such is the power of clear thought that it penetrates things; it removes obstructions, the reason being that there is nothing but consciousness, nothing but Mind. The only instrument of Mind is idea. See with perfect clearness and never become discouraged nor overcome by a sense of limitation. Know this—that the Truth with which you are dealing is absolute. All of God, all of Truth, all there is, is at the point of man's recognition; and every time you give a treatment, and all the way through it, keep bringing this back to your remembrance.

Never struggle; say, "There is nothing to struggle over; everything is mine by Divine Right; Infinite Intelligence is my Intelligence; Divine Love is my Love; Limitless Freedom is my Freedom; Perfect Joy is my Gladness; Limitless Life is my Energy."

Let us BLIND OURSELVES TO NEGATION, as far as we are mentally able to. LET US NOT TALK, THINK, OR READ ABOUT ANYTHING DESTRUCTIVE, whether it be war, pestilence, famine, poverty, sickness, or limitation of any kind. Looking at this from a practical standpoint, there is all to win and nothing to lose. The rapid progress we would make if we should do this would be wonderful.

We are always dealing with First Cause. Nothing else can equal the satisfaction that comes to one when he perceives himself, from the silence of his own soul and the activity of his own thought, actually bringing about a condition without the aid of visible instrumentalities. There is nothing else as satisfying as to heal some disease purely by the power of thought; this shows that we are dealing with First Cause.

We must definitely neutralize confusion and doubt. We should take time, daily, to conceive of ourselves as being tranquil, poised, powerful—always in control of every situation; as being always the highest concept of the Divine which we can imagine. We should never hesitate to think of ourselves in this way. The Ancients used to teach their pupils to say to themselves—"Wonderful, wonderful, wonderful me!"—until they lost sight of themselves as Mary Smith or John Jones, and perceived themselves as Divine Realities.

Then, when they came back to the objectivity of Mary Smith and John Jones, they brought with them that subtle power which distinguishes Spiritual Growth—the Atmosphere of Reality.

THE INFINITE IS PERSONAL TO ALL

Undoubtedly the power of Jesus lay in His recognition of the Infinite Person as a Responsive, Conscious, Living Reality;

while, on the other hand, He recognized the Law as an arbitrary force, which was compelled to obey His will. He combined the personal and the impersonal attributes of Life into a perfect whole. The Infinite is Personal to every soul who believes in the Infinite. It is a mistake to so abstract the Principle that we forget the Living Presence; it is the combination of the two that makes work effective.

THE CHRIST

Who is man? He is the Christ. Who is the Christ? The Son, begotten of the only Father—not the only begotten Son of God. Christ means the Universal Idea of Sonship, of which each is a Member. That is why we are spoken of as Members of that One Body; and why we are told to have that Mind in us "which was also in Christ Jesus." Each partakes of the Christ Nature to the degree that the Christ is revealed through him, and to that degree he becomes the Christ. We should turn to that Living Presence within, Which is the Father in Heaven, recognize It as the One and Only Power in the Universe, unify with It, declare our word to be the presence, power and activity of that One, and speak the word as if we believed it; because the Law is the servant of the Spirit.

If we could stand aside and let the One Perfect Life flow through us, we could not help healing people. This is the highest form of healing.

We have gone through all of our abstract processes of reasoning and have found out what the Law is and how It works; now we can forget all about It, and know that there is nothing but the Word; the Law will be working automatically. We must forget everything else, and let our word be spoken with a deep inner realization of love, beauty, peace, poise, power, and of the great Presence of Life at the point of our own consciousness.

REALIZATION

We do not dare to throw ourselves with abandonment into a seeming void; but if we did, we would find our feet planted firmly on a rock, for there is a place in the mentality, in the heights of its greatest realizations, where it throws itself with complete abandonment into the very center of the Universe. There is a point in the supreme moment of realization where the individual merges with the Universe, but not to the loss of his individuality; where a sense of the Oneness of all Life so enters his being that there is no sense of otherness; it is here that the mentality performs seeming miracles, because there is nothing to hinder the Whole from coming through. We can do this only by providing the great mental equivalents of Life, by dwelling and meditating upon the immensity of Life; and yet as vast, as immense, as limitless as It is, the whole of It is brought to the point of our own consciousness.

We comprehend the Infinite only to the degree that It expresses Itself through us, becoming to us that which we believe It to be. And so we daily practice in our meditations the realizations of Life—"Infinite, indwelling Spirit within me, Almighty God within me, Perfect Peace within me, Complete Satisfaction within me, Real Substance within me; that which is the Truth within me." "I am the Truth," Jesus said. He said: "I am the way; I am the Life; no man cometh unto the Father but by Me." How true it is! We cannot come unto the Father Which art in Heaven except through our own nature.

Right here, through our own nature, is the gateway and the path that gradually leads to illumination, to realization, to inspiration, to the intuitive perception of everything.

The highest faculty in man is intuition, and it comes to a point sometimes where, with no process of reasoning at all, he realizes the Truth intuitively. So we should daily meditate, particularly if we are practicing right along.

MEDITATION

Any practitioner should take a certain time every day to meditate within himself, to realize that the words which he speaks are the words of Truth. Being the words of Truth, they cannot fail to be fulfilled; they are a law unto themselves within the Great Law. They know themselves to be what they are.

They are immutable, irresistible, unassailable; they are eternal and complete, having intelligence, knowledge and understanding within themselves.

Every treatment must be a complete thing within itself. It is an unqualified statement of Being and pays no attention to appearances. If it did, it would not be efficacious. It rises above all appearance and may contradict every experience the human race has ever had; but it is real just the same. *The treatment begins and ends within the mentality of the one giving it; and the demonstration takes place within the mentality of the one giving it; and, to the degree that it does take place there, it is a good treatment and will be a good demonstration.*

If you have a patient who says: "I am sick," and you are able to neutralize your belief of that man as being sick, or any man as being sick, and can see him perfect, he will come to you and say: "I am healed." *The practitioner must know within himself.* He never thinks of projecting his thought, sending it out or holding it. He simply takes the whole condition and brings it into the great realization of Life.

Declare—"Perfect Life within me, God within me, Spirit within me, Good within me, Almightiness within me, Loving Intelligence within me, Peace, Poise, Power, Happiness and Joy within me, Life, Truth and Love within me, Omniscient Instinctive I am within me, Almighty God within me." It is not enough to say that God is. The concept must be brought home to the mentality of the individual and unified with it, in order to have it expressed through him.

If we need financial healing, we should say: "Infinite Substance within me, Infinite Activity within me, flowing through me into everything I do, say or think, quickening into action all those things that my mentality touches; Infinite Activity within me, unerring, never mistaking, always doing the right thing at the right time, always knowing what to do, knowing how to do it and doing it; Infinite Executive Power within me, the Great Executive, the great I am, the All-Knowing and All-Seeing, the All-Wise within me; Infinite Substance within me, forever expressing Itself through me; Infinite Supply flowing through me and flowing to me; irresistible supply, unassailable supply, limitless." As you say this, stop and think of the things you want—seeing them as realities—much as one would look at pictures on the wall.

Repeat—"Infinite Substance within me, Infinite Supply flowing through me and to me, Infinite Activity around me and within me, Infinite Intelligence within me, directing me, guarding me, governing me, controlling me; the One and Only within me and through me, that is, Almighty God within me. There is no other, or beside which there is none other. Infinite love within me, seeing all, knowing all, loving all, One in and through all." Carry this concept out until you see that you live in everybody and everybody lives in you. Then continue: "Infinite One, comprehending, seeing, knowing, understanding, living in and including the All, within me." Realize what this means. "I am One with all people. There are no enemies. There is only the One, in all and through all."

If we would spend half the time making such affirmations that we spend complaining, finding fault, fussing, being sad and sorry for ourselves, we would soon be healed. "Infinite Wisdom within me"—stop and think what this means—the Intelligence that operates through everything, visible and invisible. "Infinite Wisdom within me; Infinite Intelligence within me; Infinite Power within me"—feel what this means: The Power that holds the planets in place; a power to which the united force of the human race is as nothing. "Infinite Intelligence and Infinite Power within me, the great Executor; Infinite Energy and Wisdom within me—the All-Knowing, the Unerring Mind of the Universe—Infinite Peace within me, Infinite Peace, undisturbed and unalterable; Infinite Life, Infinite Peace within me"; that means there is no disturbance, no commotion, no trouble. There is only Infinite Peace; the power that stilled the waves and told the winds to be calm is the Power with which we deal. "Infinite Peace within me, Infinite Joy within me, the Joy that causes the leaves of the trees to clap their hands." It is the Joy that sings in the brook, the music of the spheres, the Joy of the sense of completion. "Infinite Joy within me, not somewhere else, but within me"; It is the Good which is urging Itself forth through every act which we call human or humane. We see it in the hand that gives and in every human act. That is the "Infinite Good that is within me"—Infinite everything, whatever the need may be. Meditate upon the abstract essence of the thing; then bring it to a concrete point within your own mentality and see what it means as it manifests, declaring that it is.

This great teaching plainly shows the way to liberty and freedom. It is a pathway continuously unfolding from a Limitless Source to a Limitless Source. "Arise, shine, for thy light is come." "I am that I am."

Note: Read and study "Cosmic Consciousness," Bucke; "Twelve Lessons in Mysticism," Hopkins; "The Impersonal Life" and "Creative Process in the Individual," T. Troward; "Bible Mystery and Meaning," T. Troward; "Sayings of Jesus," Red Letter Testament.

LESSON SIX

THE LAW OF PSYCHIC PHENOMENA

INTRODUCTION

It is taken for granted that the average person of today is more or less acquainted with the facts concerning psychic phenomena. It would be useless, in a course such as this, to attempt any exhaustive research work; this has already been done by those eminently able to furnish the data.

There is within man a power that can communicate without the tongue, hear without the ear, see without the eye, talk without the mouth, move ponderable objects and grasp things without the hand; and perform many other feats that are usually connected only with the physical instrument. All these facts have been completely proved, and it is no longer necessary to produce evidence to substantiate these facts.

While the above stated facts have all been proved, the reason for their being has not been so thoroughly or logically discussed, and it is the purpose of this article to explain the fundamental reasons behind the law of mental action which is called psychic; for if a thing happens, there must be a reason for its happening and a law through which it operates.

The only excuse for taking up this topic in a course of

lessons in Mental Science is that, being the phenomena of Mind, it should come under the category of known mental actions.

PSYCHIC PHENOMENA AND IMMORTALITY

Psychic phenomena are closely associated with immortality in people's minds for the reason that they deal with those unseen powers which we think of as being attributes of the soul; and also because many people have attributed the phenomena largely to the agency of discarnate spirits.

NO APOLOGIES

While no apologies are made for the ensuing pages, yet, in justice to the Truth, it must be said that many of the world's eminent scientists have investigated the subjects to be discussed, and so far, to the author's knowledge, none of them have ever refuted the ensuing facts.

The powers which are exhibited through the psychic life do really exist in man, and someday he will make conscious use of them and will, thereby, be greatly benefited. Meanwhile, every one is urged to be most careful in his approach to the subject. A little knowledge is a very dangerous thing, and it is to be regretted that very few people exhibiting psychic powers appear to know what the law is that underlies the phenomena. Many are led astray through ignorance, and one should be most careful in handling the topic. But, as stated above, this subject, coming under the known laws of mental action, must be dealt with.

God has given us a mind with which to know, and a power with which to discern, the Truth, and it is a terrible mistake to misuse that power. The whole end and aim of evolution is to produce a man who, in his self-conscious state, may depict the Divine Nature. We can do this only to the degree that we remain ourselves at all times.

We will take up the study of this subject just as we would approach the study of any other law, with an open mind, without any superstition and free from any sense of the unnatural. Nature is always natural, and only those things are mysteries which we do not understand.

LESSON SIX

METAPHYSICAL MEANINGS OF WORDS
USED IN CHART NO. VI

The upper section represents the Conscious Mind, the Self-Knowing Mind, which we call Spirit. The middle section represents the Psychic Sea, that is, the Subjective World; this is the world of thought forms and mental pictures. This has been called "The illusion of Mind," because it contains many pictures, which are pictures only, and have no real form behind them. As a picture that is hung on the wall is not really a person—but is simply a picture—so the Psychic Sea may contain pictures which, while they are real as pictures, are not real from any other sense. It does not follow that everything in the psychic world is an illusion, for it contains much that is true. We should be very careful to distinguish the false from the true.

The lower section of the chart represents the objective world. This world also reflects many false forms, such as disease and limitation. They are not things of themselves, but are the results of wrong mental pictures in the Subjective World.

Neither the psychic pictures nor the world of forms are self-creative; both are effects.

SPIRIT OR CONSCIOUS MIND
ONE AND ONLY KNOWING
POWER IN GOD OR MAN

THE PSYCHIC SEA – SUBJECTIVE
FALSE OR TRUE – MIRROR OF MIND
MEDIUM OF ALL PSYCHIC PHENOMENA
THOUGHT FORMS OR MENTAL PICTURES

OBJECTIVE
ILLUSION OF MATTER
FALSE OR TRUE
MIRROR OF MATTER

Lesson Six: Metaphysical Chart No. VI.

This is the psychic's chart and should be carefully considered, as it shows that the Spirit, or Conscious Mind, operates through a mental field, or law, which is a world of reflections. Thought is first reflected into Mind and then into matter. Read again the meaning of the conscious and the subconscious aspects of being. The world of Subjectivity is the Psychic Sea and the Medium of all subjective action. From the standpoint of man's thoughts it may be false or true, according to the way in which he thinks. It is the picture gallery of the soul, both from the universal and the individual sense. The illusion of matter means that the false mental pictures will produce a false form in the world of objectivity. Mind is not an illusion, but might contain false pictures which would be illusions; matter is not an illusion but may take on false conditions. We must learn to separate the false from the true.

LESSON SIX

PSYCHIC PHENOMENA

Psyche means soul; psychic phenomena are the phenomena of the soul. We have already seen that what we call the soul is, really, the subjective part of us. We do not have two minds, but we do have a dual aspect of mentality in what we call the objective and subjective phases of mind. The objective mind is that part of the mentality which functions consciously; it is the part of us which really knows itself; and without it we would not be real or conscious entities.

THE SUBJECTIVE MIND

Our subjective mind is our mental emanation in Universal Subjectivity; it is our individual use of mental law. It is also the avenue through which Instinctive Man works, carrying on the functions of the body; for it is the silent builder of the body. The subjective mind of the individual is the working of Instinctive Man within him, plus all of his conscious and subconscious experiences.

SEAT OF MEMORY

The subjective mind is the seat of memory and of instinctive emotion. Being the seat of memory, it contains a remembrance of everything that has ever happened to the outer man. This memory is perfect and retains every experience of the individual life. The subjective mind also contains many of the family and race characteristics which have been experienced by individualized man. It retains these memories, partly, at least, as mental pictures or impressions. This is proven by the fact that pictures have been taken of the subjective thought and definite outlines developed. This does not necessarily mean that every impression is retained as a mental picture, but that, in all probability, anything that the outer eye has definitely seen is retained as a more or less distinct picture.

The subjective mind is a picture gallery, upon whose walls are hung the pictures of all the people whom the individual has ever known and all the incidents which he has ever experienced.

SUGGESTION AND SUBJECTIVITY

The subjective mind being deductive only in its reasoning powers is compelled by its nature to retain all the mental impressions that it has ever received. It, therefore, contains much that the objective mind has never consciously known. When we realize that the individual's subjectivity is his use of the One Subjective Mind, we shall see that a subjective unity is maintained between all people, and that individual mentalities which are in sympathetic vibration with each other must, more or less, mingle, and receive suggestions from each other. This is the meaning of mental influence, which is, indeed, a very real thing. This also means that the subjective mind receives suggestions from the race and is, more or less, influenced by its environment; all this takes place on the silent side of life and is mostly unknown to the receiver.

Race-suggestion is a very real thing, and each individual carries around with him, and has written into his mentality, many impressions that he never consciously thought of or experienced; for there is a silent influence going on at all times between people under this law.

SUBJECTIVE COMMUNICATION

It is almost certain that between friends there is, at all times, a silent communication, a sort of unconscious mental conversation going on subjectively. When this rises to the surface of conscious intelligence, it is called mental telepathy. This communication with others is going on at all times, whether the conscious mind is aware of the fact or not. We are always receiving impressions that are more or less vague, and it is seldom that they come to the surface; but they are there nevertheless and are gradually building into our mentalities impressions and forms of thought that are unconsciously and silently perceived.

SUBJECTIVE MIND AND INSPIRATION

Since the subjective mind is the storehouse of memory, it retains all that the eye has seen, the ear heard or the mentality conceived. Since it contains much that the outer man never consciously knew, and is the receptacle of much of the race-knowledge, through unconscious communication, it must, and does, have knowledge that far surpasses the objective faculties.

Realizing that the subjective draws to itself everything that it is in sympathy with, or vibrates to, we see that anyone who is sympathetically inclined toward the race, or vibrates to the race-thought, might pick up the entire race-emotion and experience, and, if he were able to bring it to the surface, he could consciously depict it. Many of the world's orators, actors, and writers have been able to do this; which explains the reason why many of them have been so erratic; for they have been more or less controlled by the emotions which they have contacted.

Our greatest speakers are able to contact the subjective mentality of their audiences and in this way, not only to tell the audience what it wishes to be told, but also to send out a strong vibration that will make an equally strong subjective impression on those who are listening. It is a well-known fact that many speakers are able to connect with the mentality of an audience in such a manner as to be able to completely control it. Napoleon seemed to be able to do this, which was one of the reasons why he had such tremendous influence over his followers.

Singers and poets generally enter into more or less of a subjective state while singing or writing. In the case of a singer or actor, this enables him to respond to the emotion of his listeners and to be able to reflect back to them an equally strong emotion. It might work the other way; that is, he might, himself, awaken the emotion in his hearers. This we call temperament, and no singer, speaker or actor can be a great success without it.

In the case of a writer, this enables him to enter into the race-thought and perfectly depict race-emotion and race-endeavor. Poets are an especially good example of this ability; for poetry, like song, is the language of the soul, and none can write good poems unless he allows the soul to come to the surface. We could not imagine a great poem written mechanically. Artists lose themselves in their work and musicians often do the same; this we call inspiration.

In preaching, it is probable that the orator of the pulpit often so enters into the longings of men's hearts that he reveals them to themselves. He is able to depict their thoughts and emotions, and coupling his own with theirs, give birth to a great discourse; we say that he is inspired.

Anyone contacting the subjective side of the race-mentality with the ability to permit it to come to the surface, will have at his disposal a knowledge that many lifetimes of hard study could not possibly accumulate. But, if one had to surrender his individuality in the process, he would be better off to remain ignorant.

Enough has been said on this subject to show the source of human inspiration. There is, of course, a much deeper seat of knowledge than the subjective mind; that is, the Spirit. But direct contact with Spirit is Illumination, and is a quality which has been developed in but few people; the few who have developed this quality have given the world its greatest literature, religion and law.

MENTAL ATMOSPHERES

Each person has a mental atmosphere which is the result of all that he has thought, said, done, and consciously or unconsciously perceived. This mental atmosphere is very real and is that subtle influence which constitutes the power of personal attraction; for personal attraction has but little to do with looks; it goes much deeper and is almost entirely subjective. This will explain the likes and dislikes for those with whom we come in daily contact. We meet some, only to turn away without a word, while others we are at once drawn toward, and without any apparent reason; this is the result of their mental atmosphere or thought vibration. No matter what the lips may be saying, the inner thought outspeaks them and the unspoken word often carries more weight than the spoken. As Emerson said: "What you are speaks so loudly that I cannot hear what you say."

In contacting people, we are instantly attracted or repelled, according to the vibrations which we feel. A person whose atmosphere is one of love and sunshine, whose nature is to be happy, who lives a clean, wholesome life in a free atmosphere, will always attract friends.

Children feel mental atmosphere very keenly and are drawn to those who are inwardly right, shunning those who are inwardly wrong. It has been truly said that people whom children and dogs do not like are dangerous. Animals are almost entirely subjective and feel mental atmospheres more keenly than do most people. A dog instinctively knows one's attitude toward him and, acting accordingly, is immediately a friend or foe. Personal atmospheres vary in their intensity, there being as many varieties as there are people; for each creates his own atmosphere in Mind.

HOW TO CREATE PERSONAL CHARM

Personal charm may be easily created by learning to love all and hate none. Truly did the great Emerson say: "If you want a friend, be one." If one wishes to have friends, he should become friendly; if he wishes love, he should learn to love. There is no excuse for anyone being without a power of attraction, since it is a mental quality and may be consciously induced through right practice.

THE ATMOSPHERE OF PLACES

As all people have a mental atmosphere, so do all places; and as the atmosphere of people is the result of their thoughts, so the atmosphere of places is the result of the thoughts that have been created in them. Places are permeated with the thoughts of the people who inhabit them; in this way, mental atmospheres are created and may be easily felt by those contacting them.

How often we have had the experience of going into a place, only to feel that we were not wanted, and became so disturbed that we wished immediately to leave. How often, on the other hand, we have gone into places where we felt such a warmth and inner glow that we wished to remain. This is the result of the mental atmosphere surrounding the place or room. This is why we love our homes; they are filled with love and affection and we feel at peace within their walls. This is why one likes to return home after his day's work; for he knows that here is a place where he will be away from the world with all of its cares and worries. It is a wise wife who understands this law and who keeps the atmosphere of the home pleasant. Such a one will seldom lose her mate, but will hold him through the strong ties of love and affection with which she floods his abode. Many an unhappy home could be harmonized if this law were better understood and practiced.

The atmosphere of the home should never be clouded with the uncertainties of the outside world. Here, in the palace of human love, all else should be forgotten and an atmosphere maintained which will be a shelter from the world. Here love should be the ruling passion and harmony should reign supreme. Here, above all other places, should the Kingdom of God be established and families should dwell together in peace and joy.

Too often, jealousy and deceit rob the home of its joy, while mistrust and doubting make it so unpleasant that it becomes an impossible place in which to live. But all this can be changed by reversing the wrong thoughts and in their place creating thoughts of love and tenderness toward one another.

There is nothing more unfortunate for a child's mind than to be compelled to live in an unhappy home. The home should stand for heaven on earth, and unless it does, it will not stand long, but will be buried in the ashes of dead hopes.

The atmosphere of the desert is wonderful, for it is free from the thoughts of men's confusion and fear, and so is a place of great peace. Here, indeed, away from the haunts of men's terrible struggles, quiet may be found and peace regained. It is the same with the mountains, the lakes and the trackless deep. This is what we love about Nature; her marvelous calm and deep peace; for she speaks to us and tells of a life undisturbed by the strife of man. She does, indeed, bear a message from On High, and happy is the one who can talk to her and learn from her, for she is wonderful and filled with light.

Even the slightest things seem to be possessed of a soul, or subjective atmosphere. How often we see a familiar coat or hat hanging on a peg, while in it we seem to see the person who wears it; it seems to look like him, and so it does, for it retains the emanation of his atmosphere, and really is permeated with his personality. Everything has an atmosphere which we sense and to which we react accordingly; if it is pleasant we like it, and if unpleasant we dislike it.

THE RACE-MIND

Just as each person, place or thing has a subjective atmosphere or remembrance, so each town, city or nation has its individual atmosphere. Some towns are bustling with life and action

while others seem dead; some are filled with a spirit of culture, while others seem filled with a spirit of commercial strife.
This is the result of the mentalities of those who live in these
places. A city given over to the pursuit of the higher endeavors
will react with an atmosphere of culture and refinement, while
one whose dominant thought is to acquire wealth will react to
an atmosphere of grasp and grab. This is very definite and is felt
by all who enter such places.

Just as a city has its atmosphere, so does a whole nation; for
a nation is made up of the individuals who inhabit it; and the
combined atmospheres of all the people who inhabit a nation
creates a national mentality which we speak of as the psychology of that people.

THE MIND OF HISTORY

When we remember that Subjective Mind is Universal, we will
come to the conclusion that the history of the race is written in
the mental atmosphere of the globe on which we live. That is,
everything that has ever happened on this planet has left its
imprint on the walls of time; and could we walk down their
corridors and read the writings, we should be reading the race
history. This should seem simple when we realize that the vibrations of the human voice can be preserved in the receptive
phonographic disc, and reproduced at will. If we were to impress one of these discs with the vibration of some one's voice
and lay it away for a million years, it would still reproduce those
vibrations.

It is not hard then to understand how the walls of time may
be hung with the pictures of human events and how one who
sees these pictures may read the race history.

TELEPATHY

Telepathy, or thought-transference, is such a commonly known
fact that it is useless to do other than to discuss it briefly. How-

ever, there are some facts which might be overlooked unless we give them careful attention. The main fact to emphasize is that mental telepathy would not be possible unless there were a medium through which it could operate. This medium is Universal Mind; and it is through this medium that all thought-transference or mental telepathy takes place. Forms in matter and solid bodies may begin and end in space, but thought is more fluent.

Telepathy is the act of reading subjective thought, or of receiving conscious thought without audible words being spoken. But there must be a mental tuning in, so to speak, just as there must be in radio. We are surrounded by all sorts of vibrations, and if we wish to catch any of them distinctly, we must tune in; but there is a great deal of interference, and we do not always get the messages clearly. We often get the wrong ones, and sometimes many of the vibrations come together and seem to be nothing but a lot of noises, without any particular reason for being. It is only when the instrument is properly adjusted to some individual vibration that a clear message may be received.

This is true of mental telepathy, which is the transmission of thought. The receiver must tune in with the sender. It does not follow, however, that the sender knows that he is being tuned in on; in other words, one might pick up thoughts just as he picks up radio messages; and just as the one broadcasting may not know who is listening in, so the one sending out thought may not know who is listening in. Happily, but few people can listen in mentally, and these few only with more or less certainty of success. It would be terrible to be compelled to listen in on all the thoughts that are floating around. But, fortunately, we can only receive those messages to which we vibrate; and so the whole thing is a matter of our own choice. We are individuals in the mental world just as in the physical; and a wise person will protect himself mentally just as he would physically.

TUNING IN ON THOUGHT

Some seem to have the ability to tune in on thought and to read it, much as one would read a book. These people we call psychics; but all people really are psychic, since all have a soul or subjective mind. What we really mean is, that a psychic or medium is one who has the ability to objectify that which is subjective; to bring to the surface of conscious thought that which lies below the threshold of the outer mind. The medium reads from the book of remembrance; and it is marvelous how far-reaching this book of remembrance is.

MENTAL PICTURES

As everything must exist in the subjective world before it can in the objective, and as it must exist there as a mental picture, it follows that whatever may have happened at any time on this planet is today within its subjective atmosphere; i.e., the experiences of those who have lived here. These pictures are hung upon the walls of time, and may be clearly discerned by those who can read them.

Accordingly, since the Universal Subjectivity is a Unit and is Indivisible, all these pictures really exist at any, and every, point within It simultaneously; and we may contact anything that is within It at any point, because the whole of It is at every point. Consequently we may contact at the point of our own subjective mind (which is a point in Universal Subjective Mind) every incident that ever transpired on this planet. We may even see a picture that was enacted two thousand years ago in some Roman arena; for the atmosphere is filled with such pictures. This has been called "The Illusion of Mind" (the psychic sea). This does not mean that Mind is an illusion, but that it might present us with an illusion unless we are very careful and are quite sure that what we are looking at is a real form and not simply a picture.

It is very important that we understand this; for each person in his objective state is a distinct and individualized center in Universal Mind; but in his subjective state every one, in his stream of consciousness, or at his rate of vibration, is universal, because of the Indivisibility of Mind. Wherever and whenever any individual contacts another upon the subjective side of life, if he is psychic, i.e., if he objectifies subjectivity, he may see a thought form of that person, but it does not necessarily follow that he would be really seeing the person.

CONDITIONS NECESSARY FOR THE BEST RESULTS

The conditions necessary for the best results in psychic work are faith and expectancy; for the subjective responds to faith and seems clouded by doubts. Doubt appears to throw dust in its eyes, while sympathetic faith and willing belief render the veil much thinner and the consequent messages much clearer. This explains why many unbelieving investigators fail to receive the desired results, and go away saying that the whole thing is a fraud. Whatever the nature of the subjective may be, we did not make and we cannot change it; we shall be compelled to use this force, like all other forces in nature, according to its own laws, and not according to the way we think it should act.

It has been completely proved that the subjective mentality responds more completely when fully believed in; and anyone wishing to investigate the psychic life would much better accept this fact and act upon it, rather than dispute it and receive no results. If the law is complied with the results will be certain.

Some psychics go into a trance while giving subjective readings, while some can do this in a normal state. The trance state varies from a slight subjectivity to a completely submerged mentality, i.e., from simply getting in tune with thought while in a conscious state of mind, to becoming completely submerged in an unconscious state in order to get in tune with thought. It is never good to lose one's self-control, but many people do this

and, in so doing, have brought to light remarkable evidence of
the ability of the inner mind to perform wonderful tasks.

DEEP TELEPATHIC MESSAGES

It is possible at times for a psychic to tell one most of the incidents that have happened in his life, and also to tell of his
friends and many of the incidents that have happened to them.
This is done by entering the subjective realm of the individual
and reading the thoughts and mental pictures that are hung on
the wall of his memory. When a psychic tells one something
about his friends, he is entering their thought through the sympathetic vibration of the one whose thought he is reading. We
are always in mental contact with our friends on the subjective
side of life; and a psychic, tuning in on these vibrations, reads
the thoughts that come over the mental wireless.

READING THE HISTORY OF THE INDIVIDUAL

Often a psychic will enter a person's mentality and give him a
fairly complete history of his past and of the family from which
he came, going back, perhaps, for several generations, naming
ancestors and the things that engaged their attention while on
earth. He is reading the records of what has already happened
and is a subjective remembrance of his family.

For instance, people have often said to me: "I saw Emerson
standing behind you this morning." Of course they did not see
Emerson; what they saw was a mental picture of him; the reason
being that I am a student of Emerson, and each is surrounded by
the forms of the people he knows and the forms of those whose
thought he studies.

PERSONAL READINGS

One is surprised when he goes to a medium and is told his own,
and perhaps his mother's name, and is told by the medium that
his mother stands beside him. The psychic often tells just how

she looked while in the flesh. Now it might or might not be, that what the medium says is true; for, while this personality might be consciously near, the chances are more than even that she is not, but that the medium is simply looking at a picture of her as she once was while in the flesh.

A medium might, by reading one's subjectivity, be able to tell something about people who were not present at the time; because each, through a sympathetic vibration of thought, is connected with the subjective emanations of those whom he likes, of those with whom he is associated and of those to whom he vibrates. These people might be in the flesh or out of it.

The personal reading appears to be limited either to the immediate individual or to some one with whom he is in contact. The value of subjective mind reading is more or less uncertain. Generally all that a psychic can tell is about something that has already happened or something that might happen as the result of a subjective tendency already set in motion. There are, however, deeper messages than these.

STREAMS OF CONSCIOUSNESS

Each, being an individual identity in Mind, is known by the name he bears, and by the vibration which he emanates. For, while we are all One in Mind and Spirit, we each have a separate and an individualized personality. This is the only way that Spirit can individualize, making it possible for many to live in the One.

Each, then, is represented by his stream of consciousness; and each, continuously functioning in Mind, builds around himself an aura or mental atmosphere, which, in its turn, is constantly flowing out as a stream of consciousness.

Because of the Unity of Mind, each is one with the All; and at the point where he contacts the All, he universalizes himself. This will be easily understood when we realize that man always uses the One Mind. He is in It and thinks into It; and because It is Universal, his thought may be picked up by anyone who is able to tune in on that thought, just as we pick up radio messages. A radio message, broadcast from New York City, is immediately present all around the world. Hard as this concept may be to grasp, we know it to be the truth.

Let us shift the basis to mentality and we shall see that the same thing happens when we think. We think into the One Mind, and this thought is immediately present everywhere. It is in this sense that each one is universal. According to the Unity of Mind, thought is everywhere present, and so long as it persists it will be. What is known in one place may be known in all places.

NO OBSTRUCTIONS TO THOUGHT

Time, space and obstructions are unknown to Mind and thought. It follows, then, that anyone tuning in on our thought will enter into our stream of consciousness, no matter where we are or where he may be. And if we still persist after the body shall have suffered the shock of physical death, this law must still hold good; for past and present are one and the same in Mind. Time is only the measure of an experience, and space, of itself, is not apart from, but is in, Mind.

ENTERING THE STREAM OF THOUGHT

A psychic can enter the stream of thought of anyone whose vibration he can mentally contact, be that person in the flesh or out of it; and since we are all psychic, all having a soul element, we are all, doubtless, communicating with each other to the degree that we sympathetically vibrate toward each other. (This explains the medium through which absent treatment takes place.)

We do not all have the ability to objectify psychic impressions, and ordinarily they never come to the surface; however, they are there just the same. This is the reason why we often feel so uneasy when in the presence of certain people, or when we mentally contract some condition, having an uneasy inner feeling but without any apparent reason.

THE VIBRATION OF A BOOK

As we read and study people's thought, we gradually enter into the current of their consciousness and begin to read between the lines; we are unconsciously reading their inner mentalities. This is why we enjoy reading the thoughts of the great mentalities of all ages. More that is unwritten comes to us than mere words could possibly convey.

WHY SAINTS HAVE SEEN JESUS

Many of the saints have seen Jesus in this way. That is, through studying His words and works, they have so completely entered His thought that they have seen a picture of Him; for the pictures of everything and everybody are hung on the walls of time and anyone who can enter may read. It does not follow that these saints have seen Jesus, but that they have, without doubt, seen His likeness, or what the world believes to be His likeness, hung on the walls of time. When we look at a picture of a person we are not looking at the person, but at a likeness of him.

MANY MENTAL PICTURES

We are all surrounded by mental pictures, and a good psychic sees these pictures clairvoyantly and reads our thoughts telepathically. A good medium has the ability, more or less clearly, to bring these pictures and thoughts to the surface and objectify them; but it does not follow that he is really communicating with the people whose pictures he sees.

THE HUMAN AURA

Every one constantly radiates some kind of a vibration, and consequently is always surrounded by some kind of a mental atmosphere. This is called the aura; it extends from a few inches to a few feet from the body and sometimes even farther. It varies in color and density with the varying degrees of consciousness. In moments of spiritual realization the aura is bright yellow, merging into almost a pure white; and in moments of rage it is dark and murky in appearance. There are as many colors in the aura as there are varying degrees of thought-activity in the mentality.

HALO

The halo which artists have portrayed around the heads of the saints is real, and not an idea of the artists. There is a more pronounced emanation from the head than from any other part of the body, because thought operates through the brain more than through any other part of the human instrument.

It is said that the face of Jesus shone so brightly, at times, that His disciples could not look upon it without becoming blinded by its brilliancy.

UNPLEASANT ATMOSPHERES

In a combat of wills the atmosphere sometimes appears to strike sparks as though a battle were being waged on the subjective side of life. Unpleasant people always have a disagreeable atmosphere and morbid people always depress. A radiant aura emanates from the one who lives a normal, happy life, and who is always at peace within himself.

HABIT

Habits are formed by first consciously thinking, and then unconsciously acting. But few realize that when one consciously thinks, something must happen to his thoughts. What one thinks today will tomorrow be a part of his memory; and since memory is active, what he thinks today as a conscious thought will tomorrow be submerged by active thought.

This is how a habit is formed; first it is a desire, then comes the expression of this desire, then the desire becomes subjective and the subconscious action of thought causes it to be performed automatically. First we control thought, then thought controls us.

"First the man takes a drink, Then the drink takes a drink, Then the drink takes the man."

Constant repetition gradually forms such a thought force on the subjective side of life that the very force created, in its turn, controls the one who created it. How careful we should be about what we let down into the deeper currents of mentality! All habits are formed in much the same way; they are at first conscious; then they become unconscious or subconscious. A person may create such a strong desire that it will compel him to put it into execution; this is called mania.

MANIA

Literally speaking, mania is a desire too strong to be controlled. We speak of one having a mania for certain things; that is, he has subjectified so much desire along some particular line that he becomes controlled by the very power which he has set in motion. Morbid people are more liable to do this than normally minded ones. For instance, let a sensitive person become despondent and he may think of committing suicide. This thought, at first, may be put aside as unworthy, but as it returns it receives a little more attention, until at last it may become so strong that it is irresistible.

Most murders are committed from this mental attitude; and most murderers are people who are mentally sick. Some day this will be better understood; such people will be considered sick and will be healed mentally. This shows how very careful we should be to control our thinking, never allowing the mentality to conceive ideas which we do not wish to see manifest. After all, these things are mental attitudes, and the best way to heal them is through mental treatment.

OBSESSION

Obsession is another form of mental control and may or may not be conscious at its inception. People may become obsessed with desires, thoughts, ambitions, habits, suggestions or other mental influences; and if the spirits of undeveloped entities surround us, it seems entirely possible that people may become obsessed by them.

The obsession of desire produces a mania to express that desire; for thought demands an outlet. Some are so obsessed by their ambitions that they are constantly driven to the accomplishment of them. Some are obsessed by the suggestion of their environment, for the mental atmosphere of places often obsesses people, compelling them to do certain things and without any apparent reason. In studying a case of obsession we should take all the facts into consideration and reason from effect back to cause.

PERSONAL INFLUENCE AND OBSESSION

People often become mildly obsessed by the mentalities of those surrounding them; this is called personal contagion. Many take on the color of their environment, and this should be guarded against, for it is a mild form of hypnotism. It is, of course, brought about through the suggestive power of unconscious mental action, and may or may not be malicious. We should never allow ourselves to become controlled by anything that we do not consciously allow to enter the thought. If one feels an influence silently demanding attention, he should at once declare that there is no power, in the flesh or out of it, that can control him except, of course, the One Perfect Mind.

OBSESSION OF DISCARNATE SPIRITS

If we are surrounded by discarnate spirits, they, also, might control us through suggestion; that is, if we allowed them to do so. By thinking toward us with a strong desire, they might so implant this desire on the subjective side of our thought that it would come up from within, causing us to do certain things which we never consciously thought of doing. This, of course, is hypnotic influence; but all mental influence is hypnotic, varying only in degree. If it is true that discarnate spirits are around us (and it appears to be true), we should carefully guard against the possibility of any mental influence from them. The statement that ONLY THE ONE MIND CONTROLS will protect us from any and all wrong mental influences of whatever nature, whether emanating from those in the flesh or out of it.

GENERAL THEORY OF OBSESSION AND MENTAL INFLUENCE

All obsession, of whatever character, is some form of mental influence, and can easily be destroyed by making the above stated affirmation. We should never for one instant allow the suggestions of other mentalities to control us. The day will come when people will choose the thoughts that they allow to enter the mind as carefully as they now choose the food they eat. Staying close to the thought of the One Mind is a safe and sure protection from any and all wrong mental influence.

INSANITY

Insanity is the complete control of the conscious mind by the unconscious or subjective mind. Dwelling too long on one idea, or some sudden shock, seems to produce this state. It is easily healed by knowing that there is but ONE MIND, AND THAT IT CANNOT FORGET ITSELF. THERE IS ONE MIND IN GOD, AND THIS MIND OUR MIND NOW.

THE PSYCHIC POWER MUST BE CONTROLLED

The psychic power should always be under full control of the conscious mind; otherwise, all sorts of influences may be picked up, which, operating under the guise of seemingly real individualities, control the one who admits them. When the psychic power is under full control of the conscious mind, it furnishes a wonderful storehouse of knowledge; for, being the seat of memory of both the individual and the race, it contains much that we do not consciously know.

NORMAL STATE

A normal condition would be a complete balance between the objective and subjective mentalities. This would give an immediate access to all the wisdom of the human race, and might even extend much farther, for it could give access to a higher state, which is now more or less clogged by contrary suggestions.

The subjective side of thought is the sole and only medium between the relative and the Absolute. If one were in full control of his inner mentality he could, at once, enter the Absolute, and his every word would bear fruit. Jesus was such an One.

In attempting to accomplish this we do not have to come under control of any power other than that of our inner selves and our higher selves; anything less than this is dangerous. Many seem to think that simply because they are under control they must be dealing with spiritual power. NO GREATER MISTAKE WAS EVER MADE. Jesus, Who was fully illumined, always kept His full state of conscious thought and personal volition.

THE AIM OF EVOLUTION

The aim of evolution is to produce a man who, at the objective point of his own self-determination, may completely manifest the inner life of the Spirit. Even the Spirit does not seek to control us, for It lets us alone to discover ourselves.

The most precious thing that man possesses is his own individuality; indeed, this is the only thing that he really has, or is; and for one instant to allow any outside influence to enter or control this individuality is a crime against man's real self.

THE STATE OF TRANCE

The trance state is any state of mentality that allows itself to become submerged. It varies in degree from simply allowing the mind to become receptive, which is harmless, to a complete self-denial of the objective consciousness, i.e., allowing any and all influences to be picked up. This is very dangerous.

There are many normal psychics who can, while in a perfectly objective state, read people's thoughts and perform many other wonderful feats of the mind. This is normal and no harm can come from it. It is, indeed, one of nature's ways of working and is most interesting.

NORMAL PSYCHIC CAPACITIES

Any psychic power that can be used while in a normal state of mind is harmless and helpful; that is, any psychic power which can be used while one is in a perfectly conscious state of mentality. Many have this power and find that it is helpful as well as interesting. This power can be developed by knowing that the WITHIN AND THE WITHOUT ARE REALLY ONE.

ABNORMAL PSYCHIC POWERS

Abnormal psychic powers are developed in the full trance state; that is, when the medium becomes controlled by surrounding influences. In this state some wonderful and hidden powers of mind are revealed.

In certain psychic states people can see, hear and read others' thoughts; travel abroad and perform many other marvelous feats, which in the conscious state seem impossible. No doubt the time will come when all these powers will be under the control of the conscious mind; man will then be much less limited.

CLAIRVOYANCE

Clairvoyance is a state of mentality wherein the medium is able to see things that the objective eye cannot see under normal conditions. It is the physical eye reproduced on the mental side of life, only with a greatly extended vision. Time, space and obstructions are swept away, and the operator can as easily look through a closed door as, in a normal state, he looks through a window.

PSYCHOMETRY

Psychometry is a clairvoyant state wherein the operator is able to psychometrize, or read from the soul or subjective side of things. Mention has already been made of the fact that everything has its mental atmosphere which is the result of the thoughts surrounding it. To psychometrize anything means to read from this mental atmosphere and to tell what it radiates. Sometimes the operator seems able to take a piece of ore or metal and give a perfect description of the location from which it was taken. This will explain why some mediums wish to hold an object which has been used by the sitter; for through this avenue the medium is able to enter the inner thought of the person sitting.

CLAIRAUDIENCE

Clairaudience may be called the ear of the soul; it is the ability to hear the inner voice speak, and is a most remarkable mental attribute. Some hear these voices silently, while to some they come as independent voices.

It appears as though the instinctive man tries to tell the outer man of certain things or to give him warnings. Sometimes these warnings come as visions and sometimes in dreams. This power is uncertain and should be carefully watched, as we are not always able to tell whether the impression is real or simply some suggestion of a surrounding mental influence. A good way to test this is to know that all impressions must come from the Perfect Mind.

INDEPENDENT VOICES

Sometimes independent voices speak forth, apparently from the air, and may be conversed with by the hour. I have talked with these voices, but, so far, have not been able to determine whether or not they ever told anything beyond the subjective knowledge of those present. I have been unable to satisfy myself as to whether they were caused by those present in the flesh or whether they were caused by some form of spirit life. The fact remains that such voices do speak and that they are real. I have held animated and interesting conversations with such voices for hours at a sitting, and it has been a most wonderful experience; but, so far, it seems impossible to determine their exact nature. Time and a more complete investigation alone can give the real proof.

APPARITIONS

Apparitions, or thought forms, often appear during mental stress. For instance, people often see some friend just before he passes from this life. Sometimes the apparition appears before the incident takes place; an explanation of this will be made later in this chapter. This type of phenomenon is not at all uncommon; nearly every one has some record of such experiences. When one is asleep he is entirely subjective, and this will explain why so many of the above referred to incidents take place during sleep. But impressions received while in the sleeping state do not always come to the surface.

GHOSTS AND PHANTASMS OF THE DEAD

People often see the forms of those who have passed from this life. Many have been alarmed over seeing such forms, as though there might be danger from them; but whether or not we believe them to be the forms of the dead or the living, they certainly can do no harm.

It is claimed by some that ghosts are always the result of some form of violent death, and that those who pass out in a state of peace never leave a ghost behind. Of the truth of this statement I am NOT absolutely sure, since all must leave behind the forms used while in the flesh, and each must leave behind him a thought form of himself.

GHOSTS SOMETIMES CAN SPEAK

It is a well-known fact that ghosts sometimes have the ability to speak or convey some kind of a message to the living. And it is also generally conceded by those who have investigated such matters, that once a ghost has had the opportunity to speak, it is seldom ever seen again.

If we suppose a ghost to be a real entity, we can easily see how it could speak or telepathically convey a message. If, on the other hand, we assume that a ghost is only a form of thought, we can imagine that it might be equipped with the power to convey a message, after which it would gradually fade away. For thought has some power to express itself. I hold no brief for either case, since I have been unable to make up my own mind as to just what a ghost really is.

In such a case as this it is a mistake to assume anything, other than the fact that such appearances do make themselves known to people under certain conditions. The matter will have to rest at this point until further investigation proves what a ghost is.

PROJECTING THE MENTALITY

Under certain states of mentality it is possible to project the mentality and travel far from the body. Just what it is that projects is difficult to say; and we are not so much concerned about what it is that projects as we are interested in the fact that there is something about the mentality which can project itself. Since there is but One Mind, perhaps nothing has to project; perhaps we simply see through the One Mind, which must have and hold, within Itself, all that is.

CRYSTAL GAZING

Crystal gazing is a form of concentrating the mentality in such a manner as to make it possible for the subjective to come to the surface. The operator, looking steadily at a bright object, gradually becomes subjective and consequently able to read thought.

BLACK MAGIC

Black Magic has been taught and practiced from time immemorial. It is the act of thinking toward some one for the purpose of doing him an injury.

THE MODERN CURSE

Today, black magic is called by another name, but "a rose by any other name would smell as sweet." Today it is called malpractice. Malpractice takes several different forms; namely, malicious, ignorant and unconscious. Malicious malpractice is the act of arguing in Mind that some certain person is something that he ought not to be. In some cases it is supposed to even take the form of saying that he is not present in the flesh. If this were persisted in, and the one being damned should receive the condemnation, he might begin to feel sick; and if this were carried to a final conclusion, he would, perhaps, "pass from this vale of tears."

Mention is made of this, not as being something to fear, but as one of those things which today is being more or less discussed and believed in by many. So far as we are concerned, we believe only in the One Mind, AND WE KNOW THAT IT CANNOT BE DIVIDED AGAINST ITSELF. This will settle the question of malicious malpractice for all time.

We hear of people who live in constant terror of malpractice, and it seems certain that some do try to use this force to do injury to others; but no one with real understanding of the Truth will be affected by it, nor seek to use it; for this would be playing with fire; and we are the servants to the things which we obey.

If our thought is still operating on a level where such things are possible, we had better find it out, straighten up our thought and be healed; for, after all, malpractice is only wrong thought suggestion, and we do not believe in wrong thought suggestion.

Innocent and ignorant malpractice causes much disease and discomfort, through sympathy with sickness and fear for people's safety. We should sympathize with the one suffering, but never with that from which he suffers; for this would make him worse instead of better.

AUTOMATIC WRITING

Automatic writing is an interesting phenomenon of the mind. It is a mental control which uses the arm and hand for the purpose of writing messages.

There are several forms of automatic writing; one, the Ouija board, which is a small smooth board, upon which is written the alphabet. Upon this board is placed a small, pear-shaped, three-legged instrument, which points to the letters and spells out words. Another form is to put a pencil through the board; and still another form, and one even more interesting, is when the pen is held in the hand which is controlled by some force not known, but supposed to be the subjective thought of either the operator or of some one present.

Some believe that the arm is under control of a discarnate spirit. Many and long have been the discussions on this point, and I do not care to enter into them; but one thing is certain, the phenomenon transpires, and many wonderful messages come through in this manner.

INDEPENDENT WRITING

The most interesting writing of all is what is called independent writing; that is, where the pencil simply tips up and writes without anyone touching it. I have seen this done and can vouch for its reality. Here, indeed, is ample cause for speculation, and we are compelled to admit that either some unconscious force of those present grasps the pencil, or that some spirit force does.

HUDSON'S THEORY

I am well aware of the theory which Hudson worked out along these lines, but I have not been able to explain everything on his basis; and I fear that he overworked his theory.

His idea was that we have no right to assume the presence of an unknown agency when there is a known one present. In other words, he said that the phenomenon is caused by some form of mental action which he called subjective; and that we have no right to assume a spirit to be the cause when we know that there are people present in the flesh; and that, since people in the flesh, as well as those out of it, have a mind, we must assume that the phenomena are caused by those present in the flesh. By the same token, and with the same logic, it could be proved either way. That psychic phenomena are caused by some form of mental power, there can be no question; and the student of the workings of mind will rest content here, knowing that mental power can operate in independence of the physical instrument; for this is the great lesson to learn.

SMELLING WHERE THERE IS NOTHING TO SMELL

A most peculiar and interesting phenomenon takes place in the act of smelling where there is, apparently, nothing to smell. The mentality, in connecting with the vibrations of a rose, can produce its odor independently of the presence of the flower.

I have seen a case where the vibrations of a certain man were brought into the room when he was in an intoxicated condition. The smell of whiskey was so strong that the influence was asked to remove its presence. Perhaps this is what is meant by occult perfume.

GRASPING OBJECTS WITHOUT THE HAND

It is a commonly known fact, to those who have spent time investigating these things, that objects are grasped and held independently of the physical touch. This is shown in independent writing and in telekinetic energy.

TELEKINETIC ENERGY

Telekinetic energy is defined as "the ability to move ponderable objects without physical contact." This form of energy is displayed in that class of mental phenomena which cause objects to move without any physical agency, and is, therefore, caused by some form of mental energy, or by some agency other than physical.

TABLE TIPPING

Table tipping is so common as to cause but little comment, but it does help to prove a principle of mind, namely, that an object can be moved about from place to place without the aid of any physical contact.

RAPPINGS

Rappings on the walls and floor are also too common to mention, but should be classed in the category of telekinetic energy.

THEORY OF ECTOPLASM

One of the investigators has advanced the theory of ectoplasm, which is a formless stuff emanating from the body of the medium. I have no doubt but this theory is correct as far as it goes; but am not willing to advance it as being sufficient to explain all the phenomena. For instance, according to this theory, if anyone stands in front of the medium the emanation is blocked and no results will follow. I have sat in a room and had a glass of water brought from another room and held to my lips while I drank it. It was a real glass and real water and I was really there, and in a perfectly normal state of mind. I could not possibly account for the above-stated incident on the theory of ectoplasm; but I could account for it through the theory of mental power.

LEVITATION

The theory of ectoplasm certainly will not account for levitation, where the body of the medium is lifted from a chair and carried to some other place in the room. This can be accounted for only on the theory that there is a power that transcends the better-known physical laws. Experience has taught that there are many things in life that cannot be accounted for on any other basis than that of a mind power which operates independent of any, and of all, physical agencies.

INTERESTING THOUGHTS

It is interesting to realize that we have such marvelous powers; and no doubt the time will come when we shall make common use of them. They are for some purpose and, as we live in a Timeless Universe, this purpose will be made known just as soon as we are ready for it.

WHAT IS THE CAUSE?

Whether psychic phenomena are caused by the agency of spirits or by some inner power of our own mentality makes no difference. That they are caused by mind power is apparent; for they are not caused by what we call physical force at all, but by some finer power than we, at present, well understand.

CAUSE FOR THOUGHT

It gives reason for thought when we realize that such inner powers exist. Some power, independent of the body, can see, hear, feel, smell, touch and taste without the aid of the physical instrument. Some power of intelligence within us can travel, communicate, project itself, recognize and be recognized, without the aid of the physical instrument. That there is a reason for this is certain; that this reason is natural and normal, no one can doubt, for nature is always natural, and only that is a mystery which is not understood.

TIME WILL PROVE ALL THINGS

Time and experience, alone, will unravel the mysteries of the human mind, with its many and varied activities. So far we have but touched the outskirts of its garments. To deny these inner attributes is not only intolerant, but is downright ignorance. It is all right to say that we do not understand them; but to openly deny them is to place us, not among the unbelievers, but among those who do not know the facts.

THE SPIRIT OF PROPHECY

Subjective mind can deduce only; it has no power of initiative or self-choice, and is compelled, because of its very nature, to retain any and all suggestions that it receives. The best illustration of this is in the creative soil, in which the gardener puts his seed. The soil does not argue nor deny, but goes to work on the seed and begins to create a plant which will represent the type of manifestation inherent, as an idea, in the seed. That is, from a cucumber seed we get cucumbers; and from a cabbage seed we get cabbages. Always the law maintains the individuality of the seed as it creates the plant; never does it contradict the right of the seed to be what it really is. Involved within the seed is the idea of the plant, as are also those lesser ideas which are to act as a medium between the seed and the plant. Involved within the seed are both cause and effect; but the seed must first be placed within the creative soil if we wish to receive a plant. In the creative soil, or in the seed, the full and perfect ideas of the plant must exist as a completed thing, else it could never be brought forth into manifestation.

The idea of the full-grown plant must exist somewhere in the seed and soil if it is ever going to materialize.

A LESSON IN SUBJECTIVITY

This teaches us a lesson in subjectivity. Thoughts going into the subjective are like seeds; they are concepts of ideas, and acting through the creative medium of Mind, have within themselves the full power to develop and to express themselves. But how could they express unless they were already known to Mind? They could not, and so Mind must view the thought as already completed in the thing; and Mind must also contain the avenue through which the idea is to be expressed. Every thought sets in motion in Mind the fulfillment of its purpose, and Mind sees the thing as already done.

Mental tendencies set in motion cast their shadows before them; and a psychic often sees the complete manifestation of an idea before it has had the time to materialize in the objective world.

This is what constitutes the average spirit of prophecy; for prophecy is the reading of subjective tendencies, and seeing them as already accomplished facts. The subjective mind can deduce only, but its power of logic and sequence appears to be perfect.

EXPLANATION

For illustration, suppose that there is a window one mile away; I am throwing a ball at this window, and the ball is halfway to it, going at the rate of one mile a minute. Now you come in, measure the distance, compute the speed with which the ball is passing through the air and say, "The ball is halfway to the window; it is traveling at the rate of one mile a minute; in just one half a minute the window is going to be broken by the ball passing through it." Let us suppose that you are the only one who sees the ball, for the rest are looking at the window; and in half a minute it is broken. How did you prophesy that the window was to be broken? By drawing a logical conclusion of an already established premise.

This is much like what happens when a psychic exercises a spirit of prophecy. They are generally unconscious as to why they do what they do, because they are getting their own subjective contact with the condition and simply interpreting what comes to them. But this is the logical, deductive, conclusive power of their subjective thought, seeing a thing completed, by first seeing a tendency set in motion, and computing the time that it will take to complete it. There are but few, however, who have any reliable spirit of prophecy.

Let us carry this thought further; the race has its subjectivity, from an individual to a nation. This is its karma, its subjective law set in motion. Each nation has its subjective causation, and the prophet of a nation could, and would, read its subjective tendency; and this is what the old prophets did, for they were psychics, every one of them, from Moses down. They were able to interpret the subjective causation of their race and so predict that certain things must follow.

There is, however, a still higher spirit of prophecy which but few have perceived, and those who have perceived it have been illumined. Within the subjective mirror of Mind there must also exist the Divine and Cosmic Purposes—the very Thoughts of God. An illumined person, who is also psychic, might read these great Cosmic Purposes; and in this manner some of the great prophets have read the destiny of the race. They have told us that the destiny of man is divine, that he is immortal now, that he need not die to become immortal, but that HE IS IMMORTAL. It was in contact with this great Law, and from It, that Moses received the Ten Commandments, the Mosaic Law. It is through the avenue of subjectivity, which is the medium between Spirit and man, between the Absolute and the intellect, that all of the prophets have prophesied and all of the sages have taught; for it contains Infinite Wisdom, Knowledge and Law.

The subjective mind is the source of much inspiration; for it contains all the thoughts which the race has ever created, and at times one contacts these thoughts and becomes inspired by them. The subjective mind is the source of much revelation because it contains the Purposes of God, and if the soul were to turn to the One, it surely would reflect into the outer mind the Light of the Eternal.

SUMMARY

We have shown that mind, independent of the body, can, and at times does, perform each and every function which we usually associate with the physical being. While most people may have to go into a trance state to perform these acts, there are a few who can produce the same results while in a perfectly normal state, that is, while in a self-conscious state. I wish to make this very plain, for there is a belief that an abnormal state must be entered into before these phenomena can be produced. I not only challenge such a statement, but entirely refute it as being altogether wrong. I have myself, while in a perfectly normal state, seen or experienced nearly everything that has been discussed under this heading.

I am willing to admit that ordinarily a trance state is developed before the best results can be obtained; but to say that it MUST be developed is to contradict my own experience and refute my own observations. I have never, at any time, gone into a trance state, and would no more consider doing so than I would consider jumping from the roof of a ten-story building. If, then, I were to refute my sanity during these experiences, by what manner of judgement could I consider myself to be sane at all? It is useless for those who know nothing at all about psychic phenomena to deny its reality. I can understand anyone saying that he does not understand it, but I cannot grasp the position of an individual who denies something of which he is entirely ignorant.

We will say then THAT EVERY ACT OF THE HUMAN INSTRUMENT WHICH WE CALL THE BODY CAN BE REPRODUCED THROUGH SOME AGENCY WHICH IS NOT PHYSICAL, OR THROUGH SOME AGENCY THAT PHYSICS CANNOT EXPLAIN. We will call this agency some power of mind with which we are not yet well familiar. It is all simple enough, anyway, for our bodies could not move unless we were here to move them, and so every act is mental, even though we use the body as an instrument.

I can find no explanation for the above-stated facts, unless we suppose that we have a mental body which reproduces the physical one; and which can function without its counterpart, and is entirely independent of it.

It makes no difference whether we attribute the phenomena to spirits or whether we say that we are unconsciously producing it ourselves, THE FACT WILL STILL REMAIN THAT THE PHENOMENA ARE PRODUCED and can be accounted for only on the basis that we either have a mental body, which acts independent of the physical one, or that the power of thought alone, and without any physical instrument, can operate upon matter. Personally, I prefer to accept the theory that we have a mental body, since this appeals to me as being more reasonable and certainly much more human.

If we assume that spirits have the ability to move ponderable objects without physical contact, we are assuming that they have a mental body, or that they operate their thought to produce the phenomena. For, once granted that the phenomena are really produced, it is self-evident that some kind of an explanation must be forthcoming.

There are but two possible answers from what is today known: either the minds of departed souls or the minds of those present in the flesh produce the phenomena. This eliminates any other possible agency, for the theory of ectoplasm cannot answer all of the facts.

LESSON SIX

PSYCHIC PHENOMENA AND IMMORTALITY

THE MEANING OF IMMORTALITY

Immortality means to the average person that man shall persist after the experience of physical death, retaining a full recollection of himself and the ability to recognize others. If his full capacities go with him beyond the grave, he must be able to think consciously, to reason, will, affirm, declare, accept, reject, know and be known, communicate and be communicated with; he must be able to travel about, see and be seen, understand and be understood; he must be able to touch, taste, smell, hear, cognize and realize. In fact, if he is really to continue as a self-conscious personality, he can do so only to the degree that he maintains a continuous stream of consciousness and self-knowingness.

This means he must carry with him a complete remembrance; for it is to the remembrance alone that we must look for the link that binds one event to another, making life a constant stream of self-conscious expression. To suppose that man can forget and still remain himself is to suppose that he could cut off the entire past and at this moment be the same personality that he was a moment ago. Remembrance alone guarantees personality. Individuality might remain without remembrance, but not so with personality; for what we are is the result of what we have been, the result of what has gone before.

Man, then, if he is to have an immortality worthy of the name, must continue, as he now is, beyond the grave. DEATH CANNOT ROB HIM OF ANYTHING IF HE BE IMMORTAL.

WHERE DID MAN COME FROM AND WHY?

It is useless to ask why man is. It can only be said of man that he is; for if we were to push his history back to some beginning, we should still be compelled to say that he is. If man's life is of God, then it comes from a source which had no beginning; and so the question as to why he is must forever remain unanswered.

God could not tell why God is; to suppose that Life could give an excuse or reason for being would be to suppose an absurdity. Life Is, and right at this point all inquiry into Truth starts, and from this point alone must this inquiry continue.

We are not so much interested in why we are, as we are interested in what we are. That we are some part of Life, no one can deny and keep faith with reason. Let us not bother about questions that can never be answered, but pay attention to those which have an answer.

MAN AWAKES WITH A BODY

When man first woke to self-consciousness, he had a body and a definite form, showing that Instinctive Life, which is God, had already clothed Itself with the form of flesh. Body, or form, is the necessary outcome of self-knowingness. In order to know, there must be something that may be known; in order to be conscious there must be something of which to be conscious. Some kind of a body or expression there always was and always will be, if consciousness is to remain true to its own nature.

WHAT IS THE BODY?

Body is a concrete idea, existing in time and space, for the purpose of furnishing a vehicle through which Life may express Itself. The physical universe is the Body of God; it is a manifestation of the Mind of God, in form. It is that Creation which, while It may have beginnings and ends, of Itself neither begins nor ends. The Manifestation of Spirit is necessary if Spirit is to come into Self-Realization; hence, Body.

MATTER

We say that body is composed of matter, but what is matter? Science tells us that matter is an aggregation of small particles arranged in some kind of form; we are also told that matter is in a continuous state of flow. Strange as it may seem, we do not have the same physical bodies that we had a few months ago; they have completely changed; new particles have taken the place of the old; and the only reason why they have taken the same form is, that Instinctive Man has provided the same mold. Our bodies are like a river, forever flowing; the Indwelling Spirit alone maintains the identity.

If we assume that immortality simply means persisting in the physical body, then we already have immortalized ourselves many times right here on earth.

THE ETHER OF SCIENCE

We are now being taught that the ether is more solid than matter. We know that the ether penetrates everything; it is in our bodies, at the center of the earth and throughout all space. This means that within our present bodies there is a substance more solid than the body which we see. This idea is very far-reaching; for it shows that we might have a body right within the physical one, which could be as real as the one of which we are accustomed to think. If Instinctive Man has molded the outer body in form, why should It not also mold the inner one into definite form? There is every reason to suppose that It does and no reason to suppose the opposite. In all probability, there is a body within a body to infinity. "In my Father's house are many mansions."

We do not depart from reason when we assume this; for, while we used to say that two bodies could not occupy the same space at the same time, we must remember that we were talking about only one plane of expression. The new idea of matter and ether has PROVED THAT MORE THAN ONE BODY MAY OCCUPY THE SAME SPACE AT THE SAME TIME; for it has been proved that there is a substance which can occupy the same space that our body does. No doubt, as time goes on, it will also be proved that there is something still finer than the ether; this may go on to infinity. There is every reason to suppose that we have a body within a body to infinity, and it is our belief that we do have.

THE RESURRECTION BODY

The resurrection body, then, will not have to be snatched from some Cosmic shelf as the soul soars aloft, but will be found to exist already WITHIN; EVERYTHING IS FROM WITHIN, FOR LIFE IS WITHIN. The resurrection body of Jesus shone so that it could not be looked upon, because it was a more spiritual one than the physical eye is used to beholding.

CONCLUSIVE FACTS

The facts are conclusive that we have a spiritual body now, and do not have to die to receive one. We now remember the past, and have already outlived the physical body many times during life. It looks as though we were already immortal and would not have to die to take on immortality.

If there are many planes of Life and consciousness, perhaps we only die from one plane to another. This thought makes a strong appeal and seems to answer the question completely.

IN WHAT MENTAL STATE DO WE GO OUT?

Some think that death robs us of the objective faculties, and that we pass out in a purely subjective state; but we are unable to follow the logic of such an assumption. To suppose that the objective faculties die with the brain, is to suppose that the brain thinks and reasons. This is proved to be false through the experience of death itself; for, if the brain could think, it would think on and on forever. No; the brain does not think; the thinker thinks through the brain, perhaps; but of itself, the brain has no power to think or feel. Detach the brain and it will not formulate ideas, nor work out plans. THE THINKER ALONE CAN THINK.

It is logical to suppose that we pass from this life to the next in full and complete retention of all our faculties. Jesus revealed Himself to His followers after His resurrection, to show them that death is but a passing to a higher sphere of life and action. To know that we maintain an identity independent of the physical body, is proof enough of immortality. This, together with the fact that remembrance maintains a constant stream of recollection, and the realization that mentality can operate independently of the body, performing all of its normal functions without its aid; and that the new theory of matter and ether furnishes proof of the possibility of a body within a body to infinity; and that the Instinctive Man is constantly forming matter into the shape of a body, should prove to anyone that we are not going TO ATTAIN IMMORTALITY; BUT THAT WE NOW ARE IMMORTAL.

WHAT CAUSES PSYCHIC MANIFESTATIONS?

It would be interesting to know whether the spirits of the supposed dead cause the manifestations which we see in the séance chamber. One thing is certain: these manifestations are either caused by those who are supposed to be dead, or else they are caused by those now in the flesh; for, since they happen, something must make them happen. Whether the manifestations are caused by the dead or the living, the agency used is either a mental body or the direct power of thought operating upon objects. Of course, in the conveyance of mental messages, telepathy explains the agency; but in physical manifestations, some kind of contact either takes place or else thought directly works on objects.

Hudson, in his "Law of Psychic Phenomena," carefully goes through an elaborate process of reasoning, the result of years of painstaking investigation, and completely proves that all of the manifestations do take place. He then goes through an extensive argument to show that they are not caused by spirits, saying that we have no reason to suppose the presence of an unknown agency, when we know that there is one present who could be producing the phenomena. Now, if our reasoning power is correct, and it is proved that physical manifestations take place through some power that is mental, and if it is proved that those who have passed on might still be near us, then we cannot see where the argument against spirit agencies could be considered perfect. We are inclined to feel that the very facts in the case prove that these manifestations could be produced by either the living or the dead; and such, we believe, to be the case.

TELEPATHY DOES NOT EXPLAIN EVERYTHING

Telepathy does not explain everything. It may explain much, but certainly not all. Telepathy could not explain certain visions which people sometimes have when passing out. We once knew a woman who practically passed out and was, indeed, thought dead for nearly a day and night; but was finally restored to consciousness to continue here for another year. She plainly saw and talked to several members of her family who had gone on some years earlier. It is not strange that those who have gone before are interested in us and wish to see us when we go over. If we had friends in London and were to send word that we were coming over, they would certainly wish to meet us. Our friends on the other side must be just as interested in us as they ever were.

Telepathy cannot explain how Jesus could take some of

His more advanced disciples aside and let them talk with the departed. It clearly states that this incident took place; and, if we cannot believe this, how can we believe any of the other events in the life and experience of this most remarkable Person?

SPIRIT COMMUNICATION

There are thousands of cases on record where people have penetrated the veil of flesh and seen into the beyond. If we cannot believe the experience of so many, how can we believe in any experience at all? Of course, there is a large field for deception, and it is not probable that all communications are real; but, to state positively that they are all illusions, is to throw the lie into the face of human thought and say that it never sees clearly. There is certainly more argument and evidence in favor of the theory of spirit communication that against it, and, so far as we are concerned, we are entirely convinced of the reality of this evidence.

If spirits really exist, and if we all live in One Mind, and if mentality can communicate with mentality without the aid of the physical instrument, then spirit communication must be possible; and since we know that the above-stated facts are true, we have no alternative other than to accept the conclusive evidence and realize that while it may be difficult to communicate with the departed, yet it is possible.

COMMUNICATION MUST BE MENTAL

It is evident that any such communication must be mental; it would be thought transference or mental telepathy, at best. Now if the supposed entity knows that we wish to communicate with it, and if it is consciously present trying to communicate with us, then it must, by the power of its thought, cause its message to come up through our subjectivity to an objective state of recognition; consequently how very difficult to receive a coherent message! For instance, suppose that one tries to think a lecture to an audience, how much would they receive? Yet this is exactly what would happen under the very best condition if the departed were trying to impress our thought. I believe that they do seek to communicate with us and that they often succeed, perhaps more often than we realize; but I repeat, "How difficult it must be!"

Whether or not the spirits are present is uncertain. Just because a psychic sees the picture of a person around us, does not mean that he is really there; for the pictures of all our friends are always in our mental atmospheres. It is quite absurd to suppose that at any time we wish we can call anyone we ever knew and make him talk to us. We are unable to do so here; and psychological and metaphysical laws are the same on every plane.

WE DO NOT CONTROL SPIRITS

To suppose that we can compel the attention of one out of the flesh, any more than of one in it, is an absurdity. And if we could, what would we hope to gain? People out of the flesh know no more than they did when in the body. I believe that we do communicate with the subjectivity of those who are departed, whether they know that we are doing so or not; but the messages that come, in our present state of evolution, are very incoherent. I believe that an unconscious communication goes on, more or less, all the time, and that those people whom we have greatly loved are still conscious of us; and are, without doubt, seeking to influence us; but it could only be a mental influence. We might feel a vague sense, much as the niece of Oom Peter did in "The Return of Peter Grimm." She felt a vague sense of her uncle; that he was trying to impress her with his thought and desire. She felt a blind groping, and that is probably the best that we would get.

THE PSYCHIC POWER SHOULD
NOT BE FORCED

We all have psychic capacities, but they should never be forced; for it is only when the subjective comes to the surface while in a normal state that a normal psychic power is produced. The average psychic must go into a semitrance to let the subjective come through; this is never good nor right, but is always destructive. The psychic capacity is normal only to the extent that it can be used while in a self-conscious state. Don't misunderstand what I am saying. It is known as the "power of darkness," but is all right if understood. Many people are bothered by their psychic powers, constantly seeing things, continually getting impressions; they are very near the surface of subjectivity, and it bothers them. This can easily be healed and should be.

There is a normal psychic capacity, and some are able to discern mental causes with perfect ease. Jesus was such an One; He was able to tell the woman that she had been married five times, and that the man with whom she was living was not her husband. He read that out of her thought; but He did it while in an objective state; for He was able to consciously and objectively exercise His subjective faculties. This is perfectly normal; but to let go of the volitional and choosing faculties, which alone constitute individuality, and become immersed in subjectivity, is very dangerous. One might become obsessed by discarnate spirits, earth-bound entities, elementals, thought forms, desires or other forces floating around; for we cannot close our eyes to the fact that all of these things do exist.

It is a crime against individuality to allow the conscious faculties to become submerged. We should control the subjective and not let it control us. The teaching of the illusion of mind sprang up because men of wisdom perceived that people might mistake the shade for the reality, the form for real substance, the hollow voice for revelation, and thereby be misled. That is why they warned against these things and against having familiar spirits; and they were absolutely right. Never let any voices speak to you unless you are in perfect control of the situation. Never admit any mental impressions or images that you do not wish to receive or that you cannot receive consciously. Say: "There is no power in the flesh or out of it but the One, which can enter my consciousness. Any thing that obeys the One, conforms to the One, believes only in the One and comes only through the consciousness of the One, is perfectly welcome, but anything other than that cannot come."

The only value that an understanding of psychic phenomena can have, is that without it we do not understand the complete workings of mind. We do not understand experiences people often have; and in a consistent philosophy which deals with mind, the lack of an understanding of psychic phenomena would be inexcusable. For anyone in this day to say that powers of clairvoyance, telepathy, thought transference, clairaudience or telekinetic energy are not exercised, is to admit his own ignorance.

These things do happen and are continuously happening in more and more instances. The thing to do is not to deny what happens, but to find a logical and scientific explanation of it. It is our business to explain all mental action, in so far as it is explainable; and so we must find and answer which will cover the law of psychic phenomena. Mind, with the laws governing It, is the whole answer, for each plane reproduces the one next to it; and psychic phenomena are reproductions of man's physical capacities on the mental plane. "What is true on one plane is true on all."

NOTE: Read and carefully study "Law of Psychic Phenomena," Hudson; "Life After Death," Hyslop; "The Unknown Guest," Maeterlinck; "Science and Immortality," Lodge; "The Hidden Power," Troward; "From the Unconscious to the Conscious," Geley.

LESSON SIX

RECAPITULATION

Psychic phenomena are the phenomena of the soul, or subjective mind. The subjective mentality is man's atmosphere in Universal Mind; it is the seat of his memory and the avenue through which Instinctive Life works.

The subjective mentality, being deductive only in its reasoning power, is compelled to retain all of the impressions that it receives, but, of course, these impressions can be erased, consciously.

Man is Universal on the subjective side of life, and in this way is connected with the subjectivity of all with whom he is in harmonious vibration.

Mental suggestion operates through the subjective mind, and a silent influence is always going on through this avenue in the form of race-suggestion. A silent communication takes place at all times between friends on the subjective side of life; when it comes to the surface, it is called mental telepathy.

The subjective mind, being in contact with the race-thought, has a much greater knowledge than the conscious mind. It is through this avenue that human inspiration comes. Orators and actors contact the subjective side of their audiences and, in this way, wield a tremendous influence. Singers, poets and writers enter the subjective race-thought and interpret it; this enables them to depict the race-emotions.

Each person has a subjective mental emanation or atmosphere which is the result of all that has ever been consciously or unconsciously said, thought or done by that person. The mental atmosphere of a person is his power of attraction. It is the result of his inner thoughts. The mental atmosphere of a place is the result of all that has been thought, said or done in that place. The mental atmosphere of a place is its power of attraction. We love those places whose mental atmosphere is one of love and peace; this is why we like our homes. The home should always be kept sacred and its atmosphere should always be one of love.

Things are possessed of a soul element and continuously emanate this atmosphere.

Each city or town has a special atmosphere which is the result of the mental emanations of those who inhabit it. The same may be said of nations; each has its national mentality.

The history of the whole race is subjectively written on the unseen walls of time, and may be reproduced by one who can read the race-mentality.

Telepathy, which is the act of reading subjective thought takes place through the medium of Universal Subjectivity. In order to mentally receive a message, and bring it to the surface, one must be in tune with the vibration of that message.

Since the whole field of subjectivity is Universal, it follows that everything that has ever been thought, said or done, is retained in the race-thought; and since this field is a unit, all of the vibrations are ever present, and may be contacted at the point of anyone's mentality.

In his objective state, man is separate and distinct, but on the subjective side of life he is universal.

The conditions necessary for the best results in psychic work are faith and expectancy; this is because the subjective mentality is the seat of the instinctive emotions and responds to feeling.

A psychic, going into more or less of a subjective state, is able to enter the vibration of an individual's thought and read from the book of his remembrance. The personal reading seems to be limited to the subjective remembrance, although this is often very far-reaching.

Each maintains a stream of consciousness in the One Mind, and anyone contacting this stream may objectify it. Because of the Universality of the Medium, the individual stream of consciousness is always omnipresent, whether the one from whom it emanated be in the flesh or out of it.

Time and space are unknown in Mind, the past and the present are one. In reading the thought of people set down in books, we enter their vibration, and in studying their thoughts we enter their stream of consciousness.

Every one who ever lived on earth has left behind a mental picture of himself; these pictures are often seen when one is in a subjective state. This does not mean that we really see the person; what we see generally is the picture.

The human aura is the mental vibration or emanation of the individual. The idea of the halo surrounding the heads of the saints is explained in this way. The personal atmosphere varies with the changing thought and emotion, and is sometimes pleasant and at other times unpleasant.

Habits are formed through conscious thought becoming subjective, and in its turn, controlling the one through whom it operates. Mania is a strong desire, subjectified, which becomes an obsession.

People may become obsessed with their own ideas or with those that operate through them from some foreign source, whether this source is from some one in the flesh or out of it. Obsession is always some form of mental suggestion. Insanity is the loss of the objective faculty.

The psychic power must always be controlled. A normal state is a perfect balance between the objective and the subjective faculties. This is the aim of evolution: to produce a man who, at the point of his objective faculty, may perfectly control the subjective. A trance state is abnormal, and only that psychic faculty is normal which is under full control of the self-discerning mind.

Clairvoyance is the ability to see without the physical eye. Psychometry is a clairvoyant state wherein the medium is able to enter the subjective side of things and read the atmospheres surrounding them; this is why mediums often wish to hold some familiar object in their hands while giving readings.

Clairaudience is the ear of the soul. Independent voices sometimes come from the air, proving that some inner power is able to express itself audibly. Apparitions are thought forms, and may come from the living or from the dead; at times they come as a warning.

Crystal gazing is for the purpose of concentrating the mind, in order that it may become subjective.

Black magic, the curse of malpractice, all mean the use of thought power for destructive purposes.

Automatic writing takes place when the arm is under control of the subjective mind of the operator or by the subconscious mind of some one else, either in the flesh or out of it; it is a form of suggestion, either conscious or unconscious. Independent writing is where the pencil writes without physical contact. This shows that some inner power has the ability to grasp solid objects without physical contact. Table tipping and rappings are from the same source. It is thought by some that these manifestations come from the agency of what is called "ectoplasm," or a subtle emanation of the body; this theory, however, does not explain all of the facts. Mind alone can do this. Levitation or the ability to move the body is another fact well known to investigators.

The power of prophecy is limited to some subjective tendency already set in motion; for mental tendencies cast their shadows before them. There is a higher power of prophecy which contacts the Cosmic Purposes and reads the thought of God.

Man reproduces, on the mental plane, all of the physical faculties.

IMMORTALITY

Immortality means that the individual shall persist after the experience of physical death, carrying with him a complete remembrance and an unbroken stream of consciousness; for if man be immortal, death cannot rob him of anything.

Man cannot conceive of himself, either as being born or as dying; he lives, and cannot think of himself from any other standpoint. Even though a person should conceive of himself as dying and imagine his own funeral, he would still have to conceive of himself as consciously being there, and so prove that he did not die at all. It is the same with birth; we can imagine being born into this world, but we cannot imagine the self as being non-existent; for, while thinking of the self as being born, we are still consciously thinking; thus proving that we were before we were physically born.

All inquiry into the Truth starts with the self-evident proposition that Life Is.

When man first woke to self-consciousness on this plane he already had a body. Consciousness always clothes itself in some kind of form.

Matter, from which the body is made, is a fluent substance, forever taking the form that intelligence gives it; it flows in and out like a river; we yearly immortalize ourselves, so far as the body is concerned.

The ether, being more solid than matter, proves that we could have a body within the one that we now occupy. Since matter in form is only a certain rate of vibration, it follows that, in dealing with Infinite Life, we are dealing with an infinite number of vibrations; consequently, we might have a body within a body to Infinity.

In reality, the body is a spiritual idea; the flesh simply covers it for the purpose of providing a physical instrument through which Spirit may function on this plane.

Man departs this body only to find himself already equipped with another one. He carries with him every attribute that he now possesses, and goes forth in complete retention of his individuality.

Since there is but One Mind, it follows that it is possible to communicate with the departed; but, as the communication must come through the subjective, it is difficult to receive clear messages; and it is impossible to know whether or not the ones with whom we think we are communicating are consciously present.

It is never safe to go into a trance state in order to communicate with the departed, as in so doing, one might subject himself to the mental influences of lesser mentalities. Individuality is sacred and must never be tampered with nor controlled, except by the conscious mind.

The value of an understanding of psychic phenomena lies in the fact that they are the phenomena of Mind and must be accounted for.

Every plane reproduces the one just below or just above it; psychic phenomena are the reproductions, on the mental plane, of the principle just below the mental, which is the physical.

PART III

SPECIAL ARTICLES

Note: It is well for the student to carefully read and study the following articles, as they have a distinct bearing on the preceding lessons.

ABSOLUTENESS AND RELATIVITY

Absolute is defined as, "Free from restrictions, unlimited, unconditioned." "The Unlimited and Perfect Being, God."

Relativity is defined as, "Existence only as an object of, or in relation to, a thinking mind." "A condition of dependence."

The Absolute, being Unconditioned, is Infinite and All; It is that Which Is, or the Truth. It is axiomatic that the Truth, being All, cannot be separated, limited nor divided; It must be Changeless, Complete, Perfect and Uncreated.

Relativity is that which depends upon something else; and if there be such a thing as relativity, it is not a thing of itself, but only that which functions within the Absolute and depends on It.

We wish to affirm relativity without destroying Absoluteness. This can be done only by realizing that the relative is not a thing apart from, but is an experience in, the All-Comprehending Mind. The relative does not contradict the Absolute, but affirms It; and the relative alone guarantees that there is an Absolute.

The Absolute is Cause, the relative is effect; the Absolute depends upon Itself, being Self-Existent; the relative must depend upon the Absolute.

We should be careful not to deny the relative, simply because it is not absolute. To suppose that there could be an Absolute without a relative, would be to suppose that there could be an unexpressed God or First Cause; this is unthinkable and impossible. The Consciousness of God must be expressed, hence the relative. The relative is not apart from, but is in the Absolute; and, as such, it is perfectly good and necessary. Time, space, outline, form, change, movement, action and reaction, manifestation and creation, all are relative; but all are real.

Relativity subsists within existence and inherent Life is potential and latent with limitless possibilities.

The relative and the Absolute do not contradict each other.

THE PROBLEM OF EVIL

Evil will remain a problem as long as anyone believes in it. This may sound rather startling until one has taken the time to think the matter through to a conclusion. Evil; of itself, is neither person, place nor thing, but is only a certain use that we make of life. We call that evil which we feel is the wrong thing to do; but our ideas of good and evil change with the unfoldment of our thought about, and belief in, life; for what was thought to be good yesterday, is today considered evil; and what, yesterday, was considered to be evil, is today called good.

Generally speaking, we may consider evil to be that which is destructive in its nature, and good to be that which is constructive.

Evil, then, will disappear in the exact proportion that we cease using destructive methods; and good will appear to the degree that we embody constructive methods. To turn from evil and do good is the desire of every soul who is consecrated to the Truth; this we can do only as we cease talking about, believing in, or doing evil.

The problem of evil will continue to be a problem just as long as we believe in it. Good will appear only as we embody it. Each soul has within a sure test, a something which directs and guides it. This Something is the Spirit of God and It knows no evil.

As there is no sin but a mistake, so there is no punishment but an inevitable consequence. As long as we make mistakes we shall be sinning; and just so long, we shall automatically be punished; for the law is certain and sure. As we turn to the Good, we will stop doing evil and, therefore, stop sinning.

The problem is solved as we turn from all that hurts, all that is destructive, all that denies the Good, and turn with our whole being into the light and toward the Truth. Evil is swallowed up in the Good as we learn to live daily in the Presence of God. "I will forgive their iniquity and I will remember their sin no more." That is, it will be completely blotted out; it will cease to be.

With our whole heart, with our whole being, in sincerity and honesty, with a complete trust in the Good, yearning toward It with a soul-desire that will be satisfied, we should turn to God, as the Supreme Presence, as the Complete Life, forsaking any belief in evil; we should turn so completely to the Spirit that our souls will become illumined by the Light Eternal.

Evil will cease to be when we stop looking at it; it never really was and is but a supposition. Let us, then, turn to the Path of Light and look to the God Within. Let us say, "Thou Infinite, Indwelling God, within me, knowing no evil, teach me of Thy ways, and in Thy wisdom make me wise. Almighty God within me, direct me into the way of the All Good." Let us turn completely from any and every belief in evil and do good. The problem will thus be solved and we shall realize that only the Good remains.

THE MEANING OF THE FALL

The story of the fall typifies race-experience as brought about through its belief in duality. Man is created perfect; that is, he starts on his journey as a perfect being, but he also starts as an individual; and this, of course, means that he starts with self-choice. Self-choice would have no real meaning unless it were backed by the power to externalize this choice and experience the effect of it. Man has the ability to choose and to externalize his choice; for he is a real individuality.

THE GARDEN OF EDEN

The Garden of Eden typifies man's original state of perfection before he began to have experience. The Tree of Knowledge means the Life Principle which can be used both ways. It bore the fruit of the knowledge of both kinds of experience, good and evil, freedom and limitation. Man must choose which kind of fruit he will eat. "Choose ye this day whom ye will serve." Man makes his choice consciously but generally in ignorance. The serpent typifies the Life Principle viewed from the materialistic viewpoint; it casts man from his perfect state through his belief in duality and separation. Man chose to depart from Good, and man alone must choose to return to It. God lets him alone; for he is a free agent and may do as he wills with himself. When man decides to return to his Father's House, he will find that his Father is still there. "Act as though I am and I will be." "Onlook the Deity and the Deity will onlook thee." "Be firm and ye shall be made firm." "As though hast believed so be it done unto thee." "Ask and it shall be given unto you; seek and ye shall find; knock and it shall be opened unto you." God's Creation is Perfect and we must wake to the fact and know that we are now in the Kingdom of Heaven.

SALVATION AND GRACE

As the fall of man was brought about through his own act, so the rise of man will be accomplished through his own act. God already Is. Salvation is not a thing but a Way; the way of salvation is through the realization of man's unity with the Whole. Grace is the givingness of the Spirit to Its Creation and is not a special law, but is a specialized one. In other words, Grace Is, but we need to recognize It. It is not something that God imposed upon us, but is the logical result of the correct acceptance of life and of a correct relationship to the Spirit.

We are saved by Grace to the extent that we believe in, accept and seek to embody, the Law of Good; for the Law of Good is ever a Law of Liberty and never one of limitation. Limitation is not a thing, but is a belief. Freedom is a Divine Reality, while limitation is an illusion, a false belief.

Salvation is an act of man and not an act of God. Man damned himself and man must save himself, if he ever is saved. He will save himself to the exact degree that he stops damning himself. He will live in Heaven when he stops living in hell. He will be healed when he stops being sick. He will become rich just as soon as he stops being poor. He will become as God when he stops masquerading as the devil. He will be happy when he stops being miserable. He will be at peace when he stops becoming confused. He will be filled with joy when he stops thinking sadness. He will live when he stops dying. He will be perfect when he stops looking upon imperfection; and he will be saved when he stops damning himself. HE WILL BE ONE WHEN HE STOPS BEING TWO. MAN, MAN, MAN, MAN, MAN, MAN, MAN; "The great Thou—I—and the great I—Thou."

THE PERFECT UNIVERSE

We must realize the Perfect Universe if we wish to embody the greatest good. If the Universe were not Perfect It could not exist for a single moment. It is self-evident that we live in a Perfect Universe; and, if so, then everything in It must also be perfect.

The Truth is Indivisible and Whole. God is Complete and Perfect. A Perfect Cause must produce a Perfect Effect. Disregarding all evidence to the contrary, the student of Truth will maintain that he lives in a Perfect Universe and among perfect people; he will regulate his thinking to meet this necessity and will refuse to believe in its opposite. At first he may appear to be weak; but as time goes on, he will prove to Itself that his position is a correct one; for that which appears imperfect will begin to slip from his experience.

To daily meditate on the Perfect Life and to daily embody the Great Ideal is the way to sure salvation; this is a royal road to freedom and is happiness to the soul of man. We cannot afford to believe in imperfection for a single instant. Let us learn to look as God must look, with a Perfect Vision; let us seek the Good and the True and believe in them with our whole heart; let us say daily to our inner selves: "Perfect God within me; Perfect Life within me, Which is God; Perfect Being within me, Which is God, come forth into expression through me and become that which I am; lead me into the paths of perfection and cause me to see only the Good."

By this practice, the soul will become illumined and will acquaint itself with God and be at peace. "Be ye therefore perfect, even as your Father Which is in heaven is Perfect."

IMAGINATION AND WILL

Coué announced a great truth when he said that imagination is superior to the will; but he did not explain the philosophy behind this truth. It is a fact that what he said is true, but we wish to analyze the fact and discover the reason back of it; for if anything is true there is always a reason for its being true.

Will is an assumption, pure and simple. We do not will to live; we live because we have life and cannot help living. The use of the will could not make us anything that we are not; for it is not possible to get out of a bag anything that the bag does not contain. We live because life is within us. Perhaps this is what Jesus meant when He said, "Which of you, by taking thought, can add one cubit to his stature?"

We did not make Life and we cannot change It, but we can use It; and the use of Life is through the imagination; because this faculty has, at its roots, the very well-spring of life and action. Imagination carries with it feeling and conviction, which mean life and action; it awakens within us all the finer forces of nature and stirs into action latent powers which otherwise would never come to the surface.

At the very root of the whole matter we find that the Creative Power of the universe does not create through will, but through imagination, imaging, feeling, and knowing. To suppose that

God must will things to happen would be to suppose that God had some opposing force to contend with.

Will power may be necessary in its place, but as a creative agency it is non-existent; it is not creative but directive; and used from this standpoint it is a wonderful force; whereas, used from any other angle, it becomes destructive and will mentally weary the one using it. To feel that we have to will things to happen casts doubt into the face of Creation and presupposes that Life is not Self-Existent and Self-Propelling.

Imagination taps the very roots of Being and utilizes the same Power that brought the worlds forth from Chaos. "The worlds were framed by the word of God." Imagination is the power of the word, while will is the directive agency, denoting the purpose for which the word is spoken.

Man reproduces the power to create and, in his own life, controls his destiny through the activity of his word. This word cannot be willed; but it can be imagined, or imaged forth, into expression.

HOW TO VISUALIZE

Visualizing means mentally seeing the things that you wish to have or to do. When you mentally see the things you desire, and see them very clearly, you are presenting Universal Mind with images of thought; and, like the creative soil of the ground, It at once tends to project them into form. If the thought image is clear it provides a good mold; if it is imperfect the mold is a poor one. This does not mean that one must set his mind or hold thought; it simply means that he must think clearly. There is no power in holding thoughts; indeed, the real secret of successful mental work is to loose thought and let Mind operate upon it.

The first thing to do is to decide what you wish to image into Mind. After having become composed in thought, begin to see the complete outcome of your desires, in mental pictures. Suppose that you wish to demonstrate a home; you should know just what kind of home you wish. Of course, if you simply thought of house you would get something, but the more definite the picture the better the results will be. In order to make the picture complete, decide just what kind of a home you wish to live in; then, in the silence of your thought, mentally look at this house; go from room to room, stopping here and there to look at some piece of furniture or at some picture on the wall. Make the whole thing real, as far as possible; enter the house, sit down and feel that you are actually living there, saying, "I am now living in this house." You have set a word in motion through the Law which will bring a realization of your desire, unless you, yourself, neutralize the picture by doubting it. Do this every day until the house appears. Use the same process in visualizing anything.

In order that you may fully understand just what I mean, I will illustrate by drawing a mental picture which I will ask you to follow as you read these lines. Imagine that you are with me; we will suppose that I am a man about six feet tall, with light hair and complexion. We are sitting on the front porch of a house that is painted green; it is a two-story house and sits quite far back from the road; there are tall trees standing in front of the house through which the sun is shining. We can see the little shadows as they play upon the porch through the open spaces between the trees. The breeze is gently blowing and the leaves are waving back and forth. I am talking to you, saying, "Let us take a walk together." We immediately rise from our seats, which are made of wicker, and walk down three stone steps to a gravel walk, leading to the street. As we go out through a stone gate we are suddenly met by a dog which is running along the street; he is a large, yellow dog, and is running rapidly. We watch him as he runs, barking, down the street, till he turns a corner—and our picture is at an end. Now, if you have carefully imaged each step in the above picture, you will understand what visualizing means.

THE SEQUENCE OF THE CREATIVE ORDER

In the creation of any form it is necessary for its image to exist in Mind before it can come into realization in the external. The Law, being only a neutral force, cannot initiate anything, and cannot, of Itself, choose to create anything. It is a Doer only, not a Knower. The Word alone knows; so we may assume that each word is a law unto itself, through the One great Law of all Life.

MAN'S CREATIVE POWER MARVELOUS

Man's creative power in his world is marvelous; for every time he thinks he sets the Law in motion. As his thought sets the Law in motion it is specializing It for some definite purpose; and in this way his word becomes the law unto the thing which he speaks. Of course man never really creates, but his use of Creative Power makes his word creative through the Medium of Mind. This should give to all a sense of freedom and a realization that there is neither competition nor monopoly. It leaves each to work out his own salvation, not with fear or even trembling, but with a calm sense of peace and assurance.

CONCENTRATION

To concentrate means to bring to a point. To concentrate the mentality means to bring the thinking to bear on one point of interest and to hold it there. Concentration has little to do with will power. Indeed, the misuse of will often renders concentration impossible.

The simplest practice for concentration is always the best. Nature always works along the lines of least resistance; and mental power is only a force of nature and should always be thought of in a natural way.

If you wish to concentrate on some particular idea or thought, bring the attention to it; then hold it there, but without effort. At first you may find that the thought wavers; do not oppose this, but mentally brush the wrong thought aside, much as you would brush a fly from the face with the hand. Be sure that you make no great mental effort, feel at ease and at peace, gently bringing the thought back to the point of attention.

Let us illustrate this by supposing that one is going to concentrate on the thought of happiness. Taking the word "happy" into the mentality, say, "I am happy"; without effort or mentally trying, just think the words, "I am happy." In a few minutes you may find that your thought has begun to wander. Right here be sure and not bring the attention back with a bang; just say again, "I am happy," making no effort to destroy the other thought, but returning to the starting point, "I am happy." Make the whole thing easy and natural, and soon you will find that you can hold the attention as long as you desire.

It is always a mistake to oppose thoughts that interfere; when one begins to do this he will at once find that he is resisting something, thereby disrupting his whole meditation.

It is unnecessary to concentrate on an external object; for CONCENTRATION IS ALWAYS FROM WITHIN AND NEVER FROM WITHOUT. The only place that the mind can know is within itself.

In concentrating, lay aside all will power and resistance, letting the thought realize the words upon which you wish to concentrate. This will be found a simple but most effective method, and by far the most prolific of results.

In teaching a child to concentrate, it is well to have him take something in which he is particularly interested. As a child's mind wanders more or less aimlessly about, it is well to have him write some thought on paper; and, looking at it, see how long he can center his interest on the mental picture that the words suggest.

THE MIRROR OF THE SUBJECTIVE

It has truly been said that Mind is a mirror. If we could realize how completely this law works, no doubt we would greatly alter our manner of thinking. It is impossible to create even the slightest thought without causing some reflex action in Mind; and the deeper the emotion the deeper will be the penetration of thought and the more complete will be the reaction.

Thought is the most subtle of all the forces which we know anything about, and but few understand what a tremendous power it has, either for good or for ill. To learn how to control one's thought means knowing how to control one's body and destiny.

Subjective mind can reason only deductively; consequently, it is compelled, by reason of its nature, to accept whatever thought gains entrance to it. So the mirror of Mind is, in reality, the working of the law of cause and effect through the mentality. The subjective mind, being the seat of memory, must contain all the thoughts which have ever gone into it, whether these thoughts have been conscious or not. But when a person is told that he has thoughts which he never consciously created it is a little hard to understand. He must realize, however, that constant contact with life opens the door to many impressions which were never consciously created. This fact, together with the realization that whatever falls into the subjective mind must be acted upon, answers the question.

Of course, we do not imagine that certain things are going to happen to us; but we do think certain kinds of thoughts which, brought to their logical conclusions, would produce definite effects. Remember that the subjective mind reasons deductively only; and all this becomes quite evident.

The subjective side of thought, being the creative agency within, must at once set to work to produce anything which is given it, no matter what the emotion may be. How wonderful! But this shows how very careful one should be in choosing the kind and type of emotion to be made into form; for something must happen to all the thoughts which submerge.

The subjective mind never argues nor contradicts what is put into it; the thought is at once accepted and acted upon. If one says that he is sick, it at once begins to create a sick condition; for, like a mirror, it reflects; and being creative, what it reflects it tends to create and to cast forth as a condition.

Like any other natural force, subjective mind was not created by man and he cannot change its mode of operation; but, while he may not change a natural force, he may change his manner of approach to it. Man cannot change his own inherent nature; but he can, and should, learn to make the best use of all his forces. Subjective mind will never change its own nature, but will always reflect to the thinker what he thinks into it. Man did not make this law nor can he change it; but, like any other law, once understood, it becomes an obedient servant.

The use of this law is entirely mental and is within the grasp of every one; it is so simple that all can understand; it is the law of mind in action, and this law is set in motion by correct thinking and knowing.

But how few know why they think or what they think!

How few control even the slightest emotion or allow the emotions to express in a constructive manner! No doubt the time will come when a complete control of the subjective will be gained and man will then be much less limited.

But the race is made up of individuals, and the place to begin is right at home. We, who have affirmed these great laws of mind to be realities in the human experience, must so prove them in our expressions of life that the rest, looking on, may read the sign and follow the signal. It is possible to do this, and the reward is great.

At first the road may be hard and beset with many difficulties; there may be failures and discouragements; but the end is certain. We fall, only to rise again into a greater realization of life and action; and, like the pilgrim of old, to renew the journey. We shall need a backbone instead of a wishbone here as in all other places. It is not in wishing but in knowing and in doing that we shall find the reward of true merit. It behooves each one to make the effort to consciously control the processes of his thought.

This does not mean sitting around in some dark corner with the hand at the brow, impersonating Socrates or Plato; it means out in the world, in the midst of affairs, at home and abroad, wherever our work takes us. We need not leave the world; for we may engage in all of its activities without being controlled by them; we may be in the world of affairs as masters and not as slaves.

Surely this hope, held before the waiting thought, will so stimulate our endeavors that we shall go forth into life and the great game of living with a new song upon our lips and a new joy within, springing forth into the dawn of a new day.

PERSONALITY

Personality is the result of man's experience; it is the sum total of all that he has said, done, felt, thought, hoped for and believed in; it is the result of his reactions to the events of life as they come and go. Factors to be considered in the development of personality are heredity, race-suggestion, environment, child training, education, auto-suggestion and, indeed, anything and everything that impinges upon consciousness. Therefore, we are what we are and where we are because of the nature of our accumulated consciousness.

FACTORS NECESSARY FOR A DYNAMIC PERSONALITY

It goes without saying that all people desire a dynamic, radiant personality; and it is self-evident that certain palates are essential to produce this result. The external personality really reflects the soul, and its building may be likened to a mental garden where the harvest depends upon the kind of seed that is sown. Each one chooses for himself just what kind of materials he will use and each builds according to the pattern of his own desires. "Whatsoever a man soweth, that shall he also reap." Just as a fine architect uses only the best materials and plans most carefully how to construct his building, so should we, in the building of personality, choose most carefully the kind of materials we wish to use.

High Character—First of all, it should be founded upon the rock of high character, high ideals, and built for Eternity as well as for today.

Sincerity—Sincerity in every human relationship is essential.

Ability—To be a master of one thing and to daily improve.

Enthusiasm—A keen interest in people and things at home and abroad; it has been called "The Fortune-Teller of Life." Enthusiasm is compelling and sweeps everything before it.

Service—Service is the keynote to success and implies constructive work; also, loyalty to your work and to all concerned in it.

Wholesomeness—A clean-minded man with high ideals is always sought after. The reading of fine books, listening to good music and becoming acquainted with the best in art and literature will soon implant in the mentality a quality of wholesomeness that is most desirable.

Success—A consciousness of success must be developed; this can be done by creating clear pictures of success and working toward them daily. Decision and assertion are aids to this end and must not be overlooked.

Self-Confidence—Implies peace and poise and knowing what to do in every situation.

Power and Strength—Are also born of peace and poise.

Sense of Humor—This is most necessary to have, as it lightens the burdens of life and makes one's self and others happy. Without it things seem dull and dreary.

This has no barb or sting and implies the ability to laugh at one's own expense.

Good Manners—Not servile but courteous.

Tact—Saying or doing the right thing at the right time.

Thoroughness—Implies system and the ability to carry things out to a definite conclusion. This quality is essential to success.

Charm—Personal charm is that indefinable something which makes every one a friend. It is the result of genuine friendliness, sympathy, kindliness and unselfish interest in others.

Magnetism—The result of an abundant vitality on the physical plane; of intellect and temperament on the mental plane; and of atmosphere or consciousness on the Spiritual plane.

Tenderness—Sympathetic union with people; real compassion.

Love—The Universal Urge to express, the Self-givingness of Spirit.

Originality—Try to create; do not imitate; think for yourself. Read Emerson's Essay on "Self-Reliance."

Incentive—Have wholesome ambitions and definite objectives which are constructive in their nature. Any ambition is wholesome which brings only good results to one's self and all concerned.

Suitable Humility, Simplicity and Genuineness—These attributes keep one from being over-ambitious and from being too aggressive.

Emotional Control—Presupposes poise and self-mastery.

Spirituality—Looking for the good in all and having faith, belief, and trust.

Health—Is a great factor in creating a dynamic, vibrant personality.

Voice—A clear, resonant, well-modulated tone at all times.

Dress—Clothes reflect one's idea of "The Eternal fitness of things." Colors particularly have a peculiarly subtle effect on the wearer and upon those with whom he comes in contact.

Strictly speaking, personality is the use that we make of our individuality. Individuality means that which we really are; it means the point in Life where we exist and can say, I AM. Perhaps it could be defined as a point in Mind where Life recognizes Itself as some Person. Each person is an Individualized Center of God-Consciousness, a self-knowing center of Life and Action.

It follows, then, that personality is much greater than it seems to be; for it is the use of Divine Individuality and has, back of it, a limitless possibility. It is the coming forth of God, or Life, into Self-Expression.

Man's personality is not a thing to be lightly spoken of or decried as human or ineffective. Within and behind it are boundless possibilities, and few, indeed, realize what a tremendous power it wields, either for good or for ill.

Today we are hearing much about this power and the way to develop it; for as yet we express only in part, being unaware of the Whole. Latent forces surge to express through man; Divine impulse seek expression through him; a Cosmic Urge forever beats against the threshold of his consciousness, demanding expression; hence, all his subtle longings and unspoken thoughts.

To develop or express the self is the great need of the human race; but though feeling, sensing, inwardly knowing and realizing a greater good, man stumbles blindly along the pathway of life, expressing only in part.

Like all the other faculties of the Great Within, personality may be consciously unfolded and expressed, if we let it come through.

We all desire a powerful personality, and all may have one if they pay attention to a few fundamental facts of Being; for personality is the expression of something that already exists and simply needs to be allowed to come forth.

Anyone wishing to develop a pleasing personality must first become pleasant. He must think pleasing thoughts. All animosity and vindictiveness must be swept aside if the soul is to express itself in terms of greatness.

There is no place for smallness in the full life and no place for meanness in the liberal mind. A broad-minded, tolerant attitude must be maintained toward all. This is not a goody-goody idea but a plain statement of fact.

A sense of calm and peace is essential to a well-rounded personality. The din and roar of the outer struggle for existence must not find entrance to the soul if Reality is to be expressed.

Poise and balance are the mainsprings of reality and cannot be overlooked. We are not attracted to people who are always fussed up and fretful, who are never satisfied and are always unhappy. Misery and unhappiness are unknown to the Spirit of man, and we should make them unknown to the outer man.

Sensitiveness and morbidity must be swept side as unworthy of the great Ideal. Refuse to have the feelings hurt. Friends do not wish to hurt the feelings of those whom they love, and none but friends need be admitted.

Personality is but half expressed until we realize that within we are complete. Wholeness is the keynote to perfection and self-esteem is not egotism but is self-realization. Completion is from within and not from without; and no one can add to, or take from, that which is already complete. The Soul and Spirit are already perfect and whole.

Love is the great loadstone of Life; and without this quality of Spirit, shining through Life's action, everything becomes dull and drear. Goodness and human kindness are the handmaids of Love and Life, and cannot be separated from Reality.

Irritation, vexation and confusion go hand in hand to rob man of his birthright to peace, comfort and harmony. As children of the dust they must be brushed aside as unfit companions of the soul.

Anger and malice, revenge and animosity cannot breathe the same atmosphere as goodness and purity, and they will fall away as we climb to those heights where the Indwelling Spirit lives.

Self-confidence and courage go hand in hand with real worth and are but the declarations of man's Wholeness. There is nothing petty or little about greatness.

Mental alertness and animation but signify that man lives in a life of everlasting interests and activities.

Honesty and sincerity show forth the fundamental principles of Being, and without them man expresses only a makeshift of himself, a false and deluded sense of Reality. No real person can be dishonest or insincere. Truth alone shines to Eternal Day.

The complete, well-rounded, dynamic personality contains all of these qualities and attributes; and they will come forth into expression to the exact degree that we allow them to flow through us.

Personality is not false but real; it is the shining through of the Real Self—the man God made.

Physical appearance has but little to do with those inner, subtle powers of attraction which decide what the Indwelling Ego is to attract to Itself. The Inner Man transcends all that is external and compels attention without effort. To be conscious of this Inner Self is to know the Real Man, to know the truth about personality and the power of attraction. As a rose unfolds, so the personality of man unfolds and blossoms forth into complete expression.

A few simple practices will soon develop such a powerful personality that it will become a magnet, drawing to its center with a force that cannot be denied. THESE PRACTICES BEGIN AND END WITHIN MAN; FOR HE IS THE CENTER OF HIS OWN UNIVERSE, AND NOTHING HAPPENS TO HIM UNLESS HE LETS IT.

Know that Life flows through you and cannot be hindered in Its expression. Know that the All Good is yours now. Act, think, believe, speak as though you were now all that you have ever dreamed. AND BE SURE THAT YOU BELIEVE THE SAME THING ABOUT ALL PEOPLE, FOR NONE OF US LIVES UNTO HIMSELF ALONE, BUT EACH LIVES UNTO ALL, WITHIN THE ONE LIFE.

Live constantly from this inner conviction, never stooping to anything less than the All Good; and you will soon discover that something is taking place that never took place before in your experience. DO NOT TRY TO MAKE THINGS HAPPEN; SIMPLY KNOW THAT THEY ARE HAPPENING.

Daily realize your Unity with the Whole and the Unity of the Whole with you. YOU WILL SOON DEVELOP SUCH A POWERFUL PERSONALITY THAT ALL WHO COME IN CONTACT WITH YOU WILL WISH TO REMAIN IN YOUR PRESENCE.

REPRESSION AND SUBLIMATION

THE SPIRIT OF SEX

We have discovered, from the preceding chapters, that the Universe is threefold in Its nature. It is Spirit, Soul and Body; Spirit as the active, projective, masculine factor; Soul as the receptive, creative, feminine factor; and Body, which is the result of the union of Spirit with Soul. The Spirit impregnates the Soul with Its Ideas, and the Soul gives form to these Ideas and clothes them with flesh. But this is the Trinity of Unity, a Triune Oneness; for the Three are really one.

Life is Androgynous, i.e., It contains within Itself both the masculine and the feminine factors. The male and the female of Creation come from One Principle; all come from the One and all will return to the One; all are now in the One and will forever remain in the One.

DESIRE

Back of all manifestation must be the desire to create, the urge to express; this is called the "Divine Urge." But this Urge, operating as Law produces energy. Desire gathers energy for creative purposes and utilizes power to express itself. So dynamic is this Urge that it will cause a little seed to break open the most solid earth, in order that it may express itself in the form of a plant. It is the coming forth of Spirit into expression, the loosing of energy into action, and is apparent in all Creation.

THE SPIRIT IS EXPRESSED

The Spirit, being Absolute, is always expressed; It has no unfulfilled desires. IT IS ALWAYS SATISFIED AND HAPPY BECAUSE IT IS ALWAYS EXPRESSED. Creation is the result of the desire of Spirit to express Itself; It is the unfoldment of the Divine Ideas, Evolution is the time and process of this unfoldment. Involution is the idea in Mind, and evolution is the coming forth of the idea into expression. Involution precedes evolution, and evolution follows involution with a mathematical precision, propelled by an Immutable Law.

That which is involved must evolve, else the Spirit would remain unexpressed. As this is unthinkable, we may set it down that evolution, or the manifestation of desire and energy, is bound to take place whenever desire sets power and energy in motion. From this law we cannot hope to escape, and it would be useless to make the attempt.

MAN REENACTS THE DIVINE NATURE

Man, as we have discussed, reenacts the Divine Nature and makes use of the same Laws that God uses. We find in man the same androgynous nature that we find in God. This nature we call his objective and subjective faculties. His objective mentality impregnates his subjective with ideas; and in its turn, the subjective, gathering force and energy, projects these ideas into forms.

Back of every act of man is some form of desire to express. This desire, of course, is purely mental in its nature. All that man is, is his mentality, both conscious and subconscious, plus what he expresses.

The Divine Urge is strong in man and constantly causes him to seek some form of self-expression. It is Divine because It

is the desire of Spirit to express Itself through him; and like all
the other forces of Nature, this energy can work through man
only at his bidding; consciously or unconsciously, for he is an
individual and has self-choice.

This Urge or Energy is called "Libido," which means "The
emotional craving, or wish, behind all human activities, the re-
pression of which leads to psycho-neuroses."

CONGESTED EMOTIONS

The energy set in motion through this urge is the dynamic
power of Mind, and unless it becomes expressed, it will congest
and cause a conflict within the mentality.

Inhibited action produces conflicts and complexes which
mentally tear and bind; and as they manifest their physical correspondents, they produce nervous disorders. It is claimed that a
large percentage of diseases is caused by the suppression of some
form of emotion. This does not necessarily mean the suppression
of the sex emotion, but might mean any desire that remains unexpressed. Some form of desire is back of every impulse that the
mind can conceive, some impulse to express life. Any unexpressed
desire will eventually cause a complex. Things will stand just so
much pressure and no more; when the limit is reached an explo-
sion will follow, unless some avenue for expression is provided.

IRRITATION, AGITATION AND FEAR

People who are constantly being irritated have suppressed some
desire to speak their minds. It may not appear as though this
were the cause, but thought is very subtle, and only a careful
study of its workings reveals the real facts. All irritation and ag-
itation are mental in their cause, and a sense of calm and peace
alone can heal them.

Fear is an intense emotion, and if bottled up, secretes poison in the system. Fear must be removed from the mentality if
one is to be healed and is to function normally.

Anger, malice, vindictiveness and kindred emotions are but subtle forms of fear arising from a sense of inferiority. All of these emotions must be swept off the board if one is to gain peace, calm and poise. The union of peace, with calm and poise, alone can give birth to power; for without these attributes of reality, power is dissipated and lost in the shuffle.

IF WE WERE EXPRESSED

If we were completely expressed we would never become sick or unhappy. The average person goes through life expressed only in part and always with a sense of incompletion and dissatisfaction. Something must be done to make the individual complete if he is to remain normal and happy and really live.

EMOTION AND INTELLECT

Emotion is strong in man, and in the well-balanced person it is controlled by the intellect; but in many people there is a conflict between the emotions and the intellect; and in too many cases the emotion gains the ascendancy.

Our strongest emotions center around the ideas of fear, hate, love, sex and worship, with all of their many ramifications and meanings.

Emotion, uncontrolled, produces chaos; unexpressed it produces confusion, conflict and complex; for energy will have an outlet. Bottled up, it creates a pressure that is the cause of much damage to the physical man, and produces most of our nervous disorders. Expression is normal when the intellect decides how the emotion is going to manifest. "He that is slow to anger is better than the mighty; and he that ruleth his spirit than he that taketh a city."

THE CONFLICT OF DESIRE

When an emotion conflicts with the will and becomes suppressed it returns to its subjective state, but remains active; it will come up in some other form; it will not be put down. It may remain in a subjective state for years; but eventually, unless neutralized, it will manifest. Let one go for years with some unexpressed longing and he will have created such a desire that it will have become irresistible in its inclination toward expression.

People often become seething caldrons within because of inhibited action. Energy must find an outlet.

THE EMOTION OF SEX

Human love and the affections often go hand in hand with sex desire, even when not recognized as such. An affectionate nature is generally a passionate one. Love is the most wonderful thing in the world and creates the highest form of energy known to the mind of man. It will be expressed at the level of the passions or else become transmuted into Spiritual Coin of real and lasting value. But the ideas on sex are likely to become over-emphasized in modern literature along these lines. Sex is normal in its proper sphere; if it were not, it would not be; for nature does nothing without some good and ample reason.

THE TRUE MEANING OF LOVE

The true meaning of love is a wonderful thing; for it is the desire of the soul to express itself in terms of creation. Creation is brought about only through the self-givingness of the lover to the object of his love. This is why, when we love people, we will go to the limit to help or serve them; nothing is too great, no sacrifice is enough. The true lover gives all and is unhappy in not having still more of himself to give to the object of his adoration.

Because of our emotional nature, love is generally expressed through the sex desire. But too great an expression of this desire is destructive, for it depletes the vitality and demagnetizes the one who overindulges. This is the meaning, and the whole meaning, of the story of Samson and Delilah. "He that hath an ear, let him hear." All people look, and occasionally someone sees.

SEX NOT NECESSARY TO THE EXPRESSION OF LOVE

The sex relationship is not necessary to the expression of real love. Love is the givingness of the self, and if this givingness is complete sex will take care of itself. But energy must have some outlet. It is only when the unexpressed desire remains in the subjective that destruction follows in its wake and strews the shores of time with human derelicts. Liberty and license, freedom and bondage, heaven and hell, happiness and misery, good and bad, all, all, are tied up in human desires. Energy is energy and will be expressed or blow the top off, just as a pipe will stand only so much pressure before bursting.

Millions are daily being blown up, mentally and physically, through the suppression of desires. Desire is a dynamic force and must be taken into account.

WHEN SEX BECOMES DESTRUCTIVE

Sex desire becomes destructive only when it remains an unexpressed longing. This theory is not put forth to encourage free love nor to advocate indiscriminate relationships; for neither the one nor the other is believed in by the writer. It is stated as a fact patent to any thinking person. "Libido," may be expressed through more than one avenue; through transmutation, freeing life's energies and lifting them into an avenue of constructive expression; or through sublimation, transfusing the essence of energy into high action and producing a magnetism that is irresistible and wonderful in its scope. The atmosphere of one thus charged is complete; for the energy then takes the form of real Love and is the highest and most powerful vibration on the physical plane.

MALE AND FEMALE

Man, coming from Unity, is both male and female, and has, within himself, both attributes of reality. In some the male predominates; in others the female. We have two distinct types in man and woman; but they are types of one fundamental principle. There is also an intermediate sex; that is, one in which the two attributes seem to be almost equally balanced. The greatest men and women of the ages have belonged to this type, for it is a more complete balance between the two which are really one. But this is too great a topic to discuss in this course of lessons.

The solution to the problem of desire is to transmute any destructive tendency into some form of action that is constructive. However, an intellectual form of expression alone will not do this, for only those things to which we may give the complete self will solve the problem. Love is the givingness of the self to the object of its adoration. We should all have something that we love to do, something that will completely express the self, something that will loosen the energies of Life into action and transmute the power into creative work. We should learn to love all people and not just some people.

It is very disastrous to feel that we cannot live unless we possess some one individual, body and soul. This is not love but is an idea of possession, which often becomes an obsession. No soul is really complete until he feels compete within himself.

This does not exclude the great human relationships which mean so much to all of us; but it does take the sting out of life and does free the individual to love all, adore some, and find happiness everywhere.

To feel that love is unrequited creates a longing so intense that it tears the very heart out of life, and throws the one so feeling into a fit of despondency from which it is, indeed, hard to recover. This feeling is met in the Truth by knowing that Love is Eternal and Real and cannot be added to nor taken from.

This may seem like a hard teaching; but the problems of humanity deal largely with the human relationships and until they are harmonized, there can be no lasting happiness.

Happiness is from within, like all the other qualities of

the Spirit. Within, Man is already complete and perfect; but he needs to realize this truth.

I can imagine some one saying: "This is too impersonal a teaching." It is not impersonal at all; this does not mean that we care less for people; indeed, we shall find that for the first time in life we shall really care; but the sting will have gone.

Refuse to have the feelings hurt. Refuse yourself the pleasure and morbidity of sensitiveness. Come out of the emotional intoxication and be YOURSELF. Never allow the thought to become depressed nor morbid. Engage in some form of activity that will express the better self. Do not attempt to draw life from others; live the life that God gave you; it is ample and complete. "But," people will say, "I believe in affinities." If by this one means that each is only one-half of a real person and must find the other half in order to be expressed, he is mistaken. Such persons usually find a second affinity as soon as the first disappears. We all have a natural affinity for each other, since we all live in One Common Mind and in One Unified Spirit. It is all right if we wish to specialize on some particular love; but the hurt will remain unless love has a broader scope than when narrowed down to one single person.

Live, love and laugh! Let the heart be glad and free; rejoice in the thought of life and be happy. Realize God, in and through all, and unify with the Whole. Why take fragments when the Whole is here for the asking?

PSYCHO-ANALYSIS

Psycho-analysis is a system of analyzing the soul, or the subjective mentality. It is a mental process of diagnosis which seems to be technically perfect when used by those who understand it. It goes into the past and unearths the objectively forgotten emotions, brings them to light and causes them to be self-seen and so dissipated. It is based upon the theory that Nature is Perfect and when let alone will flow through man in a perfect state of health. The purpose of the analysis is to uncover the complex and heal the conflict, through removing it. It takes into account every experience that the individual has ever had, paying much attention to his early training, and more especially to his mental reactions to life.

It is a wonderful system, and in the hands of the right people, is prolific of much good. But, in the thought of the writer, it is a thing without a soul, a skeleton without flesh. It lacks the warmth, the fire and the reality of spiritual re-alization. It is useless to remove a mental complex, unless at the same time we place in its stead a real realization of what life means. It is useless to tear down unless, at the same time, we build up. The proper analysis of the soul, coupled with real spiritual recognition, will do wonders, however, and is well worth while.

SELF-ANALYSIS

Go through a process of self-analysis; look into your own past and carefully remove every complex. This is easily done by the one who is not afraid to look himself in the face. Find out what you are afraid of and convince the mentality that there is noth-ing to fear. Look the world squarely in the face; sift the mentality to its depths, removing every obstruction that inhibits the free flow of those great spiritual realizations, such as will be found in the meditations that follow these lessons.

METAPHYSICS

The right kind of mental work will go beneath the surface and destroy the subjective cause of the complex, thereby easing the conflict. It will then supply a Spiritual Realization that will open the avenues of thought to the great Whole. This alone is real and lasting.

THE ATONEMENT

Atonement is defined as reconciliation: "To make an expiation for sin or a sinner," and "To be at one." The definition for sin is, "To commit sin, transgress, neglect or disregard the Divine Law; to do wrong or offend." Literally speaking, sin means missing the mark or making a mistake. "There is no sin but a mistake and no punishment but a consequence." To assume that man could sin against God would be to suppose that a Divine Law could be broken. To suppose that Divine Law could be broken would be to assume that man has the power to destroy Divine Harmony and wreck the universe with his actions.

Man may have power to go contrary to Law, but certainly he has no power to break it. Man cannot break a law, but the law can break him if he goes contrary to it.

There is no doubt but that all of man's troubles come from his disregard of law, through ignorance. There can be no doubt that much of his trouble will be over when he comes to understand the law, and to consciously cooperate with it.

We live in a Universe of Law and a Universe of Love. The Law of God is Perfect, and the Love of God is also Perfect. The Law of God is the way in which the Spirit works; the Love of God is the Self-Givingness of the Spirit to Its Creation. The unity of Love and Law produce a harmonious Universe and a Perfect Creation.

Man, because of his individuality and the use that he makes of it, may go contrary to both Love and Law; but so long as he does this he will suffer. This is the real meaning of sin and punishment.

Man has gone contrary to the Law of Harmony and Love, and no doubt this is the reason for all his troubles. He will be saved to the degree that he returns to a state of harmony and unity with God and with Life. He can do this only as he first comes to realize that God is Love and that he lives in a Universe of Law.

The greater lesson that can be taught to the race is the lesson of Love and of Law. The lesson of Love teaches us that Life gives and that God is Good; while the lesson of Law teaches that there is a way to freedom through real Love.

If Love is the Self-Givingness of Spirit, then that man who most completely loves, will most completely give of himself to Life. The man who loves his work gives himself to it; the one who loves his art gives himself to it. We give ourselves to our friends and to our families and to the causes which we really love. Love is always the giving of the self to something; but the idea of self-givingness is not a morbid one and should never be thought of in this light.

We have always thought of the Atonement of Jesus as the act of His giving Himself, through suffering on the cross, as a sacrifice for the sins of the world. But God surely does not need that any man shall suffer for Him, nor sacrifice himself to please Him. This would, indeed, be a limited idea of the Divine Being. God does not need an At-one-ment, since He is already at one with himself and with all Creation. It is man, not God, who needs an At-one-ment. The act of atonement must be on the part of man and not of God. Man may need salvation, but God is already conscious of Complete Life and Being.

MAN'S WHOLE TROUBLE

Man's whole trouble lies in the fact that he believes himself to be separated from the Source of Life. He believes in duality. The At-one-ment is made to the degree that he realizes the Unity of Good. Man needs, and always has needed, to know the Truth about himself and God; and anything that helps to fill this need would be an act of atonement.

Now a man who had reached the understanding at which Jesus must have arrived would find the ordinary channels of expression inadequate to portray His concept of Life. Jesus could have had no desire to become rich; neither did He wish to be made a king, nor to receive the plaudits of the world. He wished to show to the world what the Love of God could really mean in the lives of men; He wished to show that the Self-Givingness of Spirit is complete; to prove that Life completely gives of Itself to Its Creation. This he could do only to the degree that He let God become Man through His own Individuality.

CAREFUL PREPARATION

The whole thought and attention of Jesus was given to the accomplishment of one supreme purpose: to show that God is a Living Reality in the lives of all men. He must show the Nature of the Divine Being; he must take the place of God and reveal the Love and tender care of the Creator for Its Creation. No more complete plan was ever organized in the mentality of an individual than the plan of Jesus to prove the reality of Spirit.

His thought, being psychic, that is, being able to read mental causes, told Him just what would happen if He did this. (See chapter on Prophecy in lesson on Psychic Phenomena.) He knew that he would have to suffer physical agony, and for a time, at least, be misunderstood and abused. He also knew that the lesson would prove for all time that God is Love. He knew that in the end the lesson which He was to teach would be accepted by all; and in this way He would become a Living Witness to the reality of Divine Love and Goodness.

Carefully He worked out His plan and patiently He waited for the right time to come to complete His life work; and when this time came, He unflinchingly gave of Himself to the necessity of the case. Man must come to understand God if he is ever to realize his own nature; he must come to know Spirit as a Living Reality and not as a myth.

THE VICARIOUS ATONEMENT

The Vicarious Atonement was the conscious giving of the Self to the needs of the human race—an example for all time that God is Love. Jesus perfectly understood the Law of Life and consciously chose to make an example of Himself that would cause all people to see what a real At-one-ment could mean. In order to do this, He had to take on the sins of the world; that is, He had to enter into men's mistakes in order to rectify them; not because God demanded this, but because man needed the example.

The suffering of Jesus, as He contacted the disorders of men's minds, was His vicarious atonement for the race. It was a wonderful example of what one man could do in proving the Unity of Good.

Any person who contacts the race-mind with the desire to lift it above its own level, will, thereby, go through a vicarious atonement. But the thought of morbidity that theology had given to the message of atonement is entirely erroneous. It is not a morbid thing but a glorious one. Atonement could not be morbid, but must always produce a realization of Unity and of Good. The life of Jesus is not a sad story, but is the account of a Man Who so completely realized His own At-one-ment that He had realization to spare and to give to all who believe in His teaching. His life was a triumphant march from the cradle into Eternity, and not from the cradle to the grave. He swallowed the grave in victory, because of His At-one-ment. Jesus left no grave and no dead man behind Him.

The At-one-ment, then, is a glorious recognition of fulfillment and completion. The vicarious part is lost in the greater realization of Unity and of Good. Jesus is the most Triumphant Figure of all history and the only Man, of Whom we have record, Who completely knew His own Nature. All thought of sin, shame, iniquity, poverty, sickness, obscurity and death are swept away with the empty tomb. No wonder that this lesson still remains and His teachings still hold good, for Reality never changes.

THE GIVINGNESS OF SPIRIT

As the human side of Jesus gave way, more and more, to the Divine Realization, He more and more completely became Divine; that is, He more completely became God, Incarnated in and through Man. In this mystic way He took the place of God, and we may, perhaps, say that through Him God proved the Love of God. Of course this is a crude way of putting it, but it does serve to point a moral and is, perhaps, the best way that we can conceive of the greatest lesson of all history.

THE WORLD HAS LEARNED ALL THAT IT SHOULD THROUGH SUFFERING

The world has learned all that it should through suffering. God does not demand that man suffer; and man suffers simply because he is ignorant of his own nature and because he misuses his power. Jesus proved the Truth and departed this life in joy, having fulfilled His Divine Mission. The lesson has been taught and the evidence is complete. The grave has been swallowed up in the Victory of Life and Love; and the tomb is empty for all time. "Why seek ye the living among the dead?" The time has come for rejoicing and not for sorrowing; for the fulfillment of that peace which was promised. "Peace I leave with you."

There need be no more sorrowing nor crying; for Reality is now known. Life is Triumphant and Love reigns Supreme.

OUR PART IN THE ATONEMENT

The Vicarious Atonement is over, but the real At-one-ment has only begun. We are just beginning to realize what Love and Life mean. Every time we give of ourselves to others, helping them to overcome their troubles, we are performing an At-one-ment; we are proving the Unity of Good.

THE PERSONALITY OF GOD

In our metaphysical abstractions we have come to the conclusion that God, or First Cause, must be Infinite; and it is difficult to perceive how a power which is Infinite can, at the same time, be personal. Yet the soul longs for a responsive universe; and the heart yearns for a God Who responds to the human desire.

To take from the individual his idea of God as a personally responsive Intelligence, and leave him only a cold, unresponsive Law, is to rob the individual of his greatest birthright and to throw him, naked and bare, into the midst of an Eternity which holds no attraction.

To think of the Universe in terms of Law only, is to make of God only an Infinite It, a cold and bitter Principle, lacking that warmth and color which the soul craves.

This difficulty is removed when we realize that the Law of Mind is like any other law; it is a natural force, and, like all law, should be thought of from this angle. But back of, and working in and through the Law, there is a responsive Intelligence and a knowing Spirit, Which is God, the Father of all; and Who responds to all.

We will think of Mind, then, as Law, and of God as Love; we will use the Law and love the Spirit back of, and through, the Law. In this way, we will be robbed of nothing, but will see that the way to freedom is through Love and by Law.

JESUS AS A SAVIOUR

Jesus stands forth from the pages of human history as the greatest Figure of all time. His teachings contain the greatest lesson ever given to the human race; and His life and works, while on earth, provide the grandest example that was ever given to man.

In the Higher Thought no attempt is made to rob Jesus of His greatness or to refute His teachings; indeed, the Higher Thought Movement is based upon the words and the works of this, the most remarkable Personality that ever graced our planet with His presence; and, until a greater figure appears, Jesus will still remain the great Wayshower to mankind, the great Saviour of the race.

Let us not waste time, then, in theological discussions which lead nowhere; but, following the example set before us, let us also do the works which He did. "The works that I do, shall he do also; and greater works than these shall he do; because I go unto my Father."

SELF-EXISTENT LIFE

The most important thing that any student of the Truth can understand is the real meaning of self-existence. Whatever the nature of First Cause is, It must be Self-Existent, or else It could not be at all. It is, perhaps, hard to comprehend that there must be, and is, a Power which exists simply because It is what It Is; and yet this is the mainspring of all right metaphysical work and endeavor.

We must come to believe in, and trust, that Power of Life and Intelligence which is God, or First Cause. We must understand that we deal with First Cause whenever we think, at any, and at all, times. If we had to gather energy with which to energize the Creative Principle of Life, where should we go to get the energy with which to energize It?

We are constantly thrown back upon the fundamental

proposition that Life already Is; and that we use a Power which already Is. Let us then, without doubt or fear, throw our word into that Great Receptivity and trust It to do the work.

THE SUPREME AFFIRMATION

Strange as it may seem, the human thought can affirm only; it can never deny; for, even at the moment of denial, it really affirms the presence of that which it denies.

We speak of denials and affirmations as though they were opposed to each other, but such is not the case. Fear and faith are but different ways of expressing positive beliefs about something. Fear is a positive belief that we will experience something that we do not wish to have happen, while faith is a positive belief that we will experience something that we do wish to have happen.

The nature of Being is such that real denial is impossible; for there is but One Mind in the Universe, and It is always "yea and amen."

We are constantly affirming our way through life; and since affirmation is the only mental action possible, it behooves us to find the greatest affirmation and use it.

The Supreme Affirmation is, "I AM"; and, as such, It was given to Moses. This affirmation is constantly with us, and every time we speak we use it in some form. We must be careful to use it only as an upbuilding force.

CHRIST AND ANTICHRIST

The Spirit of Christ is the spirit of one who understands the Law and who uses It for constructive purposes only.

The spirit of Antichrist is the spirit of one who, understanding the Law, uses It for destructive purposes.

The Law, of Itself, is neither good nor bad, but is a Neutral Force, obeying all, and may be used for any purpose. But those truly instructed in the Law will never attempt to use It destructively; for they will understand that, by so doing, they would subject themselves to the very power which they have set in motion.

There is a power surrounding us which can be used either way, that is, constructively or destructively; but one instructed in the Truth will use this power only for the good of all. A most solemn warning is given to anyone who would be so rash as to misuse his power.

If the thought is kept close to Good, to Love and to the Spirit, and if there is never any desire to do other than that which is constructive, there is no danger.

The Law is there to use and It is a Law of Liberty to all who constructively contact It. Anything which makes for a greater expression of life, either for the individual or for the race, and which has no element of destruction in it, is good.

We should not hesitate to use the Law for the benefit of our personal affairs or those of our friends or for any who ask our help; but we should be very careful to use It constructively.

EVOLUTION

All emerge from that One Whose Being is ever present and Whose Life, robed in numberless forms, is manifest throughout all Creation.

Creation is the logical result of the outpush of Life into self-expression. It is the coming forth of Spirit into manifestation, the externalization of an internal idea, through the objectification of a subjective image.

The One encompasses and flows through the All, spilling Itself into numberless forms and shapes. These forms and shapes, propelled by a Divine Urge which brings them into being, seek still further expression because of the dynamic power with which they are equipped.

This is the real meaning of evolution; for evolution is the result of intelligence and not its cause.

Each evolving thing has, within itself, an impulse implanted by the Divine; and since the Divine is Limitless and Perfect, It must and will, ultimately, bring all Creation to a state of perfect manifestation.

That which, to the human eye, appears as imperfect, is imperfect only because the human eye sees imperfectly or in part; i.e., the human does not see the real idea back of the external image.

There is a philosophy which states that there is a "Becoming God," and which attempts to prove this assertion through evolution; but this philosophy is inconsistent with the ultimate nature of Reality; for, if ultimate Reality were in a state of "becoming," from what source would It gather Its impulse to become, and from whence would It draw Its power to express Itself?

A "becoming" or evolving God, or First Cause, is not consistent with true philosophy; while, on the other hand, an unfolding God, or First Cause, is consistent with Reality.

It is one thing to say that God is unfolding through His Idea of Himself but quite another thing to say that He is gradually becoming conscious of Himself. One is true while the other is false.

A "becoming" God implies a state of imperfection, or a state of being which does not recognize its perfection, at the very root of all being. An unfolding God implies a forever-outpouring Spirit and a forever-manifesting Deity, or First Cause.

The unfoldment of this First Cause is what we call evolution. Since this unfoldment is not yet complete, i.e., since the idea is still in an unfolding state, it appears as though we lived in an imperfect universe.

To a few, who have been able to see behind the veil of matter, the perfect idea has been apparent; and these few have given to the world its greatest code of law, morals and ethics. These few have been the great mystics of the race, and to them the world owes a debt which can be paid only to the degree that the world comes to understand their teachings.

Evolution is the time and the process through which an idea unfolds to a higher state of manifestation; and since ideas are Divine Realities, evolution will forever go on.

PART IV

DAILY MEDITATIONS FOR SELF-HELP
AND HEALING

In these short meditations I have tried to set forth some ideas which my experiences in mental healing have given me. I have found that a few brief statements, mentally affirmed, followed by a silent meditation, have been most effective in the healing work.

Most of the meditations have been written in the first person in order that those using them may be able to do so just as they are written.

It is not claimed that there is any occult power in these words, but that words similar to these are effective in inducing a greater realization of life. They contain thoughts which I have found to be most helpful.

Try them, my good reader, and see if they will not bring to life a deeper meaning and a greater joy. Whatever brings to the mentality a greater realization of life has, within itself, a healing power. I believe that these meditations will help all who take the time to use them.

First, decide which meditation you wish to use; then become quiet and composed. The body should be relaxed but the mentality should be active. Then, carefully read the meditation several times, phrase by phrase, endeavoring to realize the meaning of the words and trying to enter into the atmosphere of the thought. After having done this, meditate upon the words, following that meditation until you feel a sense of realization.

BODILY PERFECTION

COME, AND LET ME HEAL YOU

Come to me and I will heal you

The inner power of Life within me is God, and it can heal anything.

I will to heal and help all who come to me.

I know that the realization of Life and Love within me heals all who come into Its presence.

I love the thought that I silently bless all who enter my atmosphere.

It is not I, but The Father Who dwelleth in me; He doeth the works.

I heal all who come near me.

HE IS MIGHTY WITHIN ME TO HEAL

God within me is mighty to heal.

He healeth me of all my diseases and cures me of all.

God within is now healing me of all my infirmities, sickness and pain and is bringing comfort to my soul.

God is my life; I cannot be sick.

I hear the voice of Truth telling me to arise and walk, for I am healed. I am healed.

I DO NOT INHERIT DISEASE

There is no inherited tendency to disease, nor ill health.

I am born of Pure Spirit and am free from the belief in material existence.

False ideas cannot be transmitted from one to another, and I am free from all race-suggestion.

My Life is from Above, and I remember that I was always Perfect and Complete.

An Inner Light shines forth and frees me from the bonds of all false belief.

I came from the Spirit.

NO CONGESTION

There is no congestion nor stoppage of action. Life, flowing through me, is Perfect and Clear;

It cannot be stopped, retarded nor hindered.

I feel the One Life flowing through me now.

It eliminates all impure secretions and washes me clean from all suggestion of false deposits in the flesh.

I am Clean, Pure and Perfect, and my Word eliminates all else.

There is no congestion.

NO FALSE GROWTH

"Every plant which my Heavenly Father hath not planted, shall be rooted up."

There is no false growth and nothing for one to feed on. I am free from all thought of, or belief in, anything false or fearsome.

I cast out all fear and with it all manifestation of Fear.

A false idea is neither person, place nor thing, and has no one to believe in it nor experience it.

I am now One with The Perfect Life of Complete Wholeness.

My Word casts out all fear.

NO WEARINESS

There is no weariness.

*Mind and Spirit do not become tired nor weary, and I am
Mind and Spirit. The flesh cannot become weary,
since it has no mind of its own.*

I am free from all illusions of weariness.

*My whole being responds to the thought of Life. I am alive
with the Great Vitality of the Spirit.*

I am alive with spirit.

PERFECT HEARING

My hearing is perfect.

It is God in me hearing His own voice.

*I hear That Voice, and no belief in inaction can hinder that
hearing.*

There are no impaired organs.

*Every idea of the body is now complete and perfect and
functions according to the Divine Law.*

I open my ears to hear.

I am receptive to Truth and can understand it. Open my
ears that I may hear.

PERFECT VISION

There is One Vision and One ability to see, One perfect seeing.

My eyes are open and I see and behold one Perfect Life.

No suggestion of imperfect vision can enter my thought.

*I perceive that all people can see, and that the One, looking
through all, sees and cannot be limited in vision.*

*I am one with that complete ability to see, to know and
understand the Truth.*

I do open my eyes and do see.

*Nothing in me can hinder this Word from operating through
me and manifesting through my eyes.*

Open my eyes that I may see.

THE ALL-SEEING EYE

*The Eye of the Spirit cannot be dimmed, neither can it be
    impaired in Its ability to see.*

*My eyes are the Vision of my Indwelling Lord; they are the
    Windows of my Inner Spirit and are always open to
    the Vision of Truth.*

*I see with the Vision of the Spirit, and that ability cannot be
    weakened nor lost; it is forever effective.*

*My word which I now speak is the Law of Perfect Sight and
    my eyes are open and I see.*

Spirit sees through me.

THE HEALING OF THE FLESH

My flesh is the Manifestation of the Spirit in my body.

It is kept perfect through the Law of God.

"In my flesh shall I see God."

The mantle of flesh is perfect and complete here and now.

*It is one with the Body of God, and cannot be sick, nor
    suffer.*

My flesh is perfect.

THERE IS NO PAIN

There is no pain nor inflammation.

All fear is swept away in the realization of Truth.

I am free from every belief in pain.

*The Spirit cannot pain, and I am Pure Spirit and cannot be
    hurt nor harmed.*

I am free from all pain.

COMPLETENESS
HAPPINESS AND COMPLETION

I am happy and complete today and forever.
Within me is that which is Perfect and Complete.
It is The Spirit of all Life, Truth, and Action.
I am happy in the sure knowledge of the Inner Light.
I cannot be sad nor sorry, but must radiate Joy and Life, For
        Life is within me now.
I am happy and complete.

HERE AND NOW

Perfection is already accomplished.
I do not have to wait for the Perfect Life.
I am that Perfect Life here and now.
Today I express the Limitless Life of the All Good.
Today I manifest my Completion in every part of me. Today
        I am saved.
Here and now I am healed.

MAJESTIC CALM

The Inner Mind is still.
The Soul reflects the Most High.
The Spirit of man is God.
In the great calm of the All Good,
I rest in peace and security.
My life is now reflecting the Perfect Whole. I am Peace; I
        am Calm.
I am security and complete satisfaction.
I am One with God.
I am filled with peace.

NO LOSS

There is no loss.
Nothing can be lost, misplaced nor forgotten.

There was never any loss nor confusion.

Creation is Perfect and Complete, and within the One are all things, and are all known to the One.

I am now in complete harmony with the Whole and I cannot lose nor misplace anything.

I am constantly finding more and more Good.

I know that there is no loss.

OH, FOR A TONGUE TO EXPRESS

Oh, for a tongue to express the Wonders which the Thought reveals!

Oh, for some Word to comprehend the boundless idea!

Would that some Voice were sweet enough to sound the harmony of Life.

But Within, in that vast realm of thought where the Soul meets God, the Spirit knows.

I will listen for that Voice and It will tell me of Life, of Love and Unity.

Speak to me, Spirit.

O SOUL OF MINE, LOOK OUT AND SEE

O Soul of mine, look out and see; look up and know Thy freedom.

Be not cast down nor dismayed; be uplifted within me and exult, for Thy Salvation has come.

Behold the wonders of the Great Whole and the marvels of the Universe.

Look out and see Thy good. It is not afar off, but is at hand.

Prepare Thyself to accept and believe; to know and live.

Let Life enter and live through Thee, Soul of mine, and rejoice that Thou hast vision so fair and so complete.

Rejoice that the Perfect Whole is so completely reflected through Thee.

My light has come.

SEEING THE PERFECT

*My eyes behold the complete and perfect in all Creation, "In
all, over all and through all."*

*I see the perfect; there is nothing else to see, and no sugges-
tion of otherness can enter my thought.*

*I know only the perfect and the complete. I am perfect and
whole, now.*

I see the Good.

THE CIRCLE IS COMPLETE

The Circle of Love is complete.

*It comprehends all, includes all, and binds all together with
cords of Everlasting Unity.*

*I cannot depart from Its Presence nor wander from Its
care.*

My Love is complete within me.

The Love of God binds me to Itself, and will not let me go.

*I shall make a home for you, O my wonderful Love, and we
shall journey through life hand in hand.*

*I shall sit in your Presence and learn the wondrous things
You will tell me; For You are God.*

Love sits within me.

THE THINGS THAT ARE

The things that are, were and evermore shall be.

Time, Chance and change begone from my thought!

*The Changeless is here to stay, and the Timeless cannot
cease from Being.*

*The things that are shall remain, though heaven and earth
should pass away.*

*I rest secure and safe within the Life of Endless Perfection
and Completion. My whole Being responds to the Realization of the Complete Whole.*

I am that which Is.

DIVINE COMPANIONSHIP
A SONG OF HOPE

My Life is in Thee, O Inner Presence.
I look upon Thee and hope springs forth into realization.
O Hope within me, undying evidence of Good,
Thou dost completely hold me in Thy loving embrace,
And from this fond caress assurance shall be born, and con-
  fidence and love.
My hope is in Thee.

BE STILL AND KNOW

"Be still and know that I am God."
I am still in Thy Presence.
I am quiet and peaceful, for I put my trust in Thee.
A great stillness steals over me and a great calm quiets my
  whole being, as I realize Thy Presence.
The heart knows of Thee, O Most High within.
It is still in Thy Presence, and it puts its whole confidence
  in Thee alone.
In Thy Presence I am still.

CAST ASIDE ALL DOUBT

Cast aside all doubt, O Soul of mine, and be unafraid, for
  Thy power is from On High.
He Who sitteth in the heavens shall be Thy champion;
Thou need not fear; Come forth, O Spirit, from within and
  express Thyself through me and let not my doubts
  hinder Thy approach.
My faith shall go forth to meet Thee, and my confidence
  shall embrace Thee.
My waiting thought shall bid Thee welcome to my house of
  Love, And Joy shall accompany us through the ages
  yet to come.
I lay aside all fear and doubt.

DIVINE COMPANIONSHIP

I have an Inner Friend who walks and talks with me daily.
He is not afar off, but is within me, a constant companion.
        I shall never become lonely, for my Friend is always
        near. I have but to speak and He answers.
Before ever my lips spoke He told me of His love.
O my kind Friend, how dear to me is Thy presence.
The Spirit within me is my Friend.

HIS EYE IS ON THE SPARROW

"His eye is on the sparrow and I know He watches me."
This is a blessed thought, for it means that we cannot wan-
        der from His Presence, nor depart from His care.
Always He will watch over us and comfort us.
Forever we shall sit in His house and ceaselessly He will
        care for us.
The All-Seeing Eye cannot overlook anyone, and all, all
        shall be kept in His care.
All are kept in His care.

HOPE CANNOT DIE

Hope cannot die. Eternal Hope is forever warm and fresh
        within me; the deathless Hope built upon the rock of
        sure knowledge.
O Hope Sublime, O Life Supreme, behold I come to Thee as
        a tired child, and Thou dost rekindle within me the
        fires of Faith.
Strong, swift and sure, Faith springs forth into action and
        my entire Being rises to meet the Dawn.
Hope, Faith and Love are in me.

I AM NOT ALONE

I am not alone, for a Presence goes with me and daily ac-
companies me on my travels.

Always I shall find this Divine Companion with me.
He will not desert nor allow me to go alone.
He will always be with me and near me, and will always
*   provide for every want.*
My life is hid with Christ in God.

I WENT TO THE MOUNTAIN

I have discovered a Secret Place within, where the thought
*   goes into a mountain high above the din of the world.*
I have found in this mountain a Place of Peace and rest,
A Place of joy and comfort to the heart.
I have found that the Secret Place of God is within my own
*   Soul.* I will listen for Thy Voice.

THE JOY OF THE SOUL

My Soul within me rejoices at the realization of Life.
I am made glad as I behold my inner Light;
I cannot be sad nor depressed, for the All Good has claimed
*   me as Its own.*
O Soul within me, rejoice and become glad, for Thy Light
*   has come and Thy Day of Salvation is at hand.*
Be still within me and behold Him Who sitteth On High.
Reflect to me Thy revelation and flood me with Thy marvel-
*   ous Light.* I rejoice in my Life within me.

FREEDOM

FREEDOM

Yes, I know that the Truth has freed me from the bonds of fear.

I am not afraid. I adore thee, Most High within me; I trust in Thee and abide in that hope that knows no fear; I am Free Spirit and cannot be bound.

The One Life flowing through me is Perfect and Complete. I am not apart from It. I am One with It in Marvelous Unity and Freedom; One with the Complete Whole.

I was born free and must always remain free. The realization of freedom permeates my whole being and sinks into the innermost parts of me.

I love it, adore it, I accept it.

I am free.

FREEDOM FROM SIN

I am free from belief in sin; there is neither sin nor sinner.

There is no judgment against anyone.

God does not condemn, and man cannot.

All fear of sin is removed from me; all theological belief in punishment is gone from me.

I do not allow myself to receive such suggestions, for I per-
*   ceive that they are lies.*
I am free from all lies and from all liars.
I live by the One Power, and no thought can enter to disturb
*   me.* There is neither sin nor sinner.

FREE FROM SENSITIVENESS

My feelings cannot be hurt.
No one wishes to harm me, and there is nothing in me that
*   can believe in any separation from the All Good.*
I perceive that I am free from all people, and I cannot be
*   harmed nor mistreated.*
I have such a sense of unity with all that the circle is com-
*   plete and perfect.*
I love my friends and they love me, and that love is in, and
*   of, God, and cannot be marred nor hindered.*
I am filled with joy and love, forever.

I KEEP THE PROMISE

I shall keep the promise that I have made to myself.
I shall never again tell myself that I am poor, sick, weak,
*   nor unhappy.*
I shall not lie to myself any more, but shall daily speak the
*   truth to my inner Soul, telling It that It is wonderful*
*   and marvelous; that It is One with the Great Cause*
*   of all Life, Truth, Power and Action.*
I shall whisper these things into my Soul until it breaks
*   forth into songs of joy with the realization of Its Lim-*
*   itless possibilities.*
I shall assure my Soul.

LOVE GLEAMS THROUGH THE MIST

Through the mist of human fear love gleams and points the
*   way to freedom.*

I now decree and declare that I am free from all sense of
    bondage.
I am made perfect and whole through knowledge of the Real
    Life within me.
No illusions can enter my thought.
I know that there is One Power, and I know that this Power
    now protects me from all harm.
As Perfect Love casts out all fear, so my fear flees before the
    knowledge of Truth.
I am not afraid.

NO BONDAGE

There is no bondage nor limitation.
Every part of me moves in perfect harmony and freedom.
I cannot be tied, bound nor made inactive, for
I am Free Spirit, and the Power of my Life is from on High.
    There is no inaction nor false action,
And I am now completely Free.
I am free.

NO CONDEMNATION

There is no condemnation in me nor operating through me.
I am free from the belief or thought of men.
I walk my own way, immune to all suggestion of condem-
    nation.
Only those thoughts can enter my mentality which I allow
    to enter.
I do not, and cannot, receive adverse thoughts.
Only those thoughts which are helpful and life-giving can
    find entrance to my house.
There is no condemnation.

NO FALSE HABIT

There are no vicious nor false habits.

Ever desire of my thought and heart is satisfied in the Truth.
I do not long for anything nor feel the lack of anything.
I am complete within myself; I am perfect within myself; I
     am happy and satisfied within myself.
I am One with All Life within me.
I am free.

NO HYPNOTISM NOR FALSE SUGGESTION

There is no hypnotism nor false suggestion.
I represent the One Mind which cannot act against Itself
     nor can It act against me.
I am immune to all suggestion and cannot receive false
     thoughts, nor harbor them.
I am surrounded with a circle of Love and Protection.
Asleep or awake, I am free from false thoughts.
I see the nothingness of all belief in, or fear of, otherness;
     and I know that The One and Only Mind, alone, can
     act.
Only the Good can enter.

NO MISTAKES

There are no mistakes; none have ever been made and none
     ever will be made.
Nothing ever happened in the past to hinder or hurt.
There is no past, and I know, and can see, that there is no
     belief in any past to rise against me.
I live in the Now, free from any yesterdays or tomorrows.
     Now, I am Happy, Free and Complete.
My Word erases any and all beliefs in mistakes and sets me
     free. I Am Free!
I am free from any beliefs in the past.

THERE ARE NO RESPONSIBILITIES

The Spirit has no responsibilities.

Its work is already accomplished and Its purposes are already fulfilled. The Spirit knows no want nor fear.

It is complete within Itself and lives by virtue of Its own Being.

I am Spirit and cannot take on the fears of the world.

My work is accomplished and my ways are made straight before me.

The pathway of Life is an endless road of Eternal Satisfaction and Perfect Joy.

My Life within me is Complete and Perfect, and has no cares nor burdens. It is Free Spirit and cannot be bound.

I rejoice in that Freedom.

I rejoice in freedom

THE TIME HAS COME

The time has come, the hour has struck.

The power from within has come forth and is expressing through my word.

I do not have to wait; today is the time.

Today I enter into all Truth; today I am completely saved and healed and made happy.

Today I enter into my inheritance.

Today the Truth has made me free.

WITHIN THY LAW IS FREEDOM

Within Thy Law is freedom to all who will believe.

I believe in Thy Law and I love Thy precepts.

I know that Thy Law is perfect and It is a delight to my Soul, for It is illumined with Thy Words of Power.

Thy Law is complete freedom to me, and to all for whom it shall be spoken.

I speak the Word of freedom to all, and all shall receive it.

I am free in Thy Law.

HARMONY OF LIFE
BEAUTY

I behold the Beautiful and the Pleasant.
My eyes see only that which is beautiful to look upon.
I will not see anything else nor believe in anything else.
I know that beauty has entered into my life, and will always
remain there. I see only the beautiful.

FRIENDSHIP OF THE SPIRIT AND OF MAN

The Friendship of the Spirit and of man is mine now and
forever.
Even now I see the countless numbers of friends coming
and going around me.
I enter into this friendship and this companionship with
gladness and rejoicing.
I receive my friends.

HE WILLS ME TO BE

It was God Himself who willed that I should be.
I have no cares nor burdens to bear.
I am reminded of the great command:
"Come unto Me all ye who labor and are heavy laden and I
will give you rest."
I do come into the Light and I do know that all cares And
responsibilities fall from me as I let the Light of Wis-
dom direct my ways.
He wills me to be; therefore, I am.

I SERVE

I serve the world.
I wait upon the Lord within all men;
I call forth glory from On High through the minds of
all people. I obey the will of Him Who inhabits
Eternity.

I do the works of Him Who dwelleth among the heavens.
My Lord within commands and I obey.
I do good to all people.

I SHALL NOT DOUBT NOR FEAR

I shall not doubt nor fear, for my salvation is from On High,
and the day of its appearing is now at hand.
I shall not doubt nor fear, for my whole being responds to
the realization of Life within and around me.
I shall not fear, for the Hosts of Heaven are waiting upon me
and the Law of the Universe is my Salvation.
I shall not fear.

I WAS TOLD TO LIVE

I was told to live and to love, to laugh and to be glad.
I was told to be still and know of the One Almighty Power,
in and through all.
I was told to let that Power work through and in me. I be-
lieved that voice and I received my Good.
I am healed—The joy of Life.

LAW

I meditate upon the Law of God.
It is a Perfect Law and is now working for me and in and
through me. "The Law of the Lord is perfect."
I speak into that Law and it is done unto me.
Thy Law is in my heart.

LOVE

The Love of the All Good is within me and through me.
That Love goes out to meet all who come into my atmo-
sphere. It radiates to all and flowing through all.
My Love within me is Perfect.
Thy Love within me is Perfect.

LOVE DISSOLVES ALL FEAR

Greater than fear is Love.

Love dissolves all fear, casts out all doubt and sets the captive free.

Love, like the River of Life, flows through me and refreshes me with its eternal blessings.

Love cannot be afraid; it is fearless and strong, and is mighty in its works.

It can accomplish all things through the Inner Light of that faith in the All Good,

Which fills my very Being with a Powerful Presence.

Love casts out all fear.

MY AFFAIRS

My affairs are in the hands of Him

Who guides the planets in their course,

And Who causes the Sun to shine.

Divine Understanding attends me on the Way,

And I shall not be hindered in my work.

My affairs are controlled by Perfect Intelligence,

And cannot be hindered from expression.

I know that all that I do is done from the One Motive: To express Life; and Life will be expressed

In and through me. I cannot hinder it.

I am controlled by Intelligence.

MY BUSINESS

My business is directed by Divine Intelligence.

The All-Knowing Mind knows what to do and how to do it. I do not hinder, but let It operate in my affairs.

It prospers and directs me and controls my life.

My affairs are managed by Love, and directed by Wisdom, and they cannot fail to prosper and expand. My affairs are in His hands.

MY PROFESSION

*My profession is the Activity of the Great Mind working
through me.*

*As such It is a Divine Activity and is constantly in touch
with Reality. I am inspired in my work from On High
with lofty ideals,*

And my thought is illumined by the All-Knowing One.

I am inspired.

NO DELAYS

There are no delays in the Divine Plan for me.

*Nothing can hinder the operation of this Law unto my Life
and Action.*

Obstructions are removed from my path, and

*I now enter into the realization and manifestation of com-
plete fulfillment of right desires.*

*I do not have to wait, for the Law waits upon me at every
turn in Life's road.*

Now it is done unto me.

NO MISREPRESENTATIONS

No one can lie to me; none can mislead me.

I am free from the belief in all lies and untruths;

*I know and speak only the Truth, and the Truth alone can
be spoken to me. I know the false and can understand
the Real.*

I cannot be fooled nor misled; I am guided by Truth alone.

There is no lie nor liar.

NO OBSTRUCTIONS

*There are no obstructions to Life's Path; no hinderance to
man's endeavors.*

*Let my Word be the Law of elimination to all thought of
hinderance or delay.*

And let the thing that I speak come forth into manifestation at once. I behold it and see that it is even now done, complete and perfect.

I receive now.

NO OVER-ACTION NOR INACTION

There is no over-action nor inaction in Divine Law, for everything moves according to perfect harmony.

Every idea of my body functions in accordance with this Law of Perfect Life.

I now perceive that the action within me is perfect, complete and harmonious.

Peace be unto every part of me, and perfect Life to every member of my body.

I act in accordance with Divine Law.

I am Perfect Life throughout my whole Being.

ONE WITH PERFECT ACTION

I am One with Perfect Action. Everything that I do, say or think is quickened into action through this right understanding and this correct knowing.

The harmonious action of the Great Whole operates through me now and at all times.

I am carried along by this Right Action and am compelled to do the right thing at the right time.

There is nothing in me that can hinder this action from flowing through me.

The action of God is the only action.

PEACE, POISE AND POWER

Peace, Poise and Power are within me, for they are the witnesses of the Inner Spirit of all Truth, Love and Wisdom.

*I am at peace within me, and all about responds to that
    Great Calm of the Inner Soul which knows its rightful
    place in the All Good.*
*Power is born from within me and passes into my experi-
    ence without effort or labor.*
*I rest in Security and Peace, for the Inner Light shines forth
    and illumines the way.*
I rest in Thee.

STILLNESS AND RECEPTIVITY

I am still and receptive to Life.
I let Life flow through me into all that I do, say or think.
*I shall let my Life be what it is, and shall not worry nor
    complain.*
*I am now entered into the Secret Place of the Soul where
    complete quiet reigns supreme and where God talks
    to me.*
I receive.

THANKSGIVING AND PRAISE

*I will give thanks to my Inner Life for all Its Marvelous
    Wonders, and for all Its Wonderful Works.*
*I will sing and be glad, for I know that I am hid with Truth
    in a Perfect Life.*
The fulness of Joy is mine.

THE DIVINE PROMISES ARE KEPT

The Divine Promises are all kept; not one is changed.
God has told me that my Life is Perfect;
*He will never desert or leave me to travel alone. I know that
    from this day on and forevermore*
I shall live under Divine Protection and Love.
I live under Divine Protection and Love.

THE INNER LIGHT

The Light of Heaven shines through me and illumines my
       Path.
The Light Eternal is my guide and my protection.
In that Light there is no darkness at all.
It is a Perfect Light shining from the altar of a perfect Love.
O Light and Love within me, Thou art welcome.
Light shines through me and illumines the Way.

THE NIGHT IS FILLED WITH PEACE

I wrap myself in the mantle of Love and fall asleep, filled
       with Peace.
Through the long night Peace remains with me, and at the
       breaking of the new day I shall still be filled with Life
       and Love.
I shall go forth into the new day confident and happy.
I rest in Thee.

THE SEAL OF APPROVAL

The Seal of Approval is upon me, and I am not condemned
       by the thought or act of man.
I will fear no evil, for I know that the Great Judge of all
       controls my every act.
Let every fear of man be removed from and let the Silence
       of my soul bear witness to the Truth.
God approves of me.

THE SECRET WAY

There is a Secret Way of the Soul which all may know.
It is the Way of Peace and Love.
This Secret Way leads into places of joy
And into the house of good.
It is the Way of the Spirit, and all may enter who will.
I tread the Secret Way of good, the Path of Peace, And I

enter into "The Secret Place of The Most High." The
Secret Place of The Most High is within me.

THE SHINING PATH

The Pathway of Life shines before me unto the Perfect
Day.
I walk the pathway of the Soul to the Gate of Good.
I enter into the fulfillment of my desires.
Nothing need be added and nothing can be taken from the
All Good which is forever expressing Itself in me.
Daily shall I receive Its great blessings and my Soul shall
rejoice forevermore.
I am now entered into my good.

THE THINGS I NEED COME TO ME

Whatever I need comes to me from the All Good.
Divine Intelligence working through me always knows just
what I need and always supplies it when I need it.
This Law is unfailing and sure, and cannot be broken.
I receive my Good daily as I go along the pathway of Life,
and I cannot be robbed of my birthright to freedom
and happiness.
I receive my Good.

THE WAY IS MADE CLEAR BEFORE ME

The Way is made clear before me; I do not falter nor fall.
The Way of the Spirit is my Way, and I am compelled to
walk in it.
My feet are kept on the Path of Perfect Life.
The Way is prepared before me, and that Way is a Path of
Peace, of Fulfillment and Joy.
The Way is bright with the light of Love and Kindness. The
Way I tread is a pleasant and a happy one.
I see the Way and I walk in It.

IMMINENT POWER
AS LOVE ENTERS, FEAR DEPARTS

As Love enters, fear vanishes.

I am so filled with Love that no fear can enter my thought.

*I am not afraid, for I know that a Perfect Intelligence guards
and governs my every act.*

Perfect Love casteth out all fear.

*I am unafraid and strong in my faith in Him Who keeps
me from all harm.* Perfect Love casteth out all
fear.

HE WILL KEEP THEE

*The Inner Spirit of man is God, and my Inner Spirit is the
Realization of my Life.*

*I know that my Inner Spirit will keep me from all harm,
and will not let destruction come near me.*

*I am unafraid in the midst of confusion, and unmoved in
the face of calamity.*

*I am confident in the presence of seeming danger, and fear-
less before any sense of trouble.*

He will keep me.

INFINITE LIFE WITHIN

*Infinite Life within me, which is God, guard Thou my feet
and keep Thou my way.*

Let me not stray from Thee, but compel me to do Thy will.

*I am guarded and governed by an Infinite Intelligence and
an Omnipotent Power.*

No mistakes can be made and none ever have been made.

*An unerring judgement operates through me and I am lead
by the Spirit of Truth into all Good and into all Peace
and Happiness.*

Infinite Life within me.

MY FEET SHALL NOT FALTER

My feet shall not falter, for they are kept upon the path of
     Life through the Power of the Eternal Spirit.
Guide Thou my feet; compel my way; direct my paths and
     keep me in Thy Presence.
My feet are guarded, and I am guided into the All Good.
He guides my feet.

NO HARM SHALL BEFALL THEE

No harm shall befall you, my friend, for a Divine Presence
     attends your way and guards you into The All Good.
Loving kindness awaits you at every turn of Life's road.
     Guidance is yours along the pathway of experience,
     And an Infallible Power protects you.
God, Himself, and no other is your Keeper.
I proclaim this for you.

POWER TO LIVE

I have the power to live the life of good.
My power is from On High; it cannot be taken from me. It
     will not leave me desolate.
Power flows through me and is in me, and
I can now feel and sense it.
The Power to live is in me and I cannot desert me. It is my
     power and is continually present.
I am the power to live.

THE CIRCLE OF LOVE

A circle of love is drawn around me and mine, and all.
No harm can enter that Sacred Circle, for it is the Love of
     God. It is a complete protection from all evil.
"I will fear no evil, for Thou art with me."
There is no evil and no harm.

I am free from all sense of fear.
Love surrounds and protects me.

THE CIRCLE OF PROTECTION

I draw around me a circle of love and protection.
No harm can enter nor find place within that charmed cir-
cle of life and love, for it represents God's Loving Care
and Eternal Watchfulness.
I will rest within me now, and I will speak comfort to my
Soul and tell It of all the wonders of its life, safe from
the din of strife and fear.
I am protected from On High.

THE POWER WITHIN BLESSES ALL

The Power within me is blessing all mankind, and is forever
healing all with whom I come in contact.
The Power within me is God, and It must bless and help
and heal all who come near It.
Silently the work goes on, and silently all are being helped
by this Inner Power which is operating through me.
I will give thanks that my Power within is silently blessing
and helping everyone to whom my thought reaches.
The Life within me blesses all mankind.

THE QUICK ANSWER

My answer comes quickly and surely back to me from On
High.
My answer will not fail me, for the Law of the Universe is
the Power through which it comes.
I shall not doubt nor fear, for the answer is swift and certain.
My answer comes.

INSPIRATION

A SONG OF JOY

*There is a Song upon my lips today; it sings of the glad
    heart and the happy ways of Life.*

*I will listen to my song, for it carols to me the glad tidings
    of Great Joy, of Love and Life.*

*It tells me of the Wondrous Journey of the Soul and the
    Boundless Life in which my life is hid.*

I am filled with joy.

BORN OF ETERNAL DAY

Child of All Good, you are born of Eternal Day.

There is no evening of the Soul, for it shall live forever.

*It is Deathless and Perfect, Complete and One with the
    Everlasting.*

*No thought of tomorrow can disturb the calm of him who
    knows that Life is one Eternal Day.*

*No fear can enter where Love reigns, and Reason keeps faith
    with Hope.*

The thoughts of the tomorrows and the yesterdays are

swallowed up in the great realization of the Perfect
Here and the Complete Now.

Today I completely accept my wholeness.

I ARISE AND GO FORTH

I arise and go forth into the Dawn of the New Day, filled
with faith and assurance in the All Good.

I arise, I arise, I sing with joy!

I proclaim the One Life: "In all and through all."

I arise, I arise, I shout with gladness that is within me. I
declare this day to be Complete, Perfect and Eternal.
I respond to Life.

INSPIRATION

Come, Thou Great and Infinite Mind and inspire me to do
great deeds.

Acquaint me with Thy knowledge and in Thy wisdom make
me wise. I would be taught of Thee, Inner Light, and
inspired by Thy presence.

I will listen for Thy Voice and it will tell me of great things
to be done. I will walk in Thy Paths and they will lead
me into All Good.

I will be inspired from On High.

O Wonderful Presence, flooding me, filling me with Thy
Light, Thou dost inspire me!

I feel the inspiration of Spirit.

THE DAWN HAS COME

Out of the darkness of the long night the Dawn has come.

I rise to meet the new day, filled with confidence and strength.

I arise and go forth into the dawn, inspired and refreshed by
the Living Spirit within me.

O Day, you shall never die; the sun shall never set upon
your perfect glory.

*For the Lamp of the Soul has been re-kindled with the oil
     of Faith,*
*And Love has cleansed the windows of Life with the spirit
     of gladness.*
*They shall nevermore grow dim with fear, for Perfect Love
     casteth out all fear.*
I am renewed in strength through knowing Good.
My light has come.

I AM COMPLETE IN THEE

*Almighty God, Everlasting Good, Eternal Spirit, Maker of
     all things and Keeper of my Life, Thou art All.*
*Infinite Presence within, in Whom all live; Joy Supreme,
     flooding all with gladness, I adore Thee.*
Eternal Peace, undisturbed and quiet, I feel Thy calm.
*O Thou Who dost inhabit Eternity and dost dwell within
     all Creation, Who Dost live through all things and in
     all people, hear Thou my prayer.*
*I would enter Thy gates with joy and live at peace in Thy
     House.*
I would find a resting place in Thee, and in Thy presence live.
*Make me to do Thy will and from Thy wisdom teach me
     the ways of Truth.*
*Compel me to follow Thee and let me not pursue the paths
     of my own counsel.*
*O Eternal and Blessed Presence, illumine my mind and
     command my will that my Soul may be refreshed
     and that my live may be renewed.*
*As deep cries unto deep, so my thought cries unto Thee and
     Thou dost answer.*
*I am renewed and refreshed; my whole being responds to
     Thy love, and I am complete in Thee.*
*All my ways are guarded and guided, and I shall live with
     Thee eternally.*

O Lover of my Soul and Keeper of my Spirit, none can separate us, for we are One.

So shall Thy Wisdom guide me, Thy Presence dwell within me, Thy Love keep me and Thy life envelop me now and forevermore.

I rest in Thee.

PRESENCE OF THE ALL GOOD

A MARVELOUS SENSE

A marvelous sense steals over him who waits on Good, and in patience bides his time.

A feeling of some Unseen Presence silently creeps over the waiting thought, and the Voice of God speaks through the mist and says: "Be not afraid."

It is all for a purpose; and when you cannot trace, you must trust. This is not an illusion, but a reality; for time proves all things, and he who will wait for his time to come shall be rewarded; and Good shall come to him, for God Himself shall be his Companion and Champion.

I wait on Thee.

COMPLETE CONFIDENCE

My confidence in The All Good is complete.
My faith in the Power of Spirit is supreme.
I have no doubts nor uncertainties.
I know that my Good is at hand, and
I realize that no fear can hinder

That Good from making Its appearance in my life and af-
*   fairs.*
I know that my Life and Good are complete.
Evil cannot touch nor hinder my work.
I rest in security, for
THE ONE MIND IS MY COMPLETE REFUGE AND
*   STRENGTH.*
I am serene and confident.

DRAWING THE GOOD

I draw my Good to me as I travel along the Way of Life, and
*   nothing can keep It from me.*
My Good will always follow me.
I accept the Good and rejoice that it is with me.
I accept the Good.

I FEAR NO EVIL

"I will fear no evil, for Thou art with me."
I will not be afraid, for the All Good is constantly with me
*   and is always near at hand to guide and comfort.*
There is no evil in the Truth, and no power of darkness to
*   hinder the Light from shining.*
I will not be afraid, for there is One within Who protects
*   and keeps me from all harm.*
I fear no evil.

I HAVE KNOWN, ALWAYS

I have always known the Truth, and no fear can keep my
*   inner knowledge from me.*
My wisdom from within comes forth into daily expression.
Knowledge from On High is given to me, and I shall always
*   be led of the Spirit.*
I know the Truth.

I MEET MY GOOD

*Today I meet my Good; it knows me and will not let me
    depart from it.*

My Good is at hand, and I cannot be robbed of it.

Good is forever expressing itself to me and mine.

*I can even now see and hear and feel the All Good in and
    around me. It presses itself against me, and fills me
    with a great surge of Life.*

My Good is at hand.

MY ATMOSPHERE

*My atmosphere is attracting the Good; it is constantly on
    the alert to see and know the Good, and to bring it
    into my experience.*

*There is that within me that calls forth abundance and
    happiness from Life. I am surrounded with an atmo-
    sphere of Peace, Poise and Power.*

*All who come in contact with that great Calm of my
    Life are made strong and confident, are healed and
    blessed.*

*"Bless the Lord, O my Soul, and all that is within me, bless
    His Holy Name."*

I am hid with Christ in God.

MY GOOD IS COMPLETE

*My Good is complete; it is finished; it is now here and is
    conscious of me and of mine.*

*I do not have to wait for my Good; it is at hand and ever
    ready to spring forth and express itself to me.*

*I accept my Good and gladly acknowledge it to be my daily
    companion. My Good is mine now, and I can see it
    and feel it and know it.*

Today I claim my Good.

MY OWN SHALL COME TO ME

From far and near my own shall come to me. Even now it
is coming to me, and I receive it.

My own is now manifesting itself to me, and I see and know
its presence. My own shall know and respond to me.

The drawing power of that inner Spirit within me is now
attracting and drawing into my experience all that
is good and perfect. There is nothing within me to
hinder nor to delay it.

My own cannot be kept from me, neither can I keep my
good away from me. I receive it now.

I now receive my good.

MY OWN SHALL FIND ME

My Own shall find me; no matter where I go, It will follow
and claim me.

I cannot hide myself from my Own.

My Own shall come to me, even though I deny it; for there
is nothing in me that can hinder it from entering and
taking possession of my Soul.

My own is now expressed.

MY SOUL REFLECTS THY LIFE

My Soul reflects Thy Life and rejoices in the happy
though[t]* that it looks on Thee alone.

O Soul of mine, look out and up and on; and reflect to me
the wondrous Life of the All Good.

Look thou upon The One, and be saved. Behold thou His
Face forevermore.

My Soul reflects Thy Life.

OUT OF THE DEPTHS OF LIFE

Out of the deep places of life my Soul has cried unto Thee
and Thou hast made answer.

Out of the turmoil and struggle and strife I have come unto Thee, and Thou hast heard me and understood.

I shall nevermore be sad, for I have found what the Soul craves—the Inner Life and Love of the All Good.

Thou hast heard.

SORROW FLEES FROM ME

As the Great Joy of Life comes into my Soul, flooding me with its wondrous light, all sorrow and sadness flee from me.

I shall not grieve, for nothing is lost nor gone from me.

My own cannot be kept from me.

My own knows me and will follow me wherever I go.

I am filled with the Joy of living and the Great Peace that comes to all who believe.

I am made glad forevermore.

SUBSTANCE AND SUPPLY

The Substance of the Spirit is my Daily Supply.

I cannot be without my Good.

I can see that the constant stream of Life flowing to me brings into my experience all that makes Life happy and worthwhile.

I rest in security, knowing that Infinite Good is within and is expressing through me.

I receive my good.

THE EVER AND THE ALL

Life always was and evermore shall be, "World without end."

All the Power there is, is mine now.

All the Life, Truth and Love of the Universe is now and forever Flowing through my Soul.

The All Good cannot change.

I shall always have access to my Eternal God within me. I
am Changeless Life within me.

THE HOUSE OF LOVE

I dwell in the house of Love;
"A house not made with hands, eternal in the heavens." My
        dwelling place is filled with peace and eternal calm.
        Love attends me in my home of the Soul, and
Joy awaits upon me in the "Secret Place of the Most High."
        My house is built for me by the hand of Love, and
I shall never leave this Home of the Spirit, for it is always
        present. I shall abide in this home forevermore.
My house is a house of love.

SPIRIT OF GOD WITHIN

ARISE, MY SPIRIT

Arise, my Spirit, arise and shine.

Let Thy light illumine my path, and let Thy wisdom direct my way. Compel my will to do Thy bidding, and command my Soul to look to Thee. I will follow Thee, my Spirit, and will learn of Thee all that I need to know. I will sit in the Silence and listen and watch, and

I will see Thy light and hear Thy voice.

I will follow Thee and will not depart from Thee, for in Thee alone is Peace.

Arise and shine.

BIRTHLESS AND DEATHLESS

The Spirit within me is Birthless and deathless;

It was not born and It cannot die.

I have no fear of death, for I perceive that Death is an illusion and not the Truth.

I was born of the Spirit, and I live in the Spirit, And shall continue to live in and by the Spirit. The Spirit within me lives forever.

COMMAND MY SOUL

Spirit within me, command my Soul to do Thy bidding;
Compel me to follow the course of Truth and Wisdom. Con-
trol my inward thoughts and my outward ways,
And make me to understand Thy Laws.
Command my Soul to turn to Thee for guidance and light;
To turn to Thee for wisdom and knowledge.
Let the paths of my Life be made straight and sure; Let
the Journey of my Soul find its completion in Thee.
Command my Soul to do Thy bidding.

DESPAIR GIVES WAY TO JOY

Despair gives way to joy at the thought of Thee, Indwelling
Good.
I cannot be sad when I think of Thee.
My sorrow is turned to gladness and my shame to rejoicing.
My tears are wiped away and the sunlight of the Spirit
shines through the clouds of depression and lights the
way to Heaven.
Thy Joy has made me glad.

FREE SPIRIT WITHIN ME

Free Spirit within me, Unbound and Perfect, teach me Thy
ways and make known to me Thy Limitless Completion.
O Spirit of Life, control my every action and thought.
Compel me to follow Thy light that I too may be free and
complete.
I will follow Thy footsteps and learn of Thee all the won-
drous secrets of Life.
I will follow Thy light into the Perfect Day.
Free spirit within me.

FULLNESS OF LIGHT

The Light of Life is full within me and around me.

It shines forth into the Perfect Day.
O Light within, lighting my path to peace,
I adore and love You and I let You shine.
Go forth and bless all who come to You, Light within.
My Light radiates to all and through all.
My light has come.

HE WHO INHABITS ETERNITY

He Who inhabits Eternity keeps watch over me and mine.
"He Who neither slumbers nor sleeps" forever keeps watch
     over all.
I will rest in the assurance of Love and Protection.
O Thou Great Overshadowing Presence,
I am conscious of Thy care; I am aware of Thy loving kind-
     ness. I rest in Thee.
Be still and know.

I LISTEN

I will listen for Thy voice, Inner Presence.
It will guide me and acquaint me with all knowledge.
Thy voice is sweet and tender; it is always kind and gentle. O
     Lover of my Soul, how I adore Thee! How I love Thee!
     How I love Thy voice; it thrills me with gladness and
     joy. It fills me with peace and calm, and it soothes me.
It quiets me and gives me wonderful rest.
I listen, O Divine Speaker, I listen to Thee alone.
I listen for Thy voice.

JOY HAS COME TO LIVE WITH ME

Joy has come to live with me. How can I be sad?
I do so love Thy presence, which is Joy within me.
It makes me glad, and I sing, for I am so filled with Thy
     Spirit that I cannot be depressed nor unhappy.
I am filled with the joy of the Spirit, and I overflow with the
     gladness of life.

Thou art a Happy Companion to travel with me through
Life, wonderful Joy, Thou art so radiant and beaming.
It is impossible to be sad in Thy presence.
I shall give myself to Thee and remain with Thee, for Thou
art complete and satisfying.
I find fulfillment in Thee and joy forevermore.
I am filled with the Spirit of Joy.

KNOWLEDGE AND WISDOM

All Wisdom and Knowledge is from within.
And my God, Who is All-Knowing, is also within.
I am guided and guarded along Life's road into the All
Good. My Mind is instructed from On High,
And my Wisdom cometh from afar.
The Spirit within me is All Wisdom.

MY THOUGHT IS IN THEE

My thought is in Thee, Inner Light.
My words are from Thee, Inner Wisdom.
My understanding is of Thee, Inner God.
I cannot be hid from Thee, my Inspiration and my Life. My
thought is in Thee.

O LOVE DIVINE

O Love Divine within me, I am overpowered by Thy Pres-
ence.
I am speechless, for words cannot utter the things that Thou
hast revealed to me.
Why dost Thou love me so, and why clasp me so close to
Thy Eternal Heart?
O Blessed Presence, I know, for Thou hast claimed me
as Thine own. I shall nevermore walk apart from
Thee.
The love of God is within me.

PEACE STEALS THROUGH THE SOUL

*Peace steals through the waiting Soul, and the comfort of
the Spirit comes into the stillness of the heart.*

*Peace, like an ocean of Infinite Life, reflects itself through me
and calms every turbulent feeling.*

*I am at peace and rest in the knowledge of the All Good
which is at hand.*

I rest in peace.

STAND FORTH AND SPEAK

Stand forth and speak, Spirit within me.

*Proclaim Thy presence, announce Thy course. Declare
through me Thy wondrous works and Let the children of men hear Thy voice. Behold, He maketh all
things new.*

*The Spirit within speaks words of Truth and Life to all. The
Spirit within me is God.*

I speak the Truth.

SUBTLE ESSENCE OF SPIRIT WITHIN ME

Subtle Essence of Spirit within me, flowing through me;

*Elixir of Life in my veins purifying me with Thy marvelous
Life, I let Thy Spirit cleanse me from all false thought
and ideas;*

*I let Thy Life flow through me in a complete and Perfect
Whole.* I feel the presence of Spirit within me.

THE CHRIST WITHIN

My Life is "hid with Christ in God";

*The Inner Man is the image and likeness of the Spirit of
God.*

*I let that Inner Man come forth into expression in my life;
He will guide my feet into all Truth and Wisdom.*

*The Christ within me is free from all worry, and cannot be
hindered by any opposing force.*

My Christ within me is now perfect.
My Christ is within me.

THE EVERLASTING ARMS

His Arms enfold me, His Strength upholds me,
His Presence fills me with Life and Joy.
I shall nevermore be sad nor depressed, for I know that I do
*   not walk Life's path alone.*
There is One Who goes with me and tells me all the things
*   that I should know.*
There is a Presence with me guiding me into the Perfect
*   Way.*
I rejoice in knowing that I am not alone.

THE MANTLE OF LOVE

Like a cloak His Love is wrapped around me. Like a warm
*   garment It shelters me from the storms of life.*
I feel and know that an Almighty Love envelops me in Its
*   close embrace.*
O Love Divine, My Love, how wonderful Thou art. I am
*   open to receive Thy great blessing.*
Love envelops me.

THE VOICE OF TRUTH

The Voice of Truth speaks to me and through me.
The Voice of Truth guides me and keeps me on the Path of
*   the Perfect Day.*
I will listen to the Inner Voice and It will tell me what to do
*   in the hour of need.*
I shall be told everything that I ought to know when the
*   time of need arrives, and I shall not be misled.*
The Voice of Truth cannot lie, but always speaks to me from
*   On High. Nothing enters but This Voice, for it is the*
*   Voice of God.*
God speaks to me.

THE WITNESS OF TRUTH

There is a Witness within me who knows the Truth and who
*   will not let me enter into falsehood.*

My Inner Guide keeps me on the Pathway of Life and
*   directs me at all times to that which is right and*
*   best.*

I shall never be without this witness of the Spirit, for I be-
*   lieve in It and accept It as the Great Companion of*
*   the Soul.*

The Spirit within me is perfect now.

THROUGH THE LONG NIGHT WATCHES

Through the long night watches Thou hast been with me.

In the dark places of human ignorance Thy hand hath
*   guided me,*

Thy light hath lighted the pathway of desolation to a land
*   of plenty.*

I have perceived Thee from afar, and my soul hath yearned
*   to Thee, O Thou Mighty One!*

The Spirit within me hath urged me on to the goal, and I
*   have not been misled.*

I have been guided and guarded through the long journey,
*   and Thy Presence hath been made known to me.*

I awake from the dream and reenter the house of my Lord
*   clothed with Peace and robed in colors of Light.*

The Spirit of Truth watches over me.

THY STRENGTH IS SUFFICIENT

O Spirit of man and God within me, Thy Power is great,
*   and Thy Knowledge goes beyond the range of human*
*   experience.*

Thy Wisdom excels that of all else, and beside Thee there is
*   none other. In Thy Strength do I daily walk and live;*

In Thy Presence do I always rest in peace and joy.

Spirit within me and without, Powerful Thou art, and
      Great; Wonderful is Thy Might, and Complete is Thy
      Understanding.
I let Thy Mighty Strength flow through me,
And out into all the paths of my human endeavors. Life
      from within expresses through me.

WAITING ON THEE

In waiting on Thee there is fulness of Life.
I wait on Thee, my Inner Lord; I listen for Thy voice.
I hear Thy word; I do Thy will; again I wait on Thee.
And listening, I hear Thee say: "Be perfect, be complete;
      live, love, be glad."
Sit thou in the stillness and let thy Lord speak.

WHOSE RIGHT IT IS TO COME

He has come Whose right it is.
He has made His home within me, and will nevermore
      depart from me.
I shall walk no more alone, for One walks with me
Who knows the path of Life, and Whose feet will never
      falter nor fail.
My Inner Light shines through the mist of human beliefs
And frees me from the bondage of fear and limitation.
I shall walk with You, my Friend, and shall learn of You the
      ways of Life and Freedom.
We shall travel together from this day, and none can part
      us, For we are united in the perfect bonds of an ever-
      lasting unity. I walk with Thee.

THE POWER OF THE WORD

I CONTROL MY MENTAL HOUSEHOLD AND CONQUER ALL FEAR AND DOUBT

I conquer my mental household and cast out all fear and doubt.

Let my Word cast out all sense of fear and doubt and let my thoughts be lifted unto Him Who lives Within.

My Word has dissolved all fear within me, and has cast out all doubt.

My Word shall guard my thought and make me receive only that which is Good and Perfect.

I control my life.

MY WORD COMES BACK TO ME

My word comes back to me laden with the fruits of its own speech.

My Word is the Law unto my Life, and the Law unto everything that I speak.

O Word, go forth and heal and bless all humanity.

Tell them of their Divine Birthright.

Tell the stranger that he is not alone, but that One goes with him Who knows and cares.

Tell the sick that they are healed and the poor that they
    cannot want.
Tell the unhappy of the joy of the Soul, and break the bonds
    of those who are in prison.
My Word shall come back to me blessed of God
    and man.

MY WORD SHALL BEAR FRUIT

The Word of my mouth shall bear fruit.
It shall accomplish and prosper, and shall not return unto
    me void.
My Word is the law unto the thing whereunto it is sent, and
    it cannot come back empty-handed.
I send out my Word, and it is law unto my life.
My Word is Power.

NOTHING CAN HINDER

Nothing can hinder my Word from working;
It will work, and nothing can stop it.
My word is the Law unto that thing whereunto it is spoken,
    and will become fulfilled in the right way and at the
    right time.
My Word is complete and perfect, and is the presence
    and the Power of the One Mind that is in and
    through all.
I speak that Word and know that it will accomplish.
I wait in perfect confidence for the Word to fulfill itself in
    my life. My Word is law.

O MAN, SPEAK FORTH THY WORD

O man, speak forth thy word and be not afraid.
Did you not know; have you not heard?
His Divinity is planted within thee, and thy word is one
    with all power.

*The Spirit of the Most High is thy Spirit, and the word of
    God is thy word.*

*Thy freedom is hid within thee, and thy inner light shall
    illumine thy way.*

Speak, man, and be free! Announce and proclaim thy works!

*Let thy word go forth with power, and thy Spirit shall con-
    quer all.* Spirit within me, speak.

THE POWER OF THE WORD

*The Word is a might Power, and that Word is in me and
    through me now.*

*My Word is one with the All Good and cannot fail to ac-
    complish the desired ends.*

*My Word goes forth with Power unto everything that I do,
    say or think.*

The Word is my Power by day and by night.

*I will speak the Word and trust in the great Law of Life to
    fulfill it.* I speak the word in full confidence.

THE WORD OF POWER

*My Word is a Word of Power, for I know that it is the Word
    of the Great God within me.*

*My Word shall accomplish and prosper, and shall do good
    unto all who call upon my name.*

*My Word is a tower of strength and cannot be denied. It is
    complete and perfect here and now.*

My Word is the Word of God.

My word is the word of God.

THE UNASSAILABLE TRUTH AND THE
IRRESISTIBLE WORD

*The Truth within me is unassailable, and the Power of the
    Word is irresistible.*

I can even now feel that my Word has gone forth with

Power and Reality, and that it will accomplish that
purpose for which it was created.
Limitless is its Power and wonderful are its works.
It can be nothing less than the Almighty working in and
through me.
I will let this Word of the Spirit go forth from my mouth,
and heal and bless the world.
It shall be as a strong tower unto all who call upon it.
The Truth is Complete and Perfect, and is within me now.
My Word is complete and perfect, now.

I BEHOLD IN THEE HIS IMAGE

I behold in thee His Image.
In thee, my friend, I see God and through you I feel His
presence. I see in the hand that gives, His hand;
And in the voice that speaks of Love, I hear Him speak.
For His lines have gone out into all places,
And from the highest to the lowest, all, all partake of His
nature. "For He is all in all, over all and through all."
I perceive that God is in all people.

UNITY

I SEE NO EVIL

I see no evil; I behold only the good.

I have seen the drunkard lying in the gutter, and the saint
    kneeling in ecstasy before the high altar of his faith;
    but I have found no difference.

I have perceived that each, in his own tongue, is seeking to
    express the One Life.

I will not separate and divide; I cannot condemn nor cen-
    sure, for I know that there is but One in All.

I know that all came from the One, and all will return to
    the One.

I know that all are now in the One, and that each is seeking
    to express the One.

I know and love all.

I SHALL NEVER DIE

I shall never die, for the Spirit within me is God and cannot
    change.

My life is hid within the Universe of Love and Light, and
    that Light shall live forever.

Go, fear of death and change; begone from my thought, fear
of death and uncertainty.
That which is cannot become that which is not; and that
which I am can never change.
The Spirit of Eternity is enthroned within me, and the Life
of Endless Ages flows through my being.
From Eternity to Eternity my Life flows along its way of
peace and harmony.
Time brings but more glory to crown me with its pleasures.
My life is forever.

LOVE TO THE WORLD

My Love goes out to everyone in the world;
I do not exclude anything, for I love all Nature and every-
thing that is.
My Love warms and lightens everything that it touches,
and it goes out into all places.
The Love flowing through me is a Power to all who come
into contact with it, and all feel and know that I love.
Love within me is Complete and Perfect.
Love within me is Complete.

MY LIFE IS ONE WITH GOD

My life is in God; it cannot be hurt nor hindered in its
expression.
God lives and expresses through me; His work is complete
and perfect in me now.
I know His life to be my life, and I know that my life is
complete and perfect.
My Life is in God.

NO MISUNDERSTANDINGS

There are no misunderstandings.

All is made clear between the ideas of Good.
No false sense of separation can come between people, nor
disturb the realization of the Unity of All Life.
I perceive that I am one with all people, and all are One with
me. There is no separation.
There is no separation.

THE DIVINE PLAN FOR ME

The Divine Plan for me is Perfect. I am held in the Mind
of God as a Complete and Perfect Expression of Life
and Truth.
No power can hinder nor mar this Inner Image of Reality,
for It is God-given and God-kept.
God gave and God will keep.

THE PERSONALITY OF GOD

The Great Personality of God is my Personality; the Limit-
less Knowingness of The Spirit is my Knowingness,
and the One Mind is my mind.
All, All live in One Infinite Person, and each manifests the
One Who is formed through and in all.
Man is the Personality of God in manifestation and cannot
be left without the Inner Witness of the Spirit.
I now realize that the Infinite Personalness of the Spirit is
my Personality, and I rejoice to know the Truth about
myself.
God is my Personality.

THE RADIATION OF LIFE

The life of God within me radiates and shines forth from me
in a constant stream of Light to all.
The One Life flowing through me is Life to all who come
near.

The One Power operating through me is flowing into every-
      thing that I contact.
Life radiates from me.

UNITY

Today I realize that I am One with the All Good; my God
      and I are One.
I cannot be hid from His face.
I behold Thee, O Most High, enthroned in my temple of
      flesh. Thy secret place is within me. I feel Thy pres-
      ence,
I hear Thy voice, I rejoice in Thy Light.
Today my body responds to the Divine Behest: "Be perfect."
I know of my perfection and wholeness; I am complete and
      perfect now.
Let every thought of disease flee from me, and let Thy Light
      shine.
O Light Eternal, O Light of my Life, I come into Thy pres-
      ence with joy and thanksgiving.
So be it.

WITHIN THEE IS FULNESS OF LIFE

Within Thee is fulness of Life.
Within Thee is complete Joy and everlasting Peace.
Within Thee is all.
Thou art in me as I am in Thee, and we are all in all.
My Life is full and complete within me, and that Life I give
      to all men freely;
And from all I receive again that which I have given, For it
      is One in All.
I am One with the fulness of All Life.

GLOSSARY

This glossary gives the Metaphysical meaning of the words as used in these lessons. It is not claimed that the definition of the words used in this glossary will, in every case, keep faith with the regular dictionary definition. The words are defined in such a way as to bring out the meaning with which they are used in this course of instruction.

It will be necessary for the student to carefully study the meaning of these words, together with the explanation of the words used in the different charts; in this way, the desired objective will be obtained, and there will be no confusion.

Absolute—"Free from restriction." (See Chart No. I.)

Accumulated Consciousness—The sum total of all that one has ever said, thought, done or seen, consciously or unconsciously.

Active Principle of Life—The Self-Conscious Spirit.

Affirmation—To state positively and maintain as being true.

All-good—God or Spirit.

Alpha—That which is first.

Analysis—Resolving things into their first elements.

Androgynous—Having the characteristics of both sexes.

Apparition—A specter or phantom. The act of appearing.

Attribute—The being, essence, nature and substance of.

Aura—The mental atmosphere surrounding a person.

Axiom—A self-evident truth.

Axiomatic Reasoning—The deductions drawn from self-evident truths.

Being—That which has existence.

Bible—"The sacred books of any race or people."

Blessing—Constructive thought directed toward anyone.

Body—The outward form.

Body of the Universe—The manifest Creation, the Body of God, both visible and invisible.

Causation—That which stands back of things as the Intelligent Cause.

Change—The appearance and disappearance of forms.

Christ—The total manifestation of God, from the plant to an angel; from a peanut to the entire Universe of expression. Christ in Man means the idea of Sonship, the Perfect Man as He must be held in the Mind of God.

Clairaudience—The ability to perceive sounds without the ear.

Clairvoyance—The ability to see mentally. See without the eye.

Coeternal—Always existing. Uncreated.

Coexistent—That which exists with.

Compensation—The law of balance in the mental world. Cause and effect.

Complex—The result of mental struggle, conscious or unconscious.

Conceive—To give birth to an idea.

Concentration—Bringing the attention to a focus.

Concept—An idea in mind.

Concrete Cause—Definite idea.

Condition—That which follows cause; the effect of law.

Conflict—Inner mental struggle, conscious or unconscious.

Conscious Mind—The self-knowing mind in God or man.

Consciousness—The perception of existence.

Contemplate—To know within the self.

Cosmic Conception—The Divine Mind giving birth to Its Ideas.

Cosmic Consciousness—Perception of The Whole.

Cosmic Mind—The Mind of God.

Cosmic Purpose—The ideas of Spirit propelling themselves into outer expression. The desire of Spirit executing itself.

Cosmic Stuff—The stuff from which all forms are made.

Cosmic Urge—The desire of Spirit to express Itself.

Cosmos—The Universal World, visible and invisible.

Correspondent—The mental picture of cause of anything.

Creation—Passing of Spirit into form.

Creative Medium—From the Universal Sense, it is the World-Soul; and from the individual sense, it is the subjective state of man's thought.

Creative Mind—The Universal Soul or Subjectivity. The Feminine Principle of the Universal Life.

Creative Series—Any particular and concrete manifestation of Spirit.

Curse—Mentally used to destroy.

Deductive Reasoning—Reasoning from the whole to a part.

Deity—God.

Denial—The mental act of denying the false appearance.

Desire—Life wishing to express Itself.

Devil—The personification of evil.

Diagnosis—Unearthing mental causes.

Discarnate Spirits—Entities out of the flesh.

Disease—The result of inhibited mental and spiritual action.

Divine Ideas—The Ideas of God.

Divine Nature—The true nature of all things.

Divine Principle—Spiritual Causation operating through Universal Law.

Divine Science—The facts known about mental and spiritual law.

Divine Urge—The inner desire to express life.

Dream World—World of thoughts that are UNexpressed.

Earth-bound—An entity unable to leave this plane.

Effect—That which follows cause. The result of some inner action.

Ego—The real self. The inner man.

Elementals—Unevolved entities in the invisible world.

Emanate—To flow forth from.

Emotion—Mental energy, set in motion through feeling.

Emmanuel—"God with us."

Entities—Anything that exists, visible or invisible.

Equivalent—The mental likeness of a thing. The mental cause back of anything. The idea of the thing in the Subjective World.

Esoteric—Inner.

Eternal—Everlasting, without beginning or end.

Ether—A universal medium which is supposed to be the last known analysis of matter; it interspheres all things and all space. The fine particles of matter, or electrons, are supposed to be cemented together by the ether. Ether seems to be, to the material world, what mind is to the mental world; i.e., a universal medium.

Evil—That which seems destructive.

Evolution—The passing of Spirit into form.

Existence—Having real being within itself. The cause of its own being, depending upon nothing but itself. Different from subsistence.

Exoteric—Outer.

Faculty—"Any mode of bodily or mental behavior regarded as implying a natural endowment or acquired power—the faculties of seeing, hearing, feeling, etc."

Familiar Spirits—Refers to the control of consciousness through the instrument of some invisible agency.

Father-Mother God—The Masculine and Feminine Principles of Being as included in the Androgynous One, or First Cause.

Feminine Principle—The Universal Soul. In man, the subjective or subconscious intelligence.

First Cause—That which is the cause of all things. The Uncreated, from which all Creation springs. The First Cause is both Masculine and Feminine in Its Nature, and includes the Intermediate Principle of Creative Activity.

Form—Any definite outline in time and space. Forms may be visible or invisible. In all probability, all space is filled with many kinds of forms.

Formless Substance—The ultimate stuff from which all forms are created, universally present, in an unformed state, and acted upon by conscious and subconscious intelligence. It is the nature of the Soul to give form to the ideas with which It is impregnated; hence, Soul contains Substance within Itself.

Function—"The normal action of any organ."

Ghost—The mental form of any person in the flesh or out of it.

God—The First Cause, the Great I Am, The Unborn One, The Uncreated, The Absolute or Unconditioned, The One and Only. Man comprehends God only to the degree that he embodies the Divine Nature.

Habit—Any act that has become a part of the subconscious mentality.

Halo—The emanation that appears around the head.

Heaven—A harmonious state of being.

Hell—A discordant state of being.

Holy Ghost—The third Person of the Trinity. The Servant of the Spirit. Used in the sense of the World, Soul or Universal Subjectivity.

Humanity—The multiplied expression of God as people. The many who live in the One.

Hypnotism—The mental control of another.

I Am—From the universal standpoint, means God; and from the individual, means the Real Man.

Idea—A concept. The Ideas of God are the Divine Realizations of His own Being. The real Ideas are eternal.

Illumination—Inspiration reaching Cosmic state. A direct contact with Reality or God. A complete intuitive perception.

Illusion of Mind—Means looking at a picture in Mind which may be real, only as a picture, but not as substance. As a picture of a person is not the person, so there are many pictures, drawn in Mind, which are real only as pictures. Mind is not an illusion, but might present us with illusions, unless we are very careful to distinguish the false from the true.

Image—The mental likeness of anything.

Imagination—The imaging faculty.

Immaculate Conception—All things are immaculately conceived, as all things come from the One.

Immortality—The Deathless Principle of Being in all people.

Immutable Law—Absolute in its ability to accomplish.

Impersonal Receptivity—The Creative Mind is impersonal receptivity, in that It receives all seeds of thought.

Incarnation—The Spirit of God in all Creation.

Individuality—The Real Idea of man, as distinguished from the outer personality.

Induce—The act of planting seeds of thought in Creative Mind.

Inductive Reasoning—Reasoning from effect to cause.

Indwelling Christ—Generic man, manifesting through the individual. The idea of Divine Sonship. The Real Man. As much of this reality appears as we allow to express through us.

Indwelling Ego—The Spirit of man as differentiated from his soul or subjective mentality. The Real Man which is the conscious part of him.

Indwelling God—The Real Man is as much of God as he is able to embody. The Divine Spark, Birthless and Deathless.

Infinite—That which is beyond all comprehension.

Inherent Life—Real life as distinguished from latent life.

Inner Sight—The spiritual capacity of knowing the Truth. It is a mental quality which brings the mentality to a comprehension of Reality.

Insanity—The loss of the objective faculties.

Inspiration—From the human side, means contact with the subconscious of the individual or the race. From the Divine, means contact with the Universal Spirit.

Instinctive Life—The One in everything.

Instinctive Man—The Spiritual Man.

Intellect—The reasoning faculty.

Intuition—The ability to know without any process of reasoning. God knows only intuitively.

Involution—Ideas involved in Mind. Involution precedes evolution.

Jesus—The name of a man. Distinguished from the Christ. The man Jesus became the embodiment of the Christ as the human gave way to the Divine Idea of Sonship.

Karma—The subjective law of cause and effect.

Latent Life—Life that depends upon reality. Distinguished from inherent life.

Law—Mind in action.

Law of Attraction—Subjective tendencies set in motion which are bound to attract.

Law of Correspondences—The subjective image of a desire. In the subjective world there is an exact image of everything that is in the objective world.

Levitation—Where the body is lifted without the aid of any physical medium.

Libido—The emotional urge within life which causes it to express itself.

Life—The animating Principle of Being.

Logic—Reasoning which keeps faith with itself.

Logos—The word of God.

Love—The givingness of the self.

Macrocosm—The Universal World.

Malpractice—The destructive use of Mind Power. It may be conscious or malicious, innocent, or ignorant.

Man—The objectification of God in the human form. The idea of God manifested in the flesh. The Sonship of the Father. Generic man is the Type, and the personal man is the concrete expression of the Type.

Mania—An irresistible desire controlling personal action.

Manifestation—The objectification of ideas.

Masculine Principle—The Self-Assertive Spirit, either in God or man.

Material Man—The objective man. Not opposed to Spirit, but the logical outcome of the Self-Knowing Mind.

Matter—Any form which substance takes in the world of sense and objectivity.

Maya—World of mental illusion.

Medium—One who objectifies subjectivity.

Memory—The subjective retention of ideas.

Mental Atmosphere—The mental emanation of anything, any person or any place. Everything has some kind of a mental atmosphere.

Mental Correspondents—The inner image in mind which balances the outer objectification of itself. Every objective thing has an inner mental correspondent.

Mental Equivalent—Having a subjective idea of the desired experience.

Mental Image—Subjective likeness.

Mental Plane—Just between the Spiritual and the physical. The three planes intersphere each other.

Mental Science—The science of Mind and Spirit. A systematic knowledge of the laws of the Mental and Spiritual World.

Mental Treatment—The act, art, and science of inducing thought in Mind, which thought, operated upon by Mind, becomes a manifested condition.

Mentality—An individual use of Universal Mind. There is One Mind, but within this One Mind are many mentalities. The One Mind is God and the mentalities are people.

Mesmerism—The influence of personality.

Metaphysical Principle—The Universal Creative Mind; as Spirit, It is conscious; as Law, It is subjective.

Metaphysics—That which is beyond the known laws of physics.

Microcosm—The individual world or universe of man.

Mind—Mind is both conscious and subconscious. Conscious Mind is Spirit, either in God or man. Unconscious Mind is the law of conscious Mind acting and is, therefore, subconscious or subjective.

Mirror of Matter—The external form of an inner concept.

Mirror of Mind—The subjective world, reflecting the images of thought that are projected into it by the conscious mind.

Money—The idea of Spiritual supply, objectified.

Multiplicity—The many things and people which come from the One. All come from the One, And all live in, and by, the One.

Mystic—One who senses the Divine Presence.

Mysticism—Not a mystery, but a mystic sense of the presence of Ultimate Reality.

Natural Man—Instinctive or Spiritual Man.

Neutral—Not caring which way it works.

Neutralizing Thought—The act of mentally erasing thought images.

Normal—Natural.

Objectification—The act of objectifying.

Objective Mind—The conscious mind.

Objective Plane—The outer world of expression.

Objective Side of Thought—The conscious side of thinking.

Obsession—Being controlled by thoughts, ideas or entities.

Occult—Hidden.

Omega—The last.

Omnipotent—All-powerful.

Omnipresent—Everywhere present.

Omniscient—All-knowing.

Omniscient, Instinctive I Am—God in man and things.

Particularization—Concrete forms produced by Spirit.

Passive Receptivity—Willing to receive any and all forms of thought.

Peace—A state of inner calm.

Percept—An external object perceived by the mind. Distinguished from a concept which is an inner idea.

Perfection—The real state of being.

Personality—The objective evidence of individuality. The man as we see him in the relative world.

Philosophy—A man's idea of life.

Planes—Different rates of vibration.

Plastic—Easily molded.

Poise—Mental balance.

Potential—Inherent possibility.

Poverty—A limited thought.

Power—The union of peace with poise.

Practitioner—One who practices mental healing or demonstration.

Prenatal—Conditions before human birth.

Primordial Substance—The ultimate formless stuff from which all things come.

Principle—Any law of nature.

Prophet—One who prophesies.

Psyche—Soul or subjective.

Psychic—Subjective capacity. All people are psychic, but all are not mediums. A medium is one who objectifies the psychic sense.

Psychic Phenomena—Phenomena of the soul or subjective mentality.

Psychic World—The world of subjectivity.

Psycho-analysis—A systematic analysis of the subjective thought.

Psychology—Study of the workings of the human mind.

Psychometry—Reading from the soul side of things.

Purpose—Definite intention.

Race-suggestion—Human beliefs, operating through the mentality of the individual.

Reality—The truth about anything.

Realization—Subjective comprehension of Truth.

Reason—The mental ability to analyze, dissect and figure out the cause of things. The human mind can reason both inductively and deductively. The Divine Mind can reason only deductively.

Reincarnation—Rebirth in the flesh.

Relative—That which depends upon something else.

Religion—A Man's idea of God or gods.

Resurrection—Rising from a belief in death.

Revelation—Becoming consciously aware of hidden things.

Riches—Idea of abundance.

Sage—One versed in spiritual truths.

Saint—A holy man.

Science—Knowledge of laws and principles.

Seer—One who sees into causes.

Self-consciousness—Personally conscious. Distinguished from Cosmic Consciousness, which is a consciousness of the Unity of the Whole.

Self-existent—Living by virtue of its own being.

Self-knowing Mind—The conscious mind.

Self-propelling—Having power within itself.

Self-realization—A consciousness of the self as a reality.

Silence—The inner realization of the One Life.

Simple Consciousness—Consciousness, as in an animal.

Sin—Missing the mark. There is no sin but a mistake and no punishment but an inevitable consequence.

Sonship—Man as the Son of God.

Soul—The Creative Medium of Spirit.

Soul of the Universe—The Universal Creative Medium.

Space—The Cosmic World. The distance between two specific forms. Space is a relative condition within the Absolute.

Specialize—To bring into concrete form.

Spirit—God, within Whom all spirits exist. The Self-Knowing One. The Conscious Universe. The Absolute.

Spirit of Man—God in man.

Spirit of the Universe—The Self-Knowing Mind of God.

Spirits—Personalities.

Spiritual—The atmosphere of God.

Spiritual Consciousness—The realization of the Divine Presence.

Spiritual Man—Man in a conscious state.

Spiritual Realization—The realization of the Divine Presence.

Stream of Consciousness—The automatic, mental emanation of the subjective state of thought.

Subconscious—The same as subjective.

Subjective—Beneath the threshold of the conscious. The inner side.

Subjective Activity—The inner action of the automatic law.

Subjective Causation—The mental law set in motion.

Subjectivity of the Universe—The Universal Soul or mental Law.

Subjective Side of Life—The inner side of life, as law.

Subjective State of Thought—The sum total of all one's thinking, both conscious and unconscious.

Subjective Tendency—The subjective trend of thought.

Subjective to Spirit—The Law is the subjective to the Spirit.

Sublimate—To transmute energy into another form of action.

Subsist—To live by virtue of spirit.

Substance—The formless back of all forms.

Suggestion—Receiving the thoughts of another. Suggestion accepts the ideas of others and believes in them. It may be conscious or unconscious.

Symbol—Mental impressions denoting spiritual or mental truths.

Telekinetic Energy—Moving ponderable objects without physical contact.

Telepathy—Thought transference.

The Only—The One Power.

Theology—That which treats of the nature of God.

Thought—The movement of consciousness.

Thought Forms—All thought has definite form on the subjective side of life.

Time—"Sequence of events in a Unitary Whole."

Trance—A subjective state.

Transmutation—Same as sublimation.

Treatment—The art, act and science of inducing thought on the subjective side of life. Setting the Law in motion.

Trinity—The Threefold Universe.

Triune Unity—The Trinity.

Truth—That which Is.

Unconscious Memory—Subjective memory.

Unconscious Thought—Unconscious subjective thought.

Unity—The Oneness of God and man.

Universal Law—Divine Principle.

Universal Mind—The Creative Medium of Spirit.

Universal Soul—The Universal Subjectivity.

Universal Spirit—The Conscious Mind of God.

Universal Subjectivity—The Creative Medium or the Universal Mind.

Universe—The Cosmic World.

Vibration—Law in execution.

Visualization—The art of mentally projecting a thought form into the Universal Creative Medium.

Word—The thought of God or man.

THE CALL

This I saw, or else some inner presence made it known to me;
The Universe is filled with life; the air, the sky, the sea
Teem with intelligence, with majesty and might;
And deep within me, some subtle inner sight
Beholds and sees, comprehends and knows the All, Nor fears nor
   falters, but answers the Divine Call To be as one beyond the
   bounds of time and space, To overcome the bondage of the
   human race,
And leap, with trust undaunted, free, Into the deeps of that Infinite
   Sea, Whose waters, calm, are ready to receive Those, who in
   simple faith, believe.

WHAT RELIGIOUS SCIENCE TEACHES

WHAT RELIGIOUS SCIENCE TEACHES

RELIGIOUS SCIENCE is not a personal opinion, nor is it a special revelation. It is a result of the best thought of the ages. It borrows much of its light from others but, in so doing, robs no one, for Truth is universal.

The Christian Bible, perhaps the greatest book ever written, truly points a way to eternal values. But there are many other bibles, all of which, taken together, weave the story of spiritual Truth into a unified pattern.

All races have had their bibles as all have had their religions; all have pointed a way to ultimate values but can we say that any of them has really pointed **The Way?** It is unreasonable to suppose that any one person, or race, encompasses all truth, and alone can reveal the way of life to others.

Taking the best from all sources, Religious Science has access to the highest enlightenment of the ages. **Religious Science reads everyman's Bible and gleans the truths therein contained.** It studies all peoples' thought and draws from each that which is true. Without criticism, without judgment, but by true discrimination, that which is true and provable may be discovered and put to practical use.

What is the Truth? Where may it be found? And how used? These are the questions that an intelligent person asks. He finds his answer in the study of Religious Science. Shorn of dogmatism, freed from superstition, and always ready for greater illumination, Religious Science offers the student of life the best that the world has so far discovered.

It has been well said that "religions are many; but Religion is one." The varying faiths of mankind are unnumbered, but the primal faith of the race is today, as of old, the One Faith; an instinctive reliance upon the Unseen, which we have learned to call God. Religion is One. Faith is One. Truth is One. There is One Reality at the heart of all religions, whether their name be Hindu, Mohammedan, Christian or Jewish. Each of these faiths, limited by its outlook upon life and the universe, evolved its own specific statements of faith called creeds and beliefs, and henceforth was governed by the same.

Spiritual experience is always a new thing; it ever seeks to express itself in a new way. The history of religion is a history of a periodic breaking away from the older body and the formulation of a new body of disciples to whom had come new light and a more satisfying experience.

While the Universal Mind contains all knowledge and is the potential of all things, only as much truth comes to us as we are able to receive. Should all the wisdom of the universe be poured over us we should yet receive only that which we are ready to understand. Each draws from the source of all knowledge that to which he inwardly listens. The scientist discovers the principle of his science, the artist taps the essence of beauty, the saint draws Christ into his being, because to each is given according to his ability to receive.

Emerson taught the immanence of God; the spiritual impulse underlying all life; the divinity of the universe including mankind, and his message gradually permeated the sodden mass of the accepted theological concepts of the day. He wrought a revolution in religious thinking, the full effects of which we are only beginning to realize in our own time. "Yourself," he said, "a new born bard of the Holy Ghost, cast behind you all conformity, and acquaint men at first hand with Deity. Look to it first and only that tradition, custom, Authority, are not bandages over your eyes, so that you cannot see. . . . Let me admonish you first of all to go alone, to refuse good models, even those sacred in the imagination of men; dare to love God without mediator and without veil." . . . "O my brothers, God exists: There is a soul at the center of Nature, and over the will of every man, so that none of us can wrong the universe. . . . things do not happen, they are pushed from behind."

The central principle of the teaching of Religious Science is this immanence of God. "God is an eternal and everlasting essence." All phenomena appearing in the natural world are manifestations of the spiritual world, the world of causes. "Our thought is an instrument of Divine Mind." "Christ is the reality of every man, his true inner self. Christ is the unseen principle in Man. God is in Man." The whole universe is the manifestation of a Unity which men call God.

Religious Science believes sincerely in what is known as "the silence," that is, it accepts the teachings of Jesus that "the Kingdom of God is within." The new sayings of Jesus from Oxyrhyncus quotes the statement as follows: "The Kingdom of Heaven is within you and whoever knows himself shall find it. Strive therefore to know yourselves, and ye shall be aware that ye are the Sons of the Almighty Father, and ye shall know that ye are in the City of God, and ye are the City."

Believing that the Universal Spirit comes to fullest consciousness in man, as his innermost Self, we strive to cultivate the inner life, knowing that religious certainty is the result of an impact of God upon the soul. Like the Methodism of old, we seek the witness of the Inner Spirit. We call this becoming Christ conscious or God conscious, meaning by that, Soul certainty.

The Purpose of Religious Science

In its practice and teachings, Religious Science endeavors to include the whole life. It is not a dreamy, mystical cult, but the exponent of a vigorous gospel, applicable to the everyday needs of our common life. Indeed, this is the one distinctive tenet of its teaching that accounts for its rapid growth. Men and women find in it a message that fits in with their daily needs.

The conventional idea of the future life, with its teachings of rewards and punishment, is not stressed; the gospel is the good news for the here and now. Religion, it says, if it means anything, means right living, and right living and right thinking wait upon no future, but bestow their rewards in this life—in better health, happier homes, and all that makes for a well-balanced, normal life.

The following is a brief Statement of Belief of the Institute of Religious Science:

The Universe is fundamentally good.

Man is a manifestation of Spirit, and for It to desire evil for him would be for It to desire evil for Itself. This is unthinkable and impossible, for it would cause Spirit to be self-destructive; therefore, we may be certain that the Spirit of Life is for, and not against, man.

All apparent evil is the result of ignorance, and will disappear to the degree that it is no longer thought about, believed in, or indulged in. Evil is not a thing in itself. It has no entity and no real law to support it.

God is Love, and Love can have no desire other than to bless all alike, and to express Itself through all.

Many that had lost faith in God have, in this new manner of thinking, found what their souls had sought. The emphasis is insistently on God, ever present, ever available; and on man's ability to make himself receptive to the inflow of the Divine Spirit. In essence, this was the primal message of the enlightened prophets of all the ages, and this is the message of Religious Science.

The thought of the ages has looked to the day when science and religion shall walk hand in hand through the visible to the invisible. A movement which endeavors to unify the great conclusions of human experience must be kept free from petty ideas, from personal ambitions and from any attempt to promote one man's opinion. Science knows nothing of opinion but recognizes a government of law whose principles are universal. These laws, when complied with, respond alike to all. Religion becomes dogmatic and often superstitious when based on the lengthened shadow of any one personality. Philosophy intrigues us only to the extent that it sounds a universal note.

The ethics of Buddha, the morals of Confucius, the beatitudes of Jesus, together with the spiritual experiences of other great minds, constitute viewpoints of life which must not be overlooked. The mystical concepts of the ancient sage of China keep faith with the sayings of Emerson, and wherever deep cries unto deep, deep answers deep.

All men seek some relationship to the Universal Mind, the Over-Soul, or the Eternal Spirit which we call God. That we are living in a spiritual universe which includes the material or physical universe has been the conclusion of most of the deepest thinkers of the ages. That this spiritual universe must be one of pure intelligence and perfect life, dominated by love, by reason and by the power to create, is an inevitable conclusion.

Science, philosophy, intuition and revelation, all must unite in an impersonal effort if Truth is to be gained and held. Ultimately that which is true will be accepted by all. The Institute of Religious Science is an educational as well as a religious movement and endeavors to co-ordinate the findings of science, religion, and philosophy, to find a common ground upon which true philosophic conclusions, spiritual intuitions and mystic revelations may agree with the cold facts of science, thus producing fundamental conclusions, the denial of which is not conceivable to a rational mind.

It goes without saying that such conclusions cannot contradict each other. No system of thought can stand which denies human experiences; no religion can remain vital which separates humanity from Divinity, nor can any science which denies the spontaneous appearance of volition and will in the universe maintain its position.

Old forms, old creeds are passing, but the eternal realities abide. Religion has not been destroyed; it is being discovered. God, the great innovator, is in His world and that means that progress is by divine authority. Through all the ages one increasing purpose runs, and that purpose can be no less than the evolution of the highest spiritual attributes of mankind. It is the unessential only that is vanishing, that the abiding may be made more clearly manifest.

What wonder that religious faith in our day is breaking from the narrow bounds of past teaching, and expanding both in breadth and depth. It is not because men believe less in God and the true essentials of spiritual life, but because they must believe more; they are literally forced by the inevitable logic of facts to build for themselves concepts of the Infinite commensurate with the greatness and glory of the world in which they live.

As Emerson so truly said—when the half gods go the great God arrives. Religious Science is reaching out to a truer concept of a God, immanent in the universe as the very substance, law and life of all that is. The difference between the older way of thinking and the new is that we have come to see that the One Supreme Cause and Source of all that is, is not a separate Being outside His world, but is in fact the actual Spirit of Life shining through all creation as its very Life Principle, infinite in Its working, and eternal in Its essence. The universe is none other than the Living God made manifest, so that Paul voiced a literal truth when he said: "In him we live, and move, and have our being." Such is the reverent conclusion of Religious Science, a faith that is winning its way in this our new day.

The religious implications of this new viewpoint of life are revolutionary. It means that there is a moral and spiritual order in the cosmos to which mankind is intimately related. Faith in God is not, as many would have us believe, a retreat from reality, a projecting of the personal wish into a cosmic postulate. Faith in God is a reasonable expanding of the facts of life to their wisest and inevitable vision and logical end; it is the logical complement of a world order, every fibre of which has a teleological meaning. Religious faith, in fact, is rooted in the facts and realities of the natural order, inwrought into the very texture of life. Since supreme wisdom and life are in reality all that exist, including Man, religious faith is but deep calling unto deep; God recognizing His own existence and presence.

The Teaching of Religious Science

The future religion will be free from fear, superstition and doubt and will ask no man where God may be found. For the "secret place of the most High" will be revealed in the inner sanctuary of man's own heart, and the eternal God will sit enthroned in his own mind. We can know no God external to that power of perception by which alone we are conscious of anything. God must be interpreted to man through man's own nature.

Who would know God, must be as God, for He who inhabits eternity also finds a dwelling place in His own creation. Standing before the altar of life in the temple of faith one learns that he is an integral part of the universe and that it would not be complete without him. That native faith within, which we call intuition, is the direct impartation of Divine Wisdom through us. Who can doubt its gentle urges, or misunderstand its meaning?

This inner life may be developed through meditation

and prayer. Meditation is quiet, contemplative thought, with a definite purpose always in mind. Prayer is a receptive mental and spiritual attitude through which one expects to receive inspiration.

There is a Presence pervading all. There is an Intelligence running through all. There is a Power sustaining all, binding all into one perfect whole. The realization of this Presence, Intelligence, Power and Unity constitutes the nature of the mystic Christ, the indwelling Spirit, the image of God, the Sonship of the Father.

Christ means the universal idea of Sonship; the entire creation, both visible and invisible. There is One Father of all. This One Father, conceiving within Himself, gives birth to all the Divine Ideas. The sum-total of all these ideas constitutes the mystic Christ.

Jesus was a man, a human being, who understood his own nature. He knew that as the human embodies the Divine it manifests the Christ nature. Jesus never thought of himself as different from others; his whole teaching was that what he did others could do. His divine nature was aroused; he had plunged beneath the material surface of creation and found its spiritual cause. This cause he called God or the Father. To this indwelling God he constantly turned for help, daily guidance and counsel. To Jesus, God was an indwelling Reality, the Infinite Person in every personality. It was by the power of this Spirit that Jesus lived. He clearly understood the unity of God and man.

Every man is a potential Christ. From the least to the greatest the same life runs through all, threading itself into the patterns of our individuality. He is "over all, in all and through all." As Jesus, the man, gave way to the Divine Idea, the human took on the Christ Spirit and became the voice of God to humanity.

Conscious of his divinity, yet humble as he contemplated the infinite life around him, Jesus spoke from the height of spiritual perception, proclaiming the deathless reality of the individual life, the continuity of the individual soul, the unity of the Universal Spirit with all men.

Religious Science, following the example of Jesus, teaches that all men may aspire to divinity, since all men are incarnations of God. It also teaches a direct relationship between God and man. The indwelling Spirit is God. It could be nothing less, since we have Spirit plus nothing, out of which all things are made. Behind each is the Infinite, within each is the Christ. There is no boundary line between the mind of man and the Mind which is God.

Religious Science teaches that human personality should be, and may become, the highest manifestation of God. There is a reservoir of life and power as we approach the center, loosed and flowing through to the circumference as we realize the unity of the whole and our relationship to it. God is incarnated in all men and individualized through all creation without loss to Himself.

To be an individual means to exist as an entity. As God is the Infinite Person, rightly understood, so the Spirit is the Infinite Essence of all individuality. Within the One Supreme Mind, since It is infinite, exists the possibility of projecting limitless expressions of Itself; but since the Infinite is infinite, each expression of Itself is unique and different from any other expression. Thus the Infinite is not divided, but multiplied.

While all people have the same origin, no two are alike except in ultimate essence—"One God and Father of us all," but numberless sonships, each sonship a unique institution in the universe of wholeness. **Man is an individualized center of God-consciousness and spiritual power, as complete as he knows himself to be, and he knows himself only as he comprehends his relationship to the whole.**

This overbrooding Presence, this inner sense of a greater Reality, bears witness to Itself through our highest acts and in our deepest emotions. Who is there who has not at times felt this inner Presence? It is impossible to escape our true nature. The voice of Truth is insistent. The urge to unfold is constant. In the long run each will fully express his divinity, for "good will come at last alike to all."

We stand in the shadow of a mighty Presence while love forever points the way to heaven. Mingled with the voice of humanity is the word of God, for Truth is a synonym for God, and whoever speaks any truth speaks the word of God. Science reveals eternal principles; mathematics, immutable laws, and illumined minds reveal the Eternal Spirit. Behind all is a unity, through all is a diversity, saturating all is a divinity.

We can no more do without religion than we can do without food, shelter or clothing. According to our belief about God will be our estimate of life here and hereafter. To believe in a God of vengeance is one thing, and to believe in a God of love and a just law of cause and effect is another.

To believe in a special dispensation of Providence robs us of our own immediate accessibility to goodness and creates the necessity of mediums, others than our own souls, through which we must gain entrance to Reality. We cannot reach beyond the vision of our own souls. We must have direct access to the Truth.

To believe in a specialized Providence is both scientific and sensible. We are always specializing some law of nature; this is the manner in which all science advances. Unless we can thus specialize the great Law of Life Itself—the Law of Mind and Spirit—we have no possibility of further advancement in the scale of being.

The unique power that Jesus expressed was a result of his conscious union with the creative Principle which is God. Jesus realized that we are living in a spiritual universe now, and like Buddha, Plato and Socrates, Swedenborg, Emerson and Whitman, he clearly understood and taught a law of parallels or spiritual correspondences. The parables of Jesus were mostly illustrations of the concept that the laws of nature and the laws of thought are identical. This has been one of the highest perceptions of the enlightened of all ages.

The universe in which we live is a spiritual system governed by laws of Mind. There are not two minds, there is but One Mind, which is God. The out-push of the Mind of God through the mind of man is the self-realization of Spirit seeking a new outlet for Its own expression. Ideas come from the Great Mind and operate through the human mind. The two are one. In this way the Infinite Mind is personal to each individual.

It is from the infinite self-knowingness of God that our power to know arises, because our mind springs from the Universal Mind. In this way the Infinite multiplies Itself through the finite.

Religious Science teaches that God is personal, and personal in a unique sense, to everyone. It teaches that conscious communion with the indwelling Spirit opens the avenues of intuition and provides a new starting point for the creative power of the Almighty.

No man ever lived who valued the individual life more than Jesus. He proclaimed his divinity through his humanity, and taught that all men are brothers. Every man comes from the bosom of the unseen Father. As the divinity of Christ is awakened through the humanity of man, the divine spark shot from the central fires of the Universal Flame warms other souls in the glow of its own self-realization.

We can give only what we have. The only shadow that we cast is the shadow of the self. This shadow lengthens as we realize the great Presence in which we live, move and have our being.

Religious Science not only emphasizes this unity of God and man, it teaches us that in such degree as our thought becomes spiritualized, it actually manifests the Power of God.

In doing this, it literally follows the teaching of Jesus when he proclaimed that all things are possible to him who believes.

It is written that "the prayer of faith shall save the sick, and the Lord shall raise him up." It is self-evident that the prayer of faith is a positive acceptance of the good we desire. Faith is a movement within the mind. It is a certain way of thinking. It is an affirmative mental attitude. Throughout the ages, and practiced by every religion, wonderful results have been obtained through the prayer of faith. There is a law governing this possibility, else it never could have been. It is the business of Religious Science to view these facts, estimate their cause, and in so doing, to provide a definite knowledge of the law governing the facts.

Religious Science teaches that right thinking can demonstrate success and abundance; can offer help to those who are in physical distress, and bring peace to those who are lost in the maze of confusion, doubt and fear.

Religious Science teaches that the Kingdom of God is at hand; that there is a perfection at the center of all things, and that true salvation comes only through true enlightenment, through a more conscious and a more complete union of our lives with the Invisible.

Religious Science does not place an undue importance either on mental healing or the law of abundance. Its main emphasis is placed not on visible things but on the Invisible. It teaches that there is an invisible law governing every man's life. This law is a law of faith or belief; it is a law of mind and consciousness. This will make a great appeal to the practical person, for when the Law of our being is understood it may be consciously used, thus providing every individual with a certain way to freedom, to happiness and to success.

Religious Science is a religion of joy; it is a religion free from fear and uncertainty; it is a religion of faith, a faith justified by results. All men are instinctively religious, and everyone has an intuition within him which, should he follow it, would lead him inevitably to a place not only of an inner sense of certainty, but to a place of the outer condition of security.

The Divine Spirit is not limited, nor does It wish to limit us. Its whole intent is to give us a more abundant life. The time has come when religion must be made practical, and when faith in the invisible must be consciously developed free from dogma, superstition and fear.

Religious Science today offers the world what the ages have been waiting for. It is the culmination of the hope, the aspiration and the faith of the enlightened of all time. The Truth it teaches is old; it has run through spiritual philosophies of the ages, but it has always been more or less handicapped by the dogmas and superstitions imposed upon it by the theology of its times.

The new age demands that the fear and superstition surrounding religious conviction be removed, and that the Truth, plain, simple and direct, be presented that men may learn to live now, in the present, with the assurance that the "eternal God is thy refuge . . ."

Our Declaration of Principles

We believe in God, the Living Spirit Almighty; one indestructible, absolute and self-existent Cause. This One manifests Itself in and through all creation. The manifest universe is the body of God; it is the logical and necessary outcome of the infinite self-knowingness of God. * * * *We believe in the incarnation of the Spirit in man and that all men are incarnations of the One Spirit.* * * * *We believe in the eternality, the immortality and the continuity of the individual soul, forever and ever expanding.* * * * *We believe that the Kingdom of Heaven is within man and that we experience this Kingdom in the degree that we become conscious of it.* * * * *We believe the ultimate goal of life to be a complete emancipation from all discord of every nature, and that this goal is sure to be attained by all.* * * * *We believe in the unity of all life, and that the highest God and the innermost God is one God.* * * * *We believe that God is personal to all who feel this Indwelling Presence.* * * * *We* *believe in the direct revelation of Truth through the intuitive and spiritual nature of man, and that any man may become a revealer of Truth who lives in close contact with the Indwelling God. * * * We believe that the Universal Spirit, which is God, operates through a Universal Mind, which is the Law of God; and that we are surrounded by this Creative Mind which receives the direct impress of our thought and acts upon it. * * * We believe in the healing of the sick through the power of this Mind. * * * We believe in the control of conditions through the power of this Mind. * * * We believe in the eternal Goodness, the eternal Loving-kindness and the eternal Givingness of Life to all. * * * We believe in our own soul, our own spirit and our own destiny; for we understand that the life of man is God.*

• • •

The following explanation, which is an analysis of our belief, illustrates how Religious Science keeps faith with the spiritual thought of the ages.

We believe in God, the Living Spirit Almighty:

God is defined as: the Deity; the Supreme Being; the Divine Presence in the universe permeating everything; the Animating Principle in everything, as Love, and the Source of all inspiration and power, the Source of guidance and of divine protection.

God has been called by a thousand different names throughout the ages. The time has now come to cast aside any points of disagreement and to realize that we are all worshiping one and the same God.

The Sacred Books of all peoples declare that God is One; a unity from which nothing can be excluded and to which nothing can be added. God is omnipotent, omnipresent and omniscient. God is our Heavenly Father and our Spiritual Mother; the Breath of our life. God is the Changeless Reality in which we live, move and have our being.

The Bible says: "I am the Lord, I change not." "Forever, O

Lord, thy word is settled in heaven." "One God and Father of all, who is above all, and through all, and in you all." "Know that the Lord he is God; there is none else beside him." "I am Alpha and Omega, the beginning and the ending . . . which is, and which was, and which is to come, the Almighty." "In whom are hid all the treasures of wisdom and knowledge." "God is Spirit: and they that worship him must worship him in spirit and in truth." "All things were made by him; and without him was not anything made that was made." ". . . there is but one God, the Father, of whom are all things, and we in him." ". . . the Lord he is God in heaven above, and upon the earth beneath: there is none else." "For with thee is the fountain of life; in thy light shall we see light." "God is light, and in him is no darkness at all." "Thy righteousness is an everlasting righteousness, and thy law is the truth."

From the **Text of Taoism:** "The Tao considered as unchanging, has no name." "There is no end or beginning to the Tao." "The great Tao has no name, but It effects the growth and maintenance of all things." "The Tao does not exhaust itself in what is greatest, nor is it ever absent from what is least; and therefore it is to be found complete and diffused in all things." "Thus it is that the Tao produces (all things), nourishes them . . . nurses them, completes them, matures them, maintains them, and overspreads them."

The **Hermetic Teaching** defines God as a ". . . Power that naught can e'er surpass, a Power with which no one can make comparison of any human thing at all . . ." This teaching defines God as a Oneness which is the ". . . Source and Root of all, is in all things . . ." "His being is conceiving of all things. . . . He ever makes all things, in heaven, in air, in earth, in deep, in all of cosmos (that is in the entire universe). . . . For there is naught in all the world that is not He." "God is united to all men as light to the sun."

From the **Sacred Books of the East:** "There is but one

Brahma which is Truth's self. It is from our ignorance of that One that god-heads have been conceived to be diverse." "As the sun, manifesting all parts of space, above, between, and below, shines resplendent, so overrules the all-glorious adorable God . . ." "The One God, who is concealed in all beings, who pervades all, who is the inner soul of all beings, the ruler of all actions, who dwells in all beings . . ." "God is permanent, eternal and therefore existence itself." "All is the effect of all, One Universal Essence." "The Supreme Soul hath another name, that is, Pure Knowledge."

The **Zend-Avesta** defines God as "Perfect Holiness, Understanding, Knowledge, The most Beneficent, The uncomparable One, The All-seeing One, The healing One, The Creator."

The **Koran** says that "He is the Living One. No God is there but He."

In **Buddhism** we find these thoughts: ". . . the Supreme Being, the Unsurpassed, the Perceiver of All Things, the Controller, the Lord of All, the Maker, the Fashioner . . . the Father of All Beings . . ."

In the **Apocrypha** we read that God is ". . . the Most High who knows . . . who nourishes all. The Creator who has planted his sweet Spirit in all . . . There is One God . . . Worship him . . . who alone exists from age to age . . ."

From the **Talmud:** "Our God is a living God." "His power fills the universe . . . He formed thee; with His Spirit thou breathest."

We believe in God, the Living Spirit Almighty; one, indestructible, absolute, and self-existent Cause.

In Religious Science **self-existent** is defined as "living by virtue of its own being." An absolute and self-existent Cause, then, means that Principle, that Power and that Presence which makes everything out of Itself, which contains and sustains everything within Itself. God is absolute and self-existent Cause.

Therefore, the **Divine** Spirit contains within Itself infinite imagination, complete volition and absolute power.

We are to think of God not as **some power,** but as **All
Power;** not as **some presence,** but as **the Only Presence;** not
merely as **a god,** but as **The God.** Spirit is the supreme and the
only Causation.

Emerson said, "There is, at the surface, infinite variety of
things; at the center there is simplicity of cause." "We are es-
corted on every hand through life by spiritual agents, and a beneficent purpose lies in wait for us." It was Emerson's belief that
we are all sleeping giants: "Sleep lingers all our life time about
our eyes, as night hovers all day in the boughs of the fir tree."
"Into every intelligence there is a door which is never closed,
through which the creator passes."

*This One manifests Itself in and through all creation but is not ab-
sorbed by Its creation.*

Our textbook defines **creation** as "the giving of form to the
substance of Mind. . . . The whole action of Spirit must be within
Itself upon Itself." Creation is the play of Life upon Itself; the
action of a limitless Imagination upon an infinite Law.

What God thinks He energizes. The universe is God's
thought made manifest. The ideas of God take innumerable
forms. The manifest universe springs from the Mind of God.

The Bible says that "the Lord by wisdom hath founded the
earth: by understanding hath he established the heavens." "In
the beginning God created the heaven and the earth." "By his
spirit he hath garnished the heavens." "For he spake, and it was
done; he commanded, and it stood fast." ". . . the worlds were
framed by the word of God . . ." "The heavens declare the glory
of God; and the firmament sheweth his handiwork."

The **Hermetic Philosophy** states that "with Reason, not
with hands, did the World-maker make the universal World . . ."

From a **Hindu Scripture:** "From the unmanifest springs

the manifest." "Mind, being impelled by a desire to create, performs the work of creation by giving form to Itself."

Everything that exists is a manifestation of the Divine Mind; but the Divine Mind, being inexhaustible and limitless, is never caught in any form; It is merely expressed by that form. The manifest universe, then, is the Body of God. As our Declaration of Principles reads: **"It is the logical and necessary outcome of the infinite self-knowingness of God."** God's self-knowingness energizes that which is known, and that which God knows takes form. The form itself has a Divine Pattern within it.

In the **Hermetic Teaching** we find this remarkable statement: "All things, accordingly, that are on earth . . . are not the Truth; they're copies (only) of the True. Whenever the appearance doth receive the influx from above, it turns into a copy of the Truth; without its energizing from above, it is left false. Just as the portrait also indicates the body in the picture, but in itself is not the body, in spite of the appearance of the thing that's seen. 'Tis seen as having eyes; but it sees naught, hears naught at all.

"The picture, too, has all the other things, but they are false, tricking the sight of the beholders,—these thinking that they see what's true, while what they see is really false. All, then, who do not see what's false see truth. If, then, we thus do comprehend, or see, each one of these just as it really is, we really comprehend and see. But if (we comprehend, or see, things) contrary to that which is, we shall not comprehend, nor shall we know aught true."

One of the problems of Religious Science is to distinguish between that which is temporal and that which is eternal. God or Spirit is the only Reality, the One Substance or Essence. The material universe is real as a manifestation of life, but it is an effect. This is why Jesus told us to judge not according to appearances.

The **Talmud** says that "unhappy is he who mistakes the branch for the tree, the shadow for the substance."

In **Hebrews** we find: "For Christ is not entered into the holy places made with hands, which are the figures of the true; but into heaven itself, now to appear in the presence of God for us."

And from **Colossians:** "Let no man therefore judge you in meat, or in drink, or in respect of an holyday, or of the new moon, or of the sabbath days: Which are a shadow of things to come; but the body is of Christ."

Back of all form there is a Divine Substance. Hid within every appearance there is an adequate cause. If we judge by the appearance alone, as though it were self-created, we are mistaking the shadow for the Substance.

In **Fragments of a Faith Forgotten** it says: "Gain for yourselves, ye sons of Adam, by means of these transitory things . . . that which is your own, and passeth not away."

We are to translate all creation into spiritual Causation. Then we shall be viewing it rightly. The created form has no being of itself, it is an effect. In **Ramacharaka** we read: "That which is unreal hath no shadow of Real Being, notwithstanding the illusion of appearance and false knowledge. And that which hath Real Being hath never ceased to be—**can never cease to be,** in spite of all appearances to the contrary."

There is a Divine Pattern, a spiritual prototype, in the Mind of God which gives rise to all form. Jesus saw through the form to the Pattern, for he was quickened by the Spirit. "It is the spirit that quickeneth: the flesh profiteth nothing . . ." "For (now) we know in part, and we prophesy in part. But when that which is perfect is come, then that which is in part shall be done away." "Now we see as through a glass darkly." That is, our spiritual vision is not quickened to a complete perception of the Divine Reality, the spiritual prototype back of the image.

All scriptures warn us to beware of false judgments; to

judge not according to appearances but to plunge beneath or through the objective form to its spiritual cause. This does not mean that the physical universe is an illusion; it does mean that it is a logical and necessary expression of the Divine Mind. If we were to think of the physical universe as the shadow of its spiritual Reality we should be rightly interpreting it.

Religious Science translates physical form into mental and spiritual causation. It does not do this by denying the form, but through a right interpretation of it. The visible is an evidence of the invisible. The invisible is the cause, the visible is the effect.

We believe in the incarnation of the Spirit in man and that all men are incarnations of the One Spirit.

All scriptures declare that man is the spiritual image and likeness of God. This is emphatically revealed in the inspiration of our own scripture which says: "God created man in his own image." "The spirit of God hath made me, and the breath of the Almighty hath given me life." "Hereby know we that we dwell in him, and he in us, because he hath given us of his Spirit." "Thou hast made him a little lower than the angels, and hast crowned him with glory and honour. Thou madest him to have dominion over the works of thy hands; thou hast put all things under his feet." "Be ye therefore perfect, even as your Father which is in heaven is perfect."

"Now there are diversities of gifts, but the same Spirit." "There is one body, and one Spirit . . . one Lord, one faith, one baptism, one God and Father of all, who is above all, and through all, and in you all." "One faith, and one baptism" means that through faith and intuition we realize that we are living in one Spirit, or, as Emerson said, "There is one Mind common to all individual men."

"Have we not all one Father? Hath not one God created us?" "To us there is but one God, the Father, of whom are all things." "Beloved, now are we the sons of God." "Ye are the sons of the living God." "And because ye are sons, God has sent forth the Spirit of his Son into your hearts." In other words, there is but one son of God which includes the whole human family, and the Spirit of this son, which is the Spirit of Christ, is incarnated in everyone. Therefore, the Bible says that "he (man) is the image and glory of God."

"Know ye not that your body is the temple of the Holy Ghost which is in you . . . therefore glorify God in your body, and in your spirit, which are God's." "That which is born of the Spirit is spirit." We could have no more definite statement of the Divine Incarnation than this. Every man is an incarnation of God. Since God is the Universal Spirit, the one and only Mind, Substance, Power and Presence that exists, and since all men are individuals, it follows that each man is an individualized center of the Consciousness of the One God.

When Jesus said, "I and my Father are one," but "my Father is greater than I," he was stating a mathematical proposition. Every man is an incarnation of God, but no single incarnation of God can exhaust the Divine Nature. Everyone can use the figure 7 to infinity without ever exhausting its possibility. The more Divine Power we use the more Divine Power is placed at our disposal, for "there is that which scattereth, and yet increaseth."

Not only is every individual an incarnation of God, and, therefore, a manifestation of Christ, but since each individual is unique, every person has access to God in a personal sense. The Spirit is most certainly personal to each one of us—individually and uniquely personal. We could not ask for a more complete union than this, for the union is absolute, immediate and dynamic.

According to the revelation of the ages, man has a spiritual birthright which gives him dominion over all evil. But the old man must be put off; that is, transmuted into the new man, which is Christ. The real spiritual man is here now could we see him. It is ignorance of this fact which produces all evil, all limitation, all fear. It is a sense of separation from our Source which begets all our troubles. In the midst of the possibility of freedom we are bound. Thus, the Hermetic philosophy states that though we are born of harmony we have become slaves because we are overcome by sleep. And our own scripture says that we must awake from this sleep; that we must arise from the dead in order that Christ may give us life.

The **Koran** says: "We created man: and we know what his soul whispereth to him, and we are closer to him than his neck-vein."

In the **Talmud** we read: "First no atom of matter, in the whole vastness of the universe, is lost; how then can man's soul, which is the whole world in one idea be lost?"

The following quotations are drawn from various **Hindu Scriptures:** "The ego is beyond all disease . . . free from all imagination, and all-pervading." "As from a . . . fire, in thousand ways, similar sparks proceed, so beloved are produced living cells of various kinds from the Indestructible." "If ye knew God as he ought to be known, ye would walk under seas, and the mountains would move at your call." (This is similar to the teaching of Jesus when he said that if we had faith the size of a grain of mustard seed, we could say unto the mountain, "Remove hence to yonder place.") "There is that within every soul which conquers hunger, thirst, grief, delusion, old age and death."

Perhaps one of the most remarkable sayings in the **Scriptures of India,** relative to the self, is the following: "Let him raise the self by the Self and not let the self become depressed; for verily is the Self the friend of the self, and also the Self the self's enemy; The Self is the friend of the self of him in whom the self by the Self is vanquished; but to the unsubdued self the Self verily becometh hostile as an enemy." This, of course, refers to the deathless Self, the incarnation of God in us.

"He who knows himself has come to know his Lord . . ."

This refers to the complete unity of the Spirit, or, as Jesus said, "I and the Father are one." "And he who thus hath learned to know himself, hath reached that Good which doth transcend abundance . . ."

From the **Text of Taoism** are gathered the following inspiring thoughts: "Man has a real existence, but it has nothing to do with place; he has continuance, but it has nothing to do with beginning or end." "He whose whole mind is thus fixed emits a Heavenly light. In him who emits this heavenly light men see the (True) man."

Referring to the one whose mind is fixed on Reality. "His sleep is untroubled by dreams; his waking is followed by no sorrows. His spirit is guileless and pure; his soul is not subject to weariness." In spiritual revelation a calm contemplation of spiritual Truth is held important. The mind must be like a mirror if it is to reflect or image forth the Divine Prototype, the incarnation of God in man. "Men do not look unto running water as a mirror, but into still water:—it is only the still water that can arrest them all, and keep them in the contemplation of their real selves."

The **Hermetic Philosophy** tells us that if we would know God we must be like Him, for "like is knowable to like alone." "Make thyself to grow to the same stature as the Greatness which transcends all measure . . ." "Conceiving nothing is impossible unto thyself, think thyself deathless and able to know all,—all arts, all sciences, the way of every life." It tells us to awake from our deep sleep, as though our spiritual eyes were dulled by too much looking on effect and too little contemplation of cause.

We believe in the eternality, the immortality and the continuity of the individual soul, forever and ever expanding.

If man is an incarnation of God, then his spirit is God individualized, and as such it must be eternal. Since it is impossible to exhaust the limitless nature of the Divine, our expansion must be an eternal process of unfolding from a limitless Center.

Immortality is not something we purchase. It is not a bargain we make with the Almighty. It is the gift of heaven. It is inherent in the divine nature of man. When the disciples of Jesus asked him what is God's relationship to the dead, he answered as we should expect one to answer who had already plunged beneath the material surface of things and discovered their spiritual cause. He said, "He is not a God of the dead, but of the living: for all live unto him."

God is Life, and that which is Life cannot produce death. What we call death is but a transition from one plane or one mode of expression into another. "In my Father's house are many mansions."

Jesus said to one who passed with him, "Today shalt thou be with me in paradise." In the philosophy of this spiritual genius, this God-saturated man, death was but a transition.

The **Gita** tells us, "He is not born, nor doth he die; nor having been, ceaseth he any more to be; unborn, perpetual, eternal and ancient, he is not slain when the body is slaughtered."

From the **Bible:** "He asked life of thee, and thou gavest it him, even length of days for ever and ever." "And this is the promise that he hath promised us, even eternal life." "To an inheritance incorruptible, and undefiled, and that fadeth not away, reserved in heaven for you."

We believe that the Kingdom of Heaven is within man and that we experience this Kingdom to the degree that we become conscious of it.

The Kingdom of Heaven means the kingdom of harmony, of peace, of joy and of wholeness. It is an inward kingdom. This is why Jesus said that we should not lay up treasures on earth, but "lay up for yourselves treasures in heaven."

Heaven is not a place but an inward state of consciousness. It is an inward awareness of Divine Harmony and Truth. It is

the "house not made with hands, eternal in the heavens." Eze-
kiel said, "The spirit took me up, and brought me into the inner
court; and, behold, the glory of the Lord filled the house." The
glory of God fills every man's consciousness who is aware of
that glory.

Jesus likened the Kingdom of Heaven to a child: "Except
ye be converted, and become as little children, ye shall not enter
into the kingdom of heaven." This refers to the childlike consciousness, to a simple trust in the goodness of God.

The Spirit has placed divine intuition within everyone. This
divine intuition is the gateway through which the inspiration of
the Almighty enters the mind. This is why the Psalms tell us to
"lift up our gates." That is, lift up the intuition and permit the
Divine Light to enter.

When Jesus said that we are to be perfect even as God
within us is perfect, he certainly implied that there is such a Divine Kingdom already established within man. "When the without shall become as the within" then the Kingdom of God shall
be established here and now. Jesus said that we should assume
a childlike attitude toward this Kingdom. "Whosoever therefore
shall humble himself as this little child, the same is greatest in
the kingdom of heaven." "And when he was demanded of the
Pharisees, when the kingdom of God should come, he answered
them and said, The kingdom of God cometh not with observation: Neither shall they say, Lo here! or, lo there! for, behold, the
kingdom of God is within you." This certainly refers to a state
of inner awareness.

The kingdom to which Jesus referred is not external but
within. It is not to be placed outside the self, "Neither Lo here!
or, lo there!" but it is to be perceived as an everlasting dominion
within. The Kingdom of Heaven is something we possess but
have not been conscious of. It is not some far off divine event,
"for the kingdom of heaven is at hand." It is neither in the mountain nor at Jerusalem, but within the mind.

Jesus likened the Kingdom of Heaven ". . . unto treasure hid in a field; the which when a man hath found, he hideth, and for joy thereof goeth and selleth all that he hath, and buyeth that field." The treasure of the inner kingdom is already hid at the center of our being and when we discover it great joy follows. Our whole desire is to possess this inner kingdom; to drill deep into the well-spring of our being and bring up the pure oil of Spirit; to tunnel the granite rock of our unbelief and at the center of our being discover "the pearl of great price."

"And the disciples came, and said unto him, Why speakest thou unto them in parables? He answered and said unto them, Because it is given unto you to know the mysteries of the kingdom of heaven, but to them it is not given." On first reading, this sounds as though Jesus were withholding his teaching from the common multitude, but such was not the case. He spoke in parables realizing that those who comprehended their meaning would understand his teaching, for he had already instructed his disciples in the mysteries of the kingdom. That is, he had directly taught them the inner meaning of life.

In Corinthians it says: "But we speak the wisdom of God in a mystery, even the hidden wisdom, which God ordained before the world unto our glory." This is a direct reference to the inseparable unity between God and man. God has ordained that forever man shall be one with His own being, that the kingdom of good shall forever be at hand. Since we are individuals, God has also ordained that our good shall make its appearance when we recognize it.

Emerson said that "Nature forevermore screens herself from the profane, but when the fruit is ripe it will fall." The inner mysteries of the Kingdom of God are hid from the vulgar, not because the Divine withholds Itself, but because only to the pure in heart, to the child-like in mind, can the Kingdom be revealed.

One of the greatest of the Greek philosophers said that this kingdom is something which every man possesses but which few men use. Encased in materiality, filled with the din of objective confusion, we do not hear the still small voice which evermore proclaims, "Look unto me, and be ye saved, all the ends of the earth."

Again Jesus likened the Kingdom unto ". . . a grain of mustard seed, which a man took, and sowed in his field . . ." He then goes on to say that very soon this small seed becomes a tree which puts forth branches. Here Jesus is referring to the Tree of Life, which means the unity of God with man. The little seed is the consciousness of the little child which becomes aware of its relationship to the Divine Parentage. Out of this inner awareness grows and blossoms a concept of harmony. The Tree of Life expands and puts forth branches; its shade provides shelter.

No matter how small our concept of heaven may be to begin with, it has the possibility of eternal unfoldment. The power to live is within the self, implanted by the Divine. Ultimately every man will realize his inner kingdom which will become to him as the Tree of Life providing food and shelter, perfection and joy.

Again Jesus said, "The kingdom of heaven is like unto leaven, which a woman took, and hid in three measures of meal, till the whole was leavened." He is referring to the action of consciousness of the Kingdom of God in the mind as yeast spreading through the whole lump of mortal thought, lifting the weight of the burdens of life into lightness. Jesus is referring to the Kingdom of God as the Bread of Life; the eternal Substance upon which the soul feeds; the everlasting Presence upon which the inner eye feasts; the house not made with hands in which the Spirit dwells forever.

"Again, the kingdom of heaven is like unto a merchant man, seeking goodly pearls: Who, when he had found one pearl of great price, went and sold all that he had, and bought it." Since the greater includes the lesser, Jesus told us that we are first to seek the Kingdom because everything is included in it. "Pearl" stands for purity and perfection. When we discover the purity and perfection at the center of our own being, we shall naturally sell the dross, the fear and the doubt that infest our thought world, in order that we may possess this inner purity, that we may become conscious of this inner perfection.

Jesus did not wish us to feel that, in seeking this inner kingdom, we are losing anything worth while in the outer life, for he said that everyone who has sought the inner kingdom shall "receive manifold more in this present time, and in the world to come life everlasting." This is in line with all the other teachings of Jesus, that the reward for right living is immediate. The Kingdom is not something reserved only for future states; it is something which we experience here and now through the manifold blessings which the Spirit automatically bestows on us when we seek first things first.

In his parable likening the Kingdom of Heaven unto the wise virgins, Jesus clearly teaches that every man possesses the Oil of Spirit and that no man need borrow from another.

The Kingdom of God is not something we create, not something we purchase, but something that we must realize—it is something we become inwardly aware of. There is a perfection at the center of man's being. Browning tells us that we must loose this imprisoned splendor, while Plato and his followers taught that "over yonder" there is a prototype of perfection. With them "over yonder" had a meaning identical with the teaching of Jesus that the Kingdom of Heaven is within. The Greek philosophers taught that when the image, that is, the external, turns to its prototype, it is instantly made whole because it is instantly unified with its inner perfection.

Let us see what other bibles of the world have taught about this inner kingdom.

In the **Text of Taoism** we find this: "Without going outside his door . . . without looking out from his window, one sees the

Tao of Heaven. The farther one goes from himself the less he knows." "What is heavenly is internal; what is human is external. If you know the operation of what is heavenly . . . you will have your root in what is heavenly . . ." "Take the days away and there will be no year; without what is internal there will be nothing external." "He who knows . . . completion . . . turns in on himself and finds there an inexhaustible store."

The **Gita** tells us: "He who is happy within him, rejoiceth within him, is illumined within, becomes eternal." And in **Fragments of a Faith Forgotten** it says: ". . . the Kingdom of Heaven is within you; and whosoever shall know himself shall find it." "Seek for the great and the little shall be added unto you. Seek for the heavenly and the earthly shall be added unto you."

In the **Upanishad** we read: "As far as mind extends, so far extends heaven." "In heaven there is no fear . . . it is without hunger or thirst and beyond all grief."

The **Pistis Sophia** says: "Be ye diligent that ye may receive the mysteries of Light and enter into the height of the Kingdom of Light."

We believe the ultimate goal of life to be a complete emancipation from all discord of every nature, and that this goal is sure to be attained by all.

The ultimate goal of life does not mean that we shall ever arrive at a spiritual destination where everything remains static and inactive. That which to our present understanding seems an ultimate goal, will, when attained, be but the starting point for a new and further evolution. We believe in an eternal upward spiral of existence. This is what Jesus meant when he said, "In my Father's house are many mansions."

The **Koran** tell us that God has made many heavens, one on top of another, which means that evolution is eternal. The Hermetic philosophy taught an infinite variation of the manifestation of life on an ever-ascending scale. All evolution proves the transition of the lesser into the greater.

The original sources of spiritual thought, from which the great religious conceptions of the ages have been drawn, have taught that evolution is an eternal manifestation of life on an ascending scale. As we ascend from a lower to a higher level, the limitations of the previous experience must drop away from us. Since the Kingdom of God or the Kingdom of Reality is already established in Spirit, our transition from one plane to another is a matter of consciousness, and since all persons are incarnations of the Divine Spirit, every soul will ultimately find complete emancipation, not through losing itself in God, but, rather, through finding God in itself.

Tagore tells us that Nirvana is not absorption but immersion. Browning said that we are all Gods though in the germ. Jesus proclaimed that the Kingdom of Heaven is within, and that we shall attain this kingdom in such degree as we become consciously aware of, and unified with, it. This does not mean that there is any finality to evolution, for every apparent ultimate is but the beginning of a new experience.

We believe in the unity of all life, and that the highest God and the innermost God is one God.

The enlightened in every age have taught that back of all things there is One Unseen Cause. This teaching of Unity ... "The Lord our God is one God ..." is the chief cornerstone of the sacred scriptures of the East, as well as our own sacred writings. It is the mainspring of the teachings of modern spiritual philosophies, such as Unity Teachings, the New Thought Movement, the Occult Teachings, the Esoteric or Inner Teachings, our own Religious Science, and even much that is taught under the name of Psychology. Science has found nothing to contradict this unity, for it is self-evident. An entire chapter in our textbook is available for further elucidation of this subject.

There is One Life of which we are a part; One Intelligence, which we use; One Substance, which takes manifold forms.

"That they all may be one; as thou, Father, art in me, and I in thee, that they also may be one in us."

In the Bible we find these passages: "Now there are diversities of gifts, but the same Spirit." "Whither shall I go from thy spirit? or whither shall I flee from thy presence? If I ascend up into heaven, thou art there: if I make my bed in hell, behold, thou art there . . . If I say, Surely the darkness shall cover me; even the night shall be light about me." "We all, with open face beholding as in a glass the glory of the Lord, are changed into the same image . . . by the Spirit of the Lord." "I shall be satisfied when I awake with thy likeness."

"Know ye not that your body is the temple of the Holy Ghost which is in you?" "That which is born of the Spirit is spirit." "The Lord our God is one God . . . He is God in heaven above and upon the earth beneath. There is none else." ". . . His word is in mine heart as a burning fire shut up in my bones." "And the Word was made flesh, and dwelt among us . . ." ". . . I will put my words in his mouth . . . the word is very nigh unto thee, in thy mouth, and in thy heart, that thou mayest do it."

All sacred scriptures have proclaimed the unity of life; that every man is a center of God Consciousness. This is the meaning of the mystical marriage, or the union of the soul with its Source. Jesus boldly proclaimed that he was one with the Father. This is the basis for all New Thought teaching, the spiritual union of all life.

The **Qabbalah** states that "every existence tends toward the higher, the first unity . . . the whole universe is one, complex. The lower emanates from the Higher and is Its image. The Divine is active in each."

Unity is a symbol of the soul's oneness with the Higher Nature, implying complete freedom from bondage to anything less than itself. All positive religions have taught that the supreme end of humanity is a union of the soul with God.

"The Atman, which is the substratum of the ego in man,

is One." The **Hermetic Teaching** tells us that "this Oneness, being source and root of all, is in all." And the **Gita** explains that "when he (man) perceiveth the diversified existence of beings as rooted in One, and spreading forth from It, then he reacheth the eternal."

Again the **Bible** tells us: "Thus saith the Lord . . . I am the first and I am the last . . ." "I am Alpha and Omega, the beginning and the ending . . . which was and which is to come . . ."

From **The Awakening of Faith:** "In the essense (of Reality) there is neither anything which has to be included, nor anything which has to be added."

In one of the **Upanishads** we find this quotation: "The One God who is concealed in all beings, who is the inner soul of all beings, the ruler of all actions . . ." "All is the effect of all, One Universal Essence." And again in Ephesians, "One God and Father of all, who is above all, and through all, and in you all."

In **Echoes From Gnosis** we find: "Oh Primal Origin of my origination; Thou Primal Substance of my substance; Breath of my breath, the breath that is in me."

From the **Bible:** "To us there is but one God, the Father, of whom are all things, and we in him . . ." And from another Bible, "All this universe has the Deity for its life. That Deity is Truth, who is the Universal Soul."

From the **Apocrypha:** "He is Lord of Heaven, sovereign of earth, the One existence." And the **Upanishads** tell us, "He who is the Ear of the ear, the Mind of the mind, the Speech of the speech, is verily the Life of life, the Eye of the eye."

Religious Science teaches an absolute union of man with his Source. So complete is this union that the slightest act of human consciousness manifests some degree of man's divinity. Man is not God, but he has no life separate from the Divine; he has no existence apart from his Source. He thinks God's thoughts after Him. He is divine neither by will nor through choice, but by necessity. The whole process of evolution is a continual process of awakening. It is an understanding of this indwelling union which constitutes the Spirit of Christ.

Our textbook defines Christ as "the Word of God manifest in and through man. In a liberal sense, the Christ means the Entire Manifestation of God and is, therefore, the Second Person of the Trinity. Christ is Universal Idea, and each one 'puts on the Christ' to the degree that he surrenders a limited sense of Life to the Divine Realization of wholeness and unity with Good, Spirit, God."

Christ is the Higher Self, the Divine Life proceeding from the Father. This Christ enters the world of manifestation and animates all things. Christ is in everything; we are rooted and centered in Him who is "the way, the truth, and the life."

Christ is the supreme ideal which Jesus made manifest through the power of his word. Christ is the Divine Nature of all being and the Supreme Goal of Union toward which all individual and collective evolution moves.

The realization of this union gives birth to the consciousness of Christ in the individual, and has been called "the light of the world." When Peter said to Jesus, "Thou art the Christ, the son of the living God," Jesus answered by telling Peter that no man had revealed this to him but that it was a direct revelation of the Spirit. This is in accord with our statement that:

We believe that God is personal to all who feel this Indwelling Presence. . . . We believe in the direct revelation of Truth through the intuitive and spiritual nature of man, and that any man may become a revealer of Truth who lives in close contact with the Indwelling God.

"Know ye not that ye are the temple of God, and that the Spirit of God dwelleth in you?" "God is in his holy temple." Augustine said that the pure mind is a holy temple for God, and Emerson that God builds His temple in the heart. Seneca said that "temples are not to be built for God with stones . . . He is to be consecrated in the breast of each."

Every man is an incarnation of God, and since each person is an individual, everyone is a unique incarnation. We believe in the Divine Presence as Infinite Person, and personal to each. God is not a person, but the Person. This Person is an Infinite Presence filled with warmth, color and responsiveness, immediately and intimately personal to each individual.

The Spirit is both an over-dwelling and an indwelling Presence. We are immersed in It and It flows through us as our very life. Through intuition man perceives and directly reveals God. We do not have to borrow our light from another. Nothing could be more intimate than the personal relationship between the individual and that Divine Presence which is both the Center and the Source of man's being.

Not **some** men, but **all** men, are divine. But all men have not yet recognized their divinity. Our spiritual evolution is a gradual awakening to the realization that the Spirit is center, source and circumference of all being. It is in everything, around everything and through everything, and It is everything.*

The main body of the Christian religion is built upon three grand concepts: first, that **God is an Over-dwelling Presence;** next, that **God is also an Indwelling Presence;** and third, that **the conscious union of the Indwelling and the Overdwelling, through the mind of man, gives birth to the divine child, the Christ, the Son of God.** It was this revelation which enabled Jesus to perform his wonderful works. He became so conscious of his union with God that the very words he spoke were the Words of God spoken through him.

The only way that the Power of God can be manifest

---

* See **Your Invisible Power,** an Institute publication. Also read carefully section on **The Perfect Whole** in **The Science of Mind,** textbook of the Institute.

through man is by man's realization that it is the Father who dwelleth in him who doeth the works. Everyone should practice this close and intimate relationship between the individual and the Universal. Everyone should practice the Presence of God. This Presence is a reality, the one, great and supreme reality of life. There is a "light which lighteth every man." Man is spoken of in the Bible as "the candle of the Lord," and Jesus said, "Let your light so shine before men, that they may see your good works, and glorify your Father which is in heaven."

Through spiritual intuition Jesus perceived his union with God. What suffering, what unuttered anguish, what persistence, effort and discipline this man may have gone through to arrive at this exalted state, we know not, but we may be gratefully aware that he passed through every gamut of human suffering and emerged triumphant, supreme. Christ is the divine and universal Emanation of the Infinite Spirit incarnated in everything, individualized in man and universalized in God.

Whatever God is in the universal, man is in the individual. This is why all spiritual leaders have told us that if we would uncover the hidden possibility within, we should not only discover the true Self, the Christ, we should also uncover the true God, the One and Only Cause, the Supreme Being, the Infinite Person.

Jesus taught a complete union of man with God. He proclaimed that all men are divine; that all are one with the Father; that the Kingdom of Heaven is within; that the Father has delivered all power unto the son; and that the son thinks the thoughts of God after Him, and imbibes spiritual power through realization of his union with his Source.

We believe that the Universal Spirit, which is God, operates through a Universal Mind, which is the Law of God; and that we are surrounded by this Creative Mind which receives the direct impress of our thought and acts upon it.

This deals with the practical use of spiritual Power.* In Religious Science we differentiate between Spirit, Mind and Body, just as all the great major religious have done. Spirit is the conscious and active aspect of God, as distinguished from the passive, receptive and form-taking aspect. Spirit imparts motion and manifests Itself through form. Thus, the ancients said that Spirit uses matter as a sheath.

Philo, often called Philo Judaeus, born about 10 B.C., one of the greatest of the Jewish philosophers of the Alexandrian school, said that the Active Principle, which is Spirit, is absolutely free and that the passive principle is set in motion by the Spirit, giving birth to form. Plotinus, considered the greatest of the Neo-Platonists, taught that Spirit, as Active Intelligence, operates upon an unformed substance, which is passive to It, and that through the power of the Word of Spirit this substance takes form and becomes the physical world.

The spiritual teachings of antiquity all taught a trinity or three-fold unity.† In order that anything may exist there must be an active principle of self-assertion, acting as law upon a passive principle, which Plotinus called an indeterminate substance whose business it is to receive the forms which the contemplation (the word or the thought) of Spirit gives to it. In Religious Science, following the example of the Christian scriptures, we have named this trinity "The Father, Son and Holy Ghost." The Father, the supreme creative Principle; the Son (the Christ) the universal manifestation of the Father; and

---

* Read carefully the definition of Universal Power, Universal Soul, Universal Spirit, and Universal Subjective Mind on pages 641 and 642 in **The Science of Mind** textbook.

† See pamphlet published by the Institute of Religious Science, **Religious Science: The Thing Itself, the Way It Works, What It Does, and How to Use It.**

the supreme Law of Cause and Effect, the servant of the Spirit throughout the ages.

The Father means Absolute Being, the Unconditioned First Cause, the Source of all that is. Jesus called this Life Force "The Father." He referred to himself, and to all other men, as "The Son." "He is the image of the invisible God . . ." The ancient Hindus referred to The Son as Atman, the innermost spiritual self. Atman is the manifestation of Brahma as individuality. Man is an individualized center of the Consciousness of God. The Christian scripture refers to the same self when it speaks of Christ in us, for the Christ Principle has a meaning identical with Atma-Buddhi, which means divine illumination, "the Light of the world."

The Bible says that "the first man (Adam) is of the earth . . . the second man is the Lord from heaven." This refers first to the physical being, formed after the manner of all creation, and next to the Christ Principle animating this being. The birth of Christ, through Jesus, was the awakening of his consciousness to a realization of his union with God—"I and my Father are one." Jesus clearly taught that all men must come to this realization if they would enter into the kingdom of harmony, into conscious union with God, and thus gain wholeness.

"The first Adam is of the earth, earthy, and liable to death. The second is 'from heaven,' and triumphant over death. For 'sin has no more dominion over him.' He, therefore, is the product of a soul purified from defilement by matter, and released from subjection to the body. Such a soul is called virgin. And she has for spouse, not matter—for that she has renounced,—but the Divine Spirit which is God. And the man born of this union is in the image of God, and is God made man; that is, he is Christ, and it is the Christ thus born in every man, who redeems him and endows him with eternal life."*

---

* From **The Perfect Way.**

From *Ibid:* "For, as cannot be too clearly and forcibly stated, between the man who becomes a Christ, and other men, there is no difference whatever of kind. The difference is alone of condition and degree, and consists in difference of unfoldment of the spiritual nature possessed by all in virtue of their common derivation. 'All things,' as has repeatedly been said, 'are made of the divine Substance.' And Humanity represents a stream which, taking its rise in the outermost and lowest mode of differentiation of that Substance, flows inwards and upwards to the highest, which is God. And the point at which it reaches the celestial, and empties itself into Deity, is 'Christ.' Any doctrine other than this,—any doctrine which makes the Christ of a different and non-human nature,—is anti-Christian and subhuman. And, of such doctrine, the direct effect is to cut off man altogether from access to God, and God from access to man."

And from Basil Wilberforce, **Problems:** "In the evolution of God's life in man there are no short cuts, but a gradual unfolding of a principle of interior vitality. And the motto from this thought is, 'Rest in the Lord and wait patiently for Him,' while the child-Christ nature within you 'increases in wisdom and stature, and in favour with God and man'."

J. Brierley, in his book **Studies of the Soul,** says: "God as the Absolute can, in the nature of things, only come into contact with man by a self limitation . . . In Christ, to begin with, we have a revelation of the Absolute in the limited. In Him, as the Church all along has joyfully confessed, we see God."

"The second coming of Christ is a symbol of the completion of the process of purification and development of the souls of humanity, when the lower consciousness rises to union with the higher." From **Mystical Religions,** and quoting from Luke, "And then shall they see the Son of man coming in a cloud with power and great glory. But when these things begin to come to pass, look up, and lift up your heads; because your redemption draweth nigh."

R. M. Jones goes on to say: "This refers to the consummation of the physical at the end of the cycle. Then as perfection of the soul-state approaches, the indwelling Christ appears in glory within the souls of the saints, or is raised above the condition wherefrom at first his descent was made. The 'cloud' signifies a temporary veil which obscures the splendour of the Highest. The 'lifting up of heads' refers to the aspiration of the minds, needful so that liberation from the lower nature may be effected." And quoting from Luke again, "Verily I say unto you, this generation shall not pass away, till all things be accomplished," he explains: "Christ here points out that each grade of evolution of qualities now existent, shall not be extinguished until the complete process of soul-growth on the lower planes has been carried out."

To return to our analysis of the Trinity, the Father is the Absolute, Unconditioned, First Cause; the Infinite Person; the Divine in Whom we live and move and have our being. The entire manifestation of the Infinite in any and all planes, levels, states of consciousness, or manifestations, constitutes the Son.

So far as we know from teachings handed down to us from antiquity, the Holy Ghost signifies the feminine aspect of the Divine Trinity. It represents the divine activity of the higher mental plane; the Breath of God, or the Law of Being. It is difficult for us to transpose the meaning of ancient symbols into modern language, but it seems to be the consensus among the scholars who have studied this subject that the Holy Ghost means the relationship between the Father and the Son, or the divine, creative fertility of the universal soul when impregnated by the Divine Ideas. If creation is to take place, there must be a Divine Imagination which is spontaneous and a creative medium through which It acts. This creative medium is the Law of Mind.

When any individual recognizes his true union with the Infinite, he automatically becomes the Christ. He is born from the lower to a higher plane and awakes to a greater consciousness of his union with the Father—"I shall be satisfied when I awake in thy likeness."

In Religious Science it is made clear that there is a universal Law of Mind which receives the impress of our thought and acts upon it. This Law is not God, but the servant of God.

The ancients called this Law the "Feminine." Realizing that there must be an active, energizing principle which is God, the Masculine, they also recognized that there must be a creative principle in nature, which they spoke of as Feminine, whose business it is to receive God's thought and bring it into creation.

This creative Law is, of course, the Law of Mind. It is what we mean when we say there is a Universal Mind through which the Universal Spirit operates. In other words, when we think of God as pure, self-knowing Spirit, as "our Father which art in heaven," as the Absolute, the Unconditioned, as Infinite Person and Limitless Being, we are thinking of Divine Intelligence. But when we think of the universe as law, we are thinking of the Principle of Mind which receives the impress of our thought and acts upon it, always creatively, always mathematically, and without any respect to persons.

All great spiritual teachings have proclaimed such a creative Principle. It has been called by a thousand names, but careful analysis will show that every scripture has differentiated between God the Spirit and God the Law.

The ancients said that Spirit is the Power that knows Itself. They also taught the karmic law, which is the medium for all thought and action. Karma means the fruit of action.

When Jesus said, "The words that I speak unto you, they are spirit, and they are life," he was speaking from the consciousness of Christ which dominates the mental plane. His mind was such a perfect transmitter that it reflected, imaged, emanated, or automatically became an instrument through which the Divine worked.

Knowing that his word was in absolute accord with Divine Harmony he found no difference between it and the Word of God. It was his implicit confidence in his divine inspiration, arrived at through a lifetime of contemplation and of conscious union with the Infinite, which gave him the confidence to say, ". . . till all these things be fulfilled. Heaven and earth shall pass away, but my words shall not pass away." Jesus was relying upon the Law of Mind to execute his word.

In the Science of Mind we are very careful to draw a distinction between Universal Spirit and Universal Mind. The Science of Mind is the tool which the Religious Scientist uses, starting with the realization that the manifest universe is, as every scripture has declared, a logical result of the Thought of God, and realizing that man is a center of God Consciousness.

The Religious Scientist knows that in such degree as he inwardly realizes the Truth, this Truth which he realizes, operating through a universal Law of Mind, will find outward or physical manifestation in the world of form. This is what we mean when we say that the Spirit operates through a Law of Mind; that we are surrounded by this Mind which receives the impress of our thought and acts upon it.

Let us see what different scriptures have had to say on this subject, starting with our own Bible. "In the beginning was the Word, and the Word was with God, and the Word was God." "Forever, O Lord, thy word is seated in heaven." "And, Thou, Lord . . . hast laid the foundation of the earth; and the heavens are the works of thine hands." "Our God is a living God. His power fills the universe . . . with his spirit thou breathest."

In referring to the Law of Mind the Bible says: "Every idle word that men shall speak, they shall give account thereof . . . for by thy words thou shalt be justified, and by thy words thou shalt be condemned." "And they were astonished at his doctrine: for his word was with power." "Be ye doers of the word and not hearers only . . ." "For there are three that bear witness in heaven, the Father, the Word, and the Holy Ghost: and these three are one."

Our Bible is based on the premise that God is pure Spirit; that He creates through the power of His word, and that the universe is a manifestation of His imagination (His imaging within Himself through knowing Himself to be what He is). God is Spirit. The Spirit speaks, the Law is invoked and a manifestation necessarily takes form. This is the first principle.

The next principle advanced is that man is the spiritual image and likeness of God, and is of like nature with God; that he is made of the essence of God, and is an individualized center in the Consciousness of God.

Then, having stated man's divine pedigree, and having carefully pointed out what happens to man through his misuse of the Law of Freedom, commonly called "the fall of man," the conclusion is devoted to man's redemption. The old prophets intuitively perceived this; the New Testament demonstrates it, for in the person of Jesus there arose a man who became so conscious of his union with good that all evil disappeared from his imagination.

Through trial, temptation, suffering, through success and failure, this glorified soul, in a sense, fought the battle of life for all men and thus automatically become the savior of mankind. But when they mistook the man Jesus for the Christ Principle, the wisdom of Jesus caused him to withdraw himself that the Spirit of Truth might awaken in them a corresponding realization of their own union with the Divine.

The whole teaching of the Bible may be simmered down to this simple statement, presented to each one of us individually as though a Divine Hand delivered it unto our individual keeping: You are one with the creative Spirit of the universe. There is a universal, divine Spirit which will inspire, guide, direct and companion you, but there is also a universal Law of Cause and Effect which sees to it that every act, every thought, every motive, must be accounted for. Finally, through suffering, you will learn to distinguish right from wrong; you will live in conscious union and in conscious communion with the Divine Spirit.

From then on your words, thoughts and acts will be constructive and you will come into complete salvation. God has done all He can for you because He has delivered His entire nature into your keeping. But, since this nature is truth, goodness, beauty, wisdom, love and power, you can never enter completely into the kingdom of harmony until you consciously unify with harmony.

This is the balance between truth and justice, between love and reason, between true divine freedom and the misuse of the Law, which is not liberty but license. This is why Moses said, "I set before you this day a blessing and a curse; a blessing, if ye obey the commandments . . . a curse, if ye will not obey the commandments."

The whole problem of evil, as stated by the different scriptures of the world, is not a problem of dealing with an entity of evil, but with the misuse of a dynamic power which, rightly used, alone guarantees freedom.

The **Koran** says that "whatsoever good betideth thee is from God and whatsoever betideth thee of evil is from thyself." And our **Bible** says of the Spirit, "Thou art of purer eyes than to behold evil, and canst not look on iniquity."

From the **Teachings of Buddha** we learn: "For the cause of the karma (cause and effect) which conducts to unhappy states of existence, is ignorance." "Therefore it is clear that ignorance can only be removed by wisdom." The **Zend-Avesta** says, "The word of falsehood smites but the word of truth shall smite it." And from **The Book of the Dead:** "It shall come to pass that the evil one shall fall when he raiseth a snare to destroy thee . . ."

From the **Text of Taoism** we learn: "Whatever is contrary to the Tao soon ends." "He who injures others is sure to be injured by them in return."

We believe in the healing of the sick through the power of this Mind.

Spiritual mind healing has long since passed the experimental stage, and we now know why it is that faith has performed miracles. We live in a universe of pure, unadulterated Spirit, of perfect Being. We are, as Emerson said, in the lap of an infinite Intelligence. There is a spiritual prototype of perfection at the center of everything. There is a cosmic or divine pattern at the center of every organ of the physical body. Our body is some part of the Body of God; it is a manifestation of the Supreme Spirit.

In the practice of spiritual mind healing we start with this simple proposition: God is perfect. God is all there is. God includes man. Spiritual man is a divine being, as complete and perfect in essence as is God. When in thought, in contemplation, in imagination, in inward feeling, we consciously return to the Source of our being, the divine pattern which already exists, springs forth into newness of manifestation. When we clear the consciousness, that is, the whole mental life, both conscious and subjective, of discord, we are automatically healed.

The Science of Mind, which is the tool of the Religious Scientist, gives us a definite technique for doing this. It teaches us exactly how to proceed on a simple, understandable basis. It is a science because it is built upon the exact laws of Mind, for the laws of Mind are as exact as any other laws in nature. They are natural laws. From a practical viewpoint, this is done by making certain definite statements with the realization that they have power to remove any obstacle, to dissolve any false condition, and to reveal man's spiritual nature.

True mind healing cannot be divorced from spiritual realization, therefore the practitioner of this science must have a deep and an abiding sense of calm, of peace, and of his union with the Spirit. He must have an unshakable conviction that spiritual man is perfect, that he is one with God, and he must know that in such degree as he realizes, senses, feels, this inner perfection, it will appear. The physical healing itself is a result, an effect, of this inward consciousness.

The laws of this science are so simple, direct and usable that anyone may demonstrate them who cares to make the effort. Read carefully the entire section on mind healing in our textbook. **The Science of Mind,** and you will discover that there is no mystery about this. The reason that throughout the ages people have been healed through a prayer of faith, is that faith complies with the Law of Mind in producing an affirmative result. Faith is an unquestioned acceptance.

Faith also is a certain definite mental attitude. When Jesus said, "It is done unto you as you believe," he implied that there is a law, a force, or an intelligent energy in the universe which acts upon the images of our belief. Faith is an affirmative way of using this Law, this Energy, this Force. Therefore, all scriptures have announced the necessity of having faith.

"Be ye transformed by the renewing of your mind." "Be renewed in the spirit of your mind." "Let this mind be in you which was also in Christ." "I will put my laws into your mind." "Hear, O earth, behold I will bring evil upon these people, even the fruits of their thoughts." "And he sent his word and healed them." "He forgetteth all thine iniquities; he healeth all thy diseases." "O Lord, my God, I cry unto thee and thou hast healed me." "Then shall thy light break forth as morning, and thine health shall speed forth speedily." "And it shall come to pass, that before they call, I will answer; and while they are yet speaking, I will hear." "I will take sickness away from the midst of thee." "The tongue of the wise is health." "Behold I will bring health . . . I will cure them . . ."

"Jesus turned him about, and when he saw her, he said,

Daughter, be of good comfort; thy faith hath made thee whole. And the woman was made whole from that hour." "Then touched he their eyes, saying, According to your faith be it unto you. And their eyes were opened." "Heal the sick, cleanse the lepers, raise the dead, cast out devils: freely ye have received, freely give." "And great multitudes followed him, and he healed them all." "And the blind and the lame came to him in the temple, and he healed them."

In spiritual mind healing thought becomes a transmitter for Divine Power, therefore, the thought must always be kept free from confusion.

It is interesting to note that, while all the great scriptures of the ages concur about the nature of God and of man, and the relationship between the spiritual and the physical, outside the Christian scriptures very little is mentioned about healing or the control of conditions through the use of Divine Power, although they all agree that when the mind reflects the Divine Perfection, healing and prosperity follow.

In the **Text of Taoism** we find: "The still mind . . . is the mirror of heaven and earth . . ." "Maintain a perfect unity in every movement of your will. You will not wait for the hearing of your ears, but for the hearing of your mind. You will not wait even for the hearing of your mind, but for the hearing of the Spirit." "Purity and stillness give the correct law to all under heaven." And from the **Koran:** "The Lord of the worlds He hath created me and guideth me; He giveth me food and drink and when I am sick He healeth me." "And never Lord have I prayed to thee with ill success."

Jesus, the last of his particular line of prophets, was the first to introduce spiritual mind healing, and definitely to instruct his followers to practice it. People have been healed through all faiths, but the great healing shrines of the Christian belief have undoubtedly emphasized this more than most others, although we do find many instances of healing through all the various beliefs.

It is more particularly since the advent of what has been called "The New Thought," which started in America and has since spread throughout the world, that we find great emphasis placed upon spiritual healing.

This has been a sincere, earnest and effective attempt to get back to some of the first principles which Jesus taught. He sent out his disciples, telling them to heal the sick as a proof, not only of their Divine Power, but their Divine Authority, and he said, "Lo, I am with you alway." Since it is self-evident that Jesus, as a human being, could not be with them always, common sense compels us to accept that when he said, "I am with you alway," he was referring to the Divine Power, the Christ Principle, which he used.

To speak of the **science** of Jesus is no misnomer, for he certainly knew what he was doing, and repeatedly stated that his words acted as spiritual law. It might be said of Jesus that he was a practical idealist. He did not believe that the Kingdom of God is some far-off event; to him it was an ever-present reality; it was always at hand waiting merely to be perceived by the inner spiritual intuition, which is the voice of God operating through man.

"Faith without works is dead." Therefore, faith should be justified through manifestation, and if we have faith we can scientifically prove this. For, after all, science is the knowledge of universal principles and laws consciously applied for definite purposes.

There is a science of Mind and Spirit because there is a principle of Mind and Spirit. There is a possibility of using this science because we now understand how the laws of Mind and Spirit work in human affairs. The Principle of Mind operates through our thought, through our faith and conviction, and, most effectively, through an attitude of love, of compassion and of sympathy constructively used. It is impossible to make the highest use of the laws of Mind without basing such use of these laws upon inward spiritual perception, upon a conscious realization of the union of man with God.

When the physician and the metaphysician come better to understand each other they will more closely co-operate. It is self-evident that each is seeking to alleviate human suffering. No intelligent person would deny the need of physicians, surgeons and hospitals. On the other hand, it is generally agreed that a large percentage of our physical troubles are mental in their origin, and that all have some relationship to mental processes. It is most important, then, that the work of the sincere metaphysician should be both understood and appreciated.

It is not at all probable that the psychologist can take the place of the metaphysician, for just as the mere healing of the body, without an adjustment of the mental and emotional states, is insufficient, so the adjusting of mental and emotional states without introducing spiritual values will be ineffectual. Hence, there is an important place for the metaphysician, and his assistance should be sought.

Physician, metaphysician and psychologist should co-operate. There should be no sense of mistrust or criticism among them. The metaphysician should appreciate both the psychologist and the physician.

In the early days of spiritual therapeutics it was believed that one could not treat people mentally with success if they were being attended by a physician, or if they were using material methods for relief. Now we know that this idea was based on superstition. We no longer give it any serious thought. The metaphysician feels it a privilege to be called into consultation with a physician or with a psychologist. He has learned to appreciate the field of medicine and surgery.

The day is certain to come when the field of medicine will

recognize, appreciate and co-operate with the metaphysical field. Even today this practice is far more common than the average person realizes. When the metaphysician stops making foolish statements or denying that his patient is ill, he will find a greater inclination toward recognition from the medical world.

Today most physicians recognize the power of thought in relation to the body. All realize the dynamic energy of the emotions. Psychiatric hospitals are being built and psychiatric wards are being added to hospitals already in existence. Just as psychology and psychiatry are being introduced into the medical world, so the metaphysical gradually will be understood, accepted and appreciated. Already many psychologists are affirming the necessity of introducing spiritual values into their practice. Who is going to meet this need unless it be the metaphysician?

Progress is inevitable and co-operation between all right-minded workers in the healing art is certain. Let us do all that we can to remove superstition, intolerance and bigotry which, after all, merely result in stupidity. We should unite in one common cause, not only to alleviate physical suffering but, in so far as possible, to remove its cause. If much of this cause lies hidden in the realm of mind, then surely those who are equipped to work in this realm are contributing their share to the meeting of a human need.

We believe in the control of conditions through the power of this Mind.
While all sacred writings affirm that when we are in harmony with the Infinite we are automatically prospered, the Christian scriptures lay greater stress on prosperity through spiritualizing the mind than any other of the bibles of the world. Our Bible, truly understood, is a book for the emancipation of man from the thralldom of every evil, every lack and limitation.

From the teaching of Moses, running through the thought of the major prophets and culminating in the brilliant manifestation of the Mind of Christ through the thought of Jesus, over and over this idea is reiterated—that if we live in harmony with the Spirit everything we do shall prosper.

Religious Science teaches that through right knowledge of the Science of Mind we may definitely and consciously demonstrate, that is, prove or show forth, practical results of spiritual thought.* Countless thousands have proved this principle and there is no longer any question about its effectiveness. The greatest guide we have for this is found in the inspired writings of the Christian scriptures.

"Prove me now herewith, saith the Lord of hosts, if I will not open to you the windows of heaven, and pour out a blessing, that there shall not be room enough to receive it." "And he shall pray unto God and he will be favorable unto him." "For every one that asketh receiveth; and he that seeketh findeth; and to him that knocketh it shall be opened." "Ask, and it shall be given you." "And all things, whatsoever ye shall ask in prayer, believing, ye shall receive."

Whether we choose to call this faith or understanding makes no difference. It really is faith based upon understanding; it is belief elevated to the mental position of unconditioned certainty. For Jesus said that whoever could believe ". . . and shall not doubt in his heart, but shall believe that those things which he saith shall come to pass; he shall have whatsoever he saith. Therefore I say unto you, What things soever ye desire, when ye pray, believe that ye receive them, and ye shall have them."

Nothing could be more definite or concise than this statement. We must actually believe that there is a power, an intelligence, a law, which will make this desire manifest in our experience.

---

* Read carefully the entire section on the control of conditions in **The Science of Mind** textbook.

There is a Law of Mind which follows the patterns of our thought. This Law works automatically. It will always respond by corresponding. Thus Jesus said that it is done unto us as we believe. The word as is important since it implies that the creative Intelligence, in working **for** us, must work **through** us at the level of our acknowledgment of It as working. This is working **in spirit and in truth,** and according to law. And there must be law even in prayer, if there is to be cosmic order.

Man's mind has been likened to the "Workshop of God" for it is here that the tools of thought consciously may fashion destiny, may carve out a new future. We have been told to do this according to the pattern shown us on the Mount.

This means that we are to formulate our ideas on the premise that there is an all-sustaining Power and an all-pervading Presence around us, and an immutable Law ever serving us when our lives are in harmony with the Divine Nature. Through an exact law, demonstration follows the word of faith. This calls for a surrender of the intellect to a spiritual conviction which dares to believe, disregarding any evidence to the contrary.

We must continue in faith until our whole mental life, both conscious and subjective, responds. If we would pray and prosper we must believe that the Spirit is both willing and able to make the gift. But since the Spirit can only give us what we take, and since the taking is a mental act, we must train the mind to believe and to accept. This is the secret of the power of prayer.

One need not have great intellectual attainment to understand these simple things. Jesus said that the Kingdom of Heaven is reached through childlike faith. Again he said, "I thank thee, O Father . . . because thou hast hid these things from the wise and the prudent, and hast revealed them unto babes."

Just as the teachings of Jesus announce the Divine Presence, so his works prove the presence of a Law which received the impress of his word and brought it forth into form. He asked no authority other than that which was demonstrated through his act. Since Jesus taught the most definite system of spiritual thought ever given to the world, as well as the most simple and direct, and since he was able to prove his teaching by his works, we could do no better than to follow his example. There are two ways in which we may do this. One is blind faith, and we cannot doubt its effectiveness; the other is through coming to understand what the teachings of Jesus really meant. Thus knowledge passes into a faith so complete that it is unshakable.

Jesus left very implicit instructions relative to prayer. He said, "Judge not according to appearances." That is, do not be confused by the conditions around you. This is the first great instruction of Jesus—to have such faith and confidence in the Invisible that appearances no longer disturb you.

Next we come to the preparation for prayer. Having shut out all appearances to the contrary, enter the closet. To enter the closet means to withdraw into one's own thought, to shut out all confusion and discord. Here in the silence of the soul, look to the all-creative Wisdom and Power, to the ever-present Substance. When we have entered the closet and shut the door to outward appearances, we are to make known our requests— "what things soever ye desire."

Next Jesus tells us that we are to **believe that we actually possess** the objects of our desire, disregarding all appearances to the contrary. We are to enter into this invisible inheritance acting as though it were true. Our faith in the substance of the Invisible is to take actual form. The Divine Giver Himself is to make the gift, but first we must believe that we have received it, and then we shall receive it—". . . believe that ye receive them, and ye shall have them."

This is a veiled statement of the Law of Cause and Effect operating in human affairs. When we have believed that we have, we have actually given birth to the form that is to be presented. Having made known our request with thanksgiving and received the answer with gratitude, we must rest assured that the Law will bring about the desired result.

"Thy Father which seeth in secret himself shall reward thee openly." Everything passes from the Invisible into the visible to be temporarily experienced and again to be withdrawn. This is the eternal play of Life upon Itself; the eternal act of creation. "Thy Father which seeth in secret himself shall reward thee openly." Rest in peace knowing that it is done. This profound principle which Jesus announced (and the simple technique of its use in which he counselled his followers) exists today in all of its fullness. It is the very cornerstone upon which our philosophy is built.

Even in divine communion we are dealing with the Law of Cause and Effect. Our prayer invokes this Divine Law and causes It to manifest in our external world at the level of our inner perception of Its working. Because this is true, prayer should always be definite, conscious and active.

Prayer ties us to a Power that is able, ready and willing to fulfill every legitimate desire; to bring every good thing to us; to do for us even more abundantly than we have expected. "Before they call, I will answer; and while they are yet speaking, I will hear." This shifting of the burden is important, for when we feel isolated, alone and struggling against tremendous odds, we are not equal to the task before us. Life becomes a drudgery rather than a **jubilant beholding.** But if we know the burden is lifted and set upon the shoulders of the Law, then power and speed come to hands and feet; joy floods the imagination with anticipation.

The reflection of an image in a mirror is an exact likeness of the image which is held before the mirror. So the Law of Cause and Effect reflects back to us a likeness of the images of our thought. Thus we are told that we reflect the glory of God. But too often we reflect the fear and limitation of man rather than the glory of God.

We must find new meanings to life if we hope to create new images which, in their turn, will supply new reflections. Jesus told us to judge not according to appearances but to judge righteously. If we judge only according to what is now transpiring, our reflection of these images will merely perpetuate the old limitation, but if we judge righteously, that is, if we look to the omnipotence of Good, we shall create new images of thought which will reflect greater abundance.

Prayer, then, is a mirror reflecting the images of our thought through the Law of Good into our outward experiences. What are we reflecting, the glory of God or the confusion of man? However, Jesus carefully pointed out that before we can reach this position of absolute power, we must first have complied with the Law of Love. For the whole impulsion of the universe is an impulsion of love, the manifestation of Divine Givingness.

The Apostle Paul said, "I will pray with the spirit and I will pray with the understanding also . . ." This is an instruction for us to combine spiritual intuition with definite mental acceptance. He is telling us that the gift of God is to be consciously used.

We are also told to pray without ceasing, to maintain a steadfast conviction, disregarding every apparent contradiction, obstruction or appearance that would deny the good we affirm. "But let him ask in faith, nothing wavering. For he that wavereth is like a wave of the sea driven with the wind and tossed." "To the righteous good shall be repaid." "The minds of the righteous shall stand." "Behold the righteous shall be recompensed in the earth." "The righteous is delivered of all trouble." A righteous man means one who is right with the universe; one who lives in accord with the Divine Will and the Divine Nature; one who lives in harmony with good.

We have the right then to expect, and we should expect, in so far as our inner thought is in tune with the Infinite, that everything we do shall prosper.

We believe in the eternal Goodness, the eternal Loving-kindness and the eternal Givingness of Life to all.

The Spirit gives Itself to everyone, the Power of God is delivered to all. "Whosoever will may come." No matter what the mistakes of our yesterdays may have been, we may transcend both the mistake and its consequence through imbibing the Spirit of Truth, which is the Power of God.

This does not mean that we may continue living in the mistake without suffering from it. We must transcend it. That is, we must transmute hate into love, fear into faith and a sense of separation into conscious union with good. When we have done this, the entire record of the past is blotted out and we are again free—freed with that freedom which the Almighty has ordained, and which man may claim as his own.

But liberty is not license and the Law of Life cannot be fooled. It is exact and exacting. "Therefore," Jesus said, "all things whatsoever ye would that men should do unto you, do ye even so to them." "Give, and it shall be given."

This is a statement of the Law of Cause and Effect which is invariable, immutable, but which is also the plaything both of God and man, for while the Law Itself cannot be broken, any particular sequence of cause and effect in It can be transcended. The same law which brought poverty, sickness and death, rightly used, will bring peace, wholeness, prosperity and life.

This is the great challenge of spiritual faith. The Christian philosophy bids us not to look with doleful introspection on previous errors, but coming daily to the Fountain of Life, to be renewed in mind, thought and spirit, we shall find that we also are renewed in bodily conditions and in physical affairs.

The Scripture boldly declares the triumph of the Spirit of Christ over all evil: Be ye transformed by the renewing of your mind; by the putting off of the old man and the putting on of the new man, which is Christ. "Lo, I am with you alway, even unto the end of the world."

We believe in our own soul, our own spirit and our own destiny; for we understand that the life of man is God.

Man is not only a center of God Consciousness; he is an immortal being, forever expanding, forever spiraling upward, forever growing in spiritual stature. Not **some** men, but **all** men are immortal, for everyone will finally overcome or transcend any misuse of the Law which he has made in his ignorance. Complete redemption at last must come, alike, to all.

What transformations must ensue, what change of consciousness must take place before this is finally brought about, the finite has not yet grasped, but through the whisperings of divine intuition we know that even though we now see as through a glass darkly, we shall some day behold Reality face to face. We shall be satisfied when we consciously awake in the likeness of that Divinity which shapes our ends.

"Beloved, now are we the sons of God, and it doth not yet appear what we shall be: but we know that, when he shall appear, we shall be like him; for we shall see him as he is." We are all in the process of spiritual evolution, but there is certainty behind us, certainty before us and certainty with us at every moment. The Eternal Light will break through wherever we permit It to.

Potentially, everything that is to be exists now, but our spiritual vision has not yet become completely in tune with the Infinite. This is the high task set before us as Religious Scientists, this is the deathless hope implanted in our mind by the Divine.

The trials and troubles of human experience; the blind

groping of the finite toward the Infinite; the sickness, poverty, death, uncertainty, fear and doubt that accompany us, constitute the cross upon which we must offer, as a sacrifice to our ignorance, that which does not belong to the Kingdom of Good. But from this cross something triumphant will emerge, for, as Emerson said, "The finite alone has wrought and suffered; the infinite lies stretched in smiling repose."

Shall we not, then, with joy, go forth to meet the new day, endeavoring so to embody the Spirit of Christ that the Divine in us shall rise triumphant, resurrected, to live forever in the City of God? More could not be asked than that which the Divine has already delivered; less should not be expected.

APPENDIX

Professor Max Muller, one of the greatest European Orientalists and author of THE SACRED BOOKS OF THE EAST, has well said that "the true religion of the future will be the fulfillment of all the religions of the past. . . . All religions, so far as I know them, had the same purpose; all were links in a chain which connects heaven and earth; and which is held, and always was held, by one and the same hand. All here on earth tends toward right and truth, and perfection; nothing here on earth can ever be quite right, quite true, quite perfect, not even Christianity—or what is called Christianity—so long as it excludes all other religions, instead of loving and embracing what is good in each."

Like many other religions of antiquity, the origin of **Taoism** is more or less obscure. According to some authorities it is said to have begun around 600 B.C. which antedates Confucius, who was born in 551 B.C. The world generally associates **Taoism** with Lao-Tze, a Chinese metaphysical philosopher who was fifty-three years older than Confucius. It was this philosopher who must have gathered together these teachings. Archdeacon Hardwick tells us that the Chinese word "Tao" ". . . was adopted to denominate an abstract cause, or the initial principle of life and order, to which worshippers were able to assign the attribute of immateriality, eternity, immensity, invisibility."

The **Upanishads,** the **Vedas,** the **Mahabharata,** the **Raja Yoga** philosophy, as well as the **Bhagavad-Gita,** are all drawn from the ancient wisdom of India.

The philosophy of **Buddha,** who was born in the sixth century B.C., is too well known to need any comment.

The Sacred Book of the Parsis is called the **Zend-Avesta,** which is a collection of fragments of ideas that prevailed in ancient Persia, five years before the Christian era and for several centuries afterwards.

The Book of the Dead is a series of translations of the ancient Egyptian hymns and religious texts. They were found on the walls of tombs, in coffins and in papyri. Like many other sacred traditions, there probably were no written copies in the earlier days; they were committed to memory and handed down from generation to generation.

Some students believe that the books of **Hermes Trismegistus,** which means "the thrice greatest," originally derived from ancient Egyptian doctrine. Hermes was a Greek god, son of Zeus and Maia, daughter of Atlas. To Hermes was attributed the authorship of all the strictly sacred books generally called by Greek authors, **Hermetic.** (Encyclopaedia Britannica) According to some scholars, the Egyptian Hermes "was a symbol of the Divine Mind; he was the incarnated Thought, the living Word— the primitive type of the Logos of Plato and the Word of the Christians . . ."

Fragments of a Faith Forgotten are taken from the Gnostics, those "who used the Gnosis as the means to set their feet upon the Way of God." Gnosticism was pre-Christian and originated in the ancient religion and philosophy of Greece, Egypt, and Jewry.

According to H. Polano, the **Talmud** contains ". . . the thoughts . . . of a thousand years of the national life of the Jewish people."

The **Koran** is the sacred book of the Mohammedans,

consisting of revelations orally delivered at intervals by Mo-
hammed and collected in writing after his death. (Oxford Dictionary) The **Koran** is considered one of the most important of
the world's sacred books.

The **Apocrypha** refers to a collection of ancient writings.
The Greek word "Apocryphos" was originally used of books the
contents of which were kept hidden, or secret, because they embodied the special teaching of religious or philosophical sects; it
was only the members of these sects who were initiated into the
secrets of this teaching. (Encyclopaedia Britannica)

ABOUT THE AUTHOR

Ernest Holmes (1887–1960) was an influential member of the New Thought movement and in 1927 he founded what would later come to be called the Centers for Spiritual Living. There are currently over 400 CSL locations throughout America.